STRANGERS
AND
NATIVES

STRANGERS
AND
NATIVES

The Evolution of the American Jew
from 1921 to the present

★ ──────────────────────────── ★

JUDD L. TELLER

DELACORTE PRESS / NEW YORK

TO FAYGELE,
AS ALWAYS FOR PATIENCE BEYOND CALL,
AND FOR SHY WISDOM.

Contents

PREFACE ix

I. IN ALIEN CORN 1
[1921 – 1930]

Chapter 1. 1921—The Watershed Year 3
Chapter 2. Press and Theater 19
Chapter 3. Orators and Writers 37
Chapter 4. The Orthodox Brethren 60
Chapter 5. Occupations 79
Chapter 6. The World Around Us 94

II. CATASTROPHE AND TRIUMPH 111
[1930 – 1948]

Chapter 1. Introducing the Nineteen-Thirties 113
Chapter 2. The Successors 128
Chapter 3. The Culture Invasion 139
Chapter 4. Many Kinds of Jews 153
Chapter 5. America Without Compass 170
Chapter 6. Struggle for Survival 193

III. THE NATIVE AND HIS ANCESTORS 217
[1948 – 1967]

Chapter 1. The Hellenists of Suburbia 219
Chapter 2. The Rabbi and His Flock 235
Chapter 3. From Yiddish to Neo-Brahmin 251
Chapter 4. The Native and His Future 273

INDEX 299

Preface

THIS BOOK is part history and part autobiography because the
author is not a professional historian, and because some of the
era is beyond his recall. In short, it is a hybrid. Its one purpose has
been to convey the flavor and fever of the years and events since 1921
which transformed the American Jew from stranger into native, from
immigrant into junior member of the American Establishment, from
the days when the majority spoke Yiddish and honored its Yiddish
poets, novelists, orators, editors, and actors, and sought sanctuary in
national and social ideologies, to the present when Jews are among
America's ranking authors and are alleged to have introduced a "Jewish cult" into American literature. This book begins with the stoppage
of Jewish mass immigration by a willful Congress which favored
"Aryans" and was apprehensive about the fecundity of Latins, Slavs,
and Semites. The Jew could be classified in all three categories, depending on his origin. It closes with the dilemma that emergent Black
Power poses to the Jew.

The book does not bypass institutions, but its concern is people and
how they relate to customs, mores, movements. Its concerns are as
diverse as those of the American Jewish community: foods, the theater,
housing, the synagogue, clothes, athletics, unions, interfaith and interracial tensions, Zionism, Socialism, Hassidism. Together, these disparate
elements constitute the flavor of American Jewish living.

The author's gratitude to Oliver Swan, who sustained faith in the
concept of this book when my own was flagging; to Richard Huett for
insightful, persuasive but not intrusive editorial suggestions; to my

brother Benjamin Teller, for recollections of some early events and people, and to the librarians of the Jewish Room of the New York Public Library, of Yivo, of the American Jewish Committee and of Zionist Archives, New York City.

JUDD L. TELLER

". . . with our bones
We left much more, left what still is
The look of things, left what we felt
At what we saw. . . ."

WALLACE STEVENS
"A Postcard from the Volcano."

I

IN ALIEN CORN

[1921–1930]

"... for ye know the heart of a stranger, seeing
ye were strangers in the land of Egypt."

EXODUS 23:4

"And if thy brother should become impoverished,
and be without means, thou shalt uphold him and
have him live beside thee. . . ."

LEVITICUS 25:36

1921–The Watershed Year

THE YEAR 1921 came on little cat's feet, like the fog in Carl Sandburg's poem. Before it passed on, it had changed the course of American Jewish history. This, however, did not become apparent until many years later.

Three germinal events compounded the year's special distinction. In 1921, America for the first time introduced rigid immigration quotas based on the principle of national origin, inspired by the belief that immigrants from Eastern and Southern Europe were of a degenerative stock that had been contaminating the country's fundamental Anglo-Saxon racial strain. Another event that set 1921 apart from its predecessors on the calendar of American Jewry was the involuntary abdication of Louis D. Brandeis' disciples from American Zionist leadership. The third was a New York State Supreme Court ruling for the International Ladies' Garment Workers' Union in an industrial dispute that had thrown thousands of New York's Jewish workers out of their jobs.

The three events had complementary effects. East Europe, haunted by pogroms, oppression, and revolution, had since the eighteen-eighties been the major source of Jewish immigration to the United States. These immigrants now constituted a majority of the Jewish community and imprinted on it the powerful stamp of East Europe's Yiddish-language culture. The new quota system dammed their tide and was a major factor in the gradual decline of Yiddish in America. The Brandeis disciples were largely *Yahudim*.[1] Their ouster was the last stage in a many-faceted revolution of the East European Yiddish-speaking immi-

---

[1] Hebrew word for Jews. However, the East European immigrant in America applied it exclusively to the German Jew and gave it a derogatory connotation.

grant against the rule of the Yahudim over American Jewish affairs. The latter, a diminishing minority, had acted as the immigrants' mediators with English-speaking America. Having ejected the Yahudim, the East Europeans were now compelled to negotiate directly with their Gentile fellow-Americans. The court's pro-labor decision reinforced the immigrants' growing confidence in American justice, their trust in trade unions as an effective instrument for raising living standards, and completed their alienation from the radical political parties based on economic and social doctrines of European origin.

America's Jewish population numbered approximately four million. Half that number were concentrated in New York City. The return address on all their correspondence to relatives bore the proud legend "Greater New York." In reality, they knew only a small portion of the city. They were widely dispersed in Brooklyn, most numerous in Manhattan where they crowded into the Lower East Side, and had leapfrogged into Harlem. The East Bronx completed their realm.

Brooklyn was also the repository of their dead. Foreseeing that someday its cemeteries would be overpopulated, entrepreneurs offered burial plots at discount rates in Richmond and Queens. They found few takers, however, the new cemeteries were too far away, and there was reluctance, furthermore, to deposit Jewish remains where the living Jew was not suffered. The two boroughs were KKK-infested. Their Jewish population was sparse and distinctly unwelcome. Gravemarkers were periodically overturned. Jews were rousted out of their sleep at midnight to discover flaring crosses on their lawns, and in the morning were delivered poison-pen missives along with their newspapers and milk. Incredibly, only two decades later, Jews would be constructing high-rise apartment houses in Queens, and populating it with synagogues, community centers, delicatessen and appetizer stores, foreign-run movie houses and PTAs.

The vanishing breed of Yahudim, concentrated primarily on Manhattan's West End Avenue and Park Avenue, had arrived in the United States in the mid-nineteenth century when the West was opening up and this country was beginning to realize its tremendous economic potential. They started as peddlers to Southern plantations and as shopkeepers in frontier towns in the West, succeeded admirably in merchandising, took flings in mining, and, along the Eastern seaboard, engaged in the manufacture of consumer goods, and in banking.

The East Europeans, disgorged by the shiploads in the last two decades of the nineteenth century, were trotted off, like herds of cattle, from the piers to jobs in Yahudim-operated garment sweatshops. Within two decades the newcomers had taken possession of the industry as the Yahudim passed on to more distinguished occupations that were not harassed by labor trouble.

The East Europeans roughly constituted two camps. The larger was comprised of those from the Czarist territories who brought with them searing memories of pogroms and oppression. A lesser number had come from the lands of the Austro-Hungarian empire, especially the hapless Galician province whose soil could never feed its population. They had fled famine, but nursed kind sentiments for Emperor Francis Joseph; convinced of his benevolence towards the Jews, they blamed all malice on his parliament. The Russian immigrants' sweet dream was the Czar's downfall, and an extension of it was their belief that he would be succeeded by the millennium which would begin on Russian soil. Hatred of the Czar was a universal Jewish passion. But the Austro-Hungarians believed that royal Vienna, so long as the Hapsburgs ruled, was very nearly the millennium realized, and on holidays, in the Lower East Side synagogues, they recited a fervent prayer for the longevity of the emperor and the welfare of his household.

Like the patriarch Abraham, the generous Russians invited all strangers into their tents. There was always a place for yet another guest at their tables. Their fare was meager, simple, and wholesome and shared as if it were plentiful—potatoes and borscht, well-baked bread, and hot tea from the samovar. The Russians ate with relish, yet absentmindedly; they could not swallow without conversation, or digest without debate, yet their impassioned arguments were without excessive acrimony. Most of them had come from the Ukraine, birthplace of Hassidism, and were tainted with a fatal mixture of Slav melancholy and Hassidic exuberance, a keen sensitivity to social injustice and an obsession with Redemption. Being the majority, they provided the immigrant population with most of its editors, authors, and teachers; actors, theater directors, and civic leaders; ideologists, agitators, and other dispensers of the Lower East Side's rich diversity of isms—Socialism, anarchism, Zionism, and vegetarianism and other fads.

Aspiring journalists, actors, and candidates for office who failed to make it alleged discrimination by the Russian Jews. This was disproved, for example, by the prominence of Galicians in the press and on the stage, yet the allegation stuck and brought a sharp drawing of ethnic frontiers.

Delancey Street divided the two Jewish "nationalities." The Russian real extended from the south side to Cherry Street which was like a minefield, populated by abusive and belligerent Irish. The Austro-Hungarian kingdom extended from Delancey northward towards Twelfth Street where the Italian quarter began with festooned streets, religious processions, church bazaars, and dancing on the pavement in celebration of their saints' days. The Italians' sidewalks always swarmed with humanity of all ages, middle-aged men pitching horseshoes, old men puffing on their pipes, matriarchs admonishing their broods, and riding on all this was passionate and gestured talk and constant (or so it seemed) disputation and reconciliation.

The first confrontations between the East European Jews and Italians were in the garment center where they worked side by side. They somehow took to each other. Perhaps it was because they shared many habits—loud speech, broad gestures, pleasure in food, and profound concern for the well-being of their families. Both the Jewish and Italian womenfolk worked alongside their husbands and wielded a stern matriarchal authority over their households.

The Poles and Ukrainians formed a disreputable little enclave within the Austro-Hungarian district. Shuttling between mass and raucous saloons, they smelled of incense, vodka, and vomit. They brought these smells and habits with them across more than three thousand miles of ocean. In their native villages they had been sharecroppers and tenant farmers who traded and bartered with the Jew, yet on a signal, when well soused, would pour into the *shtetl* to pillage, rape, and massacre the very Jew with whom they traded. In America, they became janitors and handymen on the Lower East Side, sweepers and porters in the garment center, too humbled and dependent on the Jew to erupt even when drunk.

Within the two general categories of Jews, there were several subdivisions. The Russians towed a number of satellites—Lithuanians, Rumanians, and Poles. The Hungarians and Galicians were divided, even as the empire itself. Both were unequivocally loyal to Francis Joseph, and their younger people were votaries of Austro-Hungarian culture. However, the Hungarians loved Budapest at least as well as Vienna, and regarded themselves as Magyar Jews, and, in their opinion, Magyars were the salt of all the empire's nationalities.

The Galician Jew knew no counterpoise to Viennese elegance and sophistication. Having always been forced to toe a precarious line between their national aspirations, he had no affection for his neighbors, the Poles and Ruthenians. Each claimed Galicia as their own, sought to involve the Jew in their conspiracies against the other and against the Crown, and threatened that unless he did their will, he faced horrendous retribution when they seized power. Under the circumstances, he had no alternative but to place his trust in Francis Joseph. Vienna, knowing that the Jews were the only loyal subjects in that contumacious province, apppointed them to responsible posts in Galicia while erecting sky-high barriers against them in the capital itself.

Hungary is partly in Europe and partly in the Levant, and these two disparate elements are mixed peculiarly in the character of its people, including the Jews. The Hungarian Yiddish is a grating jabber, dominated by Magyar accents which, with Latvian and Finnish, are rooted in esoteric Ugric. Coming from a bountiful country and from among a sensuous peoples, the Hungarian Jews were more fleshed than any other Jewish immigrant group. Their walk was languorous, their footsteps heavy. Their men barbered themselves frequently and were heavy gamblers, and the elder among them wore handlebar moustaches and side burns à la the emperor and walked huge dogs, a suspiciously non-Jewish custom. Their womenfolk had a Gypsy quality about them which even the clothes they copied from Viennese fashion magazines could not subdue. They fancied huge earrings, beads and bracelets which tinkled like Christmas trees, and read palms and cards for a hobby, another non-Jewish custom.

The Hungarians, sternly clannish, were gregarious among their own, however. They had a generous conception of familial relationship. Anyone who spoke Magyar was welcome at their weekend "orgies" of goulash, wine, fiddling, songs, and card games.

They were notoriously unpredictable, reputedly produced more apostates from Judaism per capita than any other Jewish community, and also Hassidim unmatched in fanaticism. The apostates came from Budapest, the inquisitorial Hassidim from the shtetlach [2] that clustered at the foot and on the slopes of the Carpathian mountains. Remnants of each breed are still found in New York City today. The Hassidic pietists have settled in Brooklyn's Williamsburg, produce their own kosher food, and rarely intermarry with families outside their own clan. The apostates, wearing elongated beards and wide rimmed hats, staff the vanishing societies that seek to proselytize the Jews.

Yet, the Hungarians, like the Galicians, had an inordinate capacity for rapid adaptation. Not emancipated until the second half of the

[2] Plural of shtetl.

nineteenth century, they brought forth almost immediately figures of international eminence in the arts and sciences. Among Hungarians in this category, defection from Judaism was the custom. The Galicians—Freud and Buber were of Galician origin—generally remained within their fold, albeit passively. They probably had learned to temporize in following a tight and perilous course between Galicia's two contentious nationalities. Affluent Galician pietists who traveled abroad for business even trimmed their beards, defying orthodoxy. Their Hassidic or miracle rabbis maintained courts of almost Continental elegance, visited Europe's fashionable spas, and retained tutors to teach their daughters German and piano.

The Galician, like the others, brought his habits with him to America. Like all aspiring provincials, he affected courtly manners. He was vain; sometimes even the most orthodox carried a pocket mirror and comb, quoting the Talmudic admonition that a scholar must not be careless about his appearance. He was a poseur. A Galician of even the most common variety used two kinds of Yiddish, one which set him apart in a manner he did not desire, and one by which he deliberately set himself apart. The first was an idiomatically rich but peculiarly accented daily speech. The other was a kind of high Yiddish, in reality ungrammatical German, which he used in correspondence and in addressing the intelligentsia—physicians, pharmacists, notaries.

The Jewish menu through East Europe was essentially the same, except for single items—goulash was specifically Hungarian, sugared fish was Polish, *karnetzlach* (fried sausages) and *mameliga* (cornmeal bread) were Rumanian. The Galician contributed nothing to the culinary arts but a manner. He preferred a variety of dishes, miniscule portions if need be, to a single filling course. He exchanged pleasantries, but avoided conversation at mealtimes. It was the equivalent of a Japanese tea ceremony, which he supported with Talmudic and exegetical quotations.

The Rumanians, among the Russian satellites, were concentrated just north of Delancey Street and constituted a bridgehead inside the Austro-Hungarian quarter. They had no sense of clan, however. Like the Russians, they were generous, especially when in high spirits which was almost always, and, like the Hungarians, coming from an ample rural hinterland they liked good food, rollicking company, sentimental fiddling, and cards. They were outgoing extroverts and capitalized on this element in their nature, as well as on their culinary skills. Two years before this narrative begins, in 1919, they owned 150 restaurants, twenty wine-cellars, and thirty coffee houses in New York City. Most of these were concentrated on the Lower East Side, featured "Rumanian" in their names, and were no doubt responsible for converting the American palate to pastrami, corned beef, horse radish and sour pickles, knishes, blintzes, matzoh balls, and noodles.

Their smoke-filled coffee houses with corrugated ceilings and fly-specked walls, was where the men gathered to play cards. The turnover at the tables was frequent. Hungarians were known to be obsessive gamblers, Rumanians—absorbed players. Their wine-cellars were restaurants with entertainment in the Continental style, no jerky comedians or high-kicking chorus lines, but a pianist, an accordionist or a violinist, and a female singer in the mid-passage of her life, well-upholstered and generously made-up. The Yiddish theater was cradled in the Jewish wine-cellars of Rumania. Some Broadway and Hollywood stars came from theatrical families whose careers began in the wine-cellars of New York's Lower East Side.

The Poles and Lithuanians were dispersed inside the Russian quarter where, however, they maintained their own synagogues. Like the biblical "half tribe of Benjamin," the Lithuanians or Litvaks were the least numerous. They were an ascetic, conceited enclave, and made no attempt to pass as Russians, which at any rate would have been difficult because of their characteristically lisping speech. The Galicians were ridiculed for lesser speech pecularities, yet the Litvaks, although they mispronounced the Divine name itself because they could not pronounce a hard S, were sought after as teachers by the finest Hebrew schools in New York City. The reason was that while Lithuania was short on food, it had the most celebrated Talmudical academies in all Europe. The Lithuanian would treat a slice of bread and herring as a full meal, but he would not suffer fools. Even the most common garden variety Litvak could turn out to be a scholar, possessed of quick wits, a stinging tongue, the ability to argue both sides of a case with equal skill, and to invent a third side which he argued even more persuasively. His sons and grandsons became mathematicians, physicists, and professors of law and philosophy.

The Poles, who were probably no less numerous than the Russians, suffered from a fragmented collective personality. The several partitionings of Poland had left them confused about their speech and sense of place. There was a distinctive Polish Yiddish. But many whose birthplaces were designated Polish territory in the peace treaties of 1918 had been Austrian or Russian nationals when they emigrated. They spoke in accents ranging from Galician to Lithuanian and rejected the Polish label. The Lithuanians wished to be just that, unadulterated Litvaks. The Galicians were masters of dissimulation. Some tried to pass as Austrians, which they thought made them cosmopolitans, but it also made them kin of the Yahudim, which invited disapprobation on the Lower East Side. More often they tried to pass as Russians, which they believed would help them achieve civic prominence. There were many such Galician marranos[3] who affected Russian or even Lithuanian accents.

The divisive ethnicism among the East Europeans crumbled rapidly in the nineteen-twenties under the impact of powerful centripetal factors. These included the Yiddish press, stage, and literatures; the various ideological movements; and the decentralization of the immigrant population which, fanning out into the Bronx and Brooklyn, also broke away from the dense ethnic concentration patterns of the Lower East Side. There were at play, also, two major ambiguous factors—the violent labor war in the garment industry which divided the East Europeans along class and ideological lines, and the triumphant struggle against the hegemony of the Germans, or Yahudim.

All mass media have the effect of bringing disparate groups together but the Yiddish press and stage were not content with this passive process. Servicing a cross-section of the Yiddish-speaking population, they deliberately lampooned all ethnic peculiarities alike, giving the Litvak and Galician an opportunity to laugh not merely at one another but also at themselves. Furthermore, they laughed together in the darkness of the same theater, and at the workbench during lunch-break read aloud from the same newspaper. The masters of Yiddish fiction, Sholem Aleichem from the Ukraine, and Sholem Asch from Poland, demonstrated that but for dialectal differences there was no true distinction between one group of Jews and another throughout the vast territory of East Europe.

Trade unionism and Zionism played a key role in bringing together the German and East European Jew. Industrial violence in the garment center erupted in headlines across the country. The Yahudim were fearful that this would damage the Jews' reputation, especially their own. Removed from the manufacture of clothes by several decades, they were now able to view the industry's problems dispassionately, and pledged strikers their full support. A strikers' rally at Carnegie Hall

[3]Converts to Christianity in Inquisitorial Spain who secretly still practiced Judaism.

in 1916 was thrown into ecstatic messianic bedlam when, among those taking their seats on the stage behind the speakers' podium, there appeared financier-philanthropist Jacob Schiff, chief dispenser of Yahudim charity, a benevolent autocrat who comported himself as the custodian of American Jewry, and Felix Warburg, a much milder man with an interest in the arts, who was Schiff's heir apparent in Jewish philanthropy. The glitter of New York society filled the loges. The garment industry's *nouveau riche* felt beyond the social pale with this combination against them.

The war for hegemony between the immigrants and the Yahudim which, paradoxically, brought them closer together, was directed by the Zionists who were sometimes joined, but more often not, by the Socialist and trade union leaders who were irreconcilably opposed to the Zionist purpose—the restoration of Jewish nationhood in Palestine. The Yahudim, who likewise opposed this nationalistic objective, nonetheless spread their money wherever it might help, including Zionist-sponsored institutions in Palestine.

The Zionist-devised strategy sought to depose the Yahudim as trustees of American Jewry's philanthropic disbursements abroad and as spokesmen for American Jewry. The first objective was difficult to achieve since philanthropic funds came primarily from "the West Side."

However, immediately after the outbreak of hostilities in 1914, it became apparent that the funds necessary to relieve the destitution of the evacuated Jewish populations and devastated Jewish communities in the East European war zones could not be raised from large contributions alone, and that popular subscription was required. "The East Side" announced its separate collection and disbursement agency because it was denied a voice on the relief body operated by the Yahudim. The latter finally yielded their strongest weapon of authority, the purse, and the JDC (The American Jewish Joint Distribution Committee) was formed, providing some representation also for the East Side.

Now the immigrants, under the Zionist banner, advanced to their second objective, which was to wrest political power from the Yahudim. The terms "East Side" and "West Side" were used pointedly to underscore also the class difference, the underprivileged versus the privileged Jew. Many of the concepts in this second assault came from the small but dynamic Socialist (Labor) Zionists, who were hosts then to two young political fugitives from Turkish-ruled Palestine. One was tall, thin, scholarly with a gentle smile and patient manner, Itzhak Ben-Zvi, who later was to become Israel's President, and the other was short, pugnacious, rosy-cheeked David Ben-Gurion, of high-pitched voice and staccato speech, who, three decades later, was to deliver Israel from the womb of a strife-torn Palestine and attend it through its post-natal period.

The Zionists called for the election of an American Jewish Congress by popular vote. The Congress convened and chose a delegation to present Jewish demands to the Paris Peace Conference: One was international endorsement of Britain's Balfour Declaration which pledged the establishment of a National Home in Palestine for the Jewish people; the other was that all treaties with the East European, Balkan, and Baltic nations guaranteed that the Jews would be accorded the same rights as all other minority nationalities in those territories.

It was obvious, to the Yahudim, that the invitation that they join the American Jewish Congress was intended to obtain their voluntary abdication from the stewardship of American Jewish affairs. But there were other issues involved. The Yahudim were seriously disturbed by the connotations of a "Jewish" Congress, a "Jewish" delegation to the Peace Conference, and recognition of any segment of the Jewish people, however remote from the United States, as a distinct and separate nationality. The terms connoted alien concepts in the American context, but were not novel in the multi-national territories of the former Austro-Hungarian and Russian empires where the Jews, de facto, were regarded as one other minority nationality.

The Yahudim fought back at every step. As in Greek mythology, the battle for leadership was dominated by two forceful adversaries. Louis Marshall, corporate attorney, was "Secretary of State" of the Yahudim Establishment and architect of its public policy. The commander-in-chief of the Zionist forces—and this was Zionism's great coup—was also a Yahudi, a non-Establishment Yahudi, however, Louis D. Brandeis, Kentucky-born Boston attorney, People's Defender against the corporate interests. Brandeis had also acquired by then a reputation among the multitudes in the garment industry. In 1910, as mediator in a strike situation, he formulated a protocol which established novel rules of labor-management relations. It provided for a permanent arbitration board, with an impartial chairman; a preferential shop which gave the union first claim to all future job vacancies and was forerunner of the closed shop, and employer recognition of a shop chairman elected by the workers in each factory as their spokesman. Brandeis assumed for several years the post of the industry's impartial chairman. It took about two decades, however, before all disruption ceased and both sides fully realized the advantage of voluntary arbitration over strikes and lockouts.

His involvement in the garment center was Brandeis' first encounter with the Yiddish-speaking people. Until then, he had only a vague and unmeaningful awareness of his Jewishness. It is on this ground that Marshall regarded him as an intruder and challenged his credentials as a spokesman on Jewish affairs.

Alongside Brandeis stood the Hungarian-born firebrand Zionist, Rabbi Stephen S. Wise. He had turned down an offer from Temple Emanu-El, citadel of wealth and influence, because it would not guarantee him freedom of the pulpit; was an unrelenting leader of the civic reform forces in New York City, and one of the most eloquent preachers of any religious denomination in America against the savage labor policies of the mining industries. Brandeis and Wise had ready access to President Wilson. In the past the East Europeans had to rely on the Yahudim to intervene at the White House.

Brandeis, furthermore, attracted to the Zionist movement a host of other non-Establishment Yahudim. They included Austrian-born Felix Frankfurter of Harvard, and his young acolyte Benjamin V. Cohen, later member of a famous team of Roosevelt's advisers. Both Frankfurter and Cohen had a hand in drafting and redrafting the Balfour Declaration. Also drawn into the Zionist orbit by Brandeis were Laurence Steinhardt, who later served this country in several important ambassadorial posts; Eugene Meyer, Jr., who was to become publisher of the *Washington Post*, a governor of the Federal Reserve Bank, and to serve in various capacities under five Presidents; the merchant princes and philanthropists Nathan Straus and Lincoln M. Kerstein; and Bernard Flexner, attorney and social worker, brother of Abraham and Simon, the celebrated educator and medical researcher, respectively.

Marshall was a realist. Seeing the odds, he surrendered and gracefully accepted co-chairmanship of the American Jewish Congress delegation to Paris.

Time worked one of its most precious ironies. Marshall learned Yiddish so that he might himself follow the vituperative polemics against him in the Yiddish newspapers and challenge their editorial inaccuracies. He began collecting Yiddish books for his private library, was seen at the premieres of the better Yiddish plays. The East Side and Marshall had become exceedingly fond of one another.

Brandeis took an opposite course. The immigrants' culture had never piqued his intellectual curiosity. He had always been an austere and remote presence, impatient with the din that greeted his appearance at Zionist mass rallies. His elevation to the Supreme Court was celebrated with heavy heart by all East Side Zionists. To them, he had deserted the cause which was to effect the redemption of Jewry.

Although retired from Zionist office, Brandeis was determined to press his differences over Zionist policy with Dr. Chaim Weizmann, later Israel's first President. The result was a savage eruption of the East Side's ambivalence. Weizmann was East European Jewry's great pride. He had risen from the shtetl to eminence as a scientist. He had acquired many languages but never lost his mastery of the idiom of his early years. East Side legend described him as moving among potentates, a first among equals, and insisted that the Balfour Declaration was a private reward to Weizmann—the only reward he requested—for his war services to Britain.

The Yiddish press opened fire on Brandeis. It charged that having callously laid down his Zionist role, he nonetheless tried to exercise it through his disciples who were then in charge of Zionist affairs in America. It accused the latter of supercilious behavior towards the Zionist rank and file, and of contempt for its opinion. Overwhelmed, the Brandeis group surrendered office. It was the ultimate in the East Europeans' self-assertion.

However, Brandeis and most of those he had enlisted remained forever concerned with Zionism's progress, and in crisis after crisis, political and financial, responded to appeals from Weizmann and his followers.

The East Side revolt might never have succeeded had there not been an East Side shadow government prepared to replace the Yahudim.

From the very outset the immigrants resented what they alleged was the arbitrary and patronizing treatment they received in the Yahudim-sponsored dispensaries, immigrant aid bureaus, and other social welfare agencies. It is true, of course, that in all their contacts with the East Side, the Yahudim sought to "correct" the immigrants' manners and thinking to conform to their own. They regarded the newcomers as their peculiar "white man's burden" but, unlike white colonials in Africa, they obtained no material gain from the immigrants. The Orthodox pietists muttered about the "missionizing" intent of the Germans who were Reform Jews, which, in the Orthodox opinion of that day, was synonymous with apostasy. The Socialists bristled at "charity ladled out by the overfed." The Zionists called for "a voice for the people, democratization of the institutions." But it was the little people, un-committed to any ideology, clinging to their dignity and determined to assert it by helping themselves, who set about altering the situation.

They transplanted a system of mutual aid that had been the key to Jewish survival through the several centuries of Jewish life in the shtetlach of East Europe and throughout diaspora history. Its prin-ciples are derived from the biblical injunctions that man is his brother's keeper, that some of the harvest should be left in the field "for the poor among thy people and for the stranger within thy gates."

On the East Side, this mutual aid was distributed, in the first in-stance, through the *landsmanschaft* which dates back to the sixth cen-tury before the Common Era. In the First Babylonian captivity, the Judean exiles organized themselves in accordance with their Palestinian towns of origin. The East European immigrants in America followed a similar pattern. No sooner were there enough landsmen for a quorum, then they formed a landsmanschaft. Its proceedings followed Cushing's Manual of Parliamentary Rules, although it is a mystery how they dis-covered its existence. Some landsmanschaften adopted Masonic features —pass words, secret oaths, special regalia for officers, and quaint rituals —the gavel was pounded once to recognize a member from the floor, twice to recognize an officer, and three times to open or adjourn a meeting. Their tests for membership reflected Jewish mores: some barred saloonkeepers, almost all societies blackballed strikebreakers.

These proceedings were irrelevant, however, to the societies' main purpose which was that landsmen help one another. The kinds and extent of benefits depended on the size of a society's membership, and embraced a wide range—medical, unemployment and strike insurance, sick benefit and disability compensation, and many benefits associated with death: a burial plot and funeral costs, and, if a member left no male heir, provisions for the recital of the kaddish, the mourner's prayer, at morning and evening services in the twelve-month period following his demise. Provisions were also made, within a society's capacities, for the widow and orphans. A "shiva fund" compensated members for wages lost during the *shiva*, the seven days' mourning period. An officer called Hospitaler visited the sick in accordance with Jewish custom. The societies also offered no-interest loans and the officers were granted a "discretionary fund" to spare members such embarrassments as eviction for non-payment of rent.

Medical insurance was provided by the "society doctor" who was paid an annual flat fee from the society's treasury, or charged its members, in the nineteen-twenties, fifty cents a visit. These "royal commissions" went to members' sons or sons-in-law at a time when patients were not easy to come by because of the widespread practice of "home medicine": grocers sold mustard for backaches, rock candy for coughs; sore throats were gargled with salt water; colds were relieved with hot tea and lemon or with a visit to a Turkish bath, and barbers displayed signs, "We do cupping." The society doctor was one form of the East Side's assertion of its independence of Yahudim charity.

When Jacob Schiff, the capricious and concerned philanthropist passed away in the final months of 1920—another reason which marks 1921 as a milestone in the East Side's struggle for hegemony—his charity had become obsolescent. He was mourned even by those who had fought him bitterly, because he had been a responsive human being who, at one time or another, supported even those Jewish causes he had opposed, such as Zionist institutions in Palestine.

Schiff had a firm but unpredictable will and the disposition of a martinet. He had tried to impose his dictates on the East Side but failed. The East Side, however, knew him also as a proud and unflinching intervener for his people. It savored and embellished the story of his encounter with President Taft, who, under pressure from commercial interests, had refused to honor an implied pre-election pledge to denounce the Russo-American Treaty of 1832. That treaty guaranteed the citizens of either country safety and courtesy in the territory of the other, but Russia decided that these guarantees did not include American Jews. The latter felt that this was sufficient ground for abrogating the Treaty, and, furthermore, that such action would provide vigorous expression of America's disgust over Czarist-inspired pogroms.

When a delegation, headed by Schiff, was told that this could not be done, Schiff reputedly took the unprecedented initiative of terminating a Presidential conference. He himself later admitted this much, "I told the President: The question will not be downed. Mr. President, we had hoped that you would see that justice was done us, but you have decided otherwise; we shall go to the American people." When, outside the White House, a member of the delegation sighed, "We are in exile," Schiff eyed him archly and swore, "We shall fight." The issue indeed, was carried to the people. Congress denounced the Treaty.

However, at the time Jacob Schiff passed away, scores of hospitals, homes for the aged, sanitariums, day nurseries, synagogues and Hebrew schools had already demonstrated the East Side's capacity to look after its own. The East Side also contributed impressively to the JDC campaign for Jewish overseas needs. But it was estimated that the total collections of JDC were exceeded by the separate disbursements of the several thousand landsmanschaften directly assisting to their devastated shtetlach abroad. Embassies from the landsmanschaften virtually shuttled between the United States and their hometowns to survey needs and distribute funds. Their concern embraced matters that a big relief apparatus might overlook, such as repairing the leaking synagogue roof, or installing a new drainage system in the mikva, the ritual bathhouse.

These circumstances diminished the power of the paternalistic philanthropist. Schiff's contributions were generous and welcome, but he could no longer impose conditions. He had been reduced from an autocratic grandfather to an ornamental grandfather's clock. The dapper small figure, with the Van Dyke beard and brightly polished, buttoned shoes, continued to the very last to visit the East Side regularly where he conversed in pidgin German. Indigent individuals still petitioned his favor as he walked in their midst, yet the East Side was no longer his duchy. It was now a flourishing independent republic.

The East Side, violent battleground of ideologies, was flying armistice flags here and there by 1921. Real stakes were involved. Garment-center labor had obtained the preferential shop. Zionism had its toehold in Palestine. The Jews' tradition of practical idealism asserted itself; the pragmatists took charge.

Old Guard Socialists were outraged and employers were baffled when Sidney Hillman, President of the Amalgamated Clothing Workers, proposed to a meeting of manufacturers that they form a national association corresponding to the labor union. This would make possible, he explained, blanket negotiations for the entire industry, thus sparing all parties the time, effort, and expense involved in separate union negotiations with hundreds of individual employers. The employers turned the proposal down, calling it a "trick." One of the old time Socialist fire and brimstone orators, Mikhail Zametkin, the father of novelist Laura Z. Hobson, denounced it as a "sellout of Socialist principles."

In the meantime, Ben-Zvi and Ben-Gurion were back in Palestine where in 1920 they helped found Histadrut, a federation of labor and association of cooperatives. Within a decade, Histadrut had become the virtual steward of the fortunes of the Palestine Jewish community, the foundation on which the Zionist enterprise and its hope for fulfillment rested. Histadrut helped create a shadow Jewish state. Its cooperative industrial workshops began the secret manufacture of small arms which were stored at its cooperative villages that served also as training grounds for a secret defense army. Contributions solicited among workers and landsmanschaften in America by the Israel Histadrut campaign helped keep the several activities of Histadrut going. Non-labor Zionists were not always even vaguely aware of all that was going on in Palestine.

Dr. Chaim Weizmann, supported by Labor, moved quickly to enlist the widest possible Jewish support for the Palestine upbuilding effort. He readily offered accommodations to non-Zionists. Samuel Untermeyer, a non-Establishment Yahudi and a leading corporate attorney, assumed the chairmanship of a fund-raising drive for the Jewish National Home. The Establishment Yahudim were offered partnership in a new body then in formation, The Jewish Agency for Palestine, which was to supervise the undertaking. In November, 1921, the whole East Side turned out into the streets to greet a motorcade carrying a special Zionist fund-raising delegation to American Jewry headed by the legendary Weizmann and the mythical Professor Albert Einstein. Many were moved to tears by elation, and religious Jews, as the caravan passed them, muttered the prayers customary in the presence of princes and sages: "Blessed art thou, O Lord, Our God, King of the universe Who bestoweth of His wisdom and dignity upon those of flesh and blood."

Establishment Yahudim rode up the elevators at the Commodore Hotel to pay their respects to Einstein and Weizmann. Jacob Fishman, managing editor of *The Jewish Morning Journal,* then the major Yiddish Zionist daily, received a surprise phone call from Bernard Baruch who invited him to dinner. At first, Fishman thought it was a hoax. They had never met before and Baruch had been remote even from the Yahudim. But it was true and throughout dinner Fishman was subjected to a long monologue which revolved about scores of scrap books that Baruch displayed. They contained an amazingly thorough collection of anti-Semitic jibes in the American press about his wartime role as Wilson's advisor. Dinner concluded, the financier, unsolicited, drew up a check which he handed over to Fishman "for the Palestine fund." He offered no explanation. It was implicit in the evening's monologue.

CHAPTER 2

Press and Theater

THE JEWS from Eastern Europe were a singular exception among the ethnic multitudes that poured into the United States before Congress imposed immigration quotas in the early nineteen-twenties. The Irish, Italian, and Slavic immigrants were the dispossessed elements among their peoples. All they were able to bring with them were caste subcultures. The Jewish immigrants were different. They were not a class but a dispossessed people, all of Jewry in microcosm—the *yichus* (Brahmins), *balebatische* (decent folks), and the *podlie* (dregs). They deposited on American soil their full culture, the shtetl gripped in the throes of transition from ghetto to freedom, which had begun long before their arrival here.

The Jewish immigrants were attracted but not overwhelmed by the American momentum. The interplay between the impact of America and Jewish adaptability resulted in an outburst of creativity among the newcomers. In the harassing circumstances of social, geographic, and economic adjustment, they managed to launch and direct an awesome culture explosion. Its verbal instrument was Yiddish. Its peak was reached in the nineteen-twenties. The immigrant had little leisure. Even the unionized worker had no more than one-and-a-half days a week that were his own, yet inexhaustible vigor compensated for indentured time. Something was always going on that piqued his curiosity, engaged his passions, and he was deeply committed to all that touched him—his newspapers, writers, rabbis, cantors, actors; and ideology, though waning, could still spark violent dissension.

Some of the time consumed by these activities was provided by the slack periods which afflicted the garment center with unfailing regularity twice a year. Even in the busy season, with all the available time consumed by overtime schedules, the pace of their cultural and social activities did not diminish.

There were several reasons for this. There was the immigrants' physical environment. The shtetlach were rural townships, almost always near rivers and woods. The East Side, by contrast, was a compound without space or vegetation, its dwellings crammed, dilapidated, and taut with tensions. However, the Jews possessed a centuries-old immunity against drabness, boredom, or irascibility. Denied opportunities for sports and occasions for levity, they cultivated an extraordinary substitute—discourse and debate, which could be practiced even in a cell, was more diverting than devised entertainment, and no less competitive than sports or business. Passed down from the scholar's lectern to the artisan's bench, and revered as an art, debate came naturally to the Jew, and the younger generation of East European Jews received post-graduate forensic training in the clandestine revolutionary movements.

This may well be an idealized portrayal. The immigrant majority was no doubt oblivious to the creative ferment which brought periodic invasions of the East Side by aristocratic Gentile liberals. Many of the immigrant proletariat and nouveau riche no doubt preferred to spend their leisure playing poker and pinochle, although the Yiddish newspapers they read unanimously branded gambling as a demeaning diversion. But it was the fervent minority that set the normative standards. Its headquarters were Second Avenue, immigrant Jewry's Broadway, and multi-faceted East Broadway, which accommodated three of the five Yiddish dailies, numerous book stores, parochial schools and rabbinical academies, the Socialist Party headquarters, and also the Zionists' headquarters before they removed themselves, under Brandeis' administration, "way up town" to Fifth Avenue and 18th Street.

The Yiddish theater had branch lines in Harlem, the Bronx, and Brownsville which presented melodramas, musicals, variety acts, and performers remaindered by Second Avenue. Occasionally they even managed to entice a real star who had overplayed his hand in bargaining over terms and at season's opening found himself without a contract on Second Avenue.

The Lower East Side was the theater's sacred grounds, however. Max Gabel's Bowery Theater was the domain of Jennie Goldstein who wrung handkerchiefs more vigorously and shed tears more copiously than any other actress on the Yiddish stage. In the role of women who had been wronged, she retained the audience's confidence in their essential virtue, even though their children were born out of wedlock, their lovers were pimps, and their husbands death-row inmates. Gabel advertised not only his star, but also his stage sets—"a real electric chair," "twenty thousand gallons of water raining down on the stage."

On Second Avenue, Molly Picon, cast as a naughty little boy in Hassidic garb, strut about the stage before ecstatic capacity audiences, which included the intellectual elite who normally would not waste their time on musical comedy.

But it was the premieres at the Yiddish Art Theater that brought out a truly elite audience—visiting Zionist eminences, Yiddish poets, the Lower East Side's foremost ideologists, academicians and surgeons, and the full Broadway galaxy—Otis Skinner, Alice Brady, Ernest Truex, and the unpredictable Barrymore clan.

The paternity and birth of the Yiddish Art Theater are somewhat in dispute. It is generally dated back to 1918 when the overbearing Maurice Schwartz, actor, director, producer, recruited his first ensemble for the Irving Place Theater. Yet, purists insist that it was founded in 1919 by gentle Jacob Ben-Ami, the "profile" of the Jewish theater, when he broke away from Schwartz. They are technically right. It was Ben-Ami who first used the term "art." In 1918 the Irving Place Theater repertoire included, in addition to Yiddish works of high caliber, plays by Shaw, Schiller, Tolstoi, and Ibsen (*Ghosts* and *Doll's House*). In 1919 plays by Schnitzler, Andreyev, Gorki, Strindberg, and Wilde were added to the repertoire, and in subsequent seasons works by Shakespeare, Maupassant, Chekhov, Gogol, Molière, Feuchtwanger, Merezhkovski, Rolland, Toller, Lope de Vega, and others were included.[1] Schwartz's closest rivals in the volume of foreign plays produced in America were the Theatre Guild whose enthusiasm was shortlived, however, and the Civic Repertory Theater founded by Eva Le Gallienne several years later.

The Yiddish Art Theater and Maurice Schwartz enjoyed a unique reputation with the Jewish audiences. Almost all, except the podlie, had an ambivalent attitude even towards their most revered actors. The Yiddish theater originated with the Purim *shpiel*—a kind of minstrel show, mixing melodrama, history and comedy—put on by amateurs on

[1] David S. Lifson, *The Yiddish Theatre in America* (New York: Thomas Yoseloff, 1965).

Purim, which commemorates the hanging of Haman, a Persian official who some two millennia ago had planned the decimation of its Jewish community. The Purim *shpieler* (actors) would stroll about the shtetl, from one rich man's home to another, performing for the entertainment of his family and of the crowds that would gather outside the windows. The Purim shpieler was a merrymaker and this has become the Jewish definition of an actor. Even Jennie Goldstein, who relieved her audiences of buckets of tears and broke their hearts, was after all only a merrymaker. Not so Maurice Schwartz and his Yiddish Art cast. They were different, serious. Wisdom was spoken from his stage and you had to apply yourself to comprehend it. Tolstoi, Schiller, Ibsen, and Shakespeare were names spoken with reverence even among learned synagogue Jews who would not be seen passing under a theater marquee.

Schwartz was royalty. He had the dark, fleshy features and soulful eyes of the mythical Arab potentate. Unfortunately his powerful, but raucous voice, his massive build and lumbering posture, fitted him for little else but the common man roles of the Yiddish repertoire. He was at his best in Peretz Hirschbein's *Greene Felder* [*Green Fields*], David Pinski's *Yenkel Schmidt* [*Yenkel the Blacksmith*], Fischel Bimko's Jewish-Polish demimonde characters, and Leon Kobrin's shtetl and immigrant sensualists. Aspiring beyond these roles, he sometimes would mar a performance of *kleine menshelach* (little people) with a sudden grandiloquent King Lear gesture. His talents as director were also best applied to the shtetl repertoire. He would assure his actors, before they signed up, that he was aware that even versatility had its limits, and that he believed, besides, in the ensemble system. He would engage experienced European directors and give them similar assurances. However, once rehearsals began, he preempted everything, and ended up starring in most of the plays and directing them himself.

Yet, notwithstanding his reputation for unkept promises, Schwartz was able to lure away some of the finest actors from the commercial stage because a season with Maurice Schwartz would establish an actor as a "serious artist," not just a Purim shpieler.

One of Schwartz's great triumphs was when he signed up Ludwig Satz, one of the highest paid stars on the Yiddish stage. The Yiddish literary elite at all times snubbed the commercial theater, except when Satz or Molly Picon performed. Menashe Skulnik's prototype, a tragicomedian, Satz's metier was the pure-hearted ne'er-do-well, the "saintly fool," that is a hallmark of Hassidic legend and Yiddish and Slavic literature. He was a member of the Adler dynasty which still endures in Hollywood and on Broadway. Its patriarch was Jacob P. Adler and myth has it that progeny bearing the old gentleman's distinctive physiognomy, if not his name, has forever preserved the aura of his presence in all the cities where he performed.

Satz broke with Schwartz after that one season, yet rumors would seasonally spread along the Avenue that he was about to sign with Schwartz again. Satz was torn between a desire to "prove" himself once more at the Yiddish Art Theater and a reluctance to forfeit the lucrative offers of the commercial theater. Furthermore, he insisted that the roles in which he would be cast at the Yiddish Art Theater be listed in a contract. Schwartz maintained that his oral pledge was sufficient and that a contrary view impugned his sterling reputation. The rumors benefited both men. They conveyed the impression that Satz would sacrifice Money for Art if Schwartz would meet his terms, and brought him an increase from his nervous producer who, before the rumor started, pretended that the star's demands would drive him into bankruptcy. It benefited Schwartz because the more capricious and important members of his cast became amenable in contract negotiations, fearing that with Satz as an attraction the Yiddish Art Theater might dispense with their services altogether.

Schwartz's unrestrained passion for starring and directing caused frequent defections from his cast. Jacob Ben-Ami and Rudolf Schild-kraut [2] intermittently tried their fortunes on Broadway and each launched his own Yiddish art theater, but after a season or two they returned chastened to Schwartz. Jacob Ben-Ami both acted and directed with the Theatre Guild and the Civic Repertory Theater. Schildkraut eventually moved on to Hollywood. Even Schwartz himself, complaining that he was unappreciated by his cast, the critics, and the audience, occasionally defected to Broadway, only to return each time to his native grounds.

However, one of the Yiddish Art Theater's major actors eventually became both a Broadway and a Hollywood star. He was Muni Weisen-

---

[2] Schildkraut had come from the Berlin stage with a great reputation. Even Gentile German actors, arriving in America and finding that there was no permanent German theater, turned to the Yiddish stage. They never learned to read the Hebrew alphabet, studying their roles from transliterated scripts. Their German-accented Yiddish was respected by the audience as a kind of Shakespearean Yiddish.

freund, the son of actors, who began his Yiddish stage career at the age of thirteen cast in gray beard roles. Ten years later he joined the Yiddish Art Theater where he stayed for seven years. He especially excelled in Sholem Aleichem roles, Schwartz's true forte. The usual pattern of Schwartz relationships with his actors developed. The older man was both paternal and solicitous and bitterly jealous. The critics demanded a fairer break for Muni Weisenfreund alleging that Schwartz was upstaging him, or assigning him roles beneath his merits. Broadway scouts became interested in Muni Weisenfreund. His first Broadway appearance was in 1926 in *We Americans,* followed in 1927 by his performance as Benny Horowitz in *Four Walls.* He then returned for two seasons to Second Avenue, but in 1929 departed for Hollywood for good. Thereafter he was known as Paul Muni. In 1932 he returned to Broadway in *Counsellor-at-Law* and acquired Hollywood stardom in *Scarface* and *I am a Fugitive from a Chain Gang,* followed, in later years, by a host of movies, including *Black Fury, The Story of Louis Pasteur, The Good Earth, The Life of Emile Zola,* and a number of Broadway hits.

It is astonishing how an essentially impecunious population, plagued by strikes, lock-outs and slack seasons, and burdened with compassionate obligations towards *landsleit* here and aboard, could nonetheless maintain so many Yiddish theaters whose influence was recorded season after season by America's drama critics. Thomas Dickson's [3] comment in 1923 was not atypical: ". . . plays written for the narrow stages of the Yiddish theatre . . . have in their genre provided some of the truest compositions of the American stage," and an unfriendly critic of Jews on the American stage, John Corbin,[4] nonetheless recommended "the Yiddish theatre . . . [as] an object lesson for Broadway" to serve the WASP [White Anglo-Saxon Protestant] audience as the Yiddish stage serves the immigrant Jew.

The Yiddish theater was financially viable in part because of its substantial advance sales. On weekdays, entire performances or substantial blocs of tickets were offered at discount prices to landsmanschaften who found this to be an effective way of raising funds for institutions here and in their "old home."

A smaller, auxiliary source of income were the Democratic and Republican captains in Jewish districts. Between the season's opening,

[3] Lifson, *op. cit.,* p. 64.
[4] *Ibid.,* pp. 64–65.

immediately after Yom Kippur and Election Eve they distributed thousands of free tickets among their loyal constituents.

News of the good fortune of the American Jewish theater spread to all corners of the diaspora.

In the nineteen-twenties two superb Jewish ensembles arrived here for a limited run, hoping to make their fortune quickly and return home. Both met with adversity. The Vilna Troupe came in 1924 from a city celebrated as 'The Jerusalem of Lithuania,' and for two centuries the world center of Talmudic learning. Its actors, for this reason perhaps, were not mere Purim shpieler. They were literary. Their Yiddish was precise, formal, almost precious. However, New York could not afford two Yiddish art theaters, not even for a single season. Financial disaster was followed by recriminations and an irreparable schism within the cast; some members returned to Vilna, some defected, yet only one of the "defectors" made it here.[5]

The other ensemble, Habimah, the first Hebrew-language theater in the world, arrived here in 1926. Its birthplace was Moscow, where it was blessed by Stanislavski, tutored by his apostle Vakhtangov, and benefited briefly from a Soviet subsidy before Hebrew was banned by the authorities. Habimah's American audiences were a most wonderful mixture: stooped, gentle-mannered teachers of Hebrew, Zionist leaders who dutifully attended without understanding a word, and Broadway celebrities who came to witness the second unfolding of Stanislavski on the American stage. His own Moscow Art Theater visited here in 1923. An unusual sight at Habimah's American performances were the bearded, skull-capped Jews, Talmudists but simultaneously also readers of modern Hebrew, orthodox but not fanatic, to whom most theater was anathema. They were never seen in a Yiddish theater, only because it was *"bittul zman,"* a purposeless waste of time. But Habimah obviously was different. It performed in the sacred tongue. The Stanislavski stylization of voice and gesture heightened the solemnity of the speech. They sat enthralled by the dialogue erupting from the stage and swirling about them. They frowned as a word escaped them in the unfamiliar Sephardic pronunciation, and as they grasped its meaning, their faces lit up.

Like the Vilna Truppe, Habimah also split. Exiled from Moscow, it was looking for a permanent home. Nahum Zemach, its founder,

[5] Joseph Buloff has had three careers—on Second Avenue, on Broadway, and in Hollywood.

and several others erroneously believed that America was its Promised Land. They were wrong. There was no place here for a permanent Hebrew theater. The majority sailed for Palestine and became the semi-official theater of the emerging Jewish state.

Yet there always were dreamers around to float new ventures. Two such dreamers were Zuni Maud, a woodcut artist, and Yosel Kotler, a painter. They were also cartoonists and authors of nonsense verse; Yosel's was amusing and set to music, Zuni's was comprehensible only to children. Zuni, squat and dark, with a comb in his hair and remotely resembling Picasso, was more likely to be mistaken for a Spanish fisherman than recognized for a Jew from the Russian Pale. His fierce black eyes contrasted with his slow manner and vague speech, and, always whittling away at something, he was as busy with his pocket knife as a woman with her knitting needles. Yosel was tall, lithe, and blond, his drowsy blue eyes contrasting with his quick, bright manner. At cafeteria tables, on a park bench, or leaning on a lamppost, Yosel would sketch quickly and automatically, and give his sketches away to startled passersby.

This was when America's Bohemia, chafing against Babbitt-restraints, curiously mistook the Soviet system for a nonconformist's paradise, and its presiding genius for another St. Francis of Assisi or Levi Yitzhak Berdichever.[6] Zuni and Yosel shared the universal simplistic faith in Communism as the redeemer of the underdog. They were underdogs themselves. Zuni had a modicum of security. His kin ran a Catskill hotel that catered to pseudo-Bohemians. To assure its success, they called it Maud's Summerei, and kept him there all summer to wander among the guests like a witless clown, his favorite imposture. Yosel had only one kin, a brother, a butcher in the Bronx, with whom he was not on speaking terms.

Yosel pretended that his frequent involuntary fasts were dietetic experiments. He once raised money for a fast-breaking gala by charging admission to "a banquet of foods bought at a discount from Rockefeller whose doctors have placed him on a diet of spinach and saliva." Although none knew what to expect, all were certain it would be great fun. The place was jammed. Some of Yosel's bohemian friends, wearing *rubashkas* (embroidered blouses) like the waiters in the Russian restaurants around town, showed the guests to tables covered with tablecloths borrowed from his non-bohemian friends. When everyone

[6] Hassidic rabbi celebrated for his humility and universal love.

was seated, Yosel stepped before a blackboard and invited his guests to call out their orders—"any victuals or viands you may desire, however rare, for the price of admission." From the rear someone called for a hot dog. Yosel acted startled, snarled "hot dogs?" then regaining his composure peered into the audience and announced that the plebeian could have his money back. Thereafter only Lucullan orders were shouted, and Yosel sketched each one with crayons on the blackboard, erased a portion, "too much is bad for the liver," and as an afterthought, sketched it in again. "We'll wrap it up in a napkin for you to take home." He warned, "It's hot, you'll burn your tongue," or advised, "You'll have to wait twenty minutes for that order."

Zuni, Yosel, and Jack Tworkow, a puppeteer from Buffalo [7] teamed up one day to launch a Yiddish puppet theater. It seemed a mad idea. The Vilna Truppe and Habimah, with live actors, had folded up. Who would want to see puppets? Yet, ensconced in a factory flat with corrugated ceiling, the puppet theater endured season after season, performing weekends only, to capacity audiences. Tworkow made the puppets, Zuni and Yosel were the directors, authors, and cast. Their mixture of satire and innocence regaled both children and adults. They were irreverent. The puppets peered into the audience, saw a celebrity and inquired, "Is .... really here?" The audience response in unison, "He is," brought the laconic reply, "So who the heck cares?" They were compassionate. "Would that cute little number that has just passed through the door please sit down in the fifth row, third seat from the aisle, near that timid young poet who has been pining for her. If she doesn't, give her her money back." The theater folded only because Yosel and Zuni quarreled for some inexplicable reason.

Satire was a major fare.

One of the most popular Yiddish journals was *Der Kundes* (*The Wild One*), a satirical weekly, perhaps the only one of its kind in America in any language to have lasted nearly a decade. Its publisher-editor Jacob Marinoff, a brother-in-law of Carl Van Vechten, was a good natured giant of a man, a former blacksmith, equally proud of his light verse and his crushing handshake. His second-in-command was *Der Lebediker*, The Live One, a short man with shrewd myopic eyes, a scholarly humorist, the father of Ezra Goodman, the Hollywood publicist who at thirteen published a volume of Yiddish verse.

[7] Now head of the Art Department at Yale University's School of Art and Architecture.

Kundes' generous fees and free-wheeling editorial policy—it spared no person, institution, or ideology—brought contributions from the ranking Yiddish writers and cartoons from aspiring young American artists, Jews and non-Jews. Its savage lampoons were supplemented with prodigiously documented exposés in the most lancing muckraker tradition. However, by the mid-nineteen-twenties the immigrants' frustrations had abated, their anger subsided, and as they each had struck their private compromise between idealistic commitment and familial interests, they lost their appreciation for public indignation. *Kundes'* circulation dwindled, and it folded before the decade was out.

The trend to moderation was everywhere, even in the Yiddish press, which was a powerhouse of influence. Its center, East Broadway, was structurally dominated by the ten-story *Jewish Daily Forward*, the tallest building on the East Side. The newspaper's name in electric lights, in Hebrew and Latin letters, could be read from all three bridges connecting with Brooklyn, and north as far as East Fourteenth Street where it was obstructed by the Consolidated Edison Company building. Even pietist Jews, who despised the *Forward*, were deeply moved when its sign was first raised. Hebrew characters flashing across Manhattan; this could happen in none of the lands from which these immigrants had come. This was how the ancient Hebrews must have felt at the sight of the Temple restored by the Maccabees.

The Yiddish press had mellowed, although on occasion its polemics could still be vituperative. The Zionist newspapers' righteous indignation which still rose to evangelic pitch against the Yahudim, matched the Socialist *Jewish Daily Forward* attacks against the Communists.

On the same block as the *Forward*, were two other Yiddish dailies, *The Day* and *The Tageblat*, each ensconced in a red-brick house. *The Day*, Democratic and Liberal-Zionist, its contributors representing a wide range of opinion, was disdained by political purists as a "department store, a bargain basement of ideologies." *The Tageblat* was Orthodox-Zionist, prissy, homiletic, but apparently there were too few readers around of this Puritan disposition, so it eventually merged with *The Jewish Morning Journal*.

The Jewish Morning Journal was a study in delightful paradoxes. Its shabby Bowery headquarters was deceptive because its revenue from advertising exceeded the combined revenue of all the other Yiddish newspapers. As the only morning newspaper it held the corner on classified advertising, so that thousands of Socialist workers were compelled to purchase this Republican daily when looking for a job. Orthodox, it did not appear on Saturdays and holidays, but its staff worked on the sacred days to prepare the next morning's edition. On those days, its personnel entered the *Journal's* offices as if it were a speakeasy, looked around furtively, rattled the door knob, and waited to be identified by the janitor who would peer out by lifting a corner of the drawn shutters. The Bowery's elevated trains were helpful, drowning out the roar of the presses. Occasionally when Orthodox vigilantes on the prowl posted themselves outside the plant till sundown, the personnel arriving for work would walk right past the building, like customers before a raided joint, and there would be no *Journal* on the stands that evening.

Orthodoxy frowns on bachelorhood. The *Journal's* editor-in-chief Peter Wiernik and its managing editor, Jacob Fishman, were both bachelors. Their only formal education had been in East European yeshivot (Talmudical seminaries) which forbade all secular studies. However, the Yeshiva's curriculum disciplined the mind in analysis, and its loose supervision compelled its students toward self-instruction. Wiernik was a self-taught scholar of encyclopaedic range. He came to America in his teens and reputedly had worked as a longshoreman and associated with anarchists. But none doubted the sincerity of his subsequent Orthodoxy and Republicanism. From his large gold-plated pen flowed every one of the newspaper's editorials, some two columns of close newsprint daily, and a Sunday feature, "Our Multilingual Literature," in which he reviewed books by Jews and about Jews in a half-dozen languages.

Five times a week, at a precise hour, he would walk half the length of East Broadway and Canal Street from his home to his office and then back. His habits were more regular than any of the clocks in the neighborhood. His outward appearance reflected the man—of average height, thin, with a scholarly stoop, a gray mustache, a watch and chain across a concave stomach, he smiled kindly and apologetically at the world from behind old fashioned gold frames. His gentility was celebrated in fact and myth. He credited "a spark of talent" to every book he reviewed and charitably assumed that all books that reached his desk merited mention. An anecdote made the rounds that he had once been stopped by a prostitute and promptly paid the price she asked for taking him to her room. Once there, however, when she in-

quired how he wished to be served, he asked what her additional
charge might be for going to bed with him.

Wiernik was only nominally the *Journal's* editor. Its true policy was
reflected in managing editor Jacob Fishman's column which was carried three times weekly on the newspaper's front page. Fishman stands
with Abraham Cahan as an architect of the Yiddish press in America.
A handsome, ramrod figure, some two decades younger than Wiernik,
he had none of the older man's erudition, and his manner was often
curt and forbidding. Yet his column, couched in somewhat clumsy
Yiddish, was trenchant, well-informed and well-reasoned. His ready
assistance to staff members in emergencies and his private charities
were legendary. A transatlantic traveler, he developed the first Jewish
foreign news service by posting correspondents in all the major Jewish
population centers abroad. He induced prominent Jewish figures to
write their memoirs for serialization in the *Journal,* which are a mine
for the Jewish historian. However, he was a passionate partisan in
intramural Zionist polemics, always siding with Chaim Weizmann who,
albeit not always generous in his memoirs, recalls Fishman as "one of
the ablest Jewish journalists [with] a special insight into the public
mind: there were few in America, or for that matter anywhere else, to
whom I stood nearer, and with whom I could discuss Zionist affairs
in a more intimate way."

The city editor, Jacob Magidoff, was another example of the *Journal's*
paradoxes. He had been involved in radical movements in Russia, with
the German Socialists in America, spoke unaccented Russian and English, but had trouble with the Hebrew roots of Yiddish, and, although
he had been with the orthodox newspaper since its founding, he was
still unfamiliar with Jewish custom. However, he had an uncanny nose
for news and for developing a story. In his western sheriff's hat,
Magidoff was more at ease with police reporters on Park Row, then
America's Fleet Street, than with his Yiddish colleagues on East Broadway. From three P.M. each working day this disheveled man, disabled
by myopia, shuttled between the newsroom and the compositors shop,
stumbling into equipment, holding copy close to his thick lenses, trail-
ing behind him reams of teleprinter tape, and causing an occasional
little fire by droppings from his soggy cigars. Always lurking for him in
his office, in the teleprinter room, or on the stairs was some hapless fellow down on his luck who had heard that the old man was an easy
touch.

The *Day's* editorial domain was run somewhat like a Central American Republic. There were frequent *coups d'état* by persons aspiring for the editor's post, assisted by "outside intervention" from one or another of the contending Zionist factions or contentious unions then engaged in internecine warfare. The *Day* was generally an unpredictable paper. It had for a while employed as its editor-in-chief Herman Bernstein, a fairly well-known American correspondent at the time, who could not even read the newspaper over which he presided because he did not know a word of Yiddish. Several years later he was appointed U.S. Minister to Albania, an event hailed by the whole East Side as a victory "for our Jews" because until then only Yahudim had held diplomatic posts.

The average *Day* reader, a post-1910 immigrant, was perhaps a decade younger than the average reader of the other Yiddish dailies. A substantial proportion of the *Day* readership in fact had arrived after World War I. These latter-day immigrants had left a more emancipated shtetl than their predecessors, restrictions having begun to relax in "the old country."

Letters from immigrants in America had contributed to the shtetl's increasing permissiveness. They enclosed photographs which revealed that men who had left for America fully bearded as required by orthodox custom were now clean-shaven. They told of a wondrous social transformation, former yachsanim (Brahmins) now worked for a wage in factories owned by former proletarians, the podlie (low caste). The shtetl had been vigorously shaken by the abortive revolution of 1905, and slightly more than a decade later by the revolution which disposed of the Czar, the war that toppled the German and Austrian monarchies, the coup which brought Lenin to power, and several years of Russian Civil War. Many of the immigrants who entered the United States just shortly before, or trickled in after the nationalities quota system went into effect, had participated or at least been directly affected by these East European events. Their predecessors had come from a milieu in which government repression and Jewish orthodox interdiction prevented young Jews from obtaining a secular education. Among the recent newcomers there was, conversely, a high proportion of gymnasium students and graduates. They had acquired a taste for the avant-garde in Russian and German art and literature and for the corresponding Yiddish renaissance which brought forth in Poland, Russia, and the United States, a multitudinous, aggressive, and variegated generation of successors to the classicists and neo-classicists Mendele Mocher Sefarim ("grandfather" of Yiddish and modern Hebrew prose), Sholem Aleichem, Yehuda Leib Peretz, and Sholem Asch.

American Yiddish speech and journalese was a patois, heavily interlarded with corrupt English. There were purists among the writers on all the newspapers, but the *Day* was their bastion. Even its news stories were in good Yiddish. This attracted many of the newcomers who found the patois of the other newspapers offensive and unintelligible. It had perhaps more poets and novelists on its staff than any other daily. The *Day* maintained a varied literary ménage, from older writers to the young veterans of two very recent revolutions in American Yiddish poetry—*Die Yunge*, strict formalists, meticulous about language, had impeached a generation of "sweatshop poets" and before they could settle down into an establishment, they were besieged by *Inzich*, advocates of Imagism and free verse.

Perhaps the greatest single contribution to Yiddish purism came from a poet who wrote for the *Day*. Yehoash was virtually cloistered by tuberculosis and by the monumental task he had singlehandedly undertaken, to translate the Bible into Yiddish, in the process of which he clarified many obscure passages, and retrieved from ancient manuscripts and regional speech a nearly forgotten Yiddish vocabulary which revealed an awesome majesty in that colloquial language. The Bible, in Yehoash's Yiddish, was serialized in the *Day*, a newspaper that published on the Sabbath and on all the holidays except Yom Kippur.

The *Day's* staff included the gentle David Pinski whose novels appeared in English translation and whose plays had been staged by The Grand Street Neighborhood Playhouse, the parent of off-Broadway. It included Peretz Hirshbein, playwright and travel-writer, a gaunt figure with a protruding Adam's apple, and flowing hair like Chagall's, who mesmerized his audience with his grandiloquent vocabulary, slow delivery, broad gestures, meaningful pauses, and a habit of shutting his eyes like a fortune teller brooding over his crystal ball. His precious mannerisms suggested frailty, but he was known to entertain friends by tearing telephone books in half with his bare hands.

Dr. Abraham Coralnik, a short, cherubic man, was the *Day's* feuilletonist, an occupation that was the Continental forerunner of the American newspaper columnist. The feuilletonist, like the columnist, chose his subjects at random and disposed of them briefly. However, he was incubated in universities, not in the sports department of newspapers. His style was elegant and deliberately casual, he was never blunt or angry, always only mildly interested, never curious or affected, and above all never irrevocably committed. Ninety percent of a feuilletonist's output was *Weltschmerz*, reflection, and esthetics, not the dense sordid matter of daily living. When a feuilletonist became passionate, he failed his craft, which is what happened at the turn of the century to one of its best practitioners, a Viennese journalist, Theodor Herzl, when he became the Messiah of Zionism.

Dr. Coralnik, a master of the genre, had a penchant for displaying his substantial erudition by quoting, in italics, at the beginning of each essay, from some ancient source, preferably Latin or Greek. Something about the caliber of his audience and himself, according to unconfirmed legend, was revealed one day when scores of readers confronted him outside the *Day* to protest that he had quoted from a non-existent authority. He reputedly replied that there wasn't enough Greek wisdom to quote from, that since the passage had been his own, self-attribution would have been vain; false attribution to one of the known wise men of the past would have been impertinent, and to have begun without a quotation, would have been indecent exposure.

Yoel Slonim, flatfooted, with swinging gait and rapid-fire speech, wore his hat with brim bent to one side the way poets wore theirs, and smoked big cigars like a politician. He belonged to both worlds. *Die Yunge* had once published his verse, and reams of it still appeared weekly in the *Day*. He covered police headquarters, the courts, and City Hall, and was on a first name basis with the judges and racket bosses of his day, as any good reporter should be. He was also Our Man At Tammany Hall who made certain that the *Day*'s endorsement of Democratic candidates was rewarded with a generous number of paid municipal notices. To the poets he was "a fallen angel," not because of his association, which tantalized bohemians, but because he spread his byline under every story. The most vivid news stories in the Yiddish press were by poets, but regarding this as demeaning work, they adamantly refused bylines.

The metropolitan newspapers could always turn to the Lower East Side for copy to fill a dry spell or provide a change of pace from that which came from police headquarters and the criminal courts. Ghetto features made WASP readers glow inside with the kind of empathy that persuaded them that they were both superior and compassionate.

Reporters sent on these safaris were always instructed to bag, above all, an interview with Abraham Cahan, editor of the *Jewish Daily Forward.*

The immigrants, having broken out of the corral of religious discipline and shtetl conventions, needed some substitute authority to command them and set values before them in their new American environment. In philanthropy they were ruled by Jacob Schiff; in Zionism, albeit briefly, by the forceful Louis D. Brandeis; in the Yiddish Art Theater movement it was Maurice Schwartz; and in the Yiddish press and labor movement, Abraham Cahan.

Cahan walked with austere authority, taller than his fellows on East Broadway, lord of the *Jewish Daily Forward,* which was a formidable citadel of power in the days when Yiddish was the spoken language of a majority of American Jewry. A man of many parts and demonic energy, he shook strike rallies with the thunder of his oratory, and poured out editorial copy, feature stories, political comment, and book and drama reviews crackling with irrevocable judgments. His utterances had the force of papal encyclicals, affecting the relations between American Socialism and the Second International, the fate of embattled factions in American labor, causing the rise and fall of union officials, and closing a play or banishing a star from Second Avenue. Apart from this, he also produced a voluminous autobiography, a half-dozen novels and short story collections in both Yiddish and English. (Cahan's *The Rise of David Levinsky,* depicting the East European immigrant milieu, has become a minor American classic.) In his middle years he underwent abdominal surgery of a kind so rare in that day that newspaper stories stressed that this curiously put the Socialist editor and the founder of the Rockefeller fortune in a class by themselves. Legend has it that in his eighties, reported dying, he sneaked out of Beth Israel hospital and surprised his editorial aides by walking in on them as they were arguing whether to lay out his obituary with a "page headline" or a "streamer." [8]

The *Forward* was his life's work, the source of his power. He had fought ferocious battles for his editorial prerogatives, put down fitful insurrections quickly, and used them as the pretext for tightening the reins of his inexorable rule. The newspaper's publisher, The Forward Association, and its editorial staff were packed with men who were

[8] Streamers run over the masthead; a page headline is the same size but below the masthead and date.

largely his pliant tools. Unlike all other Yiddish editors he was not answerable to cost-conscious private proprietors. He shocked doctrinaire Socialists by mixing the lurid and the highbrow and adapting features from the Hearst and Pulitzer newspapers. He introduced crime reporting and an advice-to-the-troubled column, which he called *Das Bintel Brief* ("A Sheaf of Letters"), and which was really quite different from its prototype—its letters were long, its responses elaborate, an authentic reflection of the changing mores of the Jewish immigrant community. He balanced this every Sunday with a rotogravure section, which included art reproductions, and an English supplement with original contributions from Bertrand Russell, George Bernard Shaw, and Mary and Sidney Webb, the founders of Fabian Socialism.

Cahan instructed his news and human interest writers to strike out of their copy all words that might exceed the comprehension of the least among his readers and applied this fiat to his own writing. He would test copy that troubled him on peddlers, waiters, and the elevator men in the *Forward* building. The resultant vocabulary came to be known as *Forward* or "*pleiner* [plain] Yiddish" as distinct from "*reiner* [pure] Yiddish." America-bound immigrants believed that by memorizing all the unintelligible words in the *Forward* they were acquiring an English vocabulary. Unfortunately, the words they learned were patois, Yiddishized or Anglicized beyond recognition.

He had trained several generations of patois writers and forever deprived them of the capacity to express themselves in literate Yiddish. He recruited these editorial apprentices from factories, union offices, and even from the professions. He offered a regular weekly salary, steady employment, the glamour of by-lines (writers enjoyed high social status in the immigrant community), and apprenticeship under the master himself. His consuming ambition was to discover someday among them at least one whom he could train to be a great writer in the tradition of Russian realism. He encouraged and cajoled them, taught them to observe, narrate, and construct; the result, at its best, was patois fiction of documentary significance. These men were his infantry.

He also had an elite corps. This corps, exempt from his vocabulary fiat, included scholars and ideologues who addressed themselves to the Socialist intelligentsia, and fiction writers of true stature like Abraham Reisen, Sholem Asch, I. J. Singer, Yona Rosenfeld. He was proud of his collection. But even as the Lord of San Simeon stored away from sight the art he had purchased, so Cahan occasionally did the same with his name writers. One day he would celebrate them as Tolstois, Dostoevskis and Chekhovs and on the next, like a wrathful god, he would turn away his countenance from them, and systematically undermine their morale by continuing them on his payroll but regularly rejecting their manuscripts as "unprintable," and unless they wished their employment terminated they could not offer their writings elsewhere. Abraham Reisen, a gentle Yiddish Chekhov, beloved by multitudes, was subjected to this treatment intermittently, but compensated by reading his rejected manuscripts at literary evenings. Yona Rosenfeld, an almost unlettered man with great intuitive psychological insights, collected his weekly check for years without seeing a line of his published. He was an introverted man and enjoyed none of the reputation, let alone affection, that made heads turn wherever Reisen appeared. Rosenfeld, who was short, with shrewd peasant features, a powerful physique and considerably younger than Cahan, contended, with diminishing faith as his manuscripts accumulated, that with his endurance he would outlive Pharaoh. He did not. Subjected to similar treatment, but in a more advantageous financial position, Sholem Asch, considerably later walked out on Cahan and left that aged lion ranting in an agony of frustration, to the end of his days.

Cahan's formula of mixing the lowbrow and highbrow was adopted, in varying degrees, by all the other Yiddish papers, with the highbrow exceeding the lowbrow in the weekend editions. The *Jewish Morning Journal,* which did not appear on the Sabbath, published enlarged editions on Friday and Sunday. The others published theirs successively on Saturday and Sunday. The caliber of their serious material surpassed anything that the metropolitan press has ever offered in its Sunday supplements. The Yiddish newspaper was the Lower East Side's equivalent of today's university extension courses for adults. A substantial portion of its population spent long hours on weekends poring over newsprint as if it were sacred writings.

CHAPTER 3

Orators and Writers

IN THE nineteen-twenties the East European immigrants, the *Yidn,* were busy consolidating their positions in the neighborhoods they had invaded in the previous decade.

Forty years had passed since the first tide of Jewish fugitives from Czarist oppression had poured into New York from Castle Garden, which preceded Ellis Island as the immigrants' gateway to the garment center. In these four decades many of the newcomers had acquired means, even wealth, and their womenfolk, looking up from their kitchen washtubs and out at their clotheslines, raised the eternal female cry about moving "into a better neighborhood, if not for our own sake, then for our children's sake, that our daughter might make a better match, for who would marry a girl from a section where they dump garbage on your head from upper-story windows?"

Thus the invasion by the "lower classes" began. In the East Bronx, the Yidn struck out towards the Grand Concourse, and in Manhattan, from the Lower East Side to the Upper West Side where they ran into another migration, the lower-middle class or lace-curtain Irish. The two ethno-social groups were moving concurrently, albeit not in concert, and were, in fact, wary of one another. Yet those who felt discomfited by this migration judged it to be a coordinated move.

Foremost among the discomfited were the WASPS. They had settled on both sides of Central Park, eastward to Lexington Avenue, and westward to Riverside Drive. Then a sprinkling of Yahudim merchant princes and bankers, and broadloom Irish, successsful lawyers and jurists, bought mansionettes in the vicinity. Small in number, reserved in manner, they caused nervousness but not alarm. They were soon followed, however, by a multitude of lower caste. The result was panic among the WASPS; some yielded the city to the enemy altogether and took off for Westchester County, thus setting the trend towards suburbia; others, determined to fight the invaders block by block, financed cooperative apartment buildings on Park Avenue that were barred to Jews and Catholics. Recent attempts to prevent a Temple Emanu-El trustee and Robert Kennedy from purchasing apartments in the older cooperatives—any housing that dates back three or four decades is old in New York—show that some WASP bastions are still holding out a half century after the migrations began.

With the WASPS gone and the Yidn crowding in, the West Side lost its meaning for the Yahudim and they too fled, abandoning their limestones on Central Park West, West End Avenue, and Riverside Drive, their brownstones on the intersecting streets. They fled east to Fifth Avenue. The term "West Side" now acquired a new meaning in the Lower East Side vocabulary. It used to connote Yahudim, remote and wealthy German Jews; it now began to connote *alreitniks,* "our own kind," pretentious Yidn who "had made it." Of the first, the Lower East Side would speak with a bitter reverence; of the second, with biting contempt.

The uneasy condominium of Yidn and Irish changed the exterior of the West Side. Catholic churches and Orthodox synagogues became more dominant than Episcopalian churches and Reform and Conservative temples. Jewish restaurants on Broadway and Irish saloons on Columbus and Amsterdam Avenues accented the geographic divisions between Irish and Jews. The latter were uncomfortable with the heavy drinking and pugnacious Catholicism of their neighbors and remembered that not so very long ago it was not unusual to see Jewish peddlers emerge bloodied with their clothes in tatters from incursions into Cherry Street, the Lower East Side Irish citadel. The side streets, therefore, were divided between them as if by design, the Jews settling west and the Irish east of Broadway.

The Yidn were not content with merely possessing real estate. They joined the building boom and began to alter the West Side in their own image. When the New York skyline burst upon him, the Jewish immigrant immediately perceived of America's greatness in vertical terms. All his letters home since the turn of the century celebrated the tallness of the buildings in *"Columbus' medina"* (country). Verticalism related remotely to his racial experience. Cramped for space, the medieval ghetto Jew built his houses narrow, and not to invite

Christian ire, built them deep, not tall. Depth is inverted height, so that combining this medieval conditioning and his reaction to it, the Jewish realtor constructed apartment buildings on the West Side and Grand Concourse that were high, wide, and ostentatious with majestic arcades, carriage lanterns at the entrances, and elevator cages appointed like throne rooms. He ran red carpets into the street, changed his awnings several times a year to correspond to the mood and color of the seasons, and outfitted his doormen and other personnel with the splendiferous uniforms of royal guardsmen.

This housing accommodated not only more tenants and hence brought larger profits per square foot, but it also made the streets alive with the movement of people—promenaders, vendors, shoppers, and outdoor debaters. Tree-lined, quiet streets with only an occasional passerby, a solemn greeting by tipping the hat without stopping for some impassioned conversation, feasting that accented service rather than food, and a social life without mass meetings was not the Yidn habit.

Thus, even for the West Side alreitnik, the real life was still on the Lower East Side. The large West Side synagogues, auditoriums, and cinemas could not lure the Downtown masses Uptown, because they had no luster for a Yid, rich or poor. The Downtowners never traveled beyond Town Hall and Carnegie Hall, which alternated between recitals and Jewish mass meetings. The preferred meeting site was still historic Cooper Union, cavernous and half-subterranean like the medieval ghetto synagogues, and associated with President Lincoln, who was bearded, whose first name was Abraham, and who had freed the slaves and who was, therefore, no doubt at all, a Jew, which the goyim would not concede, of course. Furthermore, Cooper Union was equally accessible to residents of Brooklyn and the East Bronx.

The West Siders delighted in these excursions Downtown. No Uptown restaurant could match the cuisine of the two Ratner's on Second Avenue and on Delancey Street, of the three varieties of Yona Shimmel's knishes—potato, kashe, and cheese—dispensed from a little establishment on East Houston Street just off Allen Street with its thundering elevated trains. Allen Street stores sold old brass-frame beds, eiderdown quilts, and pillows which somehow recalled its turn-of-the-century past as a red-light district.

The Lower East Side's restaurants were the reason also that the landsmanschaften still met regularly once a month on given evenings in shabby downtown meeting-halls hung with flags, charters, and plaques

of scores of societies who used these quarters in rotation. Luchow's on
Fourteenth Street, and Jager's on East 85th Street, where the elder
Yahudim dined, had large curtained windows, dim lights, and properly
reverential waiters. The Yidn liked their restaurants brightly lit, windows with a full view of the street scene and waiters that were agile
sparring partners and a challenge to pomposity. The East Side waiter
was rude, impertinent, but also solicitous about his customers, and if
he knew them, he prescribed the meal like a doctor. "Just a bit of this
won't give you heartburn." "I won't serve you that if you stand on your
head; it's not for a man with kidney trouble. How I know you have
kidney trouble? Such things are no secret. It's not a social disease." He
was solicitous even of new customers which sometimes would get him
into trouble. "Mister, I know the chicken is on the menu, but I don't
recommend it. You insist? What's the matter, you want to give the
undertaker business? You wonder why I am so concerned for you—
first because I have a Jewish heart; second because the boss here pays
me *makos* (the plagues); thirdly because you look like a sport, and I
live from tips." He would recite the menu from memory and took
offense, if the customer insisted on a printed menu. "Look mister, the
kitchen is in my head the way the stars are in Einstein's. What's on the
menu is for decoration only. The chef can't even read."

Debate was still a major feature of Lower East Side entertainment.
But some of the once contentious issues had lost their topicality. Now
that there was ample housing, that more people had jobs and could
afford marriage, and immigration restrictions had balanced the male
and female populations, conventional patterns reasserted themselves.
Free love and atheism had altogether lost their appeal for lecture
audiences, and birth control was practiced without publicly debating
its merits or even seeking Margaret Sanger's counsel. There were still
two popular kinds of debate—the gala occasions when the East Side's
last great Zionist and radical ideologues were matched in the Cooper
Union arena; and the street-corner soap-box around election time.
Socialists' taunting occasionally compelled a Democratic or Republican
candidate to consent to argue the campaign issues, but almost always,
at the last moment, he would send a message claiming illness. The
Socialist speaker would carry on anyhow, addressing a phantom an-
tagonist. Better than a direct confrontation, it was a public hanging
and the crowd howled with delight, and, when it was all over, would
crowd around the speaker, congratulating him and assuring him, "Mister, you're the right candidate on the wrong ticket."

Sometimes, with the crowd behind him, the Socialist would prowl the district and track down the Democratic or Republican fugitive at his home or his clubrooms and vow not to leave until the coward emerged from his lair. Middling lawyers at best, the candidates of the two major parties could easily be defeated not only by the Socialist's argument, but by their inability to understand his vocabulary. Whenever the Socialists put on one of their top performers, the neighborhood's candy stores, generally humming with customers and loafers, would be deserted for that one evening as everyone flocked to the rally. The candy store nearest the rally, conversely, would be in a stage of siege as drifters from the crowd queued up for cigarettes and soft drinks. The Socialists' star performer was Norman Thomas, their featured players were August Claessens and Jacob Panken. Each of these speakers had his own particular audience, although he attracted all kinds.

A sudden crackling mockery in his steely eye and his voice rising from rumbling brass to high pitch alerted the audience to expect a vicious direct hit from Norman Thomas. As these hits increased they became a fusillade. New immigrants, young men only recently graduated from the European gymnasium and preparing at Eron Prep School on East Broadway for college entrance exams, were Thomas' special fans. Hoping to become lawyers some day, they gathered to learn the art of polemics and English rhetoric from a master, a former minister who had become a Socialist orator.

August Claessens, a short, red, and baldheaded Scotsman—Jews called him affectionately "little Esau"—attracted Orthodox Jews who knew no English but who enjoyed his wit which he communicated in a mixture of Yiddish-English, real *Forward* patois. Here was a goy with a Jewish head, they told each other, and when he berated landlords and bosses he spoke from the heart. These same people would deliberately gather in front of the speakers platform and then walk out when Jacob Panken, a Jew, spoke. He had the high-boned facial structure of an American Indian, the low brow and tight lips of an artisan, striking white hair, wore a midwesterner's sheriff's hat and shoelace tie and was the Public Defender in eviction suits. He delighted the podlie with his fierce attacks on Zionism and "religious fanatics"— no matter what the major theme of his address. The learned Orthodox Jew spoke of Thomas and Claessens as "Sozialisten" (Socialists), but applied to Panken the contemptuous diminutive "Sozialistl." He symbolized for them the arrogant, all-knowing proletarians who quoted the

Forward and its editor Abraham Cahan as the fount of all knowledge and harassed and incessantly tortured the garment center's devout workers with savage practical jokes.

The most revered speakers were multilingual, yet spoke only in Yiddish and almost never outdoors. The ideologists spoke in the formal surroundings of the East Side's meeting halls. Men of strange genius from out of the shtetl, they had fled to Switzerland and Germany after early bouts with the Czarist police, prison terms, and Siberian exile for anti-Czarist activity. Somehow, in the midst of this chaos, they managed to publish original socio-economic doctrines, acquire encyclopaedic knowledge, found and disband political parties, starve in garrets and, almost absent-mindedly, obtain doctorates in philosophy from strict European university faculties who were overwhelmed by the foreigners' outrageous waste of their prodigious talents.

Some of these ideologists managed to reach the United States in the midst of World War I and briefly exercised their influence on the American Jewish community. After World War I, only two of them remained in America—Dr. Nachman Syrkin (1867–1924) and Dr. Chaim Zhitlovsky (1865–1943). In their youth both had tackled Lenin in debate on the right of Jews to survive as a distinctive people. They had even shared some of the same ideas. Syrkin was the founder of Labor Zionism; Zhitlovsky had briefly subscribed to the doctrine although his restless intellect had reshaped it, as it did all ideas. Otherwise, the two men were contrasts. Syrkin was smallish, volatile, distraught and otherworldly; some people found his manner "funny," yet as one admirer has remarked, it did not detract from his authority. He made his living as a lecturer but was always underpaid because he was too shy to name his fee or even to collect it. Zhitlovsky was a man of commanding presence and dignity—tall and broad shouldered with a square face and a triangular beard, in appearance and manner a typical specimen of the Russian intelligentsia. He charged steep fees that were beyond Syrkin's dreams, and insisted on payment in cash before stepping up to the lectern.

Syrkin's projections of the future Jewish state have in some measure been realized. He prophesied that cooperative villages would be the country's economic base and that the government would be comprised of villagers summoned to the city for brief periods of public service. The cooperative villages, moshavim and kibbutzim, provide eighty percent of Israel's agricultural products and a high percentage of the army officers, and their members have indeed often been called to serve in the Israeli cabinet and in ambassadorial posts, especially in Africa and Asia.

Zhitlovsky became the high priest of Yiddishism, a doctrine which mixed a cult of the Yiddish language with political radicalism and indifference and, in some cases, outright hostility to religion. It was conceived by members of the Russian Jewish intelligentsia who, disenchanted with the promise of the radical movements to achieve equality for the Jews, turned back to the Jewish proletarian and assured him of his human worth by celebrating the tongue he spoke as a dignified language, not a mere low-caste dialect. Yiddishism maintained that Yiddish could preserve the modern secular Jewish generations as a distinctive people, even as religious ritual had preserved their predecessors in the course of two millennia. The language cult broke into several warring sects, but whatever their political differences they shared one essential— the worship and mystique of Yiddish.

By the nineteen-twenties abstract ideology surrendered to practical politics and to a struggle for power between the Zionists, soliciting funds for the Jewish National Home in Palestine, and the Communists, seeking funds for Jewish colonization schemes in Soviet Russia, and between *Forward-* and *Freiheit*-supported labor leaders for the control of the garment center unions. The *Freiheit* was a Communist daily founded by former writers for the Socialist *Forward*.

This concern with politics and power was paralleled by a concern with esthetics and style. It was best illustrated on the lecture platform by Hayim Greenberg, an emigré from Russia after the Revolution, who became the chief theoretical spokesman for Labor Zionism on Nachman Syrkin's passing. He was not an ideologue. He was a lecturer and feuilletonist who improvised on the theme of the ambiguities of the human predicament. He left behind very little of a theoretical nature. However, his essays are regarded by a young generation of conservative and reform rabbis as masterpieces of homiletics. He discoursed on nonviolence; his spare frame, his black hair parted in the center and combed backward along the temples, high cheekbones, and a reddish tint in his eyes gave his appearance an Oriental cast, confirming his status as a Gandhi disciple. His gestures on the public platform and in private had the delicacy of a Japanese tea ceremony. He would have been a strange weed in Labor Zionism a decade earlier, in the era of violent struggle for the right to unionize. But that period was fading away; the Yidn were beginning to evolve again as a middle class.

A decade earlier Moishe Nadir [1] might have been contemptuously dismissed by workers. He was now a regular contributor to the Communist *Freiheit* and the darling of the large audiences it corralled for literary evenings. Moishe Nadir, whose real name was Isaac Reiss primarily a satirist, was the most celebrated pseudonym in Yiddish since Sholem Aleichem. With Roman nose, olive skin and incandescent eyes, he was easily the most handsome man in Yiddish bohemia. He sported velvet jackets, handpainted cravats and, occasionally, a cape. His peculiar pseudonym might have, but did not provoke familiarity. His studied gestures did not detract from the reverence for him. He was accepted precisely for what he was, a passionate poseur, the embodiment of the mythical poet. At the center of his legend was his reputation as a lover and his legerdemain with words. His appearance in writers' hangouts was rare because he did not wish to demean his legend and he always amply prepared himself for such appearances with bon mots, epigrams and newly coined words.

The Communist *Freiheit,* capitalizing on the Yiddish readers' disposition, went deliberately and painstakingly about the task of recruiting the ranking younger Yiddish writers as its contributors. It succeeded well. There was hardly an important writer who did not, at one time or another in the nineteen-twenties, contribute to the *Freiheit* although it offered little or no remuneration. The Socialist *Forward,* and the Forward Association's literary monthly, *Die Zukunft,* conversely, paid handsomely by the standards of that day. However Abraham Cahan, as already pointed out, ruled his newspaper with an iron hand and by subjective standards. Abraham Liessin, the poet-scholar who edited *Die Zukunft,* was similarly arbitrary which, perhaps, is why the two men could not tolerate each other.

Liessin rarely put in an appearance on East Broadway. He was a mythical figure whom some of his contributors had never even seen. Manuscripts were submitted and months later often returned, without comment, through a meek deputy editor who sometimes, without reporting on the manuscript, extended an invitation from the legendary editor to meet him at a fixed time at his home in a Bronx cooperative housing project.

A widower, prematurely aged, grouchy and acidulous, Liessin presided over a gloomy household of booklined walls and a paralytic

[1] *Nadir* can mean either of two things in Yiddish—"You Can Have It," or "Give 'em Hell." He never explained which meaning he intended in adopting this pseudonym.

daughter to whom he personally attended. Deceptively gracious, plying his visitor with tea and cakes, the formidable editor would draw him out, hour after fatiguing hour, on the latest gossip from the Yiddish literary Rialto, make devastating remarks on all his contributors, but offer no comment on the visitor's manuscript. Then, when the latter felt relaxed and at ease, the editor would suddenly rise, indicating that the interview was over, and casually advise him, "Young man, you are lacking the spark, better engage in some more purposeful endeavor."

The *Freiheit's* taste was catholic. Vladimir Mayakovsky and other avant-garde writers were still tolerated in Moscow, and the *Freiheit* accordingly published all kinds of experimental writing which no author would dream of submitting to the other dailies. It also provided enthusiastic audiences for books and literary readings that had its imprimatur. The Zionist movement, by contrast, now barely took notice of Yiddish writers, except of journalistic moulders of public opinion. The *Freiheit* was attractive to Yiddish literary men also because most of them were still engaged in proletarian occupations. Before their flight to America they had been engaged in anti-Czarist activity. The full enfranchisement of Russia's Jews by the short-lived Kerensky government was extended by the Soviet regime which placed Yiddish on a par with the other national languages in its domain and subsidized Yiddish schools, newspapers, theaters and book publishing houses. This confirmed the writers' belief that the Jewish people would be delivered from anti-Semitism by the combination of Communism and Yiddishism. Very few of these writers, nonetheless committed themselves to Communist doctrine, but on the other hand they could spare no compassion for the persecution of Zionism in the U.S.S.R. and the suppression of Hebrew, Yiddishism's great rival.

The Yahudim were only dimly aware of the goings on in the "ghetto," yet they were profoundly apprehensive about this ferment. They were sincerely concerned about the welfare of the Yidn. Samuel Untermeyer, the authoritarian corporation attorney who built a chapel for his Christian wife on his estate; the kindly Mr. and Mrs. Nathan Straus, whose special concern was to provide milk for children; and the Warburg banking family, led a long roster of Yahudim who contributed generously to American Jewish charities and to Jewish effort in Palestine. Some of them also sat on the board of the American Jewish Committee, the Yahudim's policy-making body. Whenever required, they dutifully protested extreme measures against Jews in foreign lands. However, their protests were *sotto voce*, like a turned-down wick, and couched in an English idiom that seemed especially designed for that purpose: simultaneously supplicant, accusatory and apologetic, seeking to define, deny, justify, and assert Jewish "difference." Their publications bore such names as *American Hebrew* and *American Israelite*, subtle reminders to the puritan conscience of Christianity's indebtedness to the Jews. They lived in a tight, involuntary ghetto, from which intermarriage offered the only escape, on the very razor edge of the American promise. They were fearful lest the untoward conduct of irrepressible Yidn jeopardized their American sanctuary. They established institutions to "uplift" and "Americanize" the Yidn. They were well-intentioned but their determination as to what was good for the immigrant was reached arbitrarily and without consulting him. The fact is that the Yahudim themselves were not yet really adjusted to America. They were accommodating themselves to the conventions of only one single American caste, the WASP upperclass, which barred them from its country clubs and even as neighbors and was itself being overwhelmed by growing Irish Catholic political power in some of the major cities.

There was a larger America, teeming with diversity, and the East European immigrant was part of this pluralistic ferment. Striking out from his Lower East Side enclave he ranged in a wide arc—geographically, occupationally, socially. There were on the staffs of the Yiddish newspapers in the nineteen-twenties, some middle-aged men, among the most softspoken and gentle on East Broadway, who in their youth had brawled with Jack London and been Jim Tully's comrades of the road. Yiddish literature, wholly unbeknown to the Yahudim, was then busy discovering America through the senses.

The new Yiddish fiction ranged from the New York ghetto (Asch, Apatoshu, Ignatov) through the American prairie (Isaac Raboi), and the south (Baruch Glazman), and depicted such novel occupations as submarine construction (L. Chanukov). J. J. Schwartz's "Kentucky," an epic poem of several hundred pages, was hailed by his colleagues as a kind of conquest, establishing the right of Yiddish to be regarded as part of American literature. A writer could then make his reputation in Yiddish by publishing even a single poem or short story revealing some new aspect of America. One mediocre poet acquired global renown as the author of the "first tennis poems" in Yiddish.

The Negro early became a concern of American Yiddish writing. The new American poetry adopted the Negro's rhythms, even as American music adopted them, but except for Carl Sandburg it was barely aware of the Negro's human existence. Yiddish poetry promptly inducted the Negro into the pantheon of its social passion. In no other language perhaps had so much poetry been written as in Yiddish on the lynchings of the Negro in the nineteen-twenties. This was within the pattern of the immigrants' political radicalism, which was proof not of alienation, as the Yahudim feared, but of the immigrants' acclimatization. They were becoming vocal American citizens.

The Yahudim elite worried about budgets for the opera, symphony, and ballet. The poetry revolt then going on in American literature was not their interest. A corresponding revolt, with identical aims, was then under way in Yiddish poetry and was very much the concern of Yidn of all classes, including factory workers. Those concerned were not large in number, perhaps, but they were a cross-section and made the entire ghetto aware of the new movement. Meyer, none knew his family name, a painter with a penchant for hanging around with Yiddish writers, formed a club of kindred souls, all workers, who called themselves Die Schnorrers (scavengers), a writers' admiration society. They celebrated poets, not fiction writers, and only practitioners of the New Poetry, sold tickets for their readings, purchased their books, memorized their verse and recited it at lunchtime in the factories.

The revolt was against the careless craftsmanship of earlier poets who were concerned with social protest, but not with the form in which it was couched, nor very much with private verse. The rebellious forces were divided against themselves. One camp, Die Yunge, who emerged immediately after World War I, were influenced by Russian and German poetry. Another school, Inzich, emerged in the early nineteen-twenties and was influenced by American and British poetry—T. S. Eliot, Ezra Pound, and Robinson Jeffers. The Inzich Group stressed Imagism, Die Yunge pure lyricism. The former operated with learned references and foreign words, the latter shunned these as "cerebral" and insisted that all poetry is wholly intuitive. Die Yunge were mostly self-educated men, engaged in menial occupations; the chief figures among the Inzich had had some academic training and worked as copy editors on the Yiddish dailies, which Die Yunge regarded as prostitution of literary talent.

The most notable figure in all Yiddish poetry, one of the great poets between the two world wars in any language, was H. Leivick, a leader of Die Yunge. Of slight stature, he nonetheless had a commanding presence and easily stood out in a crowd; his face mixing the proletarian and ascetic, taut skin over sharp bones, thin lips and close-set eyes, prematurely white hair and a remote half-smile, both stern and forgiving. He was the saint of the proletariat, and intellectuals argued over the inner meaning of his metaphors, which grew out of a traumatic spell of Siberian exile in his youth, and a lifetime struggle with tuberculosis. In his latter years he was concerned with the mythical fate of Israel, but before that primarily with revolution. His verse was unceasingly preoccupied with the Messianic-masochistic, with deliverance through self-immolation, and steeped in the Russian literary tradition; heavy with an imagery reminiscent of Christian mysticism and of the Eastern Orthodox ikons.[2] His was a less patent, but profounder obsession with Christology than Asch exercised in his latter-day writing. Thus some of the seemingly parochial Yiddish literature was more deeply involved in interfaith than the Yahudim with their formal "Brotherhood Week" efforts to reduce tensions and barriers.

The favorite of Die Schnorrers was another leader of Die Yunge, Moshe Leib Halpern, who was rarely called by his last name. He was a kind of vagabond poet, whose love verse was tender but also daring in its candor. The bravado element was underscored by his use of Yiddish slang and folk idiom. This is probably the reason the Schnorrers declared him their poet laureate. His mixture of irony and tenderness recalled Heine, but his irregular rhythms were entirely his own and his range was wide. He wrote of the shtetl and of the savage beat of coins dropping in the slot machines as multitudes passed through the clicking subway turnstiles during the rush hour; he wrote of a comely young female on the beach at Coney Island, of anti-Semitism and of the inadequacies of Jewish life. All his verse, or most of it, was cast as a dialogue with himself. "This garden where, with a microscope, you might discover three blades, is it our garden?" "Of course, it's ours. How else?"

Moshe Leib and Leivick had worked as paperhangers before two Yiddish dailies, the *Freiheit* and *The Day* respectively, placed them on the weekly payroll not as newswriters, which they would have rejected, but as poets. Legend has it that when Schwartz premiered one of

---

[2] Chagall has so completely succumbed to this imagery that his dominant symbol of Jewish martyrdom is the Crucifixion, his Jewish family is a Holy Family, and the only thing Jewish about his work is the garb and facial features of his characters, but their destiny and posture are Christian.

Leivick's plays, the poet, having come away late from work, checked his ladder at the box office, entering the theater in his overalls as the curtain was rising.

Leivick was a taciturn shy figure; Halpern, tall and swinging his cane, moved like a hurricane, his sharp eyebrows lifted quizzically, his head with its sensuous mouth turning hungrily in all directions, and speaking at the top of his voice in broad Galician Yiddish, as regional as the southern drawl and western twang in American speech.

The leader of Inzich was Yaacov Glatshtein, a blond Apollo, a dropout from Brooklyn Law School, the fastest man with words on the news staffs in the Yiddish press, a passionate gambler and, in a kind of perverse dissent from Bohemian conformism, an incessant smoker of cigars, which would have marked any other person entering the literary café as a trespassing bourgeois presence. He has remained throughout his life a sharp critic of Moshe Leib, yet he is clearly in the Moshe Leib tradition, although he has gone far beyond it. He began, at the outset, to duplicate in Yiddish the linguistic experiments of Pound, Eliot and Joyce, and with great success, which has been no small accomplishment in a language as colloquial as Yiddish.

Scores of poets, male and female, clustered around the two schools but some "loners" belonged to no school. There were piquant characters among them. A. M. Dillon, a follower of Die Yunge, would compose a complete poem in his mind, recite it to colleagues whose opinion he respected, rewrite in his memory in accordance with their advice, and only then, after several weeks of this procedure, would he set it down on paper. He was a walking anthology of poetry in several languages—Yiddish, Hebrew and Russian, because whatever he liked he memorized and remembered it forever. None quite knew how he got along; he was among writers all day, from noon till after midnight, none ever saw him eat, and, a proud man, he refused to be treated. Through him opera lovers among the Yiddish writers were assured free entrance to the Metropolitan. However, they saw the opera not from the front, looking towards the stage, but from the rear looking out at the audience. Dillon had arranged to have them included in mass scenes. On gala evenings, he would bring a score of Yiddish poets to the opera and when the mob raised a din, they would be shouting at each other snatches of Yiddish verse. Thus, for many years, Yiddish provided the background sound for all the Met's operas.

Aaron Lutsky was one of the few Yiddish poets who had served in the U.S. Army, the others had either arrived after World War I and had seen service with the German, Austro-Hungarian or Russian armies, or had joined the Jewish Legion under British command by enlisting in Canada, or had been disqualified on medical grounds. A monthly disability check, which he exhibited like a Congressional medal, compensated Lutsky for the loss of an eye. This income he supplemented by peddling watches which he shined up to to make them look like new, and by merchandising his books which never bore a price mark. "Name your own price," he would say, "I want to see whether you know quality." If the purchaser's price was unsatisfactory, Lutsky ripped the book out of his hands; if it was right, he autographed the volume, and if it was better than right he inscribed a dedication. *Take It, It's Good For You* was the title of one of his books. He was a public performer like Vachel Lindsay, but his rhythms were considerably richer and more varied. His Yiddish syllables conveyed the hissing of kettles, the patter of rain, the lapping of a lake at eventide, the roar and splashing of showers. Some of his poems are like directions for choreography, which he alone could execute. His seasonal recitals drew a large and loyal audience. Leivick's audience came to be edified, Lutsky's to be entertained.

Herman Gold, the "Joe Gold" of Second Avenue, was a true writer, the author of a popular book of children's tales and contributor of avant-garde verse, fiction, and essays, sometimes intelligible, sometimes not. He had once been a member of Inzich but for some inexplicable reason, perhaps because his clowning impugned their earnestness at a time when they were struggling for recognition, the Inzich group ceased publishing his work. His prickly hair, upturned little beard and fair-skinned, pixy face were indispensable to the Bohemian decor which attracted Uptowners to the celebrated Café Royal. He was therefore tolerated by its waiters, although he never, in all the time he spent there, had ordered anything. He would appear early in the evening, briefly reconnoiter, then go home to Brooklyn by subway to reappear when the theaters let out, and stayed thereafter till the café's closing time. He spoke in rhymes, mostly utter nonsense, and responded to taunting with an infectious smile and giggle. He was coatless and hatless even in the deep of winter. He pretended know-nothingness, yet sometimes inadvertently startled people with his erudition, even as he mooched dimes from colleagues and strangers, and snatched morsels from other peoples' plates although widely known across the country as a dealer in rare Americana literature. President Wilson had been among his clients. Under oaths of secrecy, broken only after his death this inveterate sponger helped out friends in need with substantial sums of money by hiring them to do work for which he knew they were not fit. He hired a man who knew little Hebrew to be his son's Hebrew teacher, and another who had never held a brush to paint his apartment. He then had to bring in a professional crew to clean up the mess, but several months later, when the "painter" was again hard-up, he hired him once more with the same unhappy results.

In the daytime the Yiddish writers would meet in some café in the vicinity of East Broadway. The newspapermen sat in one section, the literati in another. Only poets who worked on newspapers crossed the no-man's land. They were suspect in both camps. Behind their backs they were called *zeidene yungermanchikes* (silken youths) by the newspapermen, and "whores" by the literati. Literati who worked for the *Forward* and were favored by Cahan were called "concubines."

The writers frequently changed these daytime hangouts which, catering to a general clientele, offered no immunity from eavesdroppers who would intrude with unsolicited opinions and, thrusting manuscripts on writers, demand an immediate opinion.

The Café Royal, where they foregathered in the evening, was different. Its Continental decor, tablecloths, high ceilings, panelled walls, and long windows discouraged the casual passerby. Strangers could not choose their tables at will. The Royal was the Yiddish writers' Algonquin, the Yiddish actors' Sardi's, and a hostel for chronic gamblers with intellectual pretensions. It was accordingly divided into three sections. In the front, to the left as one entered the café, sat the writers, and to the right the actors. In a rear room, shut off from sight by a curtain and a large credenza, chessplayers mixed with card experts and horse-race bettors.

The Royal attracted celebrities from everywhere. They always sat on the left, in the literary section. Here E. E. Cummings would drop in, on occasion, for an evening of conversation with the Inzich poets. He publicly remarked on the rejuvenative effect of these talks, but foreclosed forever on these relationships when acidulous remarks about Jews broke out like sores in his verse. Russian visitors were especially attracted to the Royal. The dancemaster Fokine glided in gracefully with a chattering retinue. The Russian baritone Chaliapin, properly stewed, would come crashing in, like a tumbling wall, filling the aisle with his enormous physique, voice, and exuberance, embracing, kissing and just as ready to brawl with the wonderful *gospoda* (gentlemen) and *tovarischi* (comrades), all of whom were Jews who had migrated from Russia. When the poet Yesenin visited this country with Isadora Duncan, his wife, he found surcease from his black moods in the companionship of Yiddish poets at the Café Royal with whom he could discuss Russian poetry as with peers because they were of the same melancholy Slav tradition. He recited his verses from memory and they translated their own into Russian for him. However, at a reception for him at the home of one of *Die Yunge*, Mani Leib, an exceedingly sensitive lyric poet, with great poetic erudition and a leather worker by trade, the Russian drank too much. Swinging furiously about him, he began to smash furniture and threatened to kill "every last all-knowing Jewish s.o.b." He was straitjacketed and removed by ambulance. Released, Yesenin tearfully offered his apologies to the Yiddish poets, but the harm could not be repaired. They now saw him in the context of his social origin, a typical peasant pogromist soliciting penance, when sober, for the unspeakable violence he had committed against the Jews when drunk.

The major domo at the Café Royal was Herman the busboy, a bald, fat and aging man with smooth eunuch-like complexion. He was a moneylender on the side. Writers had no credit with him; on the other hand, the stars of the Yiddish theater were in permanent hock to him. None of his debtors could really escape him because they could not long endure without the companionship available only at the Royal. Yet, because he liked to receive the installments and interest on time, he made the rounds of all theaters when the payroll was being distributed. He eavesdropped on the gossip about plays in rehearsal so that he might gauge in advance how much credit to extend. He was alleged to be a Hungarian Jew, a *meshumad* (converted to Christianity), and part owner of the café. All waiters deferred to him, checked with him on conflicting instructions issued by the owner's wife who sat behind the cash register which, together with a large console table in which the cutlery was stored, and heavy drapes, concealed the gambling room from the dining area.

There were two kinds of *stamgast* (regulars) at the Royal. Those who ordered and those who lingered around long enough till someone else ordered for them. If the result was two orders, not one, it did not matter to Herman how this was accomplished. If nothing else, the inveterate non-orderer kept the well-heeled stamgast entertained, which also had its purpose. However, when the place was really crowded, the malingering non-orderers were shunted into the gaming room where they stood around among the kibbitzers and occasionally popped their heads through the drapes to scan the dining room for an easy touch who might feed them.

Herman was tolerant, but hardly gracious. Yet, in his own rude way, he was solicitous of his paying regulars, defending them against usurpers from Uptown who tried to bribe him to seat them at a table at which a stamgast was expected at that hour. He sometimes waited as much as twenty minutes before ceding a regular's table to a casual diner, and then sent out messengers to find out what happened to the stamgast who, at the very least, was a source of good tips and very often also a borrower.

In the Austro-Hungarian tradition, Herman revered titles, royal and academic, and bowed from the waist in dead earnest when approaching "the doctors' table" which was the second from the front, near the window facing on East Twelfth Street, in the writers' section of the dining room. The men at this table were encyclopaedists in the Voltairean sense. When their full complement was present they could instantly provide information dispersed in a myriad of reference books and relate it with anecdotes racier than army barracks talk.

The first to arrive at the doctors' table was Dr. Neumann, a medical practitioner. A thick, gray-flecked beard, tobacco-stained around the mouth, wreathed his chubby face, and another wreath in the rear cradled his bald pate. His waistcoat, with stained lapels, was always unbuttoned displaying a watch and chain across his vest, which sheathed an ample midriff. He was reputed to have been a physician on the personal staff of Franz Joseph, Emperor of Austria and Hungary, and still practiced medicine occasionally, but in his own time. He anticipated present-day doctors' aversion to house calls by refusing to climb beyond the second floor of the East Side's walk-up tenements and deplored "that almost everything else can be delivered in a basket, except the human tongue for a doctor to examine."

While waiting for his cronies at their table in the Café Royal he would pore alternately over two leather-bound volumes he always carried with him, Plato's *Republic* in Greek and the Bible in Hebrew. The first to join him at the table was Gershom Bader, an elephantine, lumbering man with a crew cut, thick lenses, and unusually thick, wet lips. With no degrees, but enough erudition for a dozen doctorates, he was a historian, a musical comedy writer, a veteran editor of Yiddish newspapers and periodicals here and abroad, an expert in several Jewish disciplines, could recite from memory passages both from *Faust,* and from obscure Talmudic law giving the precise tractate and page. He was also an excellent raconteur. At a funeral for a Yiddish poet who had died in his forties, Bader was overheard consoling a fellow octogenarian, "We have nothing to fear my friend, death is still calling up the lower numbers."

Dr. Neumann and Bader were always joined by Dr. Kopilevich, a Heidelberg Ph.D., part-time Hebrew tutor, occasional lecturer to Zionist groups. Slender as a flute, with a fine head and thin long beard, he felt that his striking resemblance to Dr. Theodor Herzl, founder of Zionism, was an act of divine grace which imposed a special obligation on him to dress neatly, comport himself with supreme dignity, and appear serene at all times. He rose occasionally to bow to a lady across the room in the actors' section of the dining room. He listened attentively or so it seemed, smiled remotely, did not protest when interrupted, but waited benignly for the intruder to finish.

The most frequent and rudest interrupter was Dr. Heller who was at least fifteen years the junior of even the youngest man at the encyclopaedists' table. He too was a Ph.D., part-teacher, and part-bookseller. His conversation gushed at high pitch; his moustache, the kind later associated with Hitler, never ceased switching and orchestrated the rest of his body, which twitched as if invaded by grasshoppers. Constantly torn between polemics over Goethe and Hegel and the interminable gambling in the rear, he sometimes headed there without even a glance at the doctors' table, as a person coming out of the cold might head for a lavatory. Shuffling the cards, his moustache performing a pantomime, he would lecture on the ethics of gambling, quoting Spinoza on ethics, and if he detected even the slightest cheating he would break off the game and demonstrate his disgust by flinging a handful of coins through the window; in the winter, when the windows were closed, he would stride across the room and fling them out of the door. The kids of the vicinity would gather outside the Royal waiting for a windfall whenever they saw the "twitching man" at the gambling table.

The actors' section of the dining room was further subdivided, each star sat at a separate table surrounded by members of his cast. A nightly visitor, retailing and wholesaling gossip was Sarah Adler, the widow and youngest of Jacob P. Adler's several wives. In her late sixties, she wore heavy makeup and still had an eye for young men passing the Royal's swinging doors. She was delegated to oblivion however on the rare occasions when Binna Abramovich, the grand old lady of the

Yiddish Art had her dinner there. Binna wore high-necked dresses, laces, and no makeup, spoke pure and precise Yiddish, and had the confident manner and grace of a *rebbetzin* (wife of a rabbi).

There were several actors who sat in the literary section, more often than in the actors'. They were all members of the Yiddish Art Theater —its director Maurice Schwartz; Dr. Ben Zion Baratov, who had a medical degree from a Russian university and spoke Yiddish with a heavy Russian accent; Mark Schweid who doubled as a poet, and Jacob Mestel, a former Austrian high school teacher and army officers' school graduate, who founded the Artef Theater. The men sat in turn with the encyclopaedists and the writers. Although they occupied the same section of the dining room and sat back to back on crowded evenings, the two groups were not exactly enamored of each other. The creative writers, awed by the quotations tossed about at the doctors' table, would whistle in the dark for courage and dismiss this learning as sterile pedantry. After a learned critic wrote of "Socratic elements in Lutsky's verse," the poet, who was a true primitive, spoke contemptuously of the encyclopaedists, "they talk Socrates, I write Socrates, who was Socrates?" Being considerate men, the encyclopaedists were never truly outspoken on the subject, but it was well known that they recognized few writers since Goethe and Heine.

Just off East Broadway and Essex Street there is a smudgy little piazza with a half dozen faded red-brick houses, which does not even have a name of its own. It is the meeting point for two streets— Division, which dealt in fur coats, and Canal, whose major trade today is in prayer books, prayer shawls, and phylacteries. In the nineteen-twenties Canal Street's major stock was secular Hebrew literature, although the same stores also sold religious articles. It was, moreover, the embattled citadel of the Hebraists, "the lovers of Hebrew." This was a uniquely Jewish phenomenon. The Irish were divided over Gaelic and English, the conqueror's tongue. The division among Jews was over two Jewish languages, Hebrew, associated with the ancestral home; Yiddish, born out of the travail of Jewry's homelessness. Yiddish was spoken by the overwhelming majority of Jews around the globe; Hebrew by the approximately 200,000 Zionist pioneers in Palestine, and nurtured by a worldwide movement of "lovers" confident that Hebrew could be retrieved from centuries of muteness and again made a living tongue. In New York the Yiddishists regarded the entire multitudinous mass of East European immigrants with its theaters, newspapers, and organizations as their preserve, the Hebraists clung desperately to a few Hebrew schools and to the bookstores on Canal Street.

The bookstore proprietors were the chief knights of the Hebrew crusade. These stores were almost always presided over by a gentle, childless couple past middle age, who alternated between Russian and Russian-accented Hebrew, corresponded in longhand with book suppliers and buyers around the world and claimed in their youth to have been of the inner circle of Chaim Nachman Bialik, the ranking figure of the modern Hebrew renascence. Bialik's circle could not have been that large, of course, or it would have been a mob, even as George Washington could not have slept in the many beds and places for which the claim is made.

They were sensitive, kind couples, these booksellers, and whenever anyone inquired about the price of a book, they would go into a huddle and come up with a figure based on their estimate of what he could afford. Underpaid Hebrew teachers sometimes got their books below cost, and the difference was passed on to one of the affluent reform rabbis, but with such scrupulous exactitude that the booksellers just about kept their heads above water. They preferred comparison shoppers, who lingered and conversed even if they bought nothing, to a customer who ordered, paid, and walked right out with his purchase wrapped under his arm. He made them feel like grocers. He also left them with a troubled conscience for they knew that no true lover of books carried his new acquisition wrapped like a candy box. He could not resist the temptation of poring over it even as he walked to the trolley or subway. To sell books to the other kind was like dealing in slaves. They atoned for it at the first opportunity, however, by lending a brand new volume to a budding author of Hebrew verse.

Each of these booksellers prayed that someday he might be granted the grace of discovering among his clientele another Chaim Nachman Bialik, which would be almost as great a station in life as being Bialik himself. They were especially on the alert for pupils from the Talmudic academies and day schools in the vicinity. These pupils came from all the boroughs; occasionally one of them would stroll in for a purchase. The bookseller and a stray customer or two—trade was always sparse—would break off their impassioned argument over a line of poetry or a point in grammar and begin a kind of toreador dance around the youth as he moved among the bookstacks, coming up close to peer at him, backing away, appraising him from all sides, then asking with studied casualness which school he attended, who his teachers were, how far he had advanced in his studies. Flattered and completely disarmed by the attention, the youth would suddenly find himself cornered by harsh examiners testing him in the complexities of Hebrew syntax. Unable to stand his torment, the bookseller's wife would finally rescue him and if he acquitted himself well he was given the book as a gift and treated to cookies from a jar which she kept with an electric samovar under the counter.

Nearly every bookseller possessed a treasure chest of his own rejected manuscripts. Reconciled to never being a writer himself, he sought, at least, to be in writers' company. There were few recognized Hebrew writers in America, and none to match the Yiddish fraternity. They made their living teaching Hebrew, presiding with an abstracted air and remote manner over generally unruly classes which later recalled with unshriven guilt and warm affection the savage tricks they had played on these wonderfully innocent men whose all-consuming love was a language. Edmund Wilson has written a *New Yorker* profile of one of these men, Daniel Persky, eccentric bachelor, grammarian, feuilletonist who knew several languages but on principle would speak none but Hebrew. That is why he ate all his meals at the Automat where he did not have to communicate with waiters. Then there was Abraham Sho'er (*The Man At The Gate*), a tiny wisp of a fairy creature, with a hat several sizes too big, a goatee which did honor to that word's origins, and large, brown, luminous eyes behind spectacles like newly washed windows, who wrote children's tales and was the father of two American artists, Raphael and Moses Soyer.

A surviving member of that generation is A. R. Malachi, a bibliographer and collector of piquant trivia, a shriveled little man with fogged glasses and in crumpled suits sprinkled with ashes and bread crumbs, who for half a century has been poring over newspapers and, like an IBM machine, feeding himself data in the Jewish room of the New York Public Library. His meager wage for proofreading a Hebrew weekly is continually threatened, he alleges, by an editor who maintains that he cannot afford a proofreader with a cataract in one eye. "But look," Malachi argues before all who would listen, "If the sight has failed in one eye, the other is better than two. It's a medical truism." The editor in turn allegedly contends that the real trouble is not Malachi's cataract but his unsolicited efforts to improve on the editor's work by revising the galleys.

These fervent Hebraists were not foes of Yiddish, in the same fanatical manner in which Yiddishists scorned Hebrew. They hoped that Yiddish would survive even after the triumph of Hebrew as "a lady-in-waiting to the Queen language." The Hebraists always spoke in hyperbole. In pursuit of their purpose these mild men could be as doggedly determined as process servers, badgering Yiddish writers to turn to Hebrew and offering to teach them the language. Bialik's visit to the United States in 1925 evidently merited in their opinion the launching of a new calendar for thereafter they divided time into Before and After Bialik's Visit.

Contemporary fiction in English about the immigrant Jew conveyed almost nothing of this rich cultural ferment. Montague Glass' *Potash and Perlmutter* was tailored for an audience that delighted in depictions of the Jew as a grotesque, shifty, mercurial character speaking pidgin English. Anzia Yezierska's intention was not comic effect. However, she mistook her ambition to be accepted by "true" Americans for the entire ghetto's ambition. She regarded herself as the ghetto voice, even as Harry Golden regards himself today as the voice of the American Jew. In autobiographical fiction, which depicts her Americanization, she uses dialect to achieve greater authenticity. However, even while she was distorting the immigrants' idiom into quaint English, Yiddish was being shaped by masters into a greater literary instrument.

But another kind of English-Jewish writing also made its appearance in the nineteen-twenties. It corresponded in felicity and dignity to the immigrants' move from the Lower East Side to the West Side. Yezierska's East Side writing was a paean to America. This new West Side writing was a polemic against Gentile America. Its prime protagonists, Ludwig Lewisohn, of Yahudim descent and by then established as a foremost American critic, and Maurice Samuel, a considerably younger man of East European origin, published in quick succession a series of *J'accuse* volumes against the Gentile world, asserting the superiority of Jewish mores, and acclaiming the promise of Zionism. Samuel's titles thundered challenges—*You Gentiles* and *I, The Jew*. The books were a mixture of essay and autobiography, and, in Lewisohn's case, autobiographical fiction. The Jew's rejection by the Gentile world they argued, was an almost irreparable condition. But what was remediable was the Jew's self-rejection. This conclusion led them to Zionism.

His harsh indictments of the Gentile world launched Samuel's literary career and made his reputation. Ludwig Lewisohn's "conversion" to

Zionism was dramatic and mysterious. He was then in mid-career as a literary critic, interpreter, translator, and sponsor of Continental literature. He was a mover and shaker, credited with helping rouse America from its insularity and parochialism. His conversion to "Jewish prophecy" jeopardized all his past associations and he was now looked upon as an obsessed bore.

Samuel, Lewisohn, and the audience that gathered about them were spurred by the Zionist promise, the intellectual pioneer farmers in Palestine who were laying the foundation for Jewish statehood, as well as by America's quota severely limiting Jewish immigration, the unofficial quotas against Jewish students and faculty at many American colleges, and the role of Henry Ford as sponsor of anti-Semitic publications. Even the weakest of Samuel's and Lewisohn's works in this genre are nonetheless impassioned and vigorous, excellent examples of the polemic produced at the beginnings of every symbiosis, throughout history, between Jewish culture and another culture. Its tradition dates back to Alexandrian Jewry before the Christian Era. The pattern since has been repeated in Spain, Germany, Russia, and France. Superior in all other respects, Samuel's and Lewisohn's polemics nonetheless were as narrow as Yezierska's apologetics. Both genres monotonously postured the Jew against the world. Yiddish writing in the nineteen-twenties, as always, was concerned with the Jew himself. This made it universal. The writing in English was primarily a literature of grievance and the absence of humor (self-ridicule is not humor) made it parochial.

CHAPTER 4

The Orthodox Brethren

THE YAHUDIM, the upper-class Jews of German origin, had Judaism; the Yidn, the East European immigrants, had *Yiddishkeit*. Judaism was a mock term in the Yiddish vocabulary, something the Yahudim had invented to demonstrate that they were distinct from their upper-class Christian neighbors in religion only, that even the religious distinctions were more apparent than real, and, therefore, there was no reason to bar them from private clubs and exclusive resorts.

All Yidn, even the non-believers, recognized Orthodox fundamentalism as the one and only valid Jewish religion. It was inextricably woven into the fabric of their ethnic environment. It contained all their characteristic bittersweet humor, impassioned concern for right, and boundless affection for Yidn, for the multitudinous Yiddish-speaking people. Those who renounced the synagogue and all religion as residual medievalism, evolved their own brand of cultural nationalism, Yiddish-based and stripped of all religion and significantly, called it *Yiddishkeit* —*weltleche* (secular or worldly) Yiddishkeit.

Judaism definitely was not Yiddishkeit. It was primarily a religious reformation movement. It sought to reconcile faith and reason in the scientific age, and by sloughing off its peculiarly East European customs, place Jewish worship in an American frame. The Yahudim, no doubt, hoped that this might also facilitate their social acceptance by the American Christian bourgeoisie. Nor was Judaism of a single pattern. It was divided into two denominations, Reform and Conservative.

Reform Judaism was a complete break with customs that had characterized Jewish life for centuries. No custom, no tradition is inviolable, according to its extreme theologians. They discarded the dietary laws, Sabbath observance and other rituals of daily life as being obsolescent. Some rabbis transposed the Sabbath with Sunday. The word "Zion" was stricken from the prayerbooks. Jewry's ancient prayers for a return to Zion through Messianic Redemption were banished. There would be no Messiah and there was no need to Return, the Reform rabbinate decreed, because the Jews' true mission was to bear witness amongst the peoples of the earth. The precise nature of that mission and the manner of its discharge were never defined. It could be deduced, however, from the rabbis' emphasis on the Prophets as the essence of Judaism. Yet, it was not easy to translate social prophecy into social critique and practical deeds from pulpits controlled by corporation attorneys, merchant princes, and stock exchange members.

Conservative Judaism was exactly what its name suggested. It did not discard; it only sought to modify and adjust traditional practices to modern circumstances. It supported the Zionists because they sought to realize Jewry's prayers for a return to Zion. It did not regard the Bible as a single revealed work, dictated to Moses by God, yet revered it in its entirety as history, prophecy, custom, and law. Many Reform rabbis rejected all but the prophets. Conservative Judaism embraced post-biblical Hebrew law, the Talmud and the vast rabbinical literature through the ages, reserving the right, however, to be discriminating and selective. It, too, held that not all tradition was inviolable, yet, it treated most of the biblical ritualistic law, the dietary and Sabbath observances, and also some of the custom law, as, in fact, inviolable. The extent of observance varied among its rabbis; some, for example, wore skullcaps (yarmelkes) in accordance with Orthodox custom, others did not, even when studying the sacred texts.

The Conservative congregations observed the ancient custom of publicly reading a portion of the Bible on Saturday mornings and calling up individual congregants, as each fragment was read, to stand by as witness. In Orthodox synagogues the men called up for the honor reciprocated by announcing precise amounts they pledged to the synagogue, rabbi, sexton, and diverse charities. Pledges were made in the Conservative synagogues as well, but the announcement of precise amounts and charities was abolished as crass commercialism. However, like the Reform temples, the Conservative congregations stressed decorum, seated men and women together, and introduced instrumental music into the religious services. Orthodox custom had proscribed this pending the Messianic restoration of the Temple.

The major theologians of Conservative Judaism in America, men like Solomon Shechter and Mordecai M. Kaplan, were East European Yidn themselves, yet they failed to communicate with their own kind. One reason was that the Conservative, like the Reform movement, was largely supported by Yahudim. This promptly labeled it upper-class. Its polemics, primarily directed at the Reform, were meaningless to the East European immigrant rebel. Its stress on synagogue decorum only offended him. The synagogue was his father's abode. He had rejected it only because he rejected all religion. "Outsiders" criticism of the synagogue was an assault on folk custom coming from persons who had displaced Yiddish, which to him was the essence of Yiddishkeit.

Before World War I, there had been implacable hostility between Orthodox and weltleche Yiddishkeit. When the crowds emerged from the synagogue on Yom Kippur eve, which inaugurated a twenty-four hour fast and the most solemn of the Jewish holidays, young anarchists would sometimes wade into them with blasphemous songs and slogans, and biting on ham sandwiches. By the nineteen-twenties the hostilities were over. The anarchists were a vanishing sect. All other ideological movements had made peace with the pious, and the Orthodox voted Reform rabbis into Zionist leadership and joined unions led by Socialists.

The public platform was ruled by the secularists. The physical environment, however, was dominated by the Orthodox. Beards, earlocks, and wide-rimmed black velvet hats, the hallmarks of the East European fundamentalist, were a common sight everywhere from downtown, around East Broadway, to the garment center, which was then located in the West 20's. On weekdays, synagogue morning services were held in several shifts, beginning at dawn, to accommodate the many worshippers. Hurriedly, the Orthodox Jew wrapped himself in his prayer shawl and placed phylacteries, containing portions of the Hebrew law, on his left arm and his forehead, to greet his God before rushing off to work. At sundown, if he found himself far from a synagogue, he would improvise, wherever he was, a minyan, the required quorum of ten for prayers, by enlisting passersby. It was a common sight to see Orthodox Jews, singly or in quorum, recite their prayers in court corridors, in judges' chambers, or near the lamp on a street corner.

The Jewish neighborhoods were considerably darker on Friday than on weekday evenings. Most of the shops were closed and their lights were off, and one was compelled to walk blocks for a soda, a pack of cigarettes, or a newspaper, through dimmed streets twitching with the flicker of Sabbath candles in thousands of windows.

Dating was virtually impossible on Friday evening. There were few private phones in those days, and most candy stores with public phones were shut down for the Sabbath. On weekday evenings there were always school kids around to summon a girl to the phone. They formed a cartel, which expected a nickel tip for each call, at a time when a Hershey chocolate bar was only a penny. A girl who tried to get away with a bargain rate of two calls for five cents, or pretended that she had forgotten her purse upstairs, risked being cut off permanently from her telephone suitors. If her suitor called, the cartel would offer one of several replies: "She is at the dentist, her bridge fell out and broke," "She is visiting her brother in jail," "She ran off with a married man," "She is embarrassed to come to the phone, her mother gave birth to a bastard." Now and then, a girl paid the cartel a weekly retainer for which she received her own calls as well as, "by mistake," calls intended for other girls. Too many calls, however, were injurious to a girl's reputation, suggesting that she was "too particular"—"she will choose until there will be none to choose from," or that she was promiscuous, "they pass her around like a salt shaker, every week another boy calls."

On Saturday morning even the non-religious would occasionally drop into a synagogue towards the end of the services because there they could have a shot of whiskey or a glass of wine even in Prohibition days. The law permitted liquor on "sacramental occasions." A *kiddush,* the serving of drinks and refreshments to celebrate a public, familial or private event, is always a sacramental occasion in Orthodox synagogues. The consummation of a business deal is sufficient pretext for serving a kiddush. But the reason generally is something more formal, such as a *yahrzeit* (the anniversary of a death), or the "calling up" of a *bar mitzvah* (the confirmation of a boy in his thirteenth year) or of a *chossen* (bridegroom) on the Sabbath preceding the wedding.

The average kiddush in the nineteen-twenties consisted of whiskey or wine served with macaroons, *fluden,* a pastry of honey and nuts; *pletzlach,* which are square cakes with either onions or poppyseeds; and raisins, nuts, and chickpeas swooped up by the fistful from deep bowls. When a celebrant family was generous with the drinks, members of the congregation would get circumspectly tipsy, and here and there one could see around midday on Saturday a bearded elder weaving his way homeward uncertainly, humming a snatch of liturgy off-key, stopping to caress a child's head, to lean on a stoop or embrace a lantern until his dizziness passed. By late afternoon, having slept it off, he would return to the synagogue and resume his study of the sacred texts, begun that morning before prayers.

Then followed the first section of the evening service and the *shalosh seudot,* the concluding communal meal which consisted of fish, tomato herring, chalah (Jewish white bread), soda pop, and beer, ordered from a Sabbath-observing grocery Friday afternoon. It was eaten amidst singing and the recital of Torah (law) or Hassidic wonder tales in the dimness of an expiring day. When the first stars could be seen outdoors, the congregation would rise for the final prayers, and then a match was applied to the *Havdalah* (differentiation) candle. Woven of heavy strands of tallow, the Havdalah has a special function. Its flame bursting forth like a bonfire, formally seals off the Sabbath, or any holiday, and ushers in the new week. A shaker of spices was passed around for every congregant to sniff, and with handshakes and wishes for "a *gute woch*" (a good week) they dispersed.

Each holiday transformed the Jewish neighborhoods in its own image.

The pious kept up an unusually busy schedule of devotions during the Penitential Ten Days which began with Rosh Hashanah (the Jewish New Year) and concluded with Yom Kippur (the Day of Atonement). On each of the interim days midnight services were held, and the dawn was ushered in with the blowing of the shofar (ram's horn) for which rehearsals had gone on all summer, with sour notes exploding into the streets at odd hours.

Grocers stocked up on honey before Rosh Hashanah because chalah dipped in honey augured a sweet year ahead.

Several days before Yom Kippur, caravans of open trucks entered the Jewish neighborhoods carrying, in tier-like arrangements, crates filled with fowl. The fowl, feet tied, were kept in the bathtub for several days to fatten. Their cackling at dawn competed with the sound of the ram's horn. Then, with the family solemnly gathered about him, the paterfamilias would swing the fowl over the heads of his household and recite a prayer, "May this fowl be a *kapara* (absolvent) for my transgressions, those of my household, and the entire household of Israel."

The kapara served the same purpose as the scapegoat in ancient Jerusalem. Well-to-do families bought a kapara for each member of the household, including infants. The struggling fowl was carried off to the nearest kosher slaughterhouse and brought back wrapped in dripping paper, cooked and served to the family at the festive meal that broke the Yom Kippur fast. However, rabbinic law provided that charity donations, any coin, could serve instead of fowl as a kapara. The poor, unable to afford fowl, and the learned who shunned the primitive custom, availed themselves of this dispensation.

Drugstores did a brisk business in smelling salts in anticipation of Yom Kippur. The thud of bodies sinking to the synagogue floor punctured the most solemn moments of the interminable day-long service. Men would emerge from beneath their entangled prayer shawls, and look about them half-annoyed, half-curious. Cries would go up, "Open a window, pass the smelling salts." Sometimes it was an old sage who fainted, having refused the rabbi's dispensation to the elderly from fasting. Sometimes it was the cantor, exhausted from his long devotions. Most of the fainting took place in the curtained women's gallery, however, and the ladies were accused of doing it deliberately to attract male attention.

There was a stir of indignation whenever girls appeared at the door with flowers for their mothers. The sexton barred them, their mothers were embarrassed. Bringing flowers to an Orthodox synagogue in the nineteen-twenties was almost as much of a scandal as dating a goy, or breaking the fast. It was considered a custom befitting the citadel of Reform Judaism, Temple Emanu-El, which "passes for a synagogue and is worse than a church." Flowers, song and dance, had been a feature of the Yom Kippur observance in ancient Jerusalem, but were barred, along with instrumental music until the Messianic restoration of the Temple.

Flowers were a feature, however, of Shevuoth, a two-day holiday in the late spring or early summer, and Sukkoth, the week-long Feast of Tabernacles. Both are partly seasonal holidays, presenting the curious spectacle of an urbanized people in a northern climate celebrating the calendar events of its distant past as a Mediterranean peasant people. Shevuoth commemorates the giving of the Law at Sinai and Palestine's first seasonal harvest; Sukkoth memorializes the Hebrews' wanderings in the desert and the Promised Land's second seasonal harvest.

On the eve of Shevuoth, Jewish florists did a brisk business in flowers and bulrushes. The latter was in remembrance of the discovery of the infant Moses by the daughter of Pharaoh in the bulrushes on the banks of the Nile. The flowers were used to garland mirrors and chandeliers; the bulrushes were spread on the floor. Shevuoth was a gastronome's delight. The mid-day meal consisted of dairy courses, borscht, and varenikes—pockets of dough filled with cheese or potatoes—which one dunked in bowls of sour cream. The evening meal was *fleischigs*— consisting of meat—the soup contained kreplach—dough filled with meat—and the entrée or dessert consisted of holobtzies—cabbage filled with sweetened meat.

Before Sukkoth, pushcarts and outdoor stands were piled with flowers and thatch. The Bible requires that for seven days the Jew live as his ancestors had lived in their desert wanderings, in thatch-roofed huts through which the stars might be visible. These were built everywhere in the Jewish neighborhoods during the Sukkoth season, in backyards and even on roofs. Inside they were hung with birds and other patterns cut from colored paper, flowers, and Japanese lanterns. All meals were eaten there, even in rainy and chilly weather. The extremely pious even slept there. The Polish and Ukrainian janitors, seeing an opportunity, as in the old country, to hound the Jew, anonymously informed housing and fire inspectors, who found these huts in violation of city ordinances and served summonses answerable in ten days if the Sukkoth were not removed by then. This was three days more than the holiday's duration. Immediately after Sukkoth the thatch was piled high on the pavement in Jewish neighborhoods just as Christmas trees are piled high in other neighborhoods after that holiday.

The cycle of seasonal holidays begins in the Spring with Passover, which marks the Exodus from Egypt. For seven days the Jew is required to eat *matzoh*, unleavened bread, and rid his household of all *chametz*—leavened matter—so that he might share his ancestors' experience as bondsmen in Egypt and their flight in haste before their dough could ferment.

Observed in strict Orthodox fashion, Passover is the most demanding and costly of all the Jewish holidays. All truly religious Jewish homes have two sets of dishes and cutlery for year-round use, one for *milchigs* (dairy), another for *fleischigs* (meat), and sealed off in a china closet or on the upper kitchen shelves, duplicate sets for Passover, each item separately wrapped in paper. Those unable to afford extra Passover sets, dumped their year-round dishes and cutlery into two pails of scalding water, with a heated, glowing iron bar inside, to cleanse them of any chametz that might cling to them. Tables, sinks, stoves, and ice boxes were thoroughly scoured and, as a further precaution, were covered or lined with asbestos. This custom still prevails among the Orthodox observers in this country, as well as abroad.

In Orthodox homes, on the night before Passover, the paterfamilias would deposit crumbs of bread on window sills, and then with candle in hand and reciting prayers, would go from darkened room to darkened room pretending to "discover" this residual chametz and brush it with a feather duster into a large wooden spoon. Before going off to work the next day, he would light a little fire along the pavement and throw in the spoon and feather duster. All that morning the pavements in Jewish neighborhoods seemed under repair, with small fires burning along their rims, and the smell of smoke and roasting feathers lingered in the air till well past noon. The Orthodox had one more ceremony to perform before leaving their neighborhoods for the day. It involved a rather complex procedure of sale, resale, and proxy. If the Jews were really to dispose of all the accumulated chametz in their possession their poor would suffer, their businesses go bankrupt. So the sages conceived of a legal safety valve. Jews may "sell" their chametz to a Gentile and "repurchase" it after Passover. The Gentile is tipped twice for his cooperation. Under Jewish law the sale is genuine and binding, and it happened on occasion, where a warehouse, grocery, or bakery were involved in the chametz transaction that the Gentile insisted on an actual, not a fictitious price before releasing the merchandise to its Jewish owner. A further safety valve was devised: the sale is arranged through a "proxy," a rabbi or sexton who sells the chametz wholesale to the Gentile without the latter knowing what he has bought and who its owners might be. The proxy ceremony is brief, the deal between the Jewish parties is sealed by each holding the end of a handkerchief as male and female do when dancing at Orthodox weddings.

Each Orthodox synagogue had shelves with sacred works, and, close by, a sink with a towel. One could tell from the smudges on the towel the menial occupations at which the congregants made their living. A sacred book was approached like a bride, in spiritual and physical purity; one washed his fingers before removing a volume, and, as a sign of love between the Jew and his Law, "kissed" the book by placing two fingers on the printed page and then carrying them to his lips on opening or shutting a book. If a volume disintegrated so badly it could not be restored, it was wrapped in cloth like human remains and interred in sanctified ground.

Every congregation aspired to have a *chevra shas,* a Talmudic study-circle which met at least once a week to debate the rich law of two thousand years ago, and with a chevra shas in its midst, it did not require the services of a rabbi, which only few congregations could afford. Ranking below it were other chevras, the *chevra mishnayot* and *chevra ein yaacov,* students of post-biblical lore, not law, and at the bottom of the pyramid was *chevra tehilim,* reciters of the Psalms.

Every congregation had a chevra tehilim, devout men who comprehended very little of the Hebrew words they recited. It was not the words that moved them but the psalmody to which they had been conditioned from childhood. Members of the shtetl proletariat, they had somehow not been touched by the Socialist and anarchist heresies, or by America's socio-economic mobility which wrenched and raised some of their peers to new status. Their chanting, in monotonous unison, was like the buzzing of flies on a breezeless afternoon. They addressed their God familiarly, interpolating a Yiddish exclamation after each textual reference to Him—"*Goteniu* (little God), help us," and "How long, *tateniu* (little father), will these tribulations be visited on us?" or "Tell us Goteniu, tateniu, will the black *golles* (diaspora, dispersion) never end for the Jew?" A stern "*sha*" ("quiet") from the chevra shas would silence them if their voices rose too high and intruded on the Talmudists' learned discussion. Yet even the chevra shas esteemed the iron in these men whom environmental blandishment could not deflect from their simple faith and from reciting psalms when others of their kind passed their time playing pinochle.

The chevra tehilim, like the fire department, was summoned in emergencies. A swarm of women would burst into the synagogue like gusts of wind and rain, tearful and wringing their hands, crying "Yidn, help a desolate family, an impending widow, imminent orphans," they would fling open the doors of the Holy Ark, which contains the sacred scrolls, and thrusting their heads inside as if they were confronting God himself, would petition for divine reprieve for a kin of whose life the doctors had despaired. "But you, tateniu, are the doctor of all doctors, only you can help. If not you, where else can we turn? Tell us, where else?" Having filled the Ark with their laments and supplications, they would pause and suddenly remember the need for supporting petitions, for *amicus curiae*. Wheeling around they would demand of the chevra tehilim, half in wrath, half pleading, "Why are you sitting here staring at us like *golems* when every precious second counts?" Taking the cue, the chevra tehilim would raise its collective voice with *kavanah* (deepest concentration) in a high tide of collective psalmody whose impact in the heavenly court of last resort has sometimes been known to snatch a man from the very jaws of the hereafter.

The various chevras met even in the middle of the week, but the chevra shas, which required considerable cerebral effort, generally met only on the Sabbath, in the morning before services, and in the late afternoon between *mincha* and *maareev*, the long intermission between the first and second half of the evening service. They studied the Talmud page by page and tractate by tractate, covering a wide range of subjects including medicine, familial morality, historical relations with Babylonia, Persia, and Rome, for these and many other topics are all within the compass of the Talmud. They argued too with the sages and with the exegetes of past centuries, as if they were confreres sitting with them at the long, bare table in the Lower East Side or East Bronx synagogue. They would counterpose one great authority to another and sometimes come up with a conclusion which seemed to invalidate hitherto widely held opinion. The enormity of it would frighten them and they would then seek out a rabbinical authority and solicit his counsel, only to learn that some great legalist of the past whom they had somehow overlooked had already recorded a similar opinion. It comforted them that they were not alone in their dissent. It took several years for a chevra shas to complete its cycle of study, and then they would commence over again, but not before the occasion was marked by a kiddush. This kind of kiddush was a major neighborhood event worthy of being reported in the Orthodox newspapers. It took place on an evening. Refreshments included fish and meatballs prepared by wives of the scholars. Sages from synagogues in the entire borough were invited, but even as they celebrated and feasted, the chevra shas and the invited dignitaries engaged in impassioned debate over obscure passages in the Talmud, for to concentrate on food alone is the pagan way, and there can be no pleasure, even in food, without Torah.

Any one of ten Jews may lead his peers in prayer, hence there was hardly an Orthodox Jew unable to chant the full service even if he did

not know its meaning. Anyone with a pleasing voice and a fair understanding of the text could perform as a cantor on weekdays, Saturdays,
and ordinary holidays. The congregations were particular, however, as
to who led them in worship on the Days of Awe—Rosh Hashanah and
Yom Kippur—not only because each congregation competed with all
the others in selling High Holiday pews and needed an attraction, but
also because it was important that he who interceded for the Household of Israel be a man of unimpeachable piety, that he possess the
physical endurance for the task, and that he understand every word
of the service, which was an advocate's brief to the heavenly court.
To spare the cantor's energies, an assistant was engaged to chant the
early portion of the morning and evening service, before the congregation was fully assembled. The *chazan* (cantor) chanted only the major
portions. This division of roles, approximated that of solicitor and
barrister in British courts.

A truly good chazan, with a distinctive voice, an expert in trills and
frills, and with sufficient knowledge of the language of liturgy not to
run its Hebrew words together meaninglessly, could command a contract for a minimum of one year, with a clause permitting him to
accept several Saturday engagements as guest cantor in other synagogues. The most eminent were signed up for life and were sold like
baseball players. They were called by diminutive first names, which in
Yiddish, depending on the context, connoted love, reverence, or contempt and censure, and were reserved for children, rabbis, and musclemen who served both sides in industrial disputes.

The first among his peers was Cantor Yossele Rosenblatt, a small man
with a powerful, broad chest, a long wide beard and, in the idiom of
the Yidn, "a voice that chirped like canaries and rolled like thunder."
At some point in the service the Holy Ark is flung open revealing the
Holy Scrolls, bunched together in their lavish garments and silver
crowns with little bells, like an assembly of midget monarchs posing
for a picture. When Yossele's voice hit a high note, the crowns trem-
bled as if shaken by a wind, and their bells gave off rippling sounds, to
the great delight of the congregation.

The Lower East Side synagogues that could not afford to have Yossele under contract would engage him for an occasional Sabbath
morning service. An overflow crowd of several thousands would gather
outside the synagogue and police would shut off the street to divert
traffic. To escape the crush, Yossele was sometimes sneaked into the
synagogue at dawn, and later was whisked off through backyards.

His Orthodox piety was eventually his undoing. He invested his life-savings, borrowed heavily, and collected in advance on several years' salary to finance two serio-comic ventures, as if lifted from the pages of Sholem Aleichem. He was less concerned with the huge returns promised him, than with promoting Yiddishkeit. He had been persuaded by smart operators that the two existing Yiddish-Orthodox dailes were not sufficiently pious and another, more Orthodox was required. He helped finance it. It folded within months. The operators then panicked him with statistics showing that the percentage of Jewish women in New York who submitted to the post-menstrual ritual of submersion was alarmingly low. They persuaded him to invest in a capacious, luxurious ritualistic pool as a means of remedying the situation. The women still stayed away, and Yossele, who had throughout his life rejected secular concert offers, now signed up to tour the vaudeville circuit in order to discharge his debts. He stipulated, however, that he was not to be accompanied on an organ and that there be no female performers on the stage with him. The regular customers were mysti-fied by diminutive Yossele alone in the spotlight, and his large personal following had no desire to see their Yossele in his degradation, a Samson shorn of his locks parading before the Philistines in their temple. Nor could Yossele bear this very long. His heart gave out.

All the celebrated cantors cut records. Some were real *schlaggers*, or hits. Every evening of the week except Fridays, holidays, and in foul weather, crowds assembled outside the phonograph stores for concerts of records, which were amplified through a horn in the transom. Liturgy and popular music were interspersed. The serious waited patiently for the moment when a cantorial record was put on. Then they exploded into a minor riot of heated polemics, drowning out the voice pouring through the horn. Each coterie of fans acclaimed the records of its favorite cantor, but was divided against itself as to which items in his albums were superior to others. These disputations involved the pitch of the cantor's voice, the clarity of his diction, the pathos of the sighs, sobs, and exclamations that interlaced his liturgy.

At the top of the Jewish hit parade was the mixed compassionate-vindictive song, *"Mein Greene Kuzine"* ("My Greenhorn Cousin"), about an immigrant beauty who had numerous suitors but turned down their marriage proposals, and then, after several seasons at sweatshop labor, "the orange blossoms have wilted from her cheeks and better not suggest dancing to her fatigued little feet." Other schlaggers were a comedy narrative about *Moishe Kapoyer* (Wrong Way Moish) who does nothing right, and Yente Telebende who gives her husband and neighbors no quarter. But one record beat all others. It was "Eli, Eli." For nearly a decade the evening air was filled with this heart-rending Hebrew-Yiddish lament. Its opening passage, "God, My God, why hast thou forsaken us? They have thrown us like kindling into the flames, they have drowned us in blood," was followed by a detailed recital of the horrors visited upon the Jews in the purgatory that was Civil War Russia. Weddings, bar mitzvahs, and all other joyous occasions opened and closed with "Eli, Eli" lest the Yidn forget the anguish of their kinsmen. When Zionist dignitaries were given official City Hall receptions in American cities, the bands struck up this lament thinking it was the Jewish anthem.

In the nineteen-twenties, the Jewish neighborhoods swarmed with recently arrived Hassidic wonder-*rebbes* who settled in grim little flats. They were each attended by a nervous, shabby aide-de-camp who went about all week soliciting from synagogues an invitation for his rebbe to be their guest for a Sabbath, in return for whatever those called up to the Torah might care to pledge for him. The rebbes, not ordained rabbis, but supposedly charismatic leaders, lived on contributions of food and money from women whom they comforted with blessings and amulets. There were Polish and Ukraine Christian women among them who remembered the old world reputation of the Jewish wonder-rebbes. Their male retinue was sparse. On Friday evening, or Saturday afternoon, after the meal, a half dozen, or so, obtuse proletarians would gather at his table and teetering on the brink of sleep struggle to follow the rebbe's learned discourse. However, when a stranger who looked like a learned man entered, the rebbes would drop their voices to a whisper—they were better at inventing quotations than at citing real sources. The truly great rebbes were erudite men; before World War I they disavowed disciples who went to America where even pious Jews surrender to pagan custom. After the war and its atrocities they relented, but did not come to America themselves until two decades later. However, the Hassidic dynasties with their offspring numerous, had many claimants to succession whenever a dynastic head passed on. Those who came to America in the nineteen-twenties were the lesser figures in the succession struggle, dubious pretenders, as their very departure from the field of battle would indicate.

Orthodox congregations imported their hometown rabbis, preachers, teachers, cantors, and kosher slaughterers. The Bialystoker Congregation, in the Lower East Side, pulled a major coup. It brought its *magid*, an old fashioned fire-and-brimstone preacher of a high order. He preferred to speak at twilight when both the light and the mood were right. In the intermission between the first and second half of the evening service, enveloped in a prayer shawl, he would mount the stairs in front of the Ark, and swaying slightly, would survey his audience of dull-faced men in working clothes and with grimy hands, and a gallery packed with women who normally attended evening services on the High Holy days only. He would sigh loudly once or twice, as his gaze swept the synagogue, and the women would begin to sob softly. He then would admonish them loudly and sternly, "Women, stop your whining, the Bialystoker magid wishes to speak," and in a tearful voice that alternately rose in lament, screamed in agony and then dropped to a whisper, he would describe "in living color" the horrors of the hereafter that awaited those "who turned away from God, denied the poor, violated the Sabbath, placed their trust in radical writers and let their offspring grow up, like goyim, without a Jewish education, and as you reap so you harvest, and hence these children, who were taught no better, end up marrying goyim." After each exclamatory passage, a wail would rise from the women's gallery, the simple menfolk would look around terrified, and the magid again would warn, "Women, stop your whining" and resume his detailed account of crime and punishment, cause and effect.

Word about him spread. He attracted auditors who had not been to a synagogue in many decades—Socialists, Communists, anarchists. They came to see whether it was really true that working-class Jews in New York could still be put into a sweating trance by an old fashioned magid. None would concede that they were also drawn by nostalgia.

From the socialist *Forward* came Dr. B. Hoffman, better known under his pseudonym Zivyon, an unregenerate free thinker. He sat pokerfaced through an entire sermon and then remarked dryly that "if the Socialist Party were to engage the *magid* to address its election rallies, it might still make a comeback."

The Yiddish newspapers interviewed the magid. He was invited to other cities. But eventually the novelty wore off. Yet he could not return to Bialystok; his style had become obsolescent there, which was why he came to America in the first place. He finally retired in total obscurity to a home for old men in the Bronx.

There arrived, from Russia, outstanding Talmudists, several of whom joined the faculty of the Yeshiva, a sprawling barracks-like building on East Broadway, which housed a rabbinical seminary, a Hebrew teachers' institute, and a secular high school. The old headquarters have since been demolished by urban renewal and the Yeshiva has acquired a far-flung campus and has evolved into the complex known as Yeshiva University and Albert Einstein Medical Center. In the nineteen-twenties, it acquired a phenomenal emigré-Talmudist, *Der Meitcheter Eeloui*,[1] the Prodigy of Meitchet, a town in Lithuania. Sparse and neat, a narrow beard elongating his high-domed forehead with prominent corners, he resembled Michelangelo's *Moses*. His responsibility at Yeshiva was the candidates for rabbinic ordination. They studied in the huge entrance hall which doubled as a synagogue, swaying all day over tomes of ancient law, debating it with themselves, arguing it with others in singsong voice and with emphatic gestures. The Meitcheter, at a lectern to the right of the Holy Ark, would stand for hours, eyes shut, almost immobile, only occasionally riffling through a folio that lay before him.

Several times a year he would deliver a public discourse, generally at noon, on a weekday. It was a gala event for the East Side's Orthodox scholars, whatever their economic station in life. Trustees whose names were embossed in gold in the entrance hall, including the father of the New York *Times* Sunday Magazine editor, Lester Markel, cancelled all their business appointments for the rest of that day; shopkeepers drew their shutters, peddlers covered their wares with tarpaulin and hastened to Yeshiva which, for an hour or two, was jam-packed with an audience whose attention was as taut as a violin string, as they bent their ears with their hands to catch the low voice of the Eeloui. As was the custom in Yeshivas, he would be interrupted in the middle of his discourse by questions and challenges that came from all corners of the hall and seemed disembodied. He would answer hastily, impatiently, and, with-

---

[1] Great rabbis were rarely known by their family names but only by the titles of their best known works, or by an honorific combined with the name of their hometown. Attached to him in his youth, the honorific Eeloui stayed with a scholar throughout his lifetime. *Gaon*, an even greater honorific, connoting genius, has been used indiscriminately in correspondence between rabbis, but only one rabbi in modern times was universally called by that title, the Gaon of Vilna, the eighteenth-century authority who ranks with the rabbinic greats of all ages. It had none of these formidable connotations in its beginnings, between the sixth and eleventh centuries, when it was simply the rank held by the heads of the Yeshivot which then were both legal academies and courts and also had the power to levy taxes on all Jews in their jurisdiction.

out losing his strand of thought, racing along his sophist way. When it was over, all walked away as if still in a trance, with enough food for learned argument for an entire season.

In the nineteen-twenties one man's orthodoxy was another man's heresy. Full-bearded Orthodox extremists were outraged by deviationists who trimmed their beards, yet some of the younger Orthodox men went beyond this slight "heresy" and were altogether clean-shaven, contending that the Bible proscribed the use of a blade but that the foul smelling depilatory powder they used was wholly permissible.

The most rigid Orthodox congregation was The Ninety-niners. Outsiders sometimes thought the number had occult significance, or that membership, for some reason, was restricted to one hundred minus one. Ninety-nine was simply part of their address. Their synagogue was located on the second floor at 99 East Houston Street, in a flat overlooking the gray bay of Hamilton Fish Park, better known as Houston Street Park.

The Ninety-niners were *melamadim* (religious tutors), collectors for Holy Land institutions, peddlers, small shopkeepers, and ironers and buttonhole makers in the garment center. But they had never a doubt that they were an elite. Scholars of the law, observers of even the least of the rituals, they wore beards and immersed themselves daily, their wives' heads were shaved and they immersed themselves monthly. Some of the most powerful and wealthy men in American orthodoxy were rejected for membership because the Ninety-niners found them wanting. They believed that most of the kosher products on the market were a fraud, and the Ninety-niners' patronage of groceries, bakeries, dairies and restaurants was among the Orthodox more important than a rabbi's seal of approval.

Most of the Ninety-niners sent their children to Yeshiva, but a minority of the brethren regarded the Yeshiva on East Broadway as a viper's nest. Why were its students permitted to wear beanies covered with election buttons instead of yarmelkes? What rabbis and teachers would these students make if it was true they leaped onto Meyer London Matzoh Bakery trucks and pitched matzoh boxes for baseball practice? And was it not rumored that despite the law providing for an intermission of six hours between fleischigs (meat courses) and milchigs (dairy) some of its students were caught gulping down malted milk in a nearby candy store almost immediately after having had stew in the institution's cafeteria?

The extremists found other things wrong as well. Some of the faculty had Ph.D.s which meant they had indulged in "heretical" studies and they detracted from the dignity of their ordination by calling themselves "doctor rabbi." The Yeshiva President, Dr. Bernard Revel, in fact was a case in point. The dean of the Teachers Institute, Pinchas Churgin, was also a Ph.D. and not even a rabbi. The curriculum of the Teachers Institute was a public scandal from the extremists' view, it provided insufficiently for Talmudic instruction and more than enough history, philosophy, and poetry. Instead of concentrating on Maimonides' legal commentaries, it taught his *Guide to the Perplexed*. *The Guide* seeks to deduce proof of God's being by rational methods. Addressed to the skeptical Jewish and Muslim intelligentsia, it was denounced in Maimonides' lifetime by extremists to whom rational deductions were a concession to heresy. Seven centuries later, in the nineteen-twenties, minority segments of New York Orthodoxy still feared its effect on impressionable young minds.

The Yeshiva made no religious demands of its secular high school faculty, which was not easy to come by. Salaries were low and irregular, the hours were odd and included Sundays, and its students, trained in casuistry and discourse could be a trial for the dull, albeit a delight for the brilliant, teacher. The faculty, in fact, consisted of a surprising collection of men. The one religious member was an American-born rabbi who taught mathematics. He was observant of all the minutiae of Orthodox ritual, had a full house of whining infants, and his wife, also American-born, shaved her head and wore a kerchief like the wives of the Ninety-niners. Latin and French were taught by Joseph T. Shipley, a placid-tempered, plumpish man with a pipe always clutched between his teeth, who wrote drama reviews for Socialist periodicals, rushed from Yeshiva to Broadway openings and Socialist Committee meetings. One youthful teacher, Joshua Kunitz, several years later, became a contributing editor to *The New Masses;* he lived intensely every moment in class, passionately listening, heatedly arguing, and was always accompanied to the subway by a swarm of disciples.

Orthodoxy ignored all other Judaic denominations. Occasionally it panicked, as when a senior student, and this happened almost once every semester, defected to the Conservative or Reform rabbinical seminaries. The rumor was that the Talmud orals there were a joyride for those who had studied at Yeshiva, and pulpits, with wealthy congregations, were for the asking. One of Orthodoxy's rudest awakenings to the existence of other denominations occurred in 1925, at the Christmas season, and it involved Dr. Stephen S. Wise, the Zionist leader and chairman of the United Palestine Appeal. Orthodox Yidn were shaken as if by an earthquake. The Yidn never held Wise's pulpit against him, and indeed, so that they might accept him as their political leader, they deliberately took his religion lightly. They called him doctor, not rabbi, for how could they call a man rabbi who held his services on Sunday, and, like a performer, from the concert stage at Carnegie Hall? They agreed that he behaved like a goy by all standards but that his heart burst with compassion for his people. But there came a day when they could no longer be facetious.

Dr. Wise with his keen sense for histrionics, and for what would make next morning's headlines, chose the Sunday before Christmas to deliver a sermon on Jews to his Carnegie Hall congregation. All agreed that pounding the pulpit for emphasis after each phrase, he had said: "Jesus was human. Jesus was a Jew. Jesus was not a Christian." The newspaper accounts reported that the rabbi had also urged the Jews to accept Jesus as a prophet and teacher. A Christian minister, in a radio address, hailed Dr. Wise's statement as the first sign of Jewish reconciliation with Jesus, "A bud that will come to fruition in the Lord's good time." The Orthodox *Tageblat*, crying "apostasy," accused Wise of directing "the younger generation to the baptismal font." *The Jewish Morning Journal*, the enlightened Orthodox newspaper, squirmed in an uncomfortable middle position while the Socialist *Forward* was delighted at the discomfiture of the Zionists. *The Day*, the liberal Zionist daily, defended Wise, not his views, against the rising demand that he resign as chairman of the United Palestine Appeal, and all his other Zionist posts. Its famous feuilletonist Dr. Abraham Coralnik asked "Where is the Jewish sense of humor? Who ever takes Wise's theology seriously? Why deny ourselves his decided ability to stir an audience to generous contributions?" Several Reform rabbis defended his right to his opinion, although they disagreed with him, but Rabbi Samuel Schulman, of Temple Emanu-El, citadel of Reform, aligned himself with the Orthodox. This was his opportunity to settle the score with the man who over the issue of free speech had placed himself above his peers by refusing an invitation to the pulpit Schulman now occupied; who disturbed the peace of the stable Reform rabbinate with his strident Zionism and tumultuous social crusades, and who had risen high above most rabbis in public prominence. "Wise's real purpose,"

Schulman said, "was to convert them [his listeners] not to Christianity of course, but to Jesus, and I claim that conversion to Jesus is the first step to Christianity."

Wise asked for an interview with the Orthodox leaders. The atmosphere must have been not unlike that which prevailed at the religious court in Amsterdam when Spinoza was summoned to answer charges of heresy. Regally tall, and for the occasion with a yarmelke on his head and walking with a slight stoop, Wise looked every bit the penitent as he assured them that he had been reprehensibly misquoted by the press and had never called upon his congregation to "accept Jesus as teacher."

He left without a verdict. It was handed down later by a solemn assembly attended by hundreds and which demanded his resignation from the United Palestine Appeal. Wise, accordingly, submitted his resignation, which promptly triggered a worldwide reaction. The Jewish Telegraphic Agency cabled statements from Jewish leaders abroad, men acceptable to Orthodoxy, asserting their confidence that Wise could not possibly have made the statements attributed to him and urging the United Palestine Appeal to reject his resignation. The resignation was rejected by a 73-1 vote.

The high excitement was fitting for the season. The controversy continued through the first month of 1926 and then subsided. Soon the Orthodox were again crowding Wise's rallies, and without comprehending his words, applauded his eloquence when it reached high pitch, for they never had a better spokesman than this rabbi whose religion they regarded as a Purim shpiel—an entertainment.

CHAPTER 5

Occupations

IMMIGRATION overturned the hierarchal pyramid among the Yidn in America. The proletarian occupations, treated with contempt by the social arbiters of East European Jewish life, acquired dignity and respect in America. The rabbi, the most prestigious figure in the shtetl, became almost wholly irrelevant to the immigrant community. The secular professions—doctor, lawyer, pharmacist and dentist, in that order—remained at the top of the list. Some of these, however, now wore slightly tarnished halos.

In the shtetl, the doctor was a remote presence, almost a myth. He rode in a carriage. His household shopping was done by domestics. His wife traveled abroad for her clothes and her cures. He was consulted by the Christian nobility, the Jewish rich, as well as the Hassidic wonder rebbes, who were healers in their own right, treating their multitudinous followers with amulets, blessings, and a laying on of hands.

Most of the Jewish poor suffered through a lifetime of illnesses content with the ministrations of a *feldsher*, a kind of medical nurse with a state qualification certificate, who was usually also the town barber. He used leeches and cups and was a specialist in setting bones and lowering fevers. The common man consulted a doctor only regarding lingering and agonizing illnesses.

In America, the physician's remoteness ceased and his myth dissipated. He lived in the same tenement neighborhoods as his patients. His wife shopped with their wives and solicited patients in his behalf. The doctor himself accepted remuneration from palm to palm like any ordinary shopkeeper. Nonetheless, the Yidn still bowed from the waist when he passed them, and were terrified by the medicinal odors in his office and at the sight of the shining instruments in his surgical cabinet.

Some of the physicians called themselves "professors" and they advertised daily in the Yiddish press, before each of the papers began to carry a medical advice column. Some of these advertisements included photographs showing the "professor" with a Van Dyke beard, which placed him in the revered Viennese tradition, American doctors being ludicrously beardless. The "ads" hinted at infections about which one did not consult a landsmanschaft physician and that were the indirect result of long family separations caused by World War I and the restrictive immigration quota system. They pledged "painless treatment in strictest confidence" and, the competition being fierce, offered "free blood tests and X-ray examinations."

The increasing familiarity with physicians did not diminish, however, the Yidn's fear of hospitals. Only if surgery were required, or if brought there unconscious by ambulance after a street accident, did Yidn permit themselves to be hospitalized. Women insisted on being delivered in their own beds by midwives. Rumor had it that poor patients were deliberately undone in hospitals to supply corpses for student autopsies.

The midwife fulfilled a function even in America. She was a kind of dilettante witch, possessing among other things the capacity to "talk away" illnesses. A migraine headache was diagnosed as an "evil eye," for which the Yiddish term was a "good eye," a deliberate refusal to give evil an identity. A midwife could talk it away by muttering unintelligible phrases with fierce concentration.

The occupation of feldsher also endured. Although it probably constituted practicing medicine without a license, little signs with the meaningful word "cupping" were displayed in all barbershop windows; and in a visible spot, was a doctor's little black bag with the barber's tools of the medical trade—cups and candles.

Actually, the druggist was the Jewish neighborhood's ersatz-doctor. Yidn would say to someone who sought their advice, not "I know a good doctor," but "I know a good druggist." He could be trusted to recommend a physician if he deemed his own skills inadequate. The druggist was a combination of the professional and the avuncular. He removed splinters from eyes, examined sore throats, prescribed salves for hemorrhoids, and patent medicine for other ills; fitted trusses, scolded hypochondriacs, and comforted the seriously ill. Patients did not merely ask him to fill a doctor's prescription, they also sought his opinion of it.

Although bearing the title "doctor," dentists somehow rated below druggists in popular esteem, perhaps because they worked in saliva, and although pledged to heal they always caused pain. Their reputation for "skinning people alive" was acquired because their patients came only for bridgework and dentures and for none of the less expensive dental services: a tooth could be extracted by tying one end of a string to a doorknob, and one applied scallions for a toothache, or obtained some painkilling pill from a druggist.

It was in America that the ordinary Yidn first became involved with lawyers. The shtetl had few uses for lawyers. Having learned in the course of centuries not to expect justice from Christian courts, Jewry submitted its litigation to rabbis or to arbitrators. The shtetl's business with the Christian magistrates was sparse and handled by a notary who was to the lawyer what the feldsher was to the physician. He filed affidavits, mortgages, marriage certificates, and wills—the kinds of transactions that could not be handled outside official channels.

The lawyer, called *advokat,* resided in the big city. His sudden appearance in the shtetl was like running up storm signals. It meant that the daughter or son of one of the better families in town had been seized, somewhere in the metropolis, for activity against the monarchy, or that the shtetl had become implicated in a ritual murder charge. If a Christian was found murdered, or a Christian child disappeared around Easter time, which corresponds approximately to the Jewish Passover, the police knew where to look for the killers; it was an "indisputable fact" that the Jews mixed Christian blood in their matzoh. Trials of Jews charged with ritual murder were an annual occurrence, and the most brilliant Jewish legal talent rushed to the side of such defendants. They took no fee. The lawyer thus became a kind of Moses in Pharaoh's court, defending the Jew from his accusers.

It was the immigrant Jews' keen disappointment that the lawyers who hung out their shingles in New York's Jewish tenement neighborhoods bore no resemblance to the mythical European advokat. Perspiring, excessively eager for clients, and talking interminably, these lawyers were more like door-to-door salesmen, and were well aware themselves that representing one spiteful neighbor against another, defending pickpockets and arsonists, and arguing accident suits was an unglamorous way of making a living, and was certainly not a calling.

Arson and accidents had their function in the immigrant economy. When a seasonal slowdown, or a strike or lockout shut down the garment center, and bills piled up and credit at the grocers ran low, an epidemic of accidents followed. Men would plump down on the side-walk in front of stores with double display windows (a sign of afflu-ence), and clutching a knee or a hip with one hand, and waving a banana peel in the other, they would cry that the pain was excruciating and that shopkeepers ought to learn not to drop banana peels on their sidewalks. Or they would lie down in front of a horse-drawn milk-wagon while the driver was making deliveries, and groan that they had just been kicked by the animal. Soon there were witnesses who swore that they had seen the accident. Borden's and Sheffield's paid out untold amounts in accident insurance before they resolved the problem by employing neighborhood kids as "watchers" while the milkmen were inside making their rounds.

Many a small storekeeper was saved from bankruptcy by collecting insurance on a fire that occurred when there was no one on the premises, had been put out even before the fire equipment arrived with its clanging, clatter, gongs, and hoses, and yet had caused sufficient damage to justify a substantial claim. The insurance companies charged arson. The jurors, however, drew a fastidious distinction, in their own minds, between a thief and an honest man in a jam, and judges were casually reminded by wardheelers that the companies had no votes in the district.

Born in the crucible of ideologies, there was hardly a Jewish law student who did not dream of becoming a defender of the common man. Some, indeed, began their practice by taking on an unusual case load without fee and worried relatives puzzled "how will he ever make a living with his heart of gold?" Cynics, however, dismissed this zeal as being a deliberate apprenticeship, "learning to shave on someone else's beard" rather than idealism. Now and then individuals became hopelessly entangled for the rest of their lives in the web of their dream. They could be seen around the lower courts, shaggy men in hand-me-down suits, their worn briefcases tied with string and bulging with briefs and paperbag lunches. Their English was bookish, their argu-ments flatulent with legal precedents, and judges brusquely cut them off with the reminder that they did not have all day and that this was not the U.S. Supreme Court. Not without a trace of vengeful satisfac-tion, former fellow students remembered them as having been at the top of their class in law school, and poor defendants shrugged off their solicitation because "better no lawyer at all than one who charges cheap or nothing" and "look at his clothes, what judge will admit him into chambers where all decisions are made?"

There were all kinds of openings for aggressive young lawyers in the nineteen-twenties. Yidn were now engaged in real estate transactions, construction, banking, business expansion, all of which required legal counsel. The unions, locked in combat with management and among themselves, scoured the lists for experts in habeas corpus, injunctions, and appeals procedures. The neighborhood political clubs had scouts in the lower courts to spot cheeky young lawyers for the bush league who, if they proved themselves, might go as high as anyone of their ethnic group was permitted to go in New York City politics four decades ago.

Bush league politics involved helping the poor, although the motivation was votes, not compassion. The political club's favors ranged from Christmas gifts, free matzoh for Passover and free turkeys on Thanksgiving Day, to free legal counsel. The rookie lawyer spent his evenings in the clubhouse hearing complaints and dispensing advice to constituents, and his days representing them in court without fee and soliciting favors for them by telephone from the "right guys" at City Hall. His only reward was some compensatory minor legal work, just enough to keep him in pin money. His name did get around, however, and all this time, without even knowing it, he was under close and critical surveillance, being marked on his legal talents and, primarily, for his ability to make friends and place them under obligation. If he proved himself in these, he was given a dry run for office in some hopeless contest, and if he stood the pace well he was nominated, next time around, for a fairer contest.

Professional politics and remunerative public office were a relatively new experience for the Yidn. Being assigned a public trust in the shtetl was the equivalent, in social status, to knighthood in the medieval Christian community. Its centuries-old social welfare work was performed by volunteers from amongst distinguished men and women in town, and it included collecting and dispensing public charity, providing dowries for penniless brides, visiting with the ill, and washing and interring the dead. Socialist propaganda spotlighting corruption in American municipal politics helped sharpen the contrast between the clubhouse politician and the public servant of Jewish tradition.

The wardheeler in Jewish neighborhoods was characteristic of his breed, uncouth and boisterous, with a soggy cigar in his mouth, as if lifted from a savage cartoon. His Jewish-comedian Yiddish, which was not deliberate, but the best he knew, offended the older Yidn, and the student immigrants, still struggling with English syntax, were particularly sensitive to his ungrammatical English.

The balanced ticket required not only an admixture of Irish, Italian, and Jewish candidates, but also of various kinds of Jews. Not that one kind of Jew would boycott another, yet it improved the odds if the candidate south of Houston Street was a Russian or Polish Jew, and the candidate north of Houston Street was a Galician, Hungarian, or even a Rumanian. It also helped if he belonged squarely in one of two camps—he was either a labor man, or was seen in synagogue, not only on High Holidays, but occasionally even on ordinary Sabbaths. In one Lower East Side district, the Democratic candidate for Congress was a bachelor, with no known synagogue affiliation. Rumors alleging a relationship with his housekeeper, a buxom *shikse*, raised indignant speculation that when he died, his monies might be bequeathed to the church. To scotch these speculations, he spoke from the rear of a truck one evening, wrapped in a prayer shawl. Unfamiliar with the Yiddish aphorism that hypocrites wrap themselves in prayer shawls, he was astonished when an angry howl went up from pious Jews: "Rascal, get off!" He finally joined a synagogue and through its portals reached Congress on his second try.

The Yidn naturally favored Jewish candidates, but not without a troubled conscience. Politics being corrupt, was it right to expose one of their own to its temptations? They were reluctant to invite an ordinary Jewish politician to address an important meeting. It was like "calling up" a bordello proprietor to the Torah. Judges were excepted, however, even if not all were Brandeis. A public function was lacking in grace unless there was a judge among the speakers. Torah and law are synonyms, and the Yidn knew of no greater glory than to have one of their brethren on the bench dispensing American law which was patently different from the goyish law they had been accustomed to. Nor did they see any discrepancy between their reverence for the law and their occasional efforts to "reach a judge" through the district captain. All they sought was dismissal of a summons issued to a peddler, or an eviction notice to a tenant. This was entirely consistent with the Torah and its customs which provide for mixing "a measure of law with a measure of compassion."

All cops in East Europe were goyim, Pharaonic supervisors of Jewish bondage. Policework was one of the new occupations that the Yidn acquired in America. They never ceased measuring American freedom by this fact alone, although they wished a better career for their sons.

All cops spoke Yiddish, whether they were Jews, Irish, or Italian. The Irish traffic cop on East Broadway and Jefferson Street wore a *mezuzah* [1] attached to his whistle for good luck. He would remind the kids who passed him on their way to the Rabbi Jacob Joseph parochial school on Henry Street to place their beanies on their heads before their teachers caught them. He would stall traffic to comfort a youngster who had been sent home from school sobbing because he had forgotten to put on the ritualistic garment with fringes which the truly orthodox wear under their shirts.

On Friday morning, cops made their rounds to collect free fish from the peddler, chalah from the baker, groceries from the grocer, sometimes enough to feed a family for a whole week. The families of Catholic cops observed meatless Friday by eating Jewish fish exclusively, and, therefore, their kids sometimes grew up with a distaste for oysters, shrimps, and lobsters.

The Talmudic prodigy of the shtetl was now replaced by other kinds of prodigies—child virtuosos, actors, chess masters, and memory wizards who were hired out for charity performances and displayed on the vaudeville circuit. Their photographs in the Yiddish press showed them with hair bobbed like Jackie Coogan's and with Lord Fauntleroy collars. Their managers insisted on this attire even after they had outgrown the little boy stage.

There obviously were not enough child wonders to go around for every set of Jewish parents. However, parents were bitter if a boy of theirs did not qualify at least as a choir singer. Choir boys were at a premium around the High Holidays and their earnings helped supplement the family income. When a youngster's voice began to change, in his teens, the family drastically curtailed its budget.

Sammy Reshevsky, the chess champion, diminutively called Shmulikl, was the envy of every Lower East Side kid in the nineteen-twenties. "If only you would concentrate half as much on chess as on baseball," a perpetual parental exhortation, was rhetorical, of course, because parents knew better: chess was a revered game; it required a "Talmudic brain." On Saturday nights, in balebatische homes, the menfolk played chess, the women played dominoes.

In the late nineteen-twenties, Yehudi Menuhin hove into the vision of Jewish parents. It made life miserable for their kids. Demands upon

---

[1] The *mezuzah*, which devout Jews nail to their doorpost, is an encased scroll which begins with the words "Hear, O Israel." The Hebrew word *Shma* (Hear) is visible through a tiny horizontal aperture.

the children were more persistent. "Music, after all, is not chess; it requires no brains, just application. Why are we, of all parents, cursed with children who will not apply themselves?" Yet, many had their misgivings about virtuosos. "It is all right for a child, but do we want him to grow up to be a *klezmer* [instrumentalist]?" parents would muse. In the shtetl, music, like cupping, was a barber's sideline. The tradition endured among the immigrant Yidn. The bandleader of the Boiberiker *kapelie* (band), which played at all important East Side weddings and led the Zionist parades, was a barber. Another barber founded the Hassidic band that dressed in caftans and *shtreimlach* (a kind of fur hat) and jazzed up the traditional laments, and played a Charleston with the zest of a Cossack hop and spin.

The deprecation of musicians applied primarily to wind instrumentalists and drummers. The social status of violinists [2] varied, and pianists were a completely exempt category. The Yidn had a peculiar affection for the *fidele* (violin) because "its sobs could tear your heart out" and, according to Yiddish legend, the violin, not the harp was King David's instrument. One of the celebrated Hassidic wonder rebbes composed on the violin and played it, occasionally, in his private devotions. His disciples thought it significant that his name also was David— Reb Dovidl Talner. The piano was a singularly aristocratic instrument, if for no other reason than that it had never formed part of the band at Jewish weddings. Few Yidn had ever actually seen a piano before their coming to America. Only its sounds had reached them, distantly and remotely, from the mansions of the Christian nobility set deep in orchards and protected by tall iron picket fences.

The Yidn decided that somehow the violin was an instrument for boys, the piano for girls. A girl who could play the piano had the odds in her favor in the marital competition. Pianos were sold on the installment plan, and at all hours of the day they could be seen dangling from ropes outside tenement windows. Whether they were being moved in or out, depended on employment conditions in the garment center. Advertisements in the Yiddish press cajoled and flattered the potential purchaser: "Our pianos are twenty-five percent cheaper than from the factory," "Brownsville Jews are celebrated for their music appreciation, that is why Krakauer pianos has opened a store on Pitkin Avenue."

[2] Mischa Elman's father relates that he suppressed his own inclination to music because of the disrespect with which his father, a violinist with a band, and his grandfather, a *badchan,* a kind of Jewish calypso singer at weddings, had been treated.

There were more conservatories of music in the Jewish neighborhoods than in all the music capitals of Europe put together. Even as nearly every rabbi claimed to be a gaon, so most music teachers claimed to be "professors." To fortify their claim they wore four-in-one cravats, dark, broad-rimmed hats, and long hair bunched up in the rear. They advertised themselves as "graduates of the royal academy" of St. Petersburg, Vienna, or Budapest. Paris was never included because its conservatory, obviously, could not be "royal."

Music was a cult among the younger immigrants. Their orthodox parents had lived by a code of *Mitzvot*.[3] The younger generation could not entirely shake off this sense of obligation. They replaced the religious with secular commandments. One of these required them to skip meals if need be in order to afford a ticket to important concerts and dance recitals. Sol Hurok, who began his impresario career as program director at the Brownsville Jewish Labor Lyceum, could always count on advertisements in the Yiddish press to fill the mezzanine and balconies for Chaliapin, Pavlova, and Fokine. In the first two decades of the century, Jewish immigrant parents named their children for Karl Marx, Friedrich Engels, and Ferdinand Lassalle; in the nineteen-twenties they named them for Mischa Elman and Jascha Heifetz.

In the shtetl none but low caste females went to work before marriage, and their range of occupations was limited to being domestics and seamstresses. It was proper, however, for a married woman to be the family breadwinner if this released her husband to pursue his study of the Torah without distraction. However, no respectable married woman worked for others. She was either a shopkeeper or kept a stall in the marketplace. In America things changed radically. If a family was to maintain itself properly and meet its installments on steamship tickets, furniture, and Hebrew Free Loan Society borrowings, it was necessary that each of its able-bodied members bring in wages. Balebatische married women took jobs as "finishers" in the garment center. A still larger number of women took "bundles" home from fly-by-night contractors, which depressed wages and impeded unionization. However, if at all possible, parents kept their unmarried daughters out of factories. Being a shop girl was something of a stigma. The right thing was to let a girl graduate from public school and then enroll her for six months in a business school, of which there were many in the Jewish

[3] There are 613 *mitzvoth* (commands) which a Jew must obey. Many of these are ritualistic, most are general good deeds, for which one is rewarded in the hereafter.

neighborhoods, so that she might learn stenography and typing to qualify as an office girl. A girl who had attended a regular high school was in a distinctive class even if she did not graduate. A high school diploma was considered part of a girl's dowry. Bookkeepers and teachers did not require dowries at all. Both were considered elite professions.

There was nothing wrong, on the other hand, in having boys obtain their working papers at the age of fourteen, even if they had not yet graduated from elementary school. They could always attend night school. The immigrant Yidn had quickly learned that this was the American way, that this was how many men in this country began their rise to eminence in politics, the professions, and business.

Large families were the envy of everybody, growing children were an asset, infants an investment in the future, and childless couples had no real equity. Parents married off a wage-earning daughter reluctantly and only because they dared not risk that she remain an *alte moid* (a spinster). But they definitely and deliberately discouraged their sons from marrying early. "What's the hurry? A man can afford to be choosy for he could not possibly become an alte moid."

In the shtetl, tailoring was a low caste occupation, watchmaking was a middle-class trade. In America, with large Ingersoll pocket watches (nicknamed tzibeles, onions) selling for only a dollar, the watchmaker became somewhat irrelevant. Tailoring, on the other hand, began to acquire respectability as a first step to becoming a garment center boss. A balebatischer (genteel) Yid could never quite learn the trade, which required a long apprenticeship begun in the 'teens. The best he could hope for was to become a presser, an ironer, near the bottom rung of the industry's occupational ladder, second only to the finishers, who were women. Both these categories were bunched together in the least comfortable area of the shop. If the finishers were podlie they would tease the pressers, mostly Orthodox Jews, in ways that both embarrassed and excited them, and all the "tailors from back home" had a rollicking time.

A man could always land a job if he could prove that he was a "tailor from back home." However, even true tailors were not of one pattern. There were the plebeians—the operators—tubercular, round-shouldered, and hunched from bowing all day over the sewing machines, myopic from closely watching the flow of material under the needle. "Back home" they used to produce an entire garment, from the first to the last stitch. Here, they sewed together only what the designers and the cutters prepared for them. The latter two groups were the true elite of the trade. They walked head high, shoulders thrown back, conscious of their worth, constantly tugging at their jackets to maintain the crease and to accent the cut and fit. Those among them with business skill became contractors, manufacturers, and jobbers and ruthlessly fought unionization. This resulted in the evolution of a new occupation: *shtarke,* or musclemen.

The musclemen were drawn from two sources, the underworld and the proletariat. East European Jewry had its share, however modest, of thieves, pimps, and burglars. The shtetl, although it deprecated physical violence, nonetheless had learned to rely on the muscle of the Jewish draymen, bricklayers, and carpenters in fighting off pogroms. Both kinds of musclemen became imperative for the garment industry in America. At first, the police and courts were on the employers' side; labor responded with volunteer strong-arm squads that raided non-union shops, threw the switch that stopped the machines, pulled the workers off, slapped the bosses around, and then took the prison rap for the strike leaders. As they observed the vote in Jewish neighborhoods turning against "bosses' judges," the politicians "wised up" and the courts began handing down injunctions not only against strikes, but also against lockouts.

No longer able to rely on the police to do their bidding, the employers began recruiting from the underworld. The unions, emboldened, placed their own strong arm men on the permanent payroll. Some of the union muscle, having become professionals of violence, defected to the bosses who offered better pay. There were rumors that the goons on both sides had entered an agreement to sustain and extend the violence so that they might have year-round employment. Garment center violence was one of the schools—bootlegging was another—from which Lepke Buchalter, Ghurrah Shapiro and other Brownsville and East New York punks graduated into the big time of Murder, Incorporated.

The immigrant Yidn had suddenly developed an admiration for strong physiques, physical prowess, and athletics, a cult which reached its peak in the nineteen-twenties. It was as if after nearly two thousand years, the descendants of the Pharisees had surrendered to the ways of the Greeks. They stuffed their children with spinach, tomatoes, and bananas, convinced that this made them grow several inches taller than their parents. Scholarship still had priority, but if a boy could both slam a home run and skip a class,[4] there was no limit to his father's

[4] The meaning here is that a bright student, at the end of a semester, is promoted two grades instead of one.

pride. If he was Orthodox, he would serve a kiddush the following Saturday, ostensibly because his son had been twice promoted, but he was really celebrating his son's versatility. The Yidn introduced new kinds of heroes into their national pantheon: boxers, circus strong men, and soccer players.

The attitude of the Yidn towards Jewish boxers was not without ambivalence. This business of two men, half nude, entering a ring to bloody one another, was repulsive, not a fitting occupation for the offspring of Jacob. Yet the Yiddish press reported lavishly the exploits of Benny Leonard, the lightweight champion, stressing less his prowess in the ring than his qualities as "a decent Jewish boy, unspoiled by success, who accorded proper respect to his mother." On fight nights, when Benny faced his contenders, the Jewish neighborhoods were tense and apprehensive, as if Jewry faced another Siege of Jerusalem. On the Sabbath following each of his triumphs, some synagogues arranged for "*gomel benshen*," the Thanksgiving prayer one offers for himself, his kin or friends after having come unscathed through peril. It is also recited for Jewry's collective escape from some dreadful danger, such as survival after a pogrom. There was resentment when Lew Tendler challenged Benny Leonard, because "one Jew should not challenge another," and there was great delight when the champion retained his title. Later Max Baer, the heavyweight, who was not a Jew, capitalized on the fervor of the Jewish fans by appearing in the ring with a Shield of David on his trunks.

In 1923, Zisha Breitbart, a European Jewish strong man, touring the vaudeville circuit in this country, was treated like a hero returning from conquests. Yidn everywhere waited in line for hours to get in to see him. The pious kept their eyes down, their eyes shut tight, not to see the females cavorting on stage in the acts that preceded Breitbart's. A blare of bugles and an explosion of flares announced his entry. A blond giant, wrapped in a Roman toga, he stood up tall and imperious in a golden chariot pulled by two teams of horses. He was introduced as "the pride of the Yidn, the modern Bar Kokhba," [5] and patriarchs rose to their feet to render him the respect accorded "princes in Israel." He was the son of a Polish Jewish blacksmith and had performed with German circuses before his solo appearances in America. He drove in nails with his fists, split rails with his hands, and, lying down, lifted a carriage full of people by slowly heaving his chest. The entire theater perspired with his effort, the thin arms of hundreds of emaciated garment workers rippled with his muscles. In halting little

[5] Leader of the second Jewish revolt against Rome (132–135 C.E.).

speeches, both before and after each performance, he pledged always to avenge the honor of the Jew and illustrated the point with tales of his encounters with anti-Semites who spoke disparagingly of Jews, or had taunted them in his presence, not knowing "that I am Breitbart." He gave them fair warning, and when they disbelieved and would not desist, "I broke them like a match, like a *papiros*" (Russian for cigarette). At this, the crowd would jump to its feet, stamping and roaring in jubilation.

From Vienna, in 1927, came Hakoah [6] a Zionist soccer team. The Yidn inquired of their kids, experts on all athletics, but they had never heard of the game. Only the immigrant students were familiar with it, and some in fact had played it abroad. However, the Yidn were content with the assurance of the Yiddish press that the team, in blue and white uniform with a shield of David near the heart, "has everywhere vindicated Jewry's honor." The Jewish neighborhoods were plastered with Hakoah posters, all the stores were ticket agencies. On the Sunday of the game, the Jewish tenements were flying American and blue and white flags. By subway, el, street car, and chartered bus, the Yidn pilgrimaged to the Polo Grounds, which had never before seen such a heavy sprinkling of scholarly patriarchs. The hot dogs peddled that afternoon were kosher, from Hebrew National and Isaac Gellis, and there were also knishes from Yona Shimmel. The crowd was enthusiastic, but its confusion unnerved the players. When a Hakoah man was encircled, the crowd roared, "Let him go"; when he scored a goal they sighed with dismay thinking he had lost the ball, and all the time they kept yelling instructions, "Use your hands, don't pretend you're a magician, with no hands." It was not till next day, when they read it in their newspapers, that the Yidn learned what the outcome had really been and that soccer was a game without hands. Yet thereafter, if their children seemed bent on sports as a career, they encouraged them to try "a Jewish game like soccer"; baseball was "Esau's game, who ever heard of it before?"

The religious practices and customs, undergoing rapid alteration, brought into being new occupations. One of these was the reverend, another was the funeral director.

The reverends reached their peak in the nineteen-twenties and vanished, almost without trace, sometime in the nineteen-forties. A reverend could be spotted at a distance. He wore, at all times, an opera

[6] Hebrew word meaning "the Force."

hat and a frock coat, and sported a full beard and a cane. Sometimes a moderately learned man, more often barely able to read the Hebrew prayers, he was self-ordained and indefinable, with an air of indisputable authority. He hung out his shingle like a doctor or lawyer, and was primarily a marriage performer, a kind of religious justice of the peace.

Quick and quiet marriages had then come into fashion, for economic and other reasons. The Orthodox rabbis refused to accommodate. They demanded all kinds of corroborative testimony, evidence that both parties were Jewish, that neither was encumbered, under Jewish law, by previous marital obligations. Judaism has no Enoch Arden law, and the separations caused by World War I and immigration complicated the rabbis' responsibilities.

The reverend stepped into the breach, the solace and sanctuary of the unwed mother, the common-law wife seeking to legitimize her status, the interfaith couple seeking to conceal it from the Jewish parents by producing a religious marriage certificate. He required no advance notice, asked no questions and "got down to business" instead. Did they want to be married in his foyer, his kitchen, or his parlor? Dignity had its price. The most expensive ceremony provided a bridal canopy and a full quorum of ten witnesses. However, all ceremonies were of equal duration—ten minutes flat, and he was eager to have the couple out the moment it was over. The "sacramental" wine and the sponge cake passed around by his wife were free, and the longer they tarried the more refreshments they consumed. Once he had them outside the door, he was sweetness again. "I am also a *mohel* [circumciser]. God willing, some months from now and it's a boy, remember me. I do a quick and neat job, like the wedding. Half the boys in the neighborhood came under my knife, and look at them today, regular Babe Ruths."

Some reverends were triple-threat men. They were also *shadchanim* (marriage brokers). This was horning in on another profession, yet the progression from marriage broker to marriage performer to circumciser was obvious and natural. The reverend offered all three services at a flat rate, suggesting that negotiating with one man was truly economical. "If you have a boy, you've got yourself a bargain immediately. And if it's a girl, you still have my five-year guarantee." The reverend's occupation required him to be on top of all gossip, tracking it down and sifting fact from fiction. As a marriage broker he would seek out parents of unwed prospective mothers and promise to find an elderly gentleman for their daughter, one who "requires not a virgin, but care, and will provide well for her."

Some forty years before The American Funeral became a public scandal, inspired a book that hit the best seller lists, and spawned TV panel discussions, a New York Jewish monthly, *Reflex*, published an exposé of the American Jewish funeral industry. In the shtetl, the rites and interment were performed by *chevra kadisha*, a volunteer burial society composed of the most pious. The cemetery was community property. The poor were charged nothing, but if the departed had been rich and a miser, the heirs were compelled to pay a high punitive fee. They had no choice. The chevra kadisha held the monopoly. In America, things were different. The cemeteries were privately owned. *Reflex* estimated that they embraced a total of 1,500 acres, half of which was still unoccupied. The wholesale price of the unoccupied area was estimated at \$56,000,000, its retail price at \$200,000,000. *Reflex* concluded that the total assets of the Jewish burial industry, including the funeral chapels, amounted to some \$500,000,000, "a figure easily sufficient to finance the establishment of a Jewish homeland anywhere."

The funeral director's social acceptance came about slowly. The Yidn insisted on being buried from their homes, not from chapels. They insisted on the traditional rites which frown upon funeral ostentation, provide that burial be immediate, and forbid laying out the dead in an open casket, this last a practice introduced by the Park Avenue Yahudim and subsequently, in the nineteen-twenties, adopted also by the "lower classes," by the Workmen's Circle, the Jewish Socialist fraternal order. However, even some of the Socialists preferred the ancient rite which wraps the corpse in a linen shroud, whatever his station, and slips him into the ground on a plain board covered over with a prayer shawl. The Socialists substituted the red flag, and replaced the memorial prayer with the *International*.

Yet the funeral director managed to interpose himself as a death broker, removing the deceased from the hospital, providing the hearse and the carriage, and collaborating with the cemetery owners and the reverends. Each director had a favored reverend or two, who chanted the prayer, offered the eulogy, and assured the family that his particular director was not a cheat like all the others. The funeral industrialists became rich, but this did not make them socially acceptable. Better to marry a poor janitor than a rich funeral broker. It was a matter of esthetics.

CHAPTER 6

The World Around Us

IN 1923,[1] in its annual report, the American Jewish Committee stated categorically: "Save for a few exceptions the last year, like that preceding it, witnessed a continuing decline of anti-Jewish propaganda." It then, paradoxically proceeded to cite a long, melancholy list of anti-Semitic episodes that had required the Committee's intervention. This was the structure of almost every one of its reports during the decade, assurances that bigotry had declined were followed by an exhaustive tabulation of protests and intercessions.

The files of its president, the combative Louis Marshall, corporation attorney and philanthropist, were spilling over with reports, memoranda, exhibits and correspondence, all of which related to anti-Semitic writing, inflammatory speeches, and discriminatory practices. The Jews were under attack from many quarters and Louis Marshall was their public defender. Some of the attacks were disguised and subtle, others direct, crude, and primitive. They were accumulative and incessant.

In October 1921, Captain Robert Rosenbluth was indicted on a charge of murder in the first degree in the death, three years before, of his commanding officer, Major Alexander P. Cronkite. The defense showed that the captain had been drilling recruits in open view some distance away when the major was killed, and that the Cronkite wounds had been self-inflicted. It showed that Captain Rosenbluth had, since that day, been pulled in for questioning an untold number of times and otherwise harassed. It branded the case as a malicious conspiracy attributable to religious prejudice. The Jewish captain's private agony

[1] All quotations in this chapter may be found in *The American Jewish Year Book*, for the periods indicated.

had thus become American Jewry's public passion. The Yahudim and the Yidn, the Committee, the Zionists, and the Yiddish press were now of one opinion (which was a phenomenon in itself) that this was America's own Dreyfus affair which had to be fought to the last. Appeals to higher courts spawned newspaper headlines that were not all sympathetic to the accused and his fellow Jews. On October 16, 1924, after three years of tortuous litigation, Captain Rosenbluth was vindicated when the highest court in New York State dismissed the indictment against him. Henry Ford's periodical, *The Dearborn Independent*, outraged, railed that the court's action resulted from "shameful interference of social organizations . . . illustrative of the length to which an alien type of mind will go to neutralize the confidence of the people in our laws and courts."

There was a brief flurry of medieval excitement in Massena, New York—with nationwide repercussions in the Jewish community—on the eve of Rosh Hashanah, September 22, 1928, over the disappearance at noon that day of a little Christian girl. She was found unharmed next morning in the woods where she had gone in search of her brother. But the day before the mayor and a state trooper had gone into a huddle and summoned the local rabbi to Town Hall, where they questioned him about ritual murder.

In 1924, *World's Work*, a periodical published by Doubleday, Page and Company launched a vigorous circulation drive with a lurid series of articles depicting the Jewish immigrants from East Europe, who had been greatly reduced in number by the nationalities quota law, as Typhoid Marys who carried infectious subversion wherever they went. Emboldened by the stir the series had caused, and undaunted by Jewish protests, the publishers put it between bookcovers, called it *The Jews in America,* and emblazoned on its jacket a query, "with their un-American creed, will they ever be absorbed into the American commonwealth?"

Hearst's magazine, *International,* capitalized on readers' interest in the same subject from an opposite angle. It published a meticulously documented exposé, containing minutes of clandestine KKK meetings and showing how deeply the hooded order had penetrated into the state and federal governments. One Southern governor, addressing a secret Klan meeting, had assured its members that if any were arrested or convicted of a felony ordered by the Klan, they could rely on him for a pardon.

The Encyclopaedia Britannica apologized and published a correction when Louis Marshall provided incontestable proof that an article it carried in 1922 on contemporary Polish Jewry, far from being factual and objective, was riddled with fabrications and malicious intent. In an address to the American Society for International Law in 1924, a Princeton professor advanced the opinion that "a great deal of the animosity, the inhospitality, the prejudice, the unfairness to the Jew has been due to the unfortunate fact that the Jew desires to keep his racial integrity," and his best course would be to affirm "the first obligation of a citizen . . . that of undivided loyalty." Marshall replied, "we admit the impeachment and we glory in it. If by assimilation is meant that we are unwilling to surrender that which has been distinctive in our civilization . . . to apostatize, to substitute hypocrisy for conviction . . . we are unalterably opposed to such assimilation and . . . not even a Princeton professor can frighten us."

It was characteristic of the tone of all Marshall's communications on such matters. No Yiddish newspaper editor, no Zionist orator could be more impassioned, proud, and contemptuous. However, like diplomatic documents, the American Jewish Committee correspondence was almost always released long after the event. It was never presented or pre-tested before large audiences. Even the facts that were protested, if Marshall and the Committee could so arrange, were released only when other ameliorative methods had failed and publicity seemed the only recourse. The Committee, consistent with the inhibitions of its social caste, was fearful of appearing to be a public nuisance, and apprehensive about the clamor the Yidn would raise if the facts were divulged.

The Zionists and all the Yidn, resenting this self-consciousness amounting to weakness, challenged the Committee's and Marshall's authority to make arbitrary determinations, however correct, to withhold information from the Jewish constituency. Furthermore, they maintained that the anti-Semite should not be coddled but exposed, whatever his station.

This explains the paradox of the American Jewish Committee's annual presentation of a detailed list of anti-Semitic episodes and calm insistence that anti-Semitism was at a safe and manageable level, and why Marshall, the Yiddish editorial writers, and Zionist orators were constantly at war over policy, although they shared the same indignation and reacted with the same promptness to anti-Semitic offenses.

There was also the matter of the long, retrospective view taken by members of a class at some remove from the firing range, and those directly within the range. To the Yahudim, ensconced in the upper middle class, the East European immigrant seemed to have achieved much. In the four decades since he began to arrive en masse from East Europe, he had advanced from steerage, Castle Garden and East Side tenements with toilets in the hallway, to limestone mansions on Riverside Drive, public office, small time banking, and big time real estate. However, those who had approached the achievements of the Yahudim were relatively few; the overwhelming majority was still tenement-housed. Lacking financial means, the young immigrants and immigrants' sons worked in the daytime, studied at night and crammed for college entrance exams in preparation for careers that would not carry them beyond law, accountancy, pharmacy and teaching because all other professional schools and professions were virtually closed to them. Western Union would not employ Jewish schoolboys as messengers during the summer vacation, the New York Telephone Company "regretted" that it could not employ Jewish women as operators (their arms allegedly were too short to handle a switchboard), and the banks did not even bother to explain why they would not hire Jews in any capacity. The Yahudim were offended, but not handicapped by this discrimination. The children of the Jewish upper class did not seek jobs as Western Union messengers, telephone operators, or bank tellers, and the quota system for Jews was just about adequate for their enrollment by the country's best professional schools. The American Negro community today provides the closest analogue to the American Jewish community forty years ago. The American Jewish Committee then, like the NAACP and the Urban League today, feared that untoward "hot-head" action might jeopardize the gains already achieved, largely by its own kind, the upper middle class. The AJC argued the merits of gradualism and private intervention, although conceding that greater progress was required. The Zionists and the various Yiddish speaking groups, always ready for public proclamation and pressing for immediate relief and direct action, embraced as wide a range of militancy as, in the Negro community today, the Southern Christian Leadership Conference, CORE, and SNCC, the now-violent Students Non-violent Coordinating Committee.

However, the analogy must not be drawn beyond this point. The situations of the Jew then and the Negro today are otherwise quite dissimilar. The Jew had arrived here with middle-class traditions, had temporarily fallen back, but was reemerging from the proletarian class. The American Negro has never had a middle class or even a proletarian tradition. His tradition has been that of the slave and the serf. An expanding American economy required the Jew's manpower, today's technological civilization has a surplus of manpower. The Jew was feared not for his numbers but for his excellence, which his numbers would compound; criticized not for his lack of initiative but for his excessive initiative.

This fear of the Jew's capacity accounted, in large measure, for the immigration restrictions which did not single him out by name, but were patently aimed at him. These immigration restrictions were the most serious of all the disabilities inflicted upon him. The celebrated Jewish familial loyalties and strict sexual mores were precariously strained among the immigrant males. The inhibitory factors that sustained Jewish moral standards in the shtetl obviously did not obtain in the chaotic metropolitan environment with its cover of anonymity.

World War I broke out before tens of thousands of these immigrant household heads had been able to set money aside for their families' passage to America. Then, almost immediately after the war, Congress voted immigration restrictions, capstoned by the nationalities quota law. For most Jews family meant parents and parents-in-law, brothers and sisters and children irrespective of age, but the sole exemptees from the quota system were wives and children under eighteen. Reunion with husbands from whom they had become estranged through years of separation made it difficult for these women to separate from the large families with whom they had been through all the vicissitudes of war. Hence many forfeited their exemptions and stayed behind until the entire family, or at least all their children, had been cleared. This meant additional years of separation.

Even those whose turn had finally come after years of waiting in the queue were never certain of achieving their goal. U.S. consular officials and U.S. Health Service physicians abroad were ingenious at demanding all kinds of affidavits, thus delaying departures until visas had expired. Bribes often, but not always, could overcome red tape, whose purpose sometimes was not venal, but malicious, to keep the "undesirable" races out. The shipping agents encouraged those with invalid visas to board the vessels anyhow. They had collected round-trip fares beforehand in the event the immigrants, for some reason, were turned back at Ellis Island, which was always jam-packed with detainees awaiting the result of all kinds of appeal from deportation orders.

This situation produced a new sort of specialty, attorneys who called themselves "immigration experts." They were a grab-bag of public defenders and mere "fixers" who, in turn, fell into two categories, those "with God in their hearts," who charged a reasonable fee and "delivered the goods," and those who pledged "the saucer from heaven," squeezed all the money they could from the immigrants' relatives and were unable to obtain even a single court order. The "immigration specialists'" strategy was to flood the Naturalization and Immigration Service with injunctions and writs of habeas corpus, exhaust it with legal harassment, and delay deportation till the fall when, with impending elections, the odds were more favorable for the immigrant. Each of the two major political parties concentrated on obtaining some commutations of deportation orders just before Election Day, especially of hard core cases in whom the Yiddish press had taken a special interest, and particularly if their kin were from districts where the race was close.

The "commuted" family, wild-eyed and shaken, their gestures contradicting the interpreter, and still wearing The HIAS (Hebrew Immigrant Aid Society) name tags on their garments, would be subjected to the flashing bulbs and interrogational cross-fire of a press conference. Over the entrance to the house where their relatives lived was a huge "Welcome" sign, and a welcome banner was strung at the first floor fire-escape level across the street. In the evening, the immigrant family was marched through the streets in a torch-light parade, led by a brass band and showered with confetti by crowds that lined the sidewalk. It all resembled a scene from the movies showing jungle preparations for a human sacrifice. The parade would end at a block party with soda pop and goodies. The district captain, beaming, shaking hands, slapping backs, was ubiquitous throughout these ceremonies and for the next several days he could be seen shepherding the "released" family on a fatiguing shopping spree, encouraging them to "pick the best, this is America," contending that his club was footing the bill, all the while pressuring the shopkeepers to give their merchandise away free.

Occasionally some hard-pressed candidate for public office, compelled to prove his personal capacity and concern, would scurry about for a family that had been recently admitted and hire them for display at his rallies as immigrants he had saved from being returned to "the Communist Czarist hell," the precise nature of the changes in Russia having escaped him. Outfitted with name-tags on their garments, so that they looked authentic, these bewildered hirelings would stand beside him on the apron of a truck like freaks alongside a circus barker, or would cluster around his ladder or soapbox like a Salvation Army band.

The nationalities quota law was brought into being by a strange and unlikely coalition of Populists, Brahmin, Labor and pseudo-scientific "race experts." The Populists, agrarian advocates of silver currency, honestly believed that the Rothschilds were manipulating world events by means of gold caches in their possession. Brahmin senators, such as John Cabot Lodge, in the words of historian Barbara Miller Solomon, "felt they were losing their country" to the immigrants and "did not want to see the American culture they know go." Of course, they had lost their country and culture long before the first large tides of immigrants arrived here; it all went when the Yankee traders made the first foray into manufacturing. Labor was fearful that the European immigrant would depress the wages of American workers.

These diverse elements had for more than three decades pressed for laws restricting immigration. They were supported by then eminent American geneticists, anthropologists, and sociologists who cited "scientific" evidence to demonstrate that God had willed mankind into inferior and superior races, and warned that unless immigration were restricted, the superb Nordic stock, which sprang from the groins of the Founding Fathers, would be overwhelmed by inferior breeds from Eastern and Southern Europe. These American pseudo-scientists were thus the forerunners of Nazi racist doctrine. The immigrant Southern stock that so alarmed them was largely Sicilian, in flight from unyielding soil and a savage hierarchal society. The East Europeans were Jews escaping the chaos of social revolution and the nationalistic frenzy of recently created states.

The American Jewish Committee confronted "science" with "science." It circulated the results of a study of 68,000 inmates in mental institutions from *The Bulletin of the U.S. Public Health Service* which suggested "that northern and West European immigrants have, during the past twenty years shown a higher percentage of mental illness." It also quoted Dr. Raymond Pearl who, citing U.S. census figures, reported that "on June 1, 1923 in alms houses in America, 26.7% [of the inmates] came from Ireland, 20.8% from Germany, 8% from England, and only 4.4% from Poland, 2.2% from Russia, 3.1% from Italy."

There was nothing inordinate about the economic circumstances in the metropolitan regions in which he lived to account for the Jew being singled out, as indeed he was, for special attention in the nineteen-twenties. His fierce resistance to restrictive immigration legislation may have been one reason. However, it is more likely that the cause was his global-mindedness, which contrasted sharply with the American national mood of the decade—isolationist, refusal to join the League of Nations, refusal to extend recognition to the U.S.S.R., adoption of the Volstead Act.

The East European Jewish immigrant by default had become almost the sole custodian of America's contacts with the world. Tens of thousands of letters were exchanged every week between American Jews and their landsmen and kin in East, West, and South Europe, in the Baltic and the Balkan countries, and, as a result of the Russian Civil War, with Jewish refugees in Harbin, Shanghai, and Tokyo. As in medieval days, when he served as an interpreter and mediator between the Christian and Muslim lands, the Jew was again the recipient of intelligence about conditions everywhere, which transformed him into a sensitive antenna of international events when the rest of America had encased itself in Puritan self-righteousness. Most of his correspondence was written in Yiddish. There was also a steady stream of money orders and food packages from the United States to relatives and landsmen abroad, and the wealthier American landsmen constituted themselves mercy missions and relief survey teams to the shtetlach where they had been born. On the wall in every Jewish kitchen there were at least a half-dozen collection boxes, mostly for overseas charities.

On Saturday nights and Sundays, except in severe weather and on Jewish holidays, the Jewish neighborhood swarmed with volunteer collectors—men, women and children—pinning lapel flags, tags, and flowers for some worthy cause, generally overseas. The license commissioner would permit only one such weekend collection per cause, and there were not enough weekends available to grant all the applications. Zionists liked to work in teams of four; posting themselves at a busy cross-section they would each hold a corner of a Jewish flag and passersby would throw coins and bills into its depression. There were also the Yiddish theater benefits and the Hudson River Sunday excursions with proceeds going mainly for causes abroad. In addition, there were the public rallies for visiting dignitaries, as well as the Zionist protests against British breaches and Arab terror in Palestine, and the Socialist protests against draconic Communist rule in Russia.

All these no doubt helped keep America *au courant* with international events to which she would become heir less than a quarter of a century later. However, they were not seen in that light at the time. The immigrants were not appreciated as keepers of the gate, whose generous charities conveyed to the Continent a priceless impression of American generosity, but, on the contrary, they somehow were suspected of treason for maintaining a dialogue long after the rest of America had pulled up the drawbridge, turned off the lights, and very nearly ceased all communication with foreign peoples.

The Jews' global-mindedness was the tireless theme of Henry Ford's *Dearborn Independent* for seven years from May 22, 1920 when that weekly began serializing, for the first time in English translation, *The Protocols of the Elders of Zion,* purporting to be the outline of a Jewish plot to seize world rule. A patent forgery, first published in 1905, it was revised after the Communist Revolution in Russia to make it appear that it had previsioned that event. In the new version Lenin is named an agent of the Jewish conspiracy and Jacob Schiff its chief financier. The extent of anti-Semitic penetration was demonstrated when the staid London *Times,* much to its later embarrassment, declared the *Protocols* to be authentic and unimpeachable.

The Jews enlisted intercessors. Arthur Brisbane, chief columnist of the Hearst newspapers and a close friend of Henry Ford, tried to dissuade him from pursuing his anti-Semitic course, pointing out that the fallacy of the campaign would inflict no less harm upon Ford than upon the Jews. The automobile manufacturer would not be diverted. The *Dearborn Independent* expatiated on the alleged Jewish-Bolshevik conspiracy week after week. Private intervention having failed, there was no alternative to public proclamation. "An Address to Their Fellow Citizens by American Jewish Organizations," issued on December 1, 1920, and appealing against the anti-Semitic myths, was signed by nine Jewish groups, including The American Jewish Committee, B'nai B'rith, and the Zionists. On December 23, 1920 former President Taft denounced anti-Semitism in a ringing address to the Anti-Defamation League. On January 16, 1921, a roster of 121 Americans headed by out-going President Wilson and former President Taft affirmed their faith in the allegiance of American Jews. But Ford would not relent. The *Dearborn Independent* maintained its attack week after week. It was more serious than the Nazi propaganda in Germany at the time. The Nazis were a local party, of no apparent consequence, their echo confined to one country. Ford was a world-famous figure of proletarian beginnings, Populist inclinations, a peace worker, a folk hero, and a global symbol of American mechanical ingenuity and opportunity.

The Jews finally decided to strike back in force. Clarence Darrow filed a million-dollar libel suit against the *Dearborn Independent* and Ford personally on behalf of a Detroit Jewish attorney. A consumers' boycott of Ford automobiles was beginning to spread in the larger cities. Ford now apparently sought the good offices of Arthur Brisbane whose counsel he had rejected seven years before. Ford's attorneys initiated secret negotiations with Louis Marshall. On July 8, 1927 Arthur Brisbane released a dramatic statement by Ford which was banner-headlined on front pages across the nation and widely featured abroad.

"I deem it my duty," Henry Ford wrote, "as an honorable man to make amends for the wrong done to the Jews as fellowmen and brothers, by asking their forgiveness for the harm I have unintentionally committed, by retracting as far as lies within my power the offensive charges laid at their door." Louis Marshall was in top form in responding to Ford's plea for forgiveness: "So far as my influence can further the end, it will be exerted simply because there flows in my veins the blood of ancestors who were inured to suffering and nevertheless remained steadfast in their belief in God. Referring to the teachings of the Sermon on the Mount, [the English novelist] Israel Zangwill once said that we Jews are after all the only Christians. He might have added that it is because essentially the spirit of forgiveness is a Jewish trait."

Jews everywhere rejoiced in this triumph. Some anti-Semites cited Ford's surrender as evidence of Jewry's invincibility, others bitterly accused him of putting profit ahead of principle. However, the *Protocols* in the original *Dearborn Independent* translation continued to circulate through the nineteen-thirties at Nazi and Christian Front meetings and all requests by Ford that this be stopped were ineffective.

In 1927 the attention of Jews everywhere was divided between Detroit, U.S.A. and a courtroom in Paris, France where Sholem Schwartzbard, a Ukrainian Jewish watchmaker, Yiddish writer of sorts, and holder of a French army *Croix de Guerre*, went on trial for the murder of Semyon Petliura. Petliura was the Hetman or commander of the Ukrainian independence army in the Russian Civil War. His troops had massacred tens of thousands of Jews. When Ukrainian civilian leaders protested, Petliura replied, "I regret the pogroms, but I know no other way of maintaining discipline in my army." His name was spoken with dread even after his resistance to the Red Army collapsed and he had fled to France. Schwartzbard told the French court, "I stalked him for six months but his wife and child were with him. I could not chance doing them harm. Then that morning in May a year ago [1926], he came towards me on Boulevard St. Michel, alone. I stopped him and asked, 'Are you Hetman Petliura?' He replied in the affirmative. 'This is for the Jews you massacred,' I told him and pulled the trigger."

Tens of thousands of American Jews who had lost kin and landsmen in the Ukrainian pogroms hailed Schwartzbard as their avenger. His trial was front-page news in the Yiddish press. Witnesses from many lands, including America, were summoned to Paris by the defense, just as more than three decades later the prosecution was to summon witnesses to Jerusalem in the trial of Adolf Eichmann. The French jury, after brief deliberation, acquitted Schwartzbard but ordered that he compensate the widow in the amount of six francs, its evaluation of the market value of a mass murderer's life.

The day his case went to the jury hundreds of chevra tehilim recited psalms around the clock and on the following Saturday morning, on instructions from the Orthodox rabbinate, all Jewish congregations in the United States recited gomel, a thanksgiving prayer that Schwartzbard's life had been spared. Yet with all this, the older generation of Orthodox Jews had its reservations. They had been conditioned to surrender life, not to take it. They turned out, like everyone else, to hail Schwartzbard when he arrived in the United States for a lecture tour. But after observing him at close range, they commented cryptically to friends of like opinion, "He looks so mild, yet he took a life," and added hastily, "not that Petliura did not merit the death of a dog, but vengeance is in the hands of the Lord." But Schwartzbard was typical of a new mental attitude among Jews. His kind, during the Russian Civil War, joined the Red Army not because of Communist conviction, but to avenge the massacre of Jews by White Russian detachments. His kind raised the flag of revolt in the doomed Warsaw Ghetto and in the Treblinka death camp, and formed partisan units that struck from swamp and forest at the Nazi forces in East Europe. They also formed the terrorist Irgun and Stern group and the official Zionist underground army, Haganah, which compelled the British to abandon Palestine and resulted in the birth of Israel.

Most American Jews had come from Russia. The Communist seizure of power, therefore, had a tremendous impact on the American Jewish community. The Red Army seemed the sole barrier between the Jews and the pogrom-conditioned remnants of the Czarist forces that were then tearing at the living flesh of Russia. Lenin did provide equality for the Jews in all fields—economic, legal, and educational. The arrest and outlawing of Zionists, the banning of Hebrew, the persecution of rabbis, may have been initiated or recommended by vindictive Jewish Communists, so some Jews in America reasoned. The true features of the Communist Government, many concluded, would become apparent only after the Civil War had ended.

Some Russian Mensheviks (Social Democrats) in the United States adopted a similar attitude of watchful waiting, although Lenin had come to power by ousting a Menshevik Premier, Alexander Kerensky. The reasoning of these Mensheviks, admittedly a minority, was that judging from the swiftness of Lenin's *coup d'état* Kerensky had perhaps been too weak to guide Russia through the turbulence of Civil War, that Lenin's ruthlessness might have been dictated by exigencies, and that he might behave differently and reestablish a parliamentary coalition after having restored order in the land.

Russian had some 2,750,000 Jews. Although all discrimination against them on religious grounds had ceased, a majority now found themselves discriminated against on class grounds. The reasons were different, the motivations were different, the effect, however, was not very dissimilar. The regime had declassed all persons under its rule who had been engaged, before the Revolution, in any of a long list of occupations. This included owners of big estates and financiers and "their lackeys," of whom there were very few Jews and these had already fled, as well as clergy and religious tutors, of whom Russian Jewry had many, and then there were the small traders, shopkeepers, and artisans who employed apprentices. Under Czarist rule the Jews had been restricted almost exclusively to the latter occupations. Consequently approximately seventy percent of Russian Jewry now found themselves declassed, which meant they were now at the bottom of the priorities list when applying for jobs, housing, and admission to schools. This forced them to illegal trade and made their presence all the more egregious among a largely anti-Semitic population. This had not been the Kremlin's intent. Lenin was not a bigot. A remedial plan was drawn up. The Jews were to be taught industrial trades and farming and organized into industrial and farm cooperatives. It would be a costly operation. Philanthropists abroad, especially in America, might be persuaded to join with the Soviet government in meeting the costs of retraining and establishing the enterprises that would employ them. Furthermore, this would bring dollars into the Soviet Union, which was then starved for hard currency. Another auxiliary feature was appended to this program. The Kremlin had promised, at first in Crimea, then in Biro Bidjan, to develop a Jewish autonomous region, perhaps even a Jewish state. The effect of this would be to deflect some of the monies and enthusiasm that was going into the upbuilding of the Jewish National Home in Palestine under British rule. The Kremlin was opposed to the Zionist undertaking, regarding it as a wedge for the British.

American Jewish philanthropists responded with great concern. The JDC stationed a permanent representative in the Soviet Union. It also formed a complementary body, Agro-Joint, to deal exclusively with the rural resettlement of Russian Jews. Non-Jews joined in this undertaking, the roster of donors included not only the Warburgs, Lehmans, and Baerwalds, but also John D. Rockefeller.

The Zionists were in a dilemma. They could not and would not object to the rescue operation. But they did feel that the Yahudim philanthropists were perilously unsophisticated about events in the Soviet Union. They took no proper precautions to prevent the Jewish Communists in Russia from seizing this operation as a means of foisting themselves more firmly on the Jewish community. They did not use the circumstance of the Kremlin's desperate need for hard currency to demand a more benign policy: cessation of the persecution of rabbis, Hebrew teachers, Zionists and communal institutions that had sustained Russian Jewry even in its darkest moments. The argument that philanthropy must not be bent to political purpose did not impress the Zionists for several reasons. A condition that persecutions cease would have been as much of a rescue operation as financing a program of job-retraining. The Jewish philanthropists maintained one standard in regard to governments, another in dealing with Jewish aid recipients. Immediately after World War I, JDC representatives tried to dictate to Polish Jewry even as to the kinds of schools they should maintain with philanthropic funds from America. This gratuitous intervention was disdainfully repelled.

Furthermore, the Kremlin was capitalizing politically on its cooperation with Jewish philanthropic bodies by deflecting attention from the pernicious aspects of Soviet policy towards the Jews, outlined above and for which Jewish Communists may have been primarily responsible. Kremlin slogans and proclamations announcing a Jewish autonomous region and possible Jewish statehood on Soviet soil served as a smokescreen for its cooperation with the Arabs in a campaign of terror against Zionist pioneers in Palestine. Moscow apparently also hoped to divert Jewish effort and monies from the Zionist undertaking in Palestine. The Communists in America, with that end in view, launched independent drives for the Soviet so-called Jewish statehood proposals. This was as grave a tactical error, resulting from the same impatience, conceit and underestimation of the opposition, as their attempt, at approximately the same time, to seize control of American labor by launching parallel unions.

Eventually, the subterfuges, or perhaps merely ambiguities and ambivalences of Soviet "Jewish" policy, at home and abroad, came into the full glare of exposure. The Jewish cooperative farm communities and urban industrial enterprises that had been launched with the assistance of American Jewish philanthropy were sequestered by the state and their Jewish membership forcibly reduced to a minimum. The Jewish commissars, whom the Kremlin had named to head its "Zionist" experiments, were liquidated in the various Stalin-directed purges. Finally, in the period between 1948 and 1953, when he launched an outright death drive against Jewish intellectuals, Stalin apparently recalled the JDC's sometime cooperation in establishing Jewish cooperative farms in Crimea. But this had now become perverted in his mind into something quite different, serving as the basis for horrendous charges of treason. In 1952, Solomon A. Lozovsky, a former Soviet Deputy Foreign Minister, and a group of Yiddish writers were found guilty and executed as the agents of an alleged plot by the JDC, Israel, and the CIA to sever the Crimea from the U.S.S.R. and establish it as a Jewish republic and an "imperialist" base; and in 1953, Stalin ordered the arrest of the most eminent Jewish physicians on the charge that at the behest of the above-named "tri-partite conspiracy" they had plotted to liquidate the entire Soviet leadership by means of medical mistreatment. These allegations, by the way, bore a curious resemblance to the *Protocols of Zion* that had originally been hatched by the Czarist secret police and circulated by Ford.

The year 1929 was crucial in Jewry's experience with the Kremlin. The Mufti of Jerusalem launched a campaign of terror against the Jews in Palestine. Snipers along the roads picked off Jewish traffic. Armed bands besieged Jewish settlements, and in the ancient town of Hebron defenseless yeshiva students, including Americans, were massacred, in the all-too-familiar pogrom style, by a frenzied Arab mob. The Communist International hailed the Mufti as a "liberator," called his terror "a war against British imperialism and its Zionist agents." The Yiddish language *Morning Freiheit* in New York adopted the same position. Jewish reaction was prompt. H. Leivick, Moshe Leib Halpern, and other eminent Yiddish writers tendered their resignations. The *Freiheit* was removed from newsstands and destroyed. Many newsdealers voluntarily refused to handle it. Violence broke out between Zionists and Communists at their respective meetings. Family relations were gravely disrupted over these differences.

The Jewish Daily Forward Association had long been divided on the Palestine issue. Some labor leaders, members of the Forward Association, helped found the Histadrut campaign which helped the Zionist labor enterprises in Palestine. Others were adamant against Zionism. Abraham Cahan, its editor, seemingly favoring Zionism, nonetheless steered a neutral course. In 1929, however, he swung his paper behind the Jewish Palestine effort, without committing it officially to Zionism. He had been, in the early days, among the Mensheviks who adopted a cautious posture towards Lenin. But in the early nineteen-twenties the *Forward* began to lead a systematic crusade against the Communists. What determined Cahan was the Communist attempt then to seize control of the garment center unions, or, failing that to launch dual or parallel unions. The garment center unions were led by *Forward* Socialists. This then was no longer a remote power struggle, but the Menshevik-Bolshevik contest re-enacted on home grounds; the Kremlin machinations were clearly visible, and jobs, patronage, and status were at issue.

Because conditions in the garment industry had become chaotic, the time was ripe for Communist infiltration. The basting machine, the steam-press, and a number of similar innovations resulted in the mass elimination of jobs which the unions were powerless to prevent. Gar·

ments were produced in separate parts by an assembly-line system which made "the tailor from back home," the single master tailor, or even teams of craftsmen, unnecessary. The only true expert required was the cutter and designer. The rest of the operation could be entrusted to pools of unskilled labor in fly-by-night shops outside the city limits, or to homeworkers, entire families slaving away for a pittance in the tenements. The separate parts were often clandestinely assembled in union shops and, although produced by sweatshop labor, bore the union label. Available jobs were becoming scarce and the unions were reluctant to accept new members. It may also be that they feared that the newcomers, more sophisticated than the earlier pre-World War I immigrant, would take control. The Communists capitalized on all these circumstances.

The struggle for hegemony over the garment unions involved assault, bullets as well as ballots. Union offices were often barricaded like fortresses. Bodyguards shadowed leaders of both factions. Pitched battles were a common sight in the West 20s, which was the garment center then. It was a profitable period for goon squads. Strange alliances were formed. The insurgent unionists had acquired a staunch friend in Arnold Rothstein, a flamboyant gambler and man-about-town whose social circle included Mayor Walker, august judges, police brass, and underworld czars, a combination which led to his death in the gutter under a fusillade of gunfire. The blacksheep son of a pious father, who was both a merchant prince and a Talmudic scholar, Rothstein had been brought up in a tradition that makes mitzvoth, good deeds, obligatory. He had apparently decided to make the Communist labor insurgents the beneficiaries of his mitzvot. They could always count on him to intervene on their behalf with judges, the police and die shtarke (the musclemen).

There is the myth that the Communists petitioned him one day to call off the union Establishment's goons, who were to raid an insurgent rally at Madison Square Garden that evening. He called the goon leaders but they argued that they would lose their contract if they did not go through with the assignment. However, they proposed that he arrange for the police to turn out in visible numbers outside and inside Madison Square Garden, which in turn would permit them to retreat with grace. The police generally were not especially concerned about preventing internecine labor riots, and particularly with protecting Communists. However, the brass could not refuse Arnold Rothstein.

There was no riot at Madison Square Garden that night. Rothstein asked no remuneration for his services. Perhaps he believed in a reward in the hereafter.

The Palestine Arab terror which erupted on August 23, and the Depression which began with the Wall Street crash on October 28, 1929, brought to a close the era of the Yiddish-speaking immigrant hegemony in American Jewish affairs. It had been a dramatic, eventful but very brief span, begun after World War I. In the next decade a first generation of native American Jews slipped into the foreground. The Depression, and the rise of Nazism as a threat at home and abroad, were their central traumatic experiences.

II

★ ──────────────────────────── ★

CATASTROPHE
AND TRIUMPH

[1930–1948]

"For in every generation they have arisen to
exterminate us . . ."
FROM THE PASSOVER SERVICE

"I advise our descendants to come into the world
with a very thick skin."
HEINRICH HEINE, Sämtliche Werke.

"And praised. Auschwitz. Be
Maidanek. The Lord. Treblinka.
And Praised. . . ."
ANDRÉ SCHWARZ-BART, The Last of the Just.

When the Lord brought back those that returned
  to Zion,
We were like unto them that dream
Then was our mouth filled with laughter,
And our tongue with singing. . . .
PSALM 126

CHAPTER 1

Introducing the Nineteen-Thirties

THE DEPRESSION which hit America in 1929 was not felt in the immigrant ghetto until 1930. The Yiddish newspapers, to be sure, had reported the Wall Street crash and its consequences in all its grim details—the shutdown of financial institutions, the erosion of great fortunes, the humbling and suicides of powerful men. But like all else involving the goyish millionaires, from prodigal debutante balls to bacchanalian yacht parties, these events were remote in time and space from the tenement neighborhoods. They were like something unfolding on another planet. The celebrated German-Jewish philanthropists, of whom the immigrants were really secretly fond, despite their many sharp differences, were, thank God, never involved in the flamboyant goings-on that made lurid newspaper headlines. They may have suffered reverses in the Wall Street crash, but not ruin; sophisticated financiers, they carried themselves with their usual staid authority.

The newspapers also reported cutbacks in production, the closing of plants, the laying off of thousands of miners, and steel and automobile workers. These events, too, were geographically remote. There were few Jews in the states in which the affected industries were located. But the experience of being laid off was not alien to the Jewish garment worker in New York and Chicago. He was accustomed to seasonal unemployment and consequently regarded the reports as indicating a discomfiting but by no means calamitous situation. He would cushion the effect of his slack periods, between seasons, by deferring the payment of rent, requesting a credit extension from his grocer, and, in extremity, pawning some household article or piece of wearing apparel.

Besides, there was President Herbert Hoover's assurance that America had suffered a dizzy spell, not a fatal seizure. He was a Republican and so his word was gold. The Yahudim invariably voted a straight Republican ticket. The Yidn, however, often split their ballot. They voted Democrats into municipal and state offices and Republicans into the White House; the former because they were accessible to poor men in need of a favor, the latter because the fate of the country could not be entrusted to informal, accessible men. The Republicans, like the Hapsburgs until their fall in 1918, represented solidity and order. The Yidn made an exception of Al Smith, it is true, but only because the Klan was determined to defeat him, and besides, many of them reasoned, although inebriated most of the time, he had shrewdly surrounded himself with level-headed Jews who would keep his administration on an even keel. Nonetheless they were happy, when the ballots were counted, that starch-collared, solemn Herbert Hoover had been elected.

Yet, slightly more than a year after the 1929 debacle, they suddenly lost all confidence in "Francis Joseph" Hoover. The full impact of the national disaster and the hollowness of his optimism were brought home to them by a single catastrophic episode which occurred on December 10, 1930. The Bank of the United States had opened at the usual hour that morning. The tellers almost immediately sensed that there was something amiss. The volume of business was larger than usual, but it was all outgoing, no deposits, only withdrawals. Long queues were forming outside. Alarm turned into panic when a telephone check revealed a similar run on all the bank's branches. The police were summoned. Armored trucks kept driving up with money. Each delivery was quickly exhausted. It was as if the tables at Monte Carlo had gone beserk, the croupiers had joined in a conspiracy, and all the odds had turned against the casino. Long before closing hours, signs had gone up at all the branches: "Bank shut till further notice."

The bank's 400,000 depositors were mostly Jews. They represented one-fifth of the Jewish population of New York City, one-tenth of all American Jewry. Untold numbers of Jews lost their life savings. Washed out were the dowries of spinsters, the tiny insurance leavings of widows, monies set aside to send sons through medical school, to pay for operations, and to buy partnerships in luncheonettes, chicken stores and newspaper stands which were advertised in the columns of *The Jewish Morning Journal*. Thousands of Jewish businesses, including garment center factories that had accounts at the bank went bankrupt. The

Yiddish poet-humorist Moishe Nadir's popular sketch, "The First Deposit," which for years was a schlager (hit) of which the public did not seem to weary, was withdrawn from the repertoire for several years. It hit too close to home. It told of an immigrant who, having opened a savings account, is seized with panic over the fate of his dollar deposit, stays away from his job and neglects his health to maintain an around-the-clock vigil at the bank; at night because burglars might break in, in the daytime because he does not trust what the bankers might think up against him during their waking hours.

No less serious than the financial shock, perhaps, was the blow to the immigrants' collective self-confidence inflicted by the closing of the Bank of the United States. It had been their special pride. They wrote letters home to the old country describing the imposing façade of the bank's Delancey Street headquarters, its exterior marble, ample entrance, brass doors, windows almost as long as the door, and the bankers who spoke Yiddish "like you and me," are called to the Torah and serve an extravagant kiddush in the synagogue on *Shabes* (Saturday). This was a milestone for the East European immigrant who had long been concerned that there was not a single *heimischer Yid* (a landsman) among the Jewish bankers. The Schiffs, the Lehmans, the Loebs, the Seligmans, the Warburgs, towards whom the immigrant felt ambivalence, were German Jews. He regarded it as almost a defect within himself. Finance admittedly required application, but since when had he been lacking in that capacity? It was strange indeed that the Jewry which had produced a Gaon of Vilna had in America not managed to produce a single life-size financier.

However, there was an East Side travel agent who had made the grade. He was Joseph S. Marcus, an immigrant who rose from garment worker to manufacturer to travel agent-banker. In 1913 he pooled resources with Saul Singer, an immigrant like himself, who went from garment worker to industry leader when he was still in his twenties. They opened the Bank of the United States with a capital of $100,000 and reserves of $50,000, excellent personal and business reputations, and a board of directors which eventually included a powerful New York State senator, members of the New York State Real Estate Commission, and the New York State Superintendent of Banking. The queues that formed before the bank demanding their monies back on that fateful December 10, 1930 were perhaps no longer than those that formed on the bank's first day, with people eager to deposit their money with

Marcus and Singer who would protect it from fire, theft, and the depositors' own temptations.

From coffee jars, from stockings, and from under mattresses, they produced their hoardings and brought them to the Bank of the United States, even as their ancestors several millennia before had brought their rings and earrings to Aaron, brother of Moses, that he might melt them down to make a golden calf. This confidence in the bank resulted from an aggressive advertising campaign in the Yiddish press, from the bands, parades and speeches by dignitaries who attended the bank's opening, from its august structure, and from the immigrants' pride in a financier of their own kind. In the criminal proceedings in the nineteen-thirties that resulted in the conviction of the bank's top officers, the prosecutor introduced yet another reason. Was not its name, and the huge framed photograph of the capitol in Washington in full view at the bank's headquarters and its branches, a deliberate subterfuge designed to have the immigrants believe that they were depositing their money with the United States government itself?

In the bank's early years when the founders, Joseph Marcus and Saul Singer, were personally and fully in charge, the atmosphere was truly heimisch. One of the two partners was almost always in the doorway greeting depositors, affixing his signature to notes by resting the paper on his knee or on someone's back. They knew thousands of their depositors by name, their family histories and woes, and remembered their credit rating without checking the records. Their banking policies, furthermore, were benign but cautious, which was proof, perhaps, of true humility. Tough, bold, aggressive in all their previous enterprises, they may have been aware that in banking they were bearers of a public trust because Yidn everywhere cited them as a living demonstration that "our kind can succeed even in finance." They may have felt that with all their background and experience it would be tempting God and good fortune to seek larger stakes than those they had already acquired. They did hope, however, that their successors might add further luster to the bank. Joseph Marcus' bright boy Bernard seemed chosen for that destiny.

In 1919, Bernard was named the bank's first Vice-President and given broad authority. He handled most of the bank's major new accounts. He discouraged his elders from standing in the doorway to greet clients. He even persuaded them that the approval of small notes was unbecoming for a bank's top officers. The founders' sudden inaccessibility somehow induced still greater public confidence in the bank. Could one expect a Schiff or Warburg, with their preoccupations, to be readily available, and would one dare engage them in small talk? Why should not the same consideration be accorded to "one of our own"?

The difference between the bank at its founding and later, under Bernard Marcus, seemed that between a feldsher and a doctor. In the four years of Bernard Marcus' vice-presidency the bank's assets increased tenfold to a total of $45,779,225, and in 1927, as a reward, his elders named him President and released him from all restraints. Unfortunately, Bernard, who had insisted on greater formality in dealing with lesser depositors, had introduced an astonishing informality in dealing with deposits. The bank's assets kept mounting, but mostly on paper. Bernard Marcus and his appointees achieved the bank's astonishing growth by flushing the same assets through a whole series of conduits so that they appeared each time as new monies.

These facts brought out in the criminal court proceedings nonetheless do not fully explain the mystery of the bank's closing. It has been suggested that the methods of Bernard Marcus, however reprehensible, were not dissimilar from those used in the mid-nineteen-twenties, before the crash, by some of the most august American financial institutions. It has been further argued that there was no good reason why the bank should have failed, that its ability to return to the depositors thirty cents on the dollar after the liquidation of its assets in the midst of the Depression is proof that it merited saving by its sister-banks, that they deliberately turned away and let the bank go under. (A myth, never set to rest, has it that the run had been engineered by WASP Wall Street tycoons who resented the first successful incursion of immigrant Jews into public banking.)

The East European immigrants had made amazing progress before the Depression hit them. Much of it was reflected in the "Business Opportunities" and "Help Wanted" columns of *The Jewish Morning Journal*, the major advertising vehicle for the Yiddish-speaking population. It was virtually a *yarid* (county fair). Yidn were buying and selling all kinds of businesses. The young man who only several years before had replied with trepidation to an "ad" for "young man, willing to hustle, opportunity to learn trade, greener [new immigrant] preferred," was now himself advertising for "young man, willing to hustle . . . greener preferred." *The Jewish Morning Journal* publishers launched their own real estate boom with the profits from the newspaper, estimated at up to $250,000 annually. They focused their boom not on Florida, but close by, on Asbury Park, offering "fantastic bargain" lots to their readers. The immigrants' progress was reflected in the expansion of charitable institutions they had founded and in the merger of some of their lesser institutions with larger ones. Yeshiva moved from its gray barracks building on East Broadway opposite the Meyer London Matzoh Bakery into an oriental-domed, stained-glass window structure in Washington Heights, then an affluent neighborhood. Excavations were under way for an entire complex of Yeshiva buildings. Then the Depression hit the *nouveau riche* East European philanthropists who were the institution's major contributors. This had been Orthodox Jewry's most ambitious educational undertaking. It now was compelled to defer further construction, prevented from accumulating additional Washington Heights acreage and took under serious consideration a proposal that some of its acquired lots be sold so that the proceeds might be used to meet maintenance costs. Yeshiva University's present-day campus, which is widely dispersed throughout the city, is visible evidence of the Depression's impact. Yet, it would have been forced to shut down altogether if the faculty of its two corner-stone institutions, the Talmudical (Rabbinical) Academy and the Hebrew Teachers Institute, had not agreed to go without salary for months. It might even be said that small neighborhood grocers throughout the city, by extending credit to these teachers, were the Yeshiva's chief supporters in those days.

This kind of devotion prevented the closing of an untold number of institutions, mostly of a neighborhood character—orphanages, homes for the aged, day nurseries, Hebrew afternoon schools, hospitals—that the East Europeans had built. Their financial supporters and their professional staffs had a strong attachment to them; having lived amidst the needs that had brought them into being, they could easily envision the hardships their closing would inflict. Unable to expand the professional staff, some of the contributors, often men and women of quite modest means, would help out with the chores, from preparing meals to changing bed linen. Furthermore, there was an unvoiced concern that the closing of these institutions would mean loss of face for the East Europeans. Their sense of rivalry with the Yahudim was still a potent factor. Eventually, of course, most of these institutions merged with the Federation of Jewish Philanthropies, founded by the Yahudim.

The synagogues fared less well in the Depression than other institutions, perhaps because supply exceeded demand. American Jews had gone on a real synagogue-building spree in the nineteen-twenties, which was duplicated in the suburbs three decades later by their sons and grandsons. The synagogue architecture of the nineteen-twenties revealed the founders' countries of origin—the Galicians adopted Viennese baroque; the Russians favored the Byzantine, and the Hungarians who were half Turk and half Austrian (and altogether Gypsy, malicious tongues would add) built in an outlandish mixture of both styles.

Elaborate ceremonies attended both the ground-breaking and the dedication; both occasions being announced with huge Yiddish press advertisements listing the contributors to the building funds, the cast of cantors who would provide the celebration liturgy, and the civic leaders who would grace the occasion. Sometimes the mayor or even the governor would put in an appearance, regale the crowd with a smattering of Yiddish, pay tribute to the Irish, Jewish, and Italian love of freedom, and to the Jews' "contribution to civilization since the days of Moses, the lawgiver," and join a kiddush—Mayor Walker's and Governor Al Smith's specialty—and depart in a monsoon of screaming sirens.

The major domo of each synagogue was the *shames*, or sexton. It was a lowly occupation in the shtetl. He swept the synagogue, emptied and polished the spitoons, ran errands for the officers, and barely had respite to join the chevra tehilim. In America, his status was considerably higher, although ambiguous. He performed all the above chores and many more. He was both handyman and synagogue administrator, and above all the keeper of the calendar of yahrzeits. Because the yahrzeits are observed in accordance with the Hebrew calendar which does not correspond with the regular calendar, of course, relatives had to be reminded annually of the date. He also kept a record of other familial events among his members that merited a kiddush, and if he could find none he would flatter and goad one of the better situated members to give a kiddush only because "when Jews foregather to praise the Lord, they should partake of that which gladdens the heart." A shames was judged by his capacity to provide a kiddush for every Sabbath of the year, as this kept members from straying off to other synagogues. He was up at dawn to serve tea to early prayer quorums. He purchased the tomato herring and soft drinks and his wife baked the chalah and prepared the fish for the weekly shalosh seudot. No matter how many visits and how much stair-climbing this required, he would not desist before he had collected every last pledge made by members or occasional visitors when they were called to the Torah. He was the synagogue's *de facto* treasurer and membership recruiter. Members could turn to him with assurance on all occasions tinged with religious ceremonial: he provided a mohel, recommended a shadchan, and a marriage performer, and sometimes he himself tripled in all these capacities. He instructed boys in preparation for their bar mitzvahs. He assembled a hired quorum to hold services, twice daily, in mourners' homes during the entire *shiva* (seven-day mourning period). He made arrangements with the funeral director and the monument engraver and provided the text for the tombstone.

The shames' job was a concession for which he paid handsomely, although his salary for the many diverse services he rendered was a mere pittance. His true income was in tips, pledges, and kickbacks. His contract stipulated that everyone called to the Torah must pledge something for the shames, and it was he who determined whom to call and in what order; the order is important, it being the highest honor to be called *shishi*, sixth, during the weekly reading of the portion of the law. He was tipped by the members for his interventions and, additionally, got kickbacks from the mohel; the shadchan; the hired quorum; the funeral director; tombstone engraver; the grocer and the candy storekeeper who provided the wherewithal for the shalosh seudot, and the wedding caterer, although very often, if the wedding or bar mitzvah were held in the synagogue, the shames and his wife did the catering themselves. He even got a cut of the monies accumulated in the charity boxes in the synagogue vestibule, and for persuading his officers to permit a speaker from one of the philanthropies to make a ten-minute appeal during the High Holiday services. Cantors waiting to be auditioned would tip him generously for turning rivals away by telling them that the position had already been filled. He carried over to America some of the subservient, sycophantic manner that corresponded with his station in life in the "old home," and that served its purpose even here in arousing compassion. But it was only a sham. Once the butt of bullies in the shtetl he was now a bully himself, and his special victim was the rabbi. Although generally quite ignorant, he nonetheless acted as a rabbi, particularly among the women and in the less learned congregations, until a rabbi was engaged and then his status suffered accordingly, including a decline in his income. However, faced by an ultimatum from the shames, the smaller congregations sometimes let the rabbi go, because the shames had paid for his concession by granting the synagogue a second mortgage and if fired, was entitled to be paid off in full.

The first mortgages, held by banks, were generally small because the banks did not see what immediate use they could make of these structures in the event of foreclosure. Yet, during the Depression, when installments were not met, they indeed threatened to foreclose, and it was then that the shames appeared in the role of redeemer. He assumed responsibility towards the bank, acquired possession of the synagogue and became his congregation's landlord. He abandoned his subservient manner but otherwise he proceeded as usual, polishing the brass, collecting pledges, accepting tips, and getting kickbacks.

Such, at any rate, has been the legend. That many took possession of their synagogues is true, but as for the rest, who can say for certain how much is fact, how much fabrication?

The Depression in America had global repercussions. It had a very nearly disastrous effect on the poor European Jewish communities and on the Zionist experiment in Palestine, both of which drew their primary support from American Jewry.

The American Jewish Year Book, reviewing the twelve-month period terminating June 30, 1932, observed: "Economic conditions in the United States during the past year were such as to compel the Jewish community to apply by far the greater part of its energies to the solution of its own domestic problems, including those of continuing the activities and, in some cases preventing the dissolution, of institutions and agencies which had been created by the community in previous years. American Jewry was prevented therefore from taking as active an interest in its sister communities overseas as in former years, especially as far as material aid was concerned."

In America, a nationwide review of thirty Jewish welfare agencies showed a 42.8 percent increase in relief recipients during the first nine months of 1931 compared with the corresponding period of the preceding year. In Baltimore there was a 77 percent increase, in Minneapolis a 100 percent increase of families receiving relief from Jewish charities in the first eight months of 1931 as against the same period the year before. A relatively small percentage of Jews in need would then think of applying to city or state relief agencies, many wavered and struggled with their embarrassment before even turning to Jewish charities.

Yet this was the time when Jewish communities abroad were most dependent on American Jewry. Poland, like the rest of the world, was in the throes of an economic depression. None in Poland was more gravely affected than its Jewish population of three million, which suffered from such additional afflictions as an economic boycott and other measures especially designed against them by either the government or anti-Semitic agencies functioning with government approval. Unemployment among Jewish artisans fluctuated between a low of 60 percent and a high of 80 percent. Some 200,000 Jewish families, nearly a third of the Jewish population, lived below the level of poverty, and half of these were utterly destitute. In Germany, the relatively obscure National Socialist German Workers' Party emerged from the September 1930 elections as a serious contender for national power. In less than two years, the Nazis would assume national power.

In Palestine, the Zionists just barely recovered from the Arab riots of 1929 and, badly hobbled by all kinds of British restrictions, would soon begin receiving as many Jewish refugees from Germany as the government would permit to enter, supplementing the credited immigrants with a steady trickle of illegal emigrés. It is at this time that contributions from America began to taper off because of the Depression. The American Palestine Campaign, in the first six months of 1931, had raised $1,000,000, but only $609,293, a decline of $390,707, in the first six months of 1932. The Palestine effort depended primarily on support from the East European immigrants, who had been the hardest hit by the Depression. The Joint Distribution Committee (JDC), supported mainly by the Yahudim and concentrating on relief for European Jewry, fared little better. Hoping to improve their receipts through joint effort, the two campaigns established the United Jewish Appeal whose total income in 1935 was less than half of its announced goal of $3,250,000. The partnership was therefore dissolved and it was not till 1939 that the United Jewish Appeal was reconstituted.

A steady source of support even in the darkest Depression years were the landsmanschaften. Their lower middle class and working class membership always responded to appeals. The cumulative result of these contributions was impressive. However, they were reluctant to hand over their monies to the giant philanthropic agencies where they could have no voice, where their contact was not with the social worker helping the needy but with a suave fund-raiser, who perhaps never even saw those for whom he solicited, and where their dollars became anonymous and were lost in the statistics of a lavishly printed annual audit report.

That is why the landsmanschaften kept their meetings bolted against solicitors representing the big campaigns. The Zionist solicitors, with fewer big contributors to rely on, were more persistent than the others. Many of the landsmanschaften conducted their meetings with the elaborate ritualism of secret societies. All had a sergeant-at-arms at their meetings. A knock on the door would bring his stern eyes to the peep-hole, which he quickly shut if the caller were a stranger. If the knocking persisted, the sergeant-at-arms would emerge, wearing a sash diagonally across his front, from shoulder to waist, listen impatiently to a hasty explanation, then affably suggest, "Try us some other time," and vanish behind the door. Inside, a raucous debate would erupt between "isola-tionists," who insisted that the visitor be kept out, and "interventionists" who wanted him admitted.

The isolationists were pre-World War I immigrants who had founded these societies for mutual aid, to maintain a synagogue, and to help the shtetl. The interventionists were younger men, mostly post-World War I immigrants who were more interested in boy-meets-girl events, such as masquerade balls on Purim and annual excursions on the Hud-son, than in maintaining a synagogue. Furthermore, ideologically com-mitted to Zionism, Socialism, or Communism they demanded support for their respective movements. Unable to move the isolationists, these younger people broke away and formed societies which, like the older ones, still retained the names of their particular shtetlach, but thought of themselves not as a sick benefit society but as a "Young Men's Benevolent Society." Although in the four decades since their founding they have been shorn of youth and members, they still retain "young men's" in their names.

It was during the Depression that the immigrant Jew suddenly be-came aware that he had never been so completely isolated from Gen-tiles as in the urban Jewish neighborhoods of America. The Gentiles he met in the big American cities were not even Americans, they were strangers like himself, some even more alien, because fewer of their children went beyond elementary school so that even their second generation could not cope too well with American speech. They spoke several kinds of "goyish," and only the Irish spoke the American kind. Besides the custom of one kind of immigrant goy was different from another, and these differences led frequently to violent eruptions between them. In the shtetl, matters were different. Jew and Christian had lived together for centuries. The Jew spoke "goyish," the peasant Yiddish. Their customs were frequently similar, even sharing a common diet, except for foods proscribed by Jewish dietary law. A great deal of Jewish commerce had been with the Christian peasantry, some of it in barter, and familiar with each other's religious calendar they brought to market goods that corresponded to their respective holiday requirements.

In America, however, the Jewish economy was like that of the medieval ghetto. The manufacturer and his employees, the doctor and his patients, the lawyer and his clients were almost all Jews, and the various auxiliary trades and occupations that served them had similarly consisted of Jews. The garments which they produced for the great American hinterlands were distributed largely through Jewish buyers and retailers.

Their interdependence resulted from a combination of circumstances, not all of them peculiar to the Jew. The Germans, the Swedes, *all* the new immigrants settled where others of their kind had preceded them, and for the same reasons as the Jew. In New York and other Eastern cities, among his own people, the Jew was reasonably certain of the cultural and religious amenities he required: early employment, assistance before he got a job and between jobs, getting along in Yiddish before he could learn English, marrying someone of his own faith, and preserving his middle class urban social status. Although Chicago and several other Midwestern cities had substantial Jewish populations and there were sparse Jewish communities across the continent, the "real" America was to the Yidn still something remote, great, festive, and awe-inspiring. It was Fourth of July firecrackers, Thanksgiving Day turkey and a little book from which they memorized the questions and answers that might come up when they appeared before a magistrate in robes, sometimes a Jew, who would pass on their title to citizenship. Those who read Yiddish literature were vaguely aware of cotton plantations and prairies, of the lushness of American vegetation and the melancholy vastness of American space. But these were few.

Their rural geography generally was confined to the Catskills and New Jersey. Nonetheless there occurred among the Yidn, during the

Depression, a brief back-to-the-soil flurry, distantly related to the nineteenth-century movement that had been a reaction to the seemingly dehumanizing effects of industrialization and urbanization. Applied to the Jew's condition, it suggested that his economic ills and the hostility which encircled him were the consequence of the urban occupations into which he had been forced and his involuntary alienation from the soil. It had inspired abortive philanthropic efforts to settle the Jews *en masse* and permanently on the soil in Russia, Argentina, and the United States and provided the dynamics, in our own century, for Zionist pioneering on the soil of Palestine.

It seemed for a while, in the nineteen-thirties, as if the movement had been resuscitated among the immigrant Jews in America. Some who had promoted themselves out of jobs as operators and pressers in the garment center into "business opportunities" began to see their trade fall off during the Depression, and hurriedly sold their furniture and clothing stores and looked around for something "more real and more wholesome." The Jewish Agricultural Society, which had long been nursing a hope that the Jews might disperse across the country and settle on land, assisted them in purchasing little truck gardening and chicken farms in New Jersey. Some cloakmakers decided that even if they continued in their occupation, it was well to do it in bucolic surroundings and they moved to Roosevelt, New Jersey where with federal assistance they were provided with housing and a plant from whose windows they had an unobstructed view of the countryside.

The Yidn had shown considerable restiveness since World War I, moving, even inside New York City, from section to section and borough to borough. This continued right through the Depression and beyond. Three sets of comparative figures based on the ten-year census illustrate the inter-borough Jewish population movement in New York City.

In 1917 Manhattan had the largest Jewish population, with Brooklyn second; in 1927, they changed places, and in 1937 Bronx was second,

	1917	1927	1937
Manhattan	696,000	465,000	351,037
Bronx	211,000	420,000	592,185
Brooklyn	568,000	797,000	974,765
Queens	23,000	75,000	107,855
Richmond	5,000	7,200	9,158

Manhattan third. The only borough with a steadily declining Jewish population, Manhattan, nonetheless still remained the heartland of America's Yidn. There were situated the Café Royal, all the Yiddish newspapers, and more than ten Yiddish theaters. The headquarters of the national Jewish organizations, however, had by then begun to move northward; on the East Side, along Madison Avenue, towards the forties, and on the West Side, from Times Square to Columbus Circle. They were still lagging behind their constituencies. The Yidn had by then virtually evacuated Harlem, which had once had several Yiddish theaters, a synagogue that employed Yossele Rosenblatt, and a café on 110th Street facing the Park, which used to be dense with smoke and the impassioned talk of Russian emigrés, including a bushy-haired, pince-nezed revolutionary journalist whose *nom-de-guerre* was Leon Trotsky.

With all the restiveness, which caused them to shift every few years to new neighborhoods inside New York, the Jews could not be persuaded, *en masse*, to trust their fate to the great spaces beyond. The slogan "Go west, young man" was to them not a challenge, but medical advice. Garment center workers with collapsed lungs traveled west to Denver to the Spivak Sanitarium. It fell to their American-born offspring to break out of New York. The Depression and the books of Jack London and Jim Tully largely account for this westward migration. Lawyers, dentists, accountants, doctors, and teachers now became hack drivers and countermen, but many others struck out across the continent. There were also the Jewish medical students. Barred by the quota system from the better American medical schools they were advised by the American Jewish Committee to enroll in less crowded professions,[1] and told by the American Jewish Congress that the only solution to their problem was the establishment of a Jewish medical school.[2]

They rejected the first advice, and the second offered no immediate alternative. Before the Depression, when their fathers could afford it, these young men circumvented American restrictions for Jewish students by enrolling in schools abroad and, because of the language

[1] Two decades later America was short of doctors.
[2] The Albert Einstein Medical Center came into being after the medical schools had abolished the quota system. The situation was difficult even in liberal arts institutions, which was the motivation for founding Brandeis University. The quotas were abolished by the time Brandeis came into being.

problem, preferably in Scottish and Irish schools. They now had to settle for second-rate medical schools in remote areas of the American South and West.

As they crossed the continent they learned many uncomfortable facts of which their parents, insulated in their metropolitan ghettos, were barely aware. They learned that even the less crowded professions, such as engineering, for example, did not welcome Jews. They learned that a New York accent disadvantageously identified anyone as a Jew, that their degrees from the City College of New York confirmed that they were subversives, and that on both scores they had little chance of obtaining even blue collar jobs in the big assembly-line industries. Yet, some of these footloose students and professionals never returned to New York again. They settled down in extant Jewish communities and presaged the westward trek of American Jewry which acquired momentum in the nineteen-forties and nineteen-fifties. It is part of a general American pattern. Los Angeles now has a large colony of Yiddish-speaking, mostly retired, garment workers, and also thousands of Hassidim. It has, of course, the normal population of young couples, employed in all kinds of industrial research. And there are the Jewish intellectuals, highly visible in Palo Alto, Berkeley, and Santa Barbara.

CHAPTER 2

The Successors

A DECADE had passed since the Yahudim had been turned out of power. The titans had long since been gathered unto their ancestors. The last two great arbiters of American Jewish affairs, Jacob Schiff and Louis Marshall, had died within a decade of one another. Their Jewish book collections were given away to the libraries of Jewish educational institutions. Jacob Schiff's prayerbook with the family genealogy on its flyleaf was discovered several years ago among the volumes that had been shipped to the Jewish Theological Seminary. Its librarian, thinking it had been sent in error, called the heirs and was told: "Really? The family Bible? You may keep it, of course."

Gone was that entire generation of the mythically penniless immigrants who had arrived in mid-century from Germany and amassed great fortunes, and whose sons had expanded these gains and established dynasties of financiers, merchant princes, and Maecenases. Many of their progeny lost interest in Jewish affairs, some have lingered on in the Ethical Culture Society, others have vanished altogether through intermarriage, and have transferred their bequests from the temple to the church where their preferences range from Unitarianism to Episcopalianism.

The Yidn were in complete charge now, yet their victory was like ashes on the tongue. Some missed the old titans, the ideologists who had been replaced by a middle generation of pragmatists, and all evidence seemed to indicate that when these in turn would retire there would be none to succeed them because the younger generation, concerned with all kinds of radical causes, had no patience with "parochialism."

Just then the labor leader in America became a new category to reckon with in Jewish affairs. Union membership was expanding at an astonishing pace in the nineteen-thirties. The so-called Jewish labor unions, the International Ladies' Garment Workers' and the Amalgamated Clothing Workers, were no exception. Their respective heads, David Dubinsky and Sidney Hillman, became potent influences in American national politics.

In their adolescence both men had served prison terms in Czarist jails for anti-Government activities. They began their careers in the American labor movement when the picket line was a firing line, labor leaders were harassed by police and the courts, maligned by the press, and treated as pariahs by society. Enrolled Socialists since their youth, Hillman and Dubinsky, each in his own union, had to fight hard for their pragmatic approaches at a time when ideologists still carried weight in labor's ranks. Each had an impressive record of achievements by the time the New Deal rolled around. They had introduced industry-wide bargaining; employment and health insurance with employer participation long before these had passed into law; had saved jobs by extending financial assistance to floundering firms with good labor-relations records; and in 1929, that fateful year for Americans, the Amalgamated completed in the Bronx the first cooperative low-income housing project undertaken by an American labor union.

Yet, until the nineteen-thirties, the reputation of both men was confined to their industries. The New Deal widened their horizons. Leading the militant CIO's interventions in state and federal elections, Hillman was drawn early into the White House circle, and in 1941 was appointed by President Roosevelt to the important wartime post of Associate General Director of the Office of Production Management. While Dubinsky never received a federal appointment, he was among the labor leaders most frequently summoned to the White House for consultation on contemplated government wage and price policy. A baker's apprentice in his 'teens, he retained the picketline leader's and sweatshop raider's faculty for direct communication with his constituents, speaking to them in a language they understood. Hillman, who came from a rabbinic family, had, however, risen to leadership from factory workers' ranks. He was a man of more formal manner than Dubinsky, and in his later years his addresses, which were almost exclusively in English and read from a prepared text, sounded like a corporation lawyer's briefs.

None of the elite of corporation lawyers, financiers, merchant princes, and social gospel rabbis who had traditionally intervened with the White House on Jewish affairs, had ever had the kind of access to presidents that these two Jewish labor leaders acquired in New Deal days. These men, especially Dubinsky, readily responded when consulted on Jewish matters. However, American Jewish leaders neither had, nor really sought, rapport with the labor leaders, and only occasionally solicited their support through the Israel Histadrut Campaign. A really serious attempt was never made to draw them into the inner councils which determined American Jewish policy.

Zionism was also led by pragmatists now, but they possessed none of the vigor of the labor leaders. Admittedly, they dealt with a somewhat peripheral and distant cause which they effectively transformed into a wholly remote cause. American Zionism's leaders, with one or two exceptions, were mediocre persons, mostly businessmen, lawyers, and lower court judges. Perhaps their major qualifications for leadership were their ambition for office and that they spoke English, however colorless, and it was consequently hoped that they might attract a younger generation. Men of conventional habit and devoid of enthusiasm, they could only alienate younger people, especially in the fermentative 'Thirties. Yet, these men who read their speeches in dry voices from ghostwritten texts, had been virtually handpicked by the brilliant Weizmann who could speak with incisive precision and in many different tongues. He had assigned to European Jewry the task of feeding brain- and manpower into the Palestine experiment, and to American Jewry the chore of raising funds. He selected for America leaders with that particular talent, who would not be deflected from their limited course. He had chosen exceedingly well.

Some of the American Zionist movement's old vigor would still manifest itself, however, in controversy over the firmness of Zionist resistance to British policy in Palestine. The ideological discussions that claimed so much time and passion of Palestine's pioneers and of Europe's Zionist movement were confined in America to a very few intellectual young men and women who had pledged to settle in Palestine and were preparing for kibbutz life by conditioning themselves to backbreaking farmwork, at first as hired workers and, later on, at a training farm of their own. They were visited by emissaries from Palestine, sunburned and tieless men in crumpled suits whose pockets bulged with books and periodicals. For evenings on end they would discuss with these young ideological apprentices the society of the future sovereign

Jewish state, which might be dominated, they hoped, by the spirit of the kibbutz that had purged itself of bourgeois values, treated menial labor as a morally regenerative commitment, and shared a common treasury. These emissaries duplicated the discussions then taking place in the labor settlements in Palestine over the relative merits of Leninist Marxism, Social Democracy, and Tolstoianism, as interpreted by A. D. Gordon, one of their own saints, and the application of these principles to the new society they were establishing in Palestine.

The names of some of these visitors from Palestine to the small core of American novitiates in kibbutz life may be unfamiliar to Israeli youth today, yet they are inseparable from the mythology of Israel's beginnings—Berl Katzenelson, writer, orator, peripatetic teacher, ideologist, who teamed up with the pragmatist David Ben-Gurion to lay the foundations of Israel's labor movement; Joseph Baratz, founder of Ein Harod, the first Zionist commune in Palestine; Dr. Chaim Arlosoroff, the German-trained sociologist, Zionism's "prodigy" statesman, who was only in his thirties when struck down by an assassin's bullet; Enzio Sereni, son of an aristocratic Italian-Jewish family, who exchanged the salons of Rome for life in a kibbutz.

The young Zionists frequently clashed with the infinitely more numerous Communists, Communist fellow-travelers and Socialists on American campuses. The Socialists dismissed them as curious sectarian relics, the Communists denounced them as "social fascists." Yet the young Zionists and the Leftists had in common their defiance of bourgeois values and the conviction that their elders had betrayed their respective ideologies. Their allegation was not without merit. The elders had indeed frequently qualified, compromised, and even deserted principles they had enthusiastically endorsed in their youth. Socialists had bartered ideology for "New Deal opportunism," Zionist parents committed to "self-realization," which meant resettlement in Palestine as pioneers, were alarmed when their children announced their intention to drop out of school and sail for Palestine to live in a kibbutz.

In their efforts to relate to the American mind the young found both the settlement houses, maintained by philanthropy, and the college classroom wanting. The settlement house offered only a vicarious relationship to America, a bland fare of supervised American sports, instructions in arts, crafts, English for citizens and clichés about the American dream. The college classroom, with some notable exceptions, of course, was formal, forbidding, as textual as any Fundamentalist church.

The Labor Temple, on Fourteenth Street off Second Avenue, seemed to suit them best. It was partly a people's university, partly the radicals' equivalent of the tent meetings of Christian evangelists. Here they communicated, or so they thought, with the American mind. It was the pulpit of scholars and pretenders, instructors and confusers of the young, popularizers and plagiarizers, professors-emeritus who could afford to speak their minds freely; inspired teachers whose outspokenness precluded their appointment to faculties. John Dewey lectured there several times, as did Thorstein Veblen. Sidney Hook was a familiar name on its billboard. The "steadies" included A. J. Muste, for a time its minister, a radical and a crusading pacifist until his recent death at a ripe old age; Scott Nearing, Marxist student of imperialism; and Harry Waton, Spinozist, and Daniel Schmalhausen, expert on sex psychology, both of whom were really "general practitioners" who lectured and published articles and books on every conceivable subject. The lesser Communist denominations that had broken with the Moscow mother church used the Labor Temple facilities frequently. This is where the three defrocked cardinals of American Communism—Jay Lovestone, Ben Gitlow and Max Schachtman—met with their disciples.

The audience was virtually the same every evening. It fell into two categories. There were those who deliberately type-cast themselves as revolutionary proletarians: the men were hirsute and lumber-jacketed, the women were bobbed and disheveled, with short, belted leather jackets that made their hips appear wider. There were also stereotype round-shouldered, bespectacled scholars in hand-me-down suits, and women with neatly braided hair and dresses that crackled with starch. The women, in either category, had at least one embroidered Russian blouse, the fashion of the day, in their sparse wardrobes. The audience was multinational—Slavs, Finns and Latins. New England males and females—social workers, librarians and editorial personnel—stood out as if under a spotlight in a police lineup—tall, thin, angular, self-conscious, with a slight flush in their cheeks and, if they accidentally jostled someone, or were jostled themselves, were excessively apologetic. The majority, however, was nonetheless the sons and daughters of that older audience which claimed the auditorium once a week, on Saturday evenings, for Yiddish symposia and literary readings.

These young people were not committed to any specific ideology.

They were only window-shopping among the rich variety of ideological orthodoxies on display at the Labor Temple. Each of these radical faiths was an absolutist, possessive, jealous God, unforgiving of errancy; choosing one meant foreclosing on all other fascinating possibilities, and these young people were not ready to foreclose on anything.

Like their parents, they too groped their way through books to a comprehension of the world about them. They would queue up daily at the counters of the New York Public Libraries on the Lower East Side, in Brooklyn, and the Bronx to borrow and return books, and argue with the librarian over the number they might take out at one time, especially for vacation which they spent working as waiters, busboys, bellboys, and children's counsellors in summer resorts.

Even in their choice of books, they were their parents' children. Continental books, in English translation, were high on their list. They shared their elders' fascination with Tolstoi, Dostoevski, Chekhov, Gorki, and added, that being the pacifist era on campus, Remarque, Barbusse, and Rolland. They discovered the Norwegian master Knut Hamsun, who was to become a collaborator during the Nazi invasion of his country. They had many reasons to delight in his writing. His gloom was like the Russians', but without their black despair and church incense atmosphere. His first novel, *Hunger*, was social protest fiction. His *Growth of the Soil* with its patriarchal figure became their canon because the urban ghetto Jews had an aching longing for the soil, transmitted from generation to generation; the familial feeling among the Jews was still overpowering, and Hamsun's Isaac, putting down his stakes in harsh soil was the prototype, curiously, of their urbanized fathers battling their way upward from the sweatshop to claim a stake in America for their children.

They were omniverous readers of fiction depicting America's topography and social conditions. Their scrambled American authors' list included, prominently, H. L. Mencken, Upton Sinclair, Sinclair Lewis, Theodore Dreiser, John Dos Passos, Erskine Caldwell, James T. Farrell. This reading was a sort of orientation course, like their death-watch outside the Governor's Mansion on the night of the Sacco-Vanzetti execution, and their union organizing efforts in the milltowns and mines. It was also their response to the reproach that they had presumed to offer counsel on American social conditions although they had never been beyond New York City, and it produced comforting evidence that the discrimination and deprivation they suffered was not peculiar to immigrants, or Jews, but was rather a universal American condition, which in a sense made them kin with all other Americans.

Their predilection for literature dealing with social conditions also had ethnic roots. They had a hearsay familiarity with the themes of Yiddish fiction. As children they heard their parents read it aloud at the kitchen table after dinner, heard it discussed with their neighbors over steaming glasses of tea, and, on hot summer evenings, amidst the chatter on neighborhood stoops. Yiddish literature had never been escapist. Even the serialized newspaper *schundroman* (the fictional equivalent of the radio soap opera) was not escapist. It dealt with real conditions and was a running social, sometimes Swiftian, commentary on its environment. Sinclair Lewis' *Babbitt* was a close cousin of the Jewish *alreitnik*, the immigrant *nouveau riche;* Henry L. Mencken's exposure of American sham compensated for their humiliating exclusion from many areas of American life; Dreiser's *An American Tragedy* was like good class-conscious Jewish melodrama, familiar to Yiddish theater audiences. John Dos Passos' fiction with its mosaics of the American scene gave them a ringside seat at the great American spectacle. This literature established their common humanity with the rest of the American population. It reassured them that they were not some alien, unassimilable breed.

They were heirs to a tradition of savage Jewish self-criticism emanating from the modern Jewish ideological movements. Both Jewish Socialism and Zionism contended that the Jew's character had become misshapen by conditions and could only be corrected if these were changed in accordance with these movements' respective prescriptions. This anesthetized them to the anti-Semitism of Thomas Wolfe, which was not social criticism at all, but an overpowering biological aversion for the Jew so boldly and aggressively evident in his depictions of students at New York University.[1] On the contrary, he seemed to them the first American goy author who really took notice of them, their own Jewish college generation, and planted them in American fiction. No other American author before him had, for that matter, paid so much attention to the Jews. He was of their own generation, and his American smells, sounds and place-names pounded like surf on their senses. They identified with his ambivalent passions, overwhelming sense of displacement (alienation, in the current vocabulary), and furious love-

---

[1] ". . . their hot and sweaty body-smells, their strong female odors of rut and crotch and arm-pit and cheap perfume."

hate relationship with his parents. Several generations of American roots notwithstanding, Thomas Wolfe, like themselves, was a stranger in the land.

A revered name among the young Jews, carried over from their older brothers of the nineteen-twenties, or their own high school days, was Louis Untermeyer, a Jew himself, and through his anthologies the mentor of several school generations in modern American poetry. British verse, to these young Jews, was like an exercise in Latin; it had too many unfamiliar allusions. American poetry communicated directly through its evocations of the American city, America's pluralistic culture, and daily speech. Their rapport with Whitman and Sandburg was immediate. The inclusion of verse about the urban ghettos by Jewish and Italian poets, some of them immigrants, and most of them since forgotten, affirmed their claim to America. They wrinkled their brows to decipher Eliot and Pound; burning up with the fever for living, they could not relate easily to these poets' ennui and refinements. Yet, Pound and Eliot had enthusiastic disciples among those who themselves wrote verse. Unable to afford steamship tickets to Paris or even half the rent for a shared room in Greenwich Village, they pursued expatriate existences in their parental households in bug-ridden tenements on the Lower East Side, Brownsville, and East New York, as well as on the fashionable Grand Concourse in the Bronx.

The ranking American Jewish writer in the nineteen-twenties and early nineteen-thirties, almost universally accepted as such, was Ludwig Lewisohn. At first the young hailed him with enthusiasm and pride. Descended from the Yahudim, he identified with the Yidn. Born in Germany, he charged that he had been doubly rejected by America, as a German during the Germanophobia of World War I, and at all times as a Jew. His celebration of Europe's cultural eminence bolstered their ego, for were they not part of that heritage, only one generation removed from the Continent? His championing of Freud was meaningful on two scores. Freudianism was a further expansion of the process of emancipation begun by their parents' immigration to America; besides Freud was a Jew, and they thirsted for testimony affirming their ethnic worth. However, except among Zionist students, there soon developed a gap between Lewisohn and the young Jewish college generation. They were beating their way to American acceptance while he was researching his Hebraic origins and acclaiming the Jewish heritage they, and in many cases their parents before them, had jettisoned. They

saw society aligned in two contending classes, he saw an apocalyptic
denouement of the Jewish-Christian relationship; they predicted the
solution of the Jewish problem in an assimilative Socialist society, he
spoke of a Messianic return to Zion, and prophesied, some one and a
half decades before Auschwitz, that "the Jewish problem is the decisive
problem of Western civilization; by its solution this world of the West
will stand or fall, choose death or life." [2]

Despite the rise of a new generation that knew no Yiddish, the latter's
decline was not at all apparent because there was still a large audience of the middle-aged and even the young, post-World War I immigrants with considerable education from the European gymnasiums,
who engaged in Yiddish activity. The one arena in which Yiddish declined rapidly was the Zionist. In the nineteen-twenties Yiddish
speakers dominated the platform at all major Zionist meetings, in the
nineteen-thirties theirs were but token appearances. There were many
reasons for this. The Zionists belonged to the East European middle-
class intelligentsia. They were not, unlike the proletariat, wholly dependent on Yiddish. A high percentage of them read *The New York
Times* [3] and a Yiddish daily regularly, checking the veracity of one
against the other.[4] The majority were Hebraists in principle, striving
quixotically to revive Hebrew as the spoken tongue of Jews everywhere. Many were disdainful of Yiddish. But even the Yiddishists
among them agreed that in order to attract younger people it was ex-
pedient to conduct Zionist meetings in English.

Nothing was more symbolic of the banishment of Yiddish from the
Zionist platform than the case of Abe Goldberg, or Abele as he was
called with affection and derision. A Yiddish speaker, he had been, in
the nineteen-twenties, one of the ranking orators in American Zionism,
often sharing the platform with Weizmann and other dignitaries.
Rotund, short, with small arms, an overlarge head and slightly Negroid
features, he reasoned with his audience, entertained them, prefaced
anecdotes with a big childlike grin, passed restless fingers with a

[2] For an appreciation of Lewisohn read reference to him in Alfred Kazin's *On
Native Grounds,* New York: Reynal Hitchcock, 1942.
[3] Girls who read *The Daily News* were advised by marriage brokers to hide the
newspaper when a suitor came calling, because even if he read it himself, he would
deem it a defect in his future bride.
[4] Zionists charged, not without cause, that *The New York Times* gave them inadequate coverage and slanted the news against them.

flourish through his curly, salt-and-pepper hair to gloss over a lapse of memory. Approaching a crescendo, his face would become contorted, and raising his arms like Moses holding the tablets, he would thunder out a wrathful jeremiad that ripped his audience out of their seats.

But when the dull businessmen, attorneys and lower court magistrates took over, in the nineteen-thirties, they crowded each other so aggressively on the Zionist speakers' roster that there was often no place for Abele. Whining to all he could buttonhole about the slights he suffered, he would appear uninvited at rallies and head straight for the platform. This was a cue for cries from the audience, "Goldberg, Yiddish, Goldberg, Yiddish," and the chant would rise again each time a speaker was introduced, compelling from the nettled chairman repeated reassurances that "We are happy, of course, that the distinguished Mr. Goldberg could come, and shall hear from him in due course." As the proceedings dragged on, those of the public not yet numbed by the speeches twisted nervously in their seats, eyed the exits, and hastened out between speeches. Introduced at a late hour, to a half-empty hall, Goldberg, bitterly offended, lost his sense of proportion and talked on interminably, this King Lear of the Yidn who in 1921 had seized Zionist power from the disciples of Justice Brandeis and in the nineteen-thirties surrendered it to police magistrates and assemblymen.

It was primarily the labor segments that kept Yiddish vigorously alive. The *Forward* Socialists, the Labor-Zionists, and the Communists maintained all manner of Yiddish-language institutions including summer camps for adults and children. The Orthodox also clung to Yiddish, and there was even the strange phenomenon at this time, of a bestselling Yiddish author of historical romances, Saul Saphire, a youthful former Hebrew school principal whose appearance—he wore pince-nez, had small features, a schoolgirl complexion, a reticent manner and blushed easily—corresponded with the late Victorian style of his writing. His lovers were ardent but chaste, and his titles reflect the entire panorama of Jewish history—*Abraham the Patriarch, Joseph in Egypt, Solomon ibn Gabiro, The Caliph of Cordoba* (Jewish, of course), *The Jewish People, The Converted Count Potozky, The Vilna Cantor* (who became an opera star), *Haim Solomon, Mordecai Manuel Noah, Moses Montefiore* and many others.

After the serialization of several of his early works established his reputation as a circulation builder, *The Jewish Morning Journal* appointed him to its staff to write historical novels so that the first install-

ment of a new Saphire novel ran in parallel columns with the concluding installment of the old. Readers were eager to preserve and reread
his works and many orders for the book poured in even before serialization had been completed. One always knew the publication date of
another Saphire volume by the queues which formed early outside the
newspaper offices, which annoyed the reputable poets and literary
novelists on the staff whose names at best were only remotely familiar
to this huge readership, the vast majority being women of the
sheitel (wig) and *tichel* (kerchief) set and chevra tehilim males who
recited the psalms without knowing their meaning. But even learned
men among the Orthodox read his novels, although pretending only to
skim them to check on his accuracy and on slips into heresy. However,
Saphire, drawing on the Talmud and Midrash, was always accurate; as
a Simon-pure Yiddish Victorian he never erred on doctrine.[5]

On Sundays Jewish readers of another kind, young men and women,
mostly new immigrants, would pilgrimage by subway and Elevated to
the Bronx which had become the home of the foremost Yiddish poets
and novelists. The pilgrims journeyed to visit sites that had been immortalized in Yiddish verse recited in Warsaw, Buenos Aires, Cernauti,
Tel Aviv—the Edgar Allan Poe House, Bronx Park, and Mosholu Park
which Yidn nicknamed Moishele's (Little Moses') Park. If they were
fortunate, they would spot one of the celebrities walking under the
trees, or an entire pack of them, some seated, some standing, passionately arguing form and substance.

Of course, there was a greater number traveling in the reverse direction, young men and women from Yiddish-speaking homes who knew
no Yiddish themselves converged upon Greenwich Village in the hope
of seeing writers of the new American verse in the flesh.

[5] His novels are now serialized in *The Jewish Daily Forward*, whose staff he joined
at Cahan's invitation.

CHAPTER 3

The Culture Invasion

IN THE AUTUMN of 1932, when Franklin Delano Roosevelt was "preparing to take over the leadership of a country on its knees, half of New York's theaters were dark." [1] Yet, even then, new talent was coursing into the American theater—playwrights, actors, directors, scenic designers, and composers who were committed to the avant garde and declared that social commentary was a legitimate function of the stage. They brought along a like-minded audience—young, vigorous, responsive, and unable to afford Broadway prices. This combination altered the American theater profoundly.

The new spirit found expression through The Group Theater, which presented its first production in the autumn of 1931 and had been initially subsidized by The Theatre Guild; The Federal Theater, launched in the autumn of 1935, which provided jobs for 12,000 unemployed stage personnel across the country; and two workers' theaters, The Theater Union, founded in 1933, which strained against the leash of Communist control, and Labor Stage, founded in 1936 by the International Ladies' Garment Workers' Union.

These four theaters served as the launching area for an invasion of Broadway. It is through them that America's ethnic minorities asserted themselves collectively for the first time on the American stage, not through dialect comedy, but through social-protest plays and dignified American speech. American audiences came under the spell of two Armenian landsmen, Elia Kazan and William Saroyan. Orson Welles, not a minority member himself, directed an all Negro cast in *Macbeth*.

But most prominent among the new forces were the Jews, sons and

[1] Howard Taubman, *The Making of the American Theatre* (New York: Coward McCann, 1965), p. 209.

grandsons of East European immigrants who brought with them the passion of the Yiddish theater, which fascinated most observers, but alarmed some. *The Literary Digest* mused whether Broadway was "taking a back seat"; [2] John Dos Passos, in a laudatory comment pointed up the order of succession from Second Avenue to the Group Theater; [3] *Time* Magazine described the Group as comprised of Jews devoted to Leftist propaganda.[4] John Corbin, at one time the *New York Times'* theater critic was alarmed long before this by the Theatre Guild, predecessor of the new spirit. Conceding that Broadway could learn from the Yiddish theater, ". . . the yids wrote plays first hand out of their daily experience and thought and their public flocked to them enthralled and illumined," he warned, however, that the influence of Jews on Broadway was of another kind, ". . . corrosive, vitriolic, animated by the spirit of a separate minority, the intellectual theater has now given itself over to the drama of acid intelligence." [5]

Jews had been prominent in all phases of the American theater since the mid-Nineteenth century. But they did not come on collectively, and did not try to instruct or alter, but only to please. To amuse their audiences they often parodied their own and other minorities, using Jewish dialect and so-called Jewish gestures, and appearing in black-face. A long roster of Jews, Burlesk comics and Bowery singing waiters, rose to stardom after World War I and through the nineteen-twenties—Al Jolson, George Jessel, Eddie Cantor, Fanny Brice, the Marx Brothers, and, as a composer of popular music, Irving Berlin. The Gershwins, S. N. Behrman and George S. Kaufman were already variously launched on their careers when the Depression rolled around. Elmer Rice introduced the avant garde play to the American stage in the mid-nineteen-twenties. The success of all these delighted many who saw in it corroborative evidence of American opportunity.

The Jews who entered the American theater in the nineteen-thirties were different, however. They did not swing on separate branches. They were imbued not merely with personal ambition, but with a sense of mission. They had come out of the Depression with a collective grievance, like the brooding and menacing figures in Orozco and Rivera murals. Members of a highly self-conscious minority, imperiled

---

[2] *Lifson, op. cit.*

[3] *Ibid.*, p. 388.

[4] Harold Clurman, *The Fervent Years* (N.Y.: Hill and Wang, 1957), p. 149; and Taubman, *op. cit.* The Group Theater's non-Jews included Elia Kazan, Franchot Tone, and co-founder Cheryl Crawford. Eugene O'Neill was among its first "angels."

[5] Lifson, *op. cit.*, p. 64–65.

by religious hatred at home and abroad, they automatically supported any social protest movement that hove into sight. Versatile, numerous, they poked into all aspects of the American theater. They brought, unlike the Jews who preceded them, a distinctive ethnic theater tradition, which had its roots on Second Avenue, but had extended into the celebrated borscht circuit. It was almost impossible for anyone with a fondness for the theater, especially a Jew, who grew up in the nineteen-twenties and nineteen-thirties not to be brushed by the Yiddish theater, however fleetingly. It was then in its most exciting experimental period. Many of the young men who entered the American theater in the nineteen-twenties and nineteen-thirties had been regular aficionados of the Yiddish stage. Some had even served their apprenticeship there. From the Yiddish theater had even come several distinguished scenic designers and lighting effects artists—Boris Aronson, Mordecai Gorelik, Sam Leve, and Abe Feder.

Located in the same area, the Catskills and the Adirondack foothills, and alike addicted to borscht, fish, and chicken soup, were two separate and distinct borscht circuits—borscht borscht and intellectual borscht. The intelligentsia looked disdainfully at the podlie (low caste) clientele of the borscht borscht circuit, which in turn fell into two categories, the alreitniks, who stayed in the high priced hotels, and the poor who crowded the boarding houses, a family to a room, several families in a bungalow, sharing kitchen and toilet facilities, under conditions comparable to those of an urban slum of our own day.

The male population, at work in the city all week, would arrive on Friday evening and depart after lunch on Sunday, and often spend the weekend at the garment center's favorite pastimes (of that day), pinochle and poker, with barely a glance at their families and surroundings. To remedy the situation and placate grumbling wives, the hotels began to offer entertainment, on a modest scale, such as a song and dance team and a double entendre comic.

The second generation of borscht circuit visitors was provided with more sophisticated relaxation, tennis courts and dramatics. It was then, also, that the hotels acquired competition: the summer camp for young adults seeking to escape the surveillance of their elders who could not conceive of courtship without an engagement ring and were suspicious of love prattle that did not include talk of marriage. These camps, privately owned, attracted a liberal-radical clientele of no definite ideological commitment and exhausted their guests with a treadmill program of hikes, hayrides, sports and "cultural events."

Proprietors and guests alike protested that these camps were not borscht circuit, not borscht borscht. They belonged, instead, with the older ideological camps, the intellectual borscht circuit.

With few exceptions, such as Unity House, run by the International Ladies' Garment Workers' Union and the Socialist Party's Camp Tamiment, the ideological camps were primarily Yiddish-speaking, and divided among Zionists, Yiddishists, Hebraists, Farband Labor Zionist, Workmen's Circle Socialists and bitter end Communists. They catered mainly to proletarian and lower-middle-class fineshmekers (literally with a fine sense of smell, i.e. connoisseurs), with intellectual pretensions and a passion for self-improvement. There were alreitniks among them too, who wished to pass, however, as members of the proletarian intelligentsia whom fate had assigned the invidious role of agents of the capitalist system, afflicting them with real estate, manufacturing plants, and bank accounts.

The clientele of the ideological camps, humbly assuming that the incomprehensible and unenjoyable are necessarily profound and significant, would piously suffer, day after day, the tedium of cultural marathons that began after breakfast and concluded after midnight, and were comprised of lectures, symposia, music recitals, poetry readings, choirs, serious dramas, the modern dance, and experimental theater. Graduates of the dramatics staged at these ideological Yiddish-speaking camps include Sidney Lumet, Jules Dassin, Martin Ritt, and Jerome Robbins. Lumet's father, Baruch, was drama director at one of the camps, and Sidney made his stage debut there under his father's direction, at the age of four.

Alumni of the greater borscht circuit, which includes better hotels and camps, are Danny Kaye, John Garfield, Arthur Kober, Phil Silvers, Moss Hart (who, in his autobiography, *Act One,* is unusually bitter about his summer resort experiences), Dore Schary, Lorenz Hart, Garson Kanin, Red Buttons, and untold others.

The fact that their initial stage experience had been acquired performing to an ethnic audience with social commitments, also helped condition the generation of the nineteen-thirties, to social commentary. Jewish summer resort audiences expected both entertainment and a message (alreitnik and proletarian alike) and had an enormous tolerance for self-ridicule. This capacity for ridicule was translated into brilliant political satire in the Broadway commercial theater of the nineteen-thirties—*Of Thee I Sing* by George S. Kaufman in 1931, and *I'd Rather Be Right* by George S. Kaufman and Moss Hart in 1937, and that same year, the Labor Stage with a cast of garment workers presented *Pins and Needles,* a satirical topical review, which promptly became a smash hit. Its material was continually revised to sustain its relevance, *Pins and Needles* lasted until the outbreak of World War II. The men who directed it and wrote its sketches, lyrics and music acquired professional eminence in the American theater—Arthur Arent, Marc Blitzstein, Harold Rome, Joseph Schrank, Emanuel Eisenberg.

Arthur Arent was also the chief writer for the Federal Theater's most original and controversial project, The Living Newspaper, which produced such stage documentaries as *One Third of a Nation,* an exposé of housing conditions, and *Triple A Plowed Under* about farm conditions, both of which shocked the nation and advanced public understanding for FDR's program to alleviate these situations. The New Deal's opponents in Congress immediately accused the administration of using the Living Newspaper for its own purposes and charged that the Federal Theater was Communist-controlled. There no doubt were Communists among the theatrical workers as everywhere else in those days. The Congressional opposition pounced even more furiously on Marc Blitzstein's *The Cradle Will Rock,* an opera that was undeniably left-wing, which forced its director-producers, Orson Welles and John Houseman, to sever the Blitzstein production from the Federal Theater and launch their own Mercury Theater. The captious elements in Congress were displeased with the entire Federal Theater, regarding its wonderful demonstration of American pluralism in supporting Yiddish, Italian, and Spanish-language theater as "mere boondoggling" and branding as "rank Communism" the dramatization of Sinclair Lewis' novel *It Can't Happen Here,* which depicted the coming of fascism to America, a high probability at that time. Simultaneously staged in twenty-one theaters and seventeen states, it piled up the equivalent of a 260 weeks' run.

It is not here suggested that Jews alone created the American theater of the nineteen-thirties, but that their participation was substantial and their ethnic influence enduring.

The centerpiece of the Jewish contribution in the nineteen-thirties is the Group Theater, although its cast by no means was all Jewish. Stella and Luther Adler, from a great Yiddish theatrical dynasty, began their careers as child actors on the Yiddish stage. Harold Clurman, The Group's co-founder and director, mentioned briefly, in his *Fervent Years* that the first play he ever saw as a child was when his father, a Lower East Side doctor and an aficionado, took him to the Yiddish theater. Joseph Buloff, who came to Broadway and Hollywood from a Yiddish theatrical career that began in the early nineteen-twenties, maintains otherwise. He states with some acerbity: "Clurman, Odets, Kazan, Paul Mann, all hung around our Yiddish theater. Luther and Stella Adler and Morris Carnovsky acknowledge this influence." [6] Buloff's reference apparently is to the Yiddish Art Theater. Clurman makes a brief reference to another Yiddish theater, Artef, which he simply describes as "esoteric" and lists it among the labor stages that helped the "progress of the revolutionary drama in New York." Artef surely merits lengthier comment.[7]

The Group's hallmark was plays of "social significance" and direction based on Konstantin Stanislavski's brand of stage realism. From this Lee Strasberg, one of The Group's directors, evolved The Method. Stanislavski's new realism was unveiled in a new and amended version, in 1926 when Habimah, the Hebrew Theater, then of Moscow, toured the United States. Habimah was trained and directed, on Stanislavski's recommendation, by his favorite pupil, Yevgeni Vakhtangov, an Armenian. Stanislavski's emphasis was on the plastic, on gesture, on stance, on continual interplay with the ensemble. He stressed improvisation under controlled conditions, paradoxically as that might seem, and warned his actors that timidity and arrogance were equally reprehensible and intolerable. Not even for a fleeting instance must an actor behave as if he were the focus of undeflected attention, nor even in a mute walk-on role or as part of a mob scene believe himself superfluous, for he is at all times part of a fluid mural. Vakhtangov added an allegorical dimension to the new realism and, lest improvisation descend into stage rivalry, he imposed a firm stylization.

Artef, which is an abbreviation of Arbeter Theater Farband (Workers Theater Organization), was founded in December 1925 as an actors' studio. Its first enrollees were factory workers who had had some experience as performers and entertainers at the left-wing Yiddish summer camp, Nitgedaiget. Its announced goal was the establishment of "a theater of social significance." Its chief sponsor, The Morning Freiheit, intended it to become an agitprop (agitation-propaganda) theater, of the kind then popular in Germany and the U.S.S.R.[8]

[6] Lifson, op. cit., p. 501.
[7] Op. cit.
[8] There was constant strife between its directors and the Communist Party commissars who insisted on agitprop. Whenever the latter prevailed, box office results were disastrous. Even the most dedicated left-wingers could distinguish between drama of social significance and rank propaganda.

Artef enlisted the services of Benno Schneider, a member of Habimah who stayed behind at the completion of its American tour. Immediately after it presented its first play in 1927, word spread around Second Avenue, Greenwich Village, and Broadway about this Yiddish theater director who had worked miracles with shopworkers, few of whom had had previous acting experience. The Artef studio became the focus of aspiring young actors, Jews and non-Jews. It offered courses in Yiddish to those who did not know the language and wished to be trained by Schneider.

Artef's performances became the "in" thing. Its audience represented a wide spectrum—interfaith and interracial, it was composed of zealots of the political left, followers of the avant garde in the arts, unkempt Greenwich Villagers, and Park Avenue culture-slummers in minks and tuxedos. Its style was primarily Vakhtangov, yet eclectic, with a touch of Brecht, agitprop, and undistilled Stanislavski. It prepared an audience for The Group, which was to make its uncertain debut in 1931, four years after Artef's first premiere. Under Benno Schneider's direction, Artef demonstrated to Second Avenue and Broadway that the star system was an impediment and that the best performance is obtainable through a true application of the ensemble concept. Focusing on the total environment, he treated scenic design as if it had a performing role, and placed even the least important performer within a tight choreographic pattern that made each moment indispensable to the whole. There was something of the Hassidic fraternity about his ensemble procedure—a vigorous, dynamic, faceless mass, yet each fragment separately visible, revolving about the director, who, like the rebbe, was a mythical presence, pervasive but invisible. This style corresponded to Yiddish fiction which is peopled by indefatigable and buffeted ordinary men and women, anti-heroes, whose dramatic significance and distinction is their profound likeness, not their individual differences.

It is inconceivable that The Group's directors with their penchant for Stanislavski and social drama and their familiarity with the Yiddish theater had been left so completely untouched by Artef in the four years preceding The Group's own first public appearance as to justify Clurman's condescending remark that Artef was merely another of the lesser labor stages of the period, essentially "esoteric," whose, perhaps, only claim to fame, he implies, was its adaptation for the Yiddish stage of Clifford Odets' *Awake and Sing*, which had made The Group's reputation.

Combining the authors of serious drama and lighter theatrical fare, musical comedy writers and play doctors, Jews writing for the American stage between the two world wars—and the list is by no means exhausted—included S. N. Behrman, Albert Bein, Moss Hart, Lillian Hellman, George S. Kaufman, Sidney Kingsley, Albert Maltz, Samson Raphaelson, Elmer Rice, Morris Ryskind, Irwin Shaw, John Howard Lawson, Sam and Bella Spewack, and John Wexley. Yet none of these had the impact of The Group's prodigious discovery, Clifford Odets.

He is of particular significance to students of Jewish cultural history in America. Most of the other Jewish playwrights dipped, from time to time, into Jewish subject matter. Odets produced a minor "human comedy" of the American Jewish middle class of the crucial nineteen-thirties.

This segment of humanity was the end result of a crisis begun in the shtetl in the mid-nineteenth century. Its manifestations were the revolt against rigid Orthodoxy, the emergence of proto-Zionist and Jewish Socialist movements, the involvement of Jews in the anti-Czarist revolutionary underground, the mass migration of Jews to America. It was as if the equivalent in Jewish life of the Reformation and the French Revolution had occurred simultaneously. It was, also, as if the Thirty Years' War had been projected into a half-century of warfare. Such were the effects of these crises on the Jewish psyche. In America, under the stress of immigrant adjustment to an industrialized and alien society, the effects were dangerously exacerbated.

From this ferment emerged the cast of characters that populates Odets' plays. Long before him, and speaking Yiddish, they strutted upon the Second Avenue stage. Their crises were recorded in the Yiddish literary novel, in the schundroman and in the *Forward's* "Bintel Brief" (advice to the troubled column). The domineering wife and mother, the male as a frustrated dreamer and ineffectual breadwinner, the aggressive worldly success who knows himself actually to be a failure, the disintegration of familial discipline and the demands of familial loyalty, were familiar themes to the Yiddish-speaking Jew. Julie Gordon in *Paradise Lost* is straight out of Sholem Aleichem—dying of sleeping sickness, scrupulously studying the financial pages of *The New York Times* and playing a continuous game of solitaire with the stock market by investing imaginary sums daily and next morning toting up his gains. Odets' sensitive ear for authentic speech prevented him from slipping into vulgar dialect and frequently endowed his dialogue with the quality of ingenuous song. He retrieved the Yiddish-English idiom from the Jewish comedian and placed it where it belongs, in the succession to Sholem Aleichem's Yiddish-Hebrew idiom, *Fiddler on the Roof* being one of the most recent examples of this influence.

Pseudo-Marxist jargon, the fashion of the day, mars almost all his plays. *Paradise Lost* is among the least tainted, but Harold Clurman's introduction to *Six Plays by Clifford Odets* [9] reads like a parody of Marxist criticism. "But consider Julie Gordon," Clurman writes, "who dreams of making fortunes in the stock market while stricken with sleeping sickness. Does he not represent an apparently normal capitalism that is dying without knowing it?" But may not Clurman's interpretation be exactly what Odets meant? Of course. Both were members of the Group Theater and the chances are they discussed the play at length, analyzing it in detail.

Jews invaded American literature even as they invaded the theater in the nineteen-thirties. Their numbers were impressive—Benjamin Appel, Nathan Asch, Edward Dahlberg, Daniel Fuchs, Michael Gold, Albert Halper, Meyer Levin, Samuel Ornitz, Henry Roth, Isidor Schneider, Nathanael West, are only some of a long list. All but West and Levin were in the tradition of so-called socialist realism applauded by *New Masses* critics, and all but West wrote, though not exclusively, fiction of Jewish life. Yet only a few of these writers of "social significance" themes are remembered today.

The reason is that conditions were not the same as in the theater. In the theater the Jew mediated between Continental and American drama and helped shape a stage of social significance. American fiction required no such mediation. It had long since completed its apprenticeship under the Russian, French, and British masters. It already had produced both minor masters and major innovators of its own. In the field of socially informed realism there was rich American precedent which included Mark Twain, Frank Norris, Stephen Crane, Theodore Dreiser, Sinclair Lewis, John Dos Passos, John Steinbeck, the early Erskine Caldwell, James T. Farrell, and this, too, is merely a partial list.[10]

Whatever its literary merits, the Jewish fiction produced by the writers of the nineteen-thirties has documentary significance. They seemed to break with the self-demeaning tendency to parody the immi-

[9] (New York: Modern Library, 1939.)
[10] Kazin, *op. cit.*

grant Jew for the readers' entertainment, or to plead his case and prove him deserving of America's trust. In the fiction of the nineteen-thirties he was cast in a new role, that of plaintiff, a victim of America's societal ills. Both Ludwig Lewisohn and Maurice Samuel, several years earlier, already had cast the Jew in the accuser's role, with this major difference, however. They had cast him against a background of nearly two millennia of Christian-Jewish relations. Proletarian fiction, on the other hand, prescribed for the Jew a considerably lesser role by narrowing the scene, confining it to America. The context was the class struggle with the Jew as only another of its victims. This placed Jewish proletarian literature curiously, after all, in the old tradition of pleading the Jew's merit. Mary Antin, of an earlier generation, argued the Jew's case with the Establishment; Gold, Ornitz, and Schneider pleaded for him with the anti-Establishment. Mary Antin pleaded for all Jews; they pleaded only for the proletarian segment and condemned all other kinds of Jews to the awful fate that is the just dessert of the members of the exploiting class. Thus the tendency of the earlier American Jewish fiction to parody the Jew was continued in proletarian fiction with the difference that the earlier fiction ridiculed the Jew as a clown and the proletarian denounced him as a villain. In Leslie Fielder's words, in Michael Gold's *Jews Without Money* ". . . the Rabbi, the landlord, the pawnbroker are treated as egregious villains, and Gold's portraits of them disconcertingly resemble both those of European Jew-baiters like Julius Streicher, and native American provincials like Thomas Wolfe." [11]

The truth is that Gold lacked the writer's requisite, powers of observation. He was astonishingly ignorant about the customs and mores of the immigrant environment in which he was raised. His *tzadik* (Hassidic rabbi) wears a frock coat and silk top hat (proscribed by Hassidim as hedonist garb); he does not know that a convert to Christianity would never be permitted interment in Jewish burial grounds; he described a widow and other mourners riding from a funeral straight to a restaurant to consume a meal of "sour cream, pot cheese and black bread, the Jewish funeral food." Jewish funeral food is eggs and ashes consumed at home immediately after the funeral. Gold's novel was written in accordance with ideological prescription. Hence the villain is a Zionist, Tammany Hall politician, and brothel landlord all rolled into one. The villain seems adapted from Asch's play "God of Vengeance," which was shown in New York, and barred by the censor,

[11] *Waiting for the End* (New York: Dell Publishing Co., 1965), p. 80.

several years before Gold's novel appeared. However, the difference between the two is that Gold's brothel landlord is a synagogue trustee, Asch's would be content if a synagogue accepted a Holy Scroll as a gift from him. It is an important difference.

Gold's and other fiction of this genre was mostly parody because the class struggle did not quite apply to the American Jewish community of the nineteen-thirties, then still largely East European immigrant. Yahudim bankers and Hungarian movie moguls comprised a thin layer of financial oligarchs who were almost not at all involved economically with the Jewish multitudes. The immigrants' own capitalists were really only small entrepreneurs, crumb-gatherers on the periphery of the American economy. Many were swept away by the Depression, others held on precariously to eroding investments—the landlord, for example, whose tenants' rents were in arrears because of unemployment, whose vacancy rate was rising, and who was threatened by the bank with foreclosure for falling behind in his mortgage payments. An immigrant society, in a state of flux, American Jewry had no fixed class divisions; its intramural relations were constantly shifting, its members bound more by their common immigrant tradition than divided by economic differences. It required an act of the imagination even for the well-to-do to divorce himself from its poverty, which had been an ineradicable experience sustained by demanding family relationships, by kin both here and abroad soliciting financial assistance or signatures on loans which the endorser would repay if the borrower failed to do so. Sholem Asch, the Yiddish writer, in *Uncle Moses*, a novel depicting the early struggle to unionize the garment industry, rightly described it not as a class, but as a family struggle with the unions winning out. Yet, by establishing a class division within the Jewish community, the proletarian writer was pushing the point of the Jews' similarity to other Americans, removing them from the domain of the mythical, liberating them from the dubious status of alien. He did this with an excessive zeal, rooted in ambivalence, which Fiedler traces to Stalinism, others to even earlier Communist attitudes, but whose true source is the parents of some of these writers.

The parents came away from the shtetl bristling with hate and rebellion. They reacted to its rigid Orthodox disciplines with an abiding contempt for religion and clergy. Zionists and Socialists alike concurred in the essential anti-Semitic myth about the alleged exploitative and immoral nature of the Jews' occupations, but blamed it on the system, with the Socialists contending that Socialism would restore the Jew to normalcy, Zionism contending that only in a state of his own could the Jew hope to choose his occupations freely, unimpeded by economic discrimination. The Socialists denounced Zionism as bourgeois deception and an instrument of imperialism. The cumulative effect of these prejudices was the negation of that complex of rituals, customs, convictions, and loyalties that constitute the Jewish ethnic personality. Thus the proletarian Jewish writer's readiness to jettison all ancestral culture and loyalties was often the result of early, parental conditioning. His eagerness to appear as an unqualified native American corresponded with a Communist policy in the nineteen-thirties, which had become so nativist that it required its Jewish functionaries to adopt *noms-de-guerre* that would suggest native ancestry. However, no burlesk comedian in baggy pants, checkered jacket with crazy-quilt patches, and brown derby, could be funnier than the occasional round-shouldered, bespectacled youth, a stereotype for the anti-Semitic caricature of the radical Jewish student of the nineteen-thirties, who would turn up as the bearer of an Irish, Scottish, or old American name.

Not all, or perhaps not even most proletarian novels about Jews lacked compassion. Gold's *Jews Without Money* was more compassionate than Fiedler indicates. Albert Halper's Chicago novel *On the Shore*, balanced and warm, was not exactly tailored to the Marxist critics' cut. Meyer Levin, a principled Zionist, working in the same realistic tradition as the proletarian novelists, produced a rich canvas, *The Old Bunch*, a Chicago Jewish *Studs Lonigan*. He peopled his canvas with a rich variety of characters—politicians, businessmen, Communists, Zionists, Neo-Hassidim—but he was neither a caricaturist nor an ideologist, but a very punctilious reporter. Having spent some time in a kibbutz he was also the author of *Yehuda*, perhaps the first novel of kibbutz life in any language.

Remotely related to the proletarian novel were Jerome Weidman's *I Can Get It for You Wholesale* and Budd Schulberg's *What Makes Sammy Run?*. Their true prototype was Ben Hecht's novel *A Jew in Love*, and the master they looked up to was the Sinclair Lewis of *Main Street* and *Babbitt*. They were also, perhaps unknowingly, in a sound Jewish tradition. Satire has been the hallmark of Yiddish and Hebrew literature since the mid-nineteenth century. Jewish tradition treats the Hebrew alphabet as sacred, and consequently has endowed Jewish literature with a didactic function. The Yiddish literary novel and the serialized schundroman preceded Weidman in satirizing the garment industry's cut-throat mores, and Schulberg's Hollywood was merely an extension of the garment center. However, Yiddish fiction, even in its most satirical aspects, had perspective, whereas the early Weidman and Schulberg characters were garish and flat. It was the difference between portraiture and caricature. Concerned critics in the Yiddish and English-language Jewish press had another objection to this fiction. The time was inauspicious for Jewish candor. The Jews were too vulnerable. In the *bierstube* (taverns) of German neighborhoods, in guttural German Kleinbürger accents, and in the beam-ceilinged, panelled rooms of the private clubs where America's plutocracy gathered, in the polished accents of the Ivy League, there was constant talk about the Jews, and the jargon in use was identical. The myths and semantics were supplied from Berlin by Goebbels' Ministry of Propaganda: The Franklin Delano Roosevelts were really a Jewish family named Rosenfelt, the New Deal was a "Jew Deal" manipulated by an international Jewish-Bolshevik conspiracy as outlined in *The Protocols of Zion*. Ezra Pound, deeply concerned about the "Jewish plot," began an extensive correspondence with bearded, brown-shirted William Dudley Pelley who doubled as spiritualist and "con-man" to wealthy widows, besides being commander of the Silver Shirts, a para-military anti-Jewish and anti-Negro organization. Theodore Dreiser, not deterred by the Communist Party membership card in his wallet, warned that "left to sheer liberalism" the Jews "could possess America by sheer number" and "really overrun the land." [12]

The danger seemed to be closing in on American Jewry. Ludwig Lewisohn, whose past contributions to the American literary intelligence went unchallenged, but whose Zionist conversion gave him the reputation of a crackpot, was the first to sound the alarm in an article in *The Nation* [13] in which he proposed that the one dignified Jewish response to the rise of Nazism was a return to Jewish religious custom and Hebrew culture, and the reestablishment of a sovereign Jewish state in Palestine. "This German persecution," he wrote, "is the first major persecution in which the persecuted have sold out spiritually to their oppressors at the latter's invitation and command. They [the German Jews] have eviscerated themselves; they have for generations extruded from their consciousness all Jewish content and from their political and moral lives all Jewish bindings. They are in fact today as Germanized as it is possible for them to be and have nothing within them with which to bear their Jewish fate. Can anyone conceive of a more cruel confusion and of a more hideous dilemma?" He cited "the

[12] *The Nation*, April 17, 1935—a reproduction of the 1933 correspondence between Dreiser and Hutchins Hapgood.
[13] May 3, 1933.

terrible *Centralverein* [14] which whines: 'With dignity and courage we shall know how to bear upon the soil of our homeland the measures inflicted by Germans upon Germans.' "

On May 14, *The Nation* began publishing rejoinders to Lewisohn, generally diatribes from Jews who counterposed their cosmopolitanism to his "chauvinism." Elmer Rice, replying in white fury, was typical. "Mr. Lewisohn's Judaism is as unthinking and as destructive as Hitler's Teutonism," he wrote, and "his diatribe against Hitlerism . . . matches in emotional abandon the utterances of Hitler himself."

Rice's prophecies compared to Lewisohn's make macabre reading today.

"On the whole the position of the Jew throughout the world today is better than it has ever been," the playwright wrote in May 1933, after Hitler had already seized full power. "True, anti-Semitism exists everywhere, but it is progressively diminishing and will continue to diminish in exact ratio to the Jew's adaptation to his environment." He thus put the onus on the Jew himself.

Retrospectively, his predictions about Zionism provide high entertainment. "After all," Rice wrote, "it is some two thousand years since Jerusalem fell. As well try to recapture its somewhat dubious glories as to rebuild and re-animate the Parthenon." This was followed by the argument that "Mr. Lewisohn's Zionism is a utopian fantasy, as anyone can determine for himself by trying to find a common denominator for Einstein, Otto H. Kahn, a Rumanian rabbi, Benny Leonard, a Leon Trotsky, George Jean Nathan, Gyp the Blood, Lord Reading, a town beggar in the Atlas Mountains, Max D. Steuer, a Bronx sweatshop worker, and Fannie Brice."

Waldo Frank characteristically offered a wonderfully irrelevant exhortation, warning that ". . . if the Jew is to survive as an organic group he must enact his modern prophets as his father (after rejecting them also) enacted the Prophets of Scriptures." This requires, he explained, that they embrace Karl Marx "who carries on Moses and Ezra, (and) Spinoza who carries on Isaiah and Jesus." He apparently forgot that even Jesus had not been embraced by the Jews.

However, the debate was not long confined to Jewish writers and the liberal journals. It flared up in religious periodicals, mass circulation magazines, and the halls of Congress. America took notice of the Jew. Some Jews felt that it was better to be cast in a controversial role, than as a clown or not to be noticed at all. Most Jews shuddered, however.

[14] *Centralverein Deutscher Staatsburger Judischen Glaubens* (Central Organization of German Citizens of the Jewish Faith.)

CHAPTER 4

Many Kinds of Jews

A TOTAL of some 111,000 refugees from Nazism entered the United States between March 1933 when Hitler received a majority of the German vote, and December 7, 1941 when the Japanese attack on Pearl Harbor plunged America into World War II. This admission rate of less than 16,000 a year was absurdly disproportionate to the magnitude of the human displacement caused by the German persecutions, and to the total population of the United States, or even of New York City. Even this relatively minute number was not all Jewish and was opposed by principled immigration restrictionists as well as by bigots of all kinds, and by non-interventionists and pro-Nazis who feared that the mere presence of these refugees would bear stirring witness and create strong feeling in America against Berlin.

The refugees fell into two categories: those who came before September 1939 were from Germany and Austria mainly; those after that date, arriving by the Far Eastern overland route and across the Pacific, were mostly East Europeans. There were also some who came across the mined waters of the Atlantic. The overwhelming majority in both categories were Jews. But there were also some Christians among them, and those who were Jews only by Nazi definition, which was based on the premise that it required three generations of untainted Christian birth before miscegenated blood could be purged of its Jewish impurities. Those who came after the outbreak of the world conflict were an unusually mixed group. They ranged from ultra-Orthodox deans of the East European yeshivot who fled with their brightest pupils and hoped to transplant their Torah, as Jews had done for two thousand years, to new and safer ground; to sophisticated cosmopolitan Jews, barely aware of their Jewishness, not really refugees, only temporary expatriates from Nazi occupied Europe, serving with the missions here of governments-in-exile or with the Office of War Information and the American intelligence services.

The refugees from Germany who trickled in during the nineteen-thirties were distinctive beyond their numbers because of the agitation in this country against their admittance, the Jewish community's pre-occupation with their welfare, their geographic concentration and their retention of a German way of life. Unlike the East Europeans even whose intelligentsia had been largely self-taught, more than half of the German refugees had graduated from a gymnasium which, in terms of its curriculum, is the equivalent of an Ivy League junior college, and one out of five had attended a university. Albeit they never quite lost their guttural German accent, most had come here with some knowledge of English, acquired as youngsters at school or by cramming while waiting for their travel papers. Helped by their German and knowledge of Latin, they qualified, immediately on arrival here, not for elementary, but intermediate and advanced courses in English. They supplemented this with intensive study at home, poring over dictionaries, thesauruses and vocabulary builders, mumbling words to themselves wherever they went and checking against lists they carried in their pocket.

Fifty-two percent of them settled on New York's West Side. The area bounded on the south by Seventy-second Street, just one block below the baroque Hotel Ansonia which has been so richly described by Saul Bellow, in *Seize the Day,* and on the north by Fort Tryon Park and its Cloisters. The area was soon nicknamed The Fourth Reich. There were two reasons for their concentration in the area: the avail-ability of accommodations, and the character of the neighborhood.

The personnel of the Jewish agencies that rented these quarters for them and provided for their needs were descendants of East European immigrants. In their youth, many had themselves lived on the Lower East Side where their parents and grandparents began their American "careers." They felt somehow that the German Jewish refugees, who had only yesterday been members of the middle and upper middle-class, and pompously conscious of their university degrees and former place in the social hierarchy could not be asked to begin the way the immigrant from the shtetlach had begun. The West Side had the kind of cultural facilities—universities and libraries—to which these people had been accustomed, and Riverside Drive, West End Avenue and Central Park West had the elegance of Continental metropolises. The building boom of the nineteen-twenties had thrown up in that area many new edifices with large, and by the standards of that day, high-rental apartments. During the Depression, young couples postponed having children, spacing them better so that families were smaller. Few people could afford or even required such spacious accommodations. Landlords adjusted to the new situation by splitting up six and seven room apartments into "efficiencies" or converting entire buildings, including brownstones purchased from banks on foreclosures, into so-called residential hotels with furnished single and double rooms and community kitchens. The quarters were cramped and the community kitchens, which have since been outlawed, often provoked petty quarrels. But "the district" was right, the refugees' status had been preserved. These kinds of accommodations were concentrated in the area below Morningside Heights and Columbia University, and were occupied by newlyweds with no children, elderly couples, and the unmarried. Those with families moved further north to Washington Heights where "efficiencies" were fewer and rentals somewhat lower.

Eventually, within a decade or so, Negroes and Puerto Ricans on welfare replaced most of the refugees who followed their children to Queens, which was just then beginning to develop. The younger immigrants moved first into Elmhurst, then to Jackson Heights and Forest Hills, assimilated quickly to their environment, and left no distinctive Continental impress on those sections.

Their parents, however, were different, and the Fourth Reich was more than a nickname, it was a visible physical presence on the Upper West Side and Washington Heights throughout the nineteen-thirties and nineteen-forties. Almost immediately upon their arrival, specialty bakery shops were opened, then cafés and cabarets. Sauerbraten, kuchen, and pastries with *schlagsahne* (whipped cream) had always been available in German neighborhood shops throughout the nation. The Jewish refugees lifted these goods, however, out of their provincial setting, endowed them with Continental glamour and raised them to national prominence. The East Europeans' cuisine of bagel, knishes, borscht, and pastrami had taken several decades, from the Lower East Side via the Catskills, Lindy's, and Miami Beach, to achieve similar recognition. The specialty bakery shops have remained a feature of New York life, although located now primarily on the fashionable East Side and in the suburbs, with only a residual few clinging to the West Side whose economic, social, and racial complexion has undergone a drastic transformation, which the high-rental Lincoln Center residential housing may again be reversing.

The cafés and cabarets were less fortunate. The cabarets were the first to meet with disaster. They featured political satire on events in *die Heimat* and personalities of the refugee colony, Viennese waltzes and other elements of *Heimweh*. Few refugees in those early days could afford an evening at the cabaret, and for Americans most of the satire was parochial and obscure. The cabarets that have survived bear no real resemblance to their prototypes.

The cafés functioned in the Continental style. European-trained waiters scraped before the stamgast (regular) as he read newspapers, played on chess sets provided by the house, and negotiated his business deals. Whether he ordered a full meal or only pastry and coffee did not really matter to the waiters, provided the stamgast had a steady stream of visitors at his table who, however small their orders, left tips. Men congregated in these cafés in the mornings until noon; women, for gossip, in the afternoons, and family groups in the evenings. Americans who dropped in occasionally for "Continental atmosphere," were almost the only ones who could then afford to have meals there, and since cafés in America cannot survive on coffee and pastry alone, only three have endured—The Eclair on West Seventy-second Street, Rumpelmeyer's, and the Café de la Paix on Central Park South.

The closing of the cafés again disrupted the emigrés' daily rhythm. The men faced empty mornings, deprived of free newspapers and office space, the women—long afternoons with nothing to do and nowhere to go. Eventually the now twice-displaced refugees discovered a melancholy substitute, the neighborhood cafeteria, its floors strewn with paper cups and napkins, its chromium table tops swept with filthy wet rags by sullen busboys, and, parked in the narrow aisles between the tables, carts laden with food leavings and dirty dishes.

Except during the peak lunch and dinner hours, with their brisk, noisy customer turnover, these cafeterias were sparsely inhabited by a motley crowd of human rejects—shriveled, tight-lipped men in loud clothes who pursued their fortunes in the close-printed columns of *The Morning Telegraph* and *Racing Form,* and bedraggled retired veterans of half a dozen radical causes and the Union Square debates of the nineteen-twenties, who still cultivated their appearance so that they might resemble leaders whose faces and names almost everyone else had forgotten. The gamblers and the superannuated rebels sat for hours here, unmolested, chain-smoking, coughing, staring blankly into space.

The refugees soon outnumbered them—men and women of shabby elegance and formal manner, overfleshed females with dramatic makeup and studied coyness, and courtly males who removed their hats in a wide arc when greeting acquaintances and bent forward from the waist to kiss ladies' fingertips and compliment them outrageously.

They took respite, several times a week, from the bland cafeteria fare by going to unlicensed restaurants operated by fellow refugees in their apartments. These limited themselves to a dozen or so customers, friends and friends of friends, and they served blutwurst and cabbage, sauerbraten and potato dumplings, and kuchen washed down with *spritz*, soda with a dash of wine. Theirs was the furtive, nervous air of gambling joints, and of speakeasies of the preceding decade. Always expecting to be raided, the proprietors pretended, when they opened the door to a stranger, that this was a gathering of friends for a family feast. Meals were charged in the fashion of the Continental family restaurants. The overextension of credit to impecunious refugees, combined with complaints to the police and health authorities from inquisitive neighbors and restaurant workers unions, eventually forced these establishments to shut down. Some hard-pressed refugees ran pensions, or boarding houses in plain English: renting large apartments they would retain the least possible space for themselves and let out rooms with board, which was hard and demanding work, but entirely within the law.

The pathos of the refugees' cultural and economic adjustments was reflected in the advertising columns of *Aufbau*, a weekly paper serving the refugees, which was established by Dr. Manfred Georg, a refugee himself and one of Germany's foremost newspaper editors before Hitler came to power. A *hausfrau* offered, those being Depression years, a home-cooked meal and "kuchen to take home" for an evening of conversational English; someone else, lessons in German for the gift of a typewriter, and a collection of classical records for instruction in cabinet making. The most pathetic kind read something like this: "Woman in her fifties, sleep-in housekeeper, governess, psychology degrees from Göttingen and Sorbonne, unaccented English," the last to reassure parents that their children would not acquire accented English while learning French.

Yet the Fourth Reich led a rich cultural life, perhaps more cosmopolitan than that of any other neighborhood in the United States. In those days, one might suddenly come face to face with near-mythical European celebrities almost anywhere on the Upper West Side. There were the intellectual best-selling German and Austrian authors, Franz Werfel, Stefan Zweig, Lion Feuchtwanger and Emil Ludwig, the Dumas of biographers, now virtually forgotten. There were, from the theater—Max Reinhardt, Erwin Piscator, Kurt Eisler, Kurt Weill, and Ernst Toller, playwright, poet and pamphleteer, who, in his early twenties at the end of World War I, had been leader of a short-lived revolutionary government in Bavaria. From Vienna came Richard Beer Hoffmann, poet, playwright, Hebrew sage, and Dr. Theodor Reik, psychoanalyst, one of the earliest acolytes of the Freudian church who, like the composer Weill, also launched in America what amounted to a second career. Of the above list, Piscator alone was not Jewish. The fastidious Zweig and the highly charged Toller later took their lives. Weill, Werfel, and Reinhardt produced *The Eternal Road,* a tribute to Jewry's long travail.

No prominent German refugee could deny himself to the Fourth Reich even if he resided on the West Coast, visited New York City sporadically and, like Werfel, always kept aloof from emigré politics, or, like Thomas Mann, most of the time. Occasionally, everyone of them felt the need to meet a German audience in the flesh, an opportunity which none but the Fourth Reich could provide. Its population included some of the most sensitive connoisseurs of art and literature in pre-Nazi Germany. It was one of the few German-inhabited "territories" on the globe that was beyond Nazi control, a visible counterpoise to the Yorkvilles across the nation, those portable Third Reichs, the "Munichs away from Munich," that were interminably engaged in calumniating the emigrant intellectuals and had always been concerned not with German culture, but with *Kultur,* that ethnic-schmaltz mixture of *bierstube* conviviality, songfests, German Day outings, parades to martial music, and the recital of classical verse memorized in their classrooms as children.

Even the half-Jews and Christians among the German scholars and scientists, luminaries but not celebrities, however useful they subsequently became to American science and scholarship, also obtained their initial assistance from Jewish agencies and Maecenas. The latter helped the New School for Social Research establish a University-in-Exile with a faculty of refugees. For Jews with strong positive feelings about their identity, the University's name had a poignant and ironic meaning. Jewish culture endured through the centuries largely because of its yeshivot, Talmudic seminaries, the prototypal universities in exile. Many of the refugee scholars in the past had bristled at the theological and Zionist views of the Jew as being in a permanent condition of "exile" from Jerusalem, yet until they applied for U.S. citizenship they saw no reason to protest their designation as "exiles" from Germany. The American Jewish lecture circuit, then in its early stages of development, favored Christian over Jewish refugees because the former could serve as living proof that Nazi crimes should concern not Jews alone but all Americans. Prince Hubertus von Löwenstein, a Catholic Centrist, was in great demand despite the handicap that, even to his Jewish audiences he "looked Jewish" despite impeccable Aryan antecedents.

The presence in this country of so many of their eminent culture heroes compensated the refugees for their sense of loss and foreignness. It cushioned their adjustment to the new environment, enabling them to pretend, even as they groped for places in American society, that their former status still obtained. They constituted a distinct enclave in the Jewish community, and this brought mutterings from American Jews that the refugees were clannish, self-centered, concerned about their own kind only—the classical, universal allegations against foreigners and minorities.

The irritation between the refugees from Germany and their American hosts was spiced by Old World animosity. Earlier in the century, this had led to tensions between the Yahudim and the immigrant Yidn in America. Now the roles were reversed, the Yidn were the hosts, the Germans were the immigrants. The latter brought with them their traditional supercilious attitude toward the *Ostjuden* whose language was "perverted German," whose Orthodoxy they labeled medieval. The East European in turn, perhaps still smarting from an inferiority complex, recalled that only several decades ago, on his way to America, he was treated by German Jews with curt hospitality as an undesirable to be rid of quickly.

The alleged rudeness and arrogance of the refugees became a conversational *pièce de résistance*. All generalizations are half truths. Solitary episodes were presented as the rule. Even Jewish physicians began passing hearsay tales about the German-Jewish refugee doctors' ruthless drive for promotion. The main sources of these tales, ironically, were immigration-restrictionists and pro-Nazis who also spread rumors that Jewish concerns discharged Christian American employees to provide jobs for refugee Jews. A study in 1941 revealed, however, that the reverse was true, that as a rule far from displacing anyone, the refugees created additional jobs for Americans. They owned or operated 239 new businesses in eighty-two cities and thirty-two states—thirty-two wholesale, jobber and export-import firms, 125 retail stores, eight restaurants, twelve farms, five hotels and sixty-two manufacturing concerns, including plants that produced optics, casings, and electronic equipment. Three-quarters of their working force was native American. Seventy-one of their enterprises each had an annual gross volume in excess of two million dollars. Physicians constituted only two and a half percent of all the refugees. America could have used many more as was demonstrated by the wartime doctors shortage.

Nothing could more effectively refute the allegation of their unconcern for other than German-Jewish affairs than their weekly *Aufbau* which, developing into perhaps the best international Jewish weekly, reported extensively and exhaustively on Jewish events both at home and abroad. It has since declined appreciably, although still an excellent publication, because of a progressive loss of readers. The younger generation has become completely assimilated within the larger American Jewish community, which makes it difficult to confirm, for that matter, the myth that the German-Jewish refugees have not contributed adequately to the Jewish philanthropies which facilitated their own rehabilitation. Their number was small to begin with, some 100,000, or less than two percent of the Jewish population in America at the time. A high percentage, especially among their intellectuals, were thoroughly assimilated and intermarried, and once recovered from the trauma of the Vaterland's rejection, relapsed into their old habit of unawareness of their Jewish antecedents. All had, in their initial years, one overriding passion, to reestablish themselves quickly and well in their new American *heimat*.

By the time they had acquired the socio-economic status that is a prerequisite for participation in American Jewish affairs, they joined their married children's exodus into the suburbs where the younger generation have simply blended with other American Jews of their age, do not conceive of themselves as separate and distinct and their involvement in the Jewish community therefore cannot be distinguished and labeled as German-Jewish, although their number appears to be considerable, relatively no less than that of the *Ostjuden*.

There can be no doubt, conversely, of the impact of the German-Jewish refugees on American culture generally. With them began that which we today call the American cultural explosion and the "brain drain" from Europe, except that in the nineteen-thirties Europe expelled these brains and America was reluctant to receive any but the most eminent, men like Einstein, Fermi, and Szillard, refugees from Germany, Italy, and Hungary respectively.

The war years brought many talented Jews to this country, exiles from countries overrun by the Germans, or members of the missions of free countries allied with the United States. Some returned home after the war, others remained here. They contributed immeasurably to America's sophistication about the arts, and to New York's emergence as not merely a city of skyscrapers, but one of the great metropolises of history. They included, from Poland, its two foremost poets, Josef Vitlin and Julian Tuvim; from Hungary—Ferenc Molnar, playwright; from France—André Maurois, novelist, biographer, social critic; Henri Bernstein, playwright; André Spier, poet, and the artists Marc Chagall, Jacques Lipchitz, and Manne Katz.

Second Avenue experienced another short season of its former glory as these refugees descended on the Café Royal with its long windows, panelled walls, and credenza, so reminiscent of the Continental cafés. There was visible hostility between its veteran habitués, the Yiddish writers, and the Polish emigrés. The assimilated Jew in Poland ingratiated himself with the Poles by repetitive acts of self-abasement, occasionally to the extent of joining in the national pastime of taunting the Jews. Yet the Jew in Poland was never permitted to forget the stigma of his origins, even if he converted to Catholicism, and had no peer as a master of the Polish language. Such Jews compensated by walking among fellow Jews with the haughty, supercilious air of pure Poles. The poets Tuvim and Vitlin recovered some pride in their origins during the war years in America when they set down in verse their horror over the gas chambers. Yet, they entered the Café Royal for the first time not as prodigal sons, or penitents, but with the condescending manner of patrons visiting their wards. They shriveled, therefore, when the Yiddish writers, many of them Polish-born, familiar with the sycophantic type and aware that Yiddish poetry could easily match Poland's best, treated them coldly.

The Yiddish and the Gallic Jewish writers had no particular affinity for each other, but there was no tension between them. Neither knew the other's language, and with the exception of André Spier, a Zionist, the French were indifferent Jews. However, a warm and intimate relationship sprang up immediately between the Yiddish literateurs and the Parisian Jewish sculptors and painters who really were East European Yiddish-speaking Jews, with a fierce loyalty to the shtetl. They illustrated Yiddish books without a fee—since Yiddish publishing is not a profitable venture and is generally financed from the author's own pocket—and if moved by a poem or short story would send the author an etching as a gift or offer to draw his portrait. They had their idiosyncrasies. Lipchitz revealed that like any Orthodox Jew he prefaced his workday by putting on his phylacteries, however, not for religious but for compulsive reasons. Chagall embarrassed the writers by soliciting their opinion of his Yiddish verse, awkward verbalizations of his magnificent canvases. He was delighted that they found literary merit in his wife Bella's Yiddish volume of childhood reminiscences. When the Chagalls sometimes were joined by Jacques Maritain, the Catholic philosopher and his wife, the Yiddish writers would feel uncomfortable. Mrs. Maritain was Bella's relative and a convert to Catholicism.[1]

None of the religious or other developments in the indigenous American Jewish community were of any concern, or even came to the attention of the cosmopolitan Jewish visitors and temporary residents who resided in a world eons removed from the middle class which constituted the identifiable Jewish community. Even the world Zionist leaders, Dr. Chaim Weizmann and David Ben-Gurion, were little concerned with its intramural affairs. They had a single overriding objective—to enlist American Jewry's maximum financial and political support for the enterprise in Palestine. American Zionist leaders, excepting the rabbis among them, were similarly oblivious to American Jewish affairs.

Perhaps the most significant developments were those in the religious field. The Reform rabbinate began moving from left field towards a middle ground, restoring some of the Jewish customs and traditions that their predecessors, Reform Judaism's founders, had scornfully discarded. In the Conservative movement, conversely, a vigorous minority took a leftward swing and demanded bold innovation and departure from "obsolescent tradition." The Orthodox, an island unto themselves, were trying to effect a situation that would have given them arbitrary control over Jewish religious affairs in America.

---

[1] Mrs. Maritain, a religious author in her own right, co-author of some of her husband's work, was a convert to Christianity and was a relative of Bella's. Another kin had married Karl Liebknecht, founder of the German Communist Party. All three were descended from a single mercantile family. Their respective grandfathers had been disciples of the rebbe of Lubavitch, or the Habad school of Hassidism, which is a kind of High Episcopalian Hassidism and has transformed a spontaneous people's movement into a formidable intellectual discipline that is reserved for the scholarly elite against whom Hassidism had initially rebelled. Habad or Lubavitch is really a counter-revolution, or counter-reformation, disguised in the plumage of the Hassidic revolution.

The founders of Reform Judaism, German-born or German-educated rabbis, had hoped that their successors in the pulpit some day would be the offspring of East European immigrants. Their dream was realized, but the young men of East European origin who entered the Reform pulpits resolutely set about altering the movement in their own image. The founders had deleted all references to the return to Zion from the prayer book and reduced the use of Hebrew to a minimum; the younger men went so far as endorsing political Zionism and restored Hebrew to greater prominence. They also reinstated candlelighting on Friday night, the use of the shofar (ram's horn) in the High Holiday services, and two minor holidays, previously deleted because of their patently "Zionist" character—Purim, commemorating Haman's abortive genocide plot against Persian Jewry, and Hannukah, which celebrates the Maccabeans' military victory over the Greco-Syrians. Two other holidays, too important to delete, had once been slighted by the Reform movement—The Feast of Tabernacles and Passover, both of which are related to that prototypal Zionist event, the Hebrews' exodus from Egypt and their wanderings in the desert. The younger men now restored some of the old dignity to the two feasts, and ordained that Passover be celebrated with communal seders in all Reform congregations.

The Conservative movement's rebels, all younger men, rallied around one of the revered elder members of the Jewish Theological Seminary faculty, Dr. Mordecai M. Kaplan, founder of the Reconstructionist movement which proposed to incorporate even secular Jewish culture, offered a theology stripped of the supernatural and described Judaism not as a religion, but a dynamic religious civilization. With two young collaborators, Rabbis Eugene Kohn and Ira Eisenstein, he offered, in 1941, a new *Haggadah* for the Passover service. A foreword explained, "We have retained the traditional framework, with its archaic charm, but we have filled it with living, compelling content of present-day idealism and aspiration. . . . Among the innovations are the inclusion of entirely new readings. . . . All references to events, real or imagined, in the Exodus story which might conflict with our own highest ethical standards have been omitted." Perhaps it was their implied ethical superiority to the anonymous editors of the ancient *Hagagah* that aroused their peers at the Jewish Theological Seminary, but some of its most distinguished faculty members signed a statement of rebuke which they presented to Kaplan.

In 1945, The Reconstructionists published their own Sabbath Prayer Book and hell broke loose. The new Prayer Book eliminated "all invidious contrast between Israel and other peoples"; taking "cognizance of the results of modern research into the Bible," it avoided "implying the historical accuracy of those Biblical episodes which relate of miracle and supernatural events"; although praying "no less earnestly for Israel's restoration and the coming of God's kingdom" it omitted however all "references to an individual Messiah"; it omitted prayers for the restoration of animal sacrifices and the hereditary priestly castes in a rebuilt Temple, and although subscribing to the belief "that righteousness is recompensed and sin punished," it rejected the suggestion that "the processes of meteorology are dependent on man's moral behavior," and while affirming "strong faith in the soul's immortality," it rejected "along with the thinking of most modern-minded religious people . . . the doctrine of corporeal resurrection."

Although its editors—Rabbis Kaplan, Eugene Kohn, Ira Eisenstein and Milton Steinberg—asserted that "the views . . . reflected in this Prayer Book commit only the Jewish Reconstructionist Foundation Inc., and no other institutions and organizations with which the editors are associated," the Orthodox made it a *casus belli* against the entire Conservative movement. That may be the reason why his peers on the faculty of the Jewish Theological Seminary who had protested the new Haggadah maintained a taciturn silence about Kaplan's audacity in assuming responsibility for reversing the collective work of many generations. Yet, any attack on Kaplan from Conservative ranks would only have brought comfort to the belligerent Orthodox.

The latter were determined on a Holy War. Reinforced by the deans of the European yeshivot (seminaries) who had arrived in the United States by way of the Pacific, just before Pearl Harbor, the Union of Orthodox Rabbis of the United States and Canada convened on June 12, 1945 to sit in judgment on The Reconstructionists Sabbath Book.

This tribunal met in public assembly. The setting was conventional—the ballroom of a midtown New York hotel with draped walls, carpeted floors, blind windows, chandeliers and mirrored double doors. The audience was a cross-section of New York's Orthodoxy—bearded men in caftans and in business suits and smooth-skinned young rabbis who used a kosher depilatory powder, instead of a blade, thus circumventing the biblical injunction against shaving. On the elevated dais sat the rabbinic elders, a formidable group with full beards and earlocks; with few exceptions, they were all in caftans, some, absentmindedly, fingered their little black velvet skullcaps which kept slipping off, others wore broadrimmed black velvet hats which gave them a stern magisterial appearance. The ancestors of these men of ancient learning and in-exorable faith have been immortalized in Rembrandt's canvases and had presided in his native city of Amsterdam at the heresy trial of one Baruch (Benedict) Spinoza, a contemporary of the painter and a lens polisher by trade.

Not all tribunal members had studied the evidence, the Reconstructionist *siddur* (prayer book). Determined, however, that none must tamper with the sacred word, they were content with the testimony of colleagues "who had exposed themselves to reading this contaminated matter." Their verdict was unanimous, as foreseen. They denounced the book as "blasphemous." The volume lay on the dais and someone in the audience stepped up and set a match to it. Then, in accordance with the provisions for a ceremony of excommunication (*cherem*), again recalling Spinoza, candles were lit for Kaplan as for a person deceased, and wrapped in their prayer shawls some rabbis intoned words that had been fateful in other centuries. They accused "this man Kaplan of repudiating the basic tenets of our faith" and demanded that "hereafter no soul in Israel shall traffic or communicate with him, and his name and presence shall be exorcised from the congregation of Israel." Several piercing notes on the shofar (ram's horn) sealed the verdict.

At the Jewish Theological Seminary, Conservative Judaism's citadel, there was apprehension that the ban against Kaplan might damage the Seminary, although it had not been consulted by him, and although his foreword dissociated it from responsibility for the siddur. Some of its faculty had found his revisions highly distasteful, and it was rumored that, in deference to the cherem, several avoided occasions that might bring them face to face with Kaplan, and passing him in the Seminary's corridors they merely nodded, but did not stop to shake hands or converse. A stenographer at the Reconstructionist Foundation, an Orthodox girl, resigned rather than take dictation from an excom-municant.

Yet, it soon became apparent that very few, and these men of no communal consequence, took the cherem seriously. It seemed that the Orthodox rabbinate itself regretted having submitted its authority to so severe a test. The rabbis who had presided at the ceremony were now evasive when questioned whether their edict was provisional, hence a mere warning, or permanent and irrevocable until the ex-communicant, besides repenting, submitted to a humiliating public recantation.

The European deans experienced a shock. In Europe their word had been holy writ to the Orthodox but American Orthodoxy, they learned, was less cohesive and rigid, and many conducted themselves like Reform Jews although paying dues to Orthodox synagogues for sentimental reasons such as their parents having belonged there.

This was the second time in less than a decade that American Orthodoxy had tried and failed to force compliance with its writ. The first time was in 1936–7. It then involved the exposure of racketeer control of the kosher poultry industry, protracted litigation in the New York State Supreme Court before an Irish judge, and intervention by Mayor Fiorello LaGuardia, "the Little Flower," a man of mixed ethnic and religious origins, an Episcopalian Italian with some Jewish blood. It all began when some unemployed *shochtim* (kosher slaughterers) charged that the union was racketeer-dominated and that it prevented their employment in the closed-shop poultry markets by refusing to enroll them as members. The union's contention that there was not enough work even for its present membership, was met with the charge that there would be enough for everyone if the speed-up system were discontinued; its effects are in violation of rabbinic regulations, so that much of the ostensibly kosher poultry sold in New York was not kosher at all.

LaGuardia summoned both sides to a hearing at City Hall. First, however, he called in several Yiddish newspapermen who waited with the shochtim in an anteroom. Pouting with his cupid mouth, and purring, castigating, and snapping in a high falsetto voice into intercoms and telephones, he disposed of an untold number of matters before turning his full attention to the newsmen. He wanted to know how a speed-up system could make poultry unkosher, and was told that to assure a fowl's quick death the blade must be sharp, without dent; the *shochet* is, therefore, required to rinse it after each operation and to test it frequently against an overgrown fingernail. This may not be possible under the speed-up, and it may well be that blunted or dented blades are used, making the fowl unkosher. The mayor then requested "technical terms connected with this." The reporters told him that a blade was called "*chalef*," a dent was called "*pgam*." The two words were spelled out for him, he wrote them down and repeated them aloud several times. Then he asked that the two delegations, the union and the unemployed, be shown in. They entered and stood apart. When he called for the union spokesman, a bearded elder stepped forward. "I don't mean you, pop," he snapped. "You're a stooge. Where is the punk who runs your union?" He then asked each one in the union group to produce his chalef, and looking like a battened sacrificial lamb among the unsheathed blades, he reached out for several at random, passed them across a fingernail and ruled that, "There are more dents in each of these then there are needles on a porcupine." Promising a thorough investigation, he abruptly dismissed both delegations. Outside the mayor's chambers, each of the union shochtim tested his chalef again and again, anxiously soliciting the opinions of colleagues. Their blades seemed in good condition, but the mayor's apparent and belligerent knowledgeability rattled the men badly.

The racketeers resigned under City Hall fire. The union's rolls were opened to new members. The Union of Orthodox Rabbis, a national organization, and the New York City Board of Orthodox Rabbis, moved in to capitalize on the turmoil. They formed, jointly with prominent laymen, a Kashrut Association which proposed, for a service charge of one cent per fowl, to place all poultry slaughter houses under central rabbinical supervision with full-time supervisory personnel posted in each. The revenue would suffice, the Association explained, to pay the salaries and all other costs involved and provide a reserve for Orthodox Jewish educational institutions. A tin tag attached to each fowl would attest that it was kosher, and, had the plan worked, would have implied that untagged poultry, albeit rabbinically supervised, was not kosher.

Some markets charged that this would eventually prove more costly than calculated and would increase the price to consumers. What they really objected to, as did some of the shochtim, was a supervision that might become arbitrary. The plan would also have placed at the Orthodox Establishment's disposal funds it could dispense as it wished, denying them to institutions that incurred its disfavor. In full control of employment in the markets, the Establishment would have been able to penalize rabbis who opposed it.

Markets that refused to sign up with the Association filed a suit in the New York State Supreme Court charging restraint of trade. Learned rabbis testified for both sides. Special interpreters were enlisted to put the convoluted Yiddish-Hebrew arguments over rabbinic jurisprudence into intelligible English for the Irish judge who, in addition, was assisted by his law secretary, an ordained rabbi.

Interrupted by long recesses, the trial dragged on for months. The Kashrut Association already was in its terminal stage when the judge handed down his ruling in its favor. Few housewives had looked for the tag; most had never even heard of it, some recalled vaguely that it figured in an intramural rabbinical struggle. The average housewife assumed that a rabbi's certificate in the window was a guarantee that an establishment was kosher, and, if such certificate was lacking, was content with the seller's oral assurance. The consumer, furthermore, was protected by a New York state law, predating the Kashrut Association, which classifies as fraud any misrepresentation in the sale of kosher products. The state payroll carries inspectors assigned to supervise this law's enforcement.

Seeing the depressing spiritual state of American Jewry, the European deans decided on a new course: they would not address themselves to the inattentive multitudes, but concentrate on creating an elite. They went about the task with astonishing executive and sales ability, acquiring buildings in small towns—Lakewood in New Jersey, Spring Valley, New York, and similar locations in the Middle West—where they set up yeshivot that were transplants from a vanished East European shtetl. Here they assembled the "rescued remnants," disciples they had brought out of Europe, and also young American-born zealots. They persuaded philanthropists, who themselves were anything but Orthodox, to set up endowment funds so that the young scholars could devote themselves to the Torah, free of mundane concerns, and, if they married, their families would be provided for, as well. There are such Torah "fortresses" across the country, manned by several thousand scholars.

Perhaps the most eminent of the wartime Orthodox emigrés was the Lubavitcher Rebbe. Martyrdom was a family tradition. The founder of the Lubavitcher or Habad dynasty lived at the time of the Napoleonic wars and had been jailed for alleged subversion against the Czar. The Rebbe who came to America in 1941 had been jailed for alleged subversion against the Soviet State. Released for ransom paid by American disciples, he was stranded in Warsaw when the Polish capital was turned into an inferno by Nazi incendiary bombs. He survived and was brought to America where thousands greeted him on arrival. Few were prepared for his condition. He was in a wheel chair, his speech indistinct, his tall fur hat underscoring the rigidity of his paralytic stare. However, his mind was lucid, his will firm. He set up headquarters on Eastern Parkway in Brooklyn, then an elegant neighborhood, now deteriorating, and with a secretary at his side, who had a degree from

Oxford, and an energetic son-in-law who acted as his Foreign and Finance Minister, soliciting funds, corraling supporters, forming an apparatus, the Rebbe soon presided over a countrywide network of study circles, seminars, and day schools. He added books and periodicals in English to his Yiddish and Hebrew publications, and sent English-speaking emissaries across the country to enlist "converts" among Jews, especially on the campuses. The emissaries piqued people's curiosity sometimes with their argumentation, sometimes with a Hassidic *nigun* (melody), and occasionally were able to report back a real conversion, as for example, that a hitherto total unbeliever had pledged hereafter to put on phylacteries every morning. Each one of these missionaries reputedly carried several sets of phylacteries in preparation for precisely such occasions.

A relative of this great charismatic sectarian cut a figure in his own right among the cosmopolitans then in New York and Washington. Whoever saw them both was struck by the family resemblance. Isaiah Berlin, the younger man by several decades, was then frequently seen in the company of Dr. Chaim Weizmann, and like the older man was a sensualist in the broader meaning, delighting in food, places, people, ideas, his face extremely mobile, his eyes settling with curiosity on everything in his line of vision. Reticent in Weizmann's company, he was otherwise a passionate conversationalist, a brilliant raconteur. His parents brought him to London from Latvia when he was fifteen, and he soon acquired an Oxonian accent so indigenous that it sounded very nearly unintelligible. Like Weizmann, he has a firm grasp of several languages, and has even received instruction in the Talmud although not to the same extent. He had an undefined diplomatic mission, reporting directly to Churchill, and shuttling across the United States made friends among all strata—scientists, writers, artists, politicians, members of exiled governments, leaders of American ethnic minorities—low-browed, tight-lipped Ukrainians, loquacious, mercurial Poles, relentless Stalinists, unyielding Mensheviks. Some knew him even then as the author of a slim, brilliant volume on Marx, as an authority on nineteenth-century Russian thought, and as an Oxford don accomplished in both philosophy and political science and torn between the two. Perhaps none, except men of Weizmann's circle, knew him to be of the family of one of the awesome figures in Hassidism.

CHAPTER 5

America Without Compass

THE MISFORTUNE of the Jewish people, with horrendous consequences in the very next decade, was the mediocrity of the American Jewish leaders in the nineteen-thirties. Their ordinariness contrasted sharply with the brilliance of their peers, also sons and grandsons of East European immigrant Jews, who flocked to Washington to serve in F.D.R.'s New Deal and to Detroit to join the commandos of the CIO under Philip Murray and Walter Reuther.

The Depression had been a great leveler, striking indiscriminately at old and new Americans alike, sparing no religious denomination, no ethnic group, no special accent, and yes, not even the Boston Brahmin. The New Deal was another great leveler. It scoured the country for young men and women with intellectual audacity and the capacity to apply it to the poignant economic and social problems of an America in ferment. They were appointed to the staffs of the many alphabet agencies spawned by the New Deal, and a sampling of these talented young people was reluctantly accepted even by the fastidious State Department which, to paraphrase Amy Lowell's poem, was, and to a large extent still is, "a rare pattern . . . no softness anywhere . . . only whale-bone and brocade."

Some of these young Jews came from Harvard, Princeton, and Yale where their percentage had been kept deliberately low, and were generally of the German-Jewish upper middle-class. But they shared the social passion of another kind of Jew who also was appointed to these Washington posts, that of the lower middle-class and the proletariat, "the sturdy, unkillable infants of the . . . poor," graduates of the University of Chicago, which had then embarked on a bold career under

Robert C. Hutchins, President of the University, and from New York's City College whose exciting students could simultaneously riot for causes, carry off academic honors, and persevere brilliantly even if forced to hold down a full-time job and attend CCNY at night. They carried recommendations from professors and deans, from Helen Hull, dean of American settlement-house workers, and Samuel Rosenman, jurist and one of F.D.R.'s closest advisers, from Sidney Hillman and David Dubinsky. Theirs had been a rich and diversified apprenticeship, which included law clerkships under eminent jurists, blue-collar work on the assemblyline, and arrests and beatings for talking union to workers in company towns. Some were callow, bookprint still on the tips of their noses, and pledged to put their professors' untested theories into practice. Others had emerged from long wrestling bouts with the most formidable radical theories of our times, with a cynical appraisal of *homo sapiens*, yet, nonetheless, determined to prove themselves wrong. All rapidly became pragmatists who judged the validity of ideas by their workability.

They teamed up in Washington with Lutherans, Methodists, Congregationalists, and Catholics; with middle-aged veterans of Theodore Roosevelt's Bull Moose movement of 1912, Farmer-Laborites, and the descendants of German Socialists who fled here after the abortive liberal revolutions of 1848; and with Scandinavian champions of farmer-cooperatives, Midwestern Populists, Wobblies, and Irish rebels. For many of the young Jews this was their first encounter with Americans of other faiths in a close day-to-day working relationship. This was also the first encounter of the others with Jews. Alarming rumors sped through all the exclusive clubs. Washington society shuddered as the "barbarians" from New York City, Madison, and Minnesota invaded its salons.

These brilliant young Jews were engaged in the great enterprise of altering American society. The American Jewish Establishment at best could offer them no comparable challenge. They saw Nazism not as a threat particularly to the Jews, but to the world, to be treated not parochially but at the root, by striking at all gross social and economic inequity.

Zionism was remote and irrelevant, its social ideals and laboratory experiments obscured by the groundfog of cigar smoke and dull oratory at its fund-raising functions. Its leaders, politicians and businessmen, waited for cues in every crisis from men of high caliber in London and

Tel Aviv, who in turn based their decisions and advice on evaluations transmitted by the mediocrities, with one or two exceptions, who held Zionist office in America.

The American Jewish Committee also had fallen on bad days. After the passing of the proud, brilliant, often rambunctious Louis Marshall, its Presidency was filled by Dr. Cyrus Adler, President of the Jewish Theological Seminary. For a quarter of a century, before being called to the Seminary post, he had been successively curator of Oriental Antiquities at the National Museum in Washington, and librarian and assistant secretary of the Smithsonian Institution. He had, besides, been engaged all his life in initiating and soliciting funds for a multitude of Jewish scholarly enterprises. This long experience with ancient artifacts and millionaire donors took its toll. He was humbly grateful for the readiness and grace with which five Presidents—Harrison, Taft, Wilson, and Theodore and Franklin Delano Roosevelt—received him when he petitioned them on Jewish matters; and was apprehensive lest some untoward gesture cause Jewry to fall out of favor in Washington, or Jewish institutions to lose the support of some short-tempered Jewish philanthropists. This colored the American Jewish Committee's policies and utterances under his regime in the crucial nineteen-thirties: a bland inoffensive prose supplanted Marshall's powerful cadences which breathed wrathful indignation and fierce outrage. Besides, Adler was born in Van Buren, Arkansas in 1863, which was then, and is still today, off the beaten track for Jews, and when his family moved to Philadelphia he was enrolled in a German-language Hebrew school whose headmaster was a British Episcopalian. This background hardly qualified him to deal with the other Jewish organizations, led by East European immigrants and their offspring.

The Jewish trade union movement in America also failed to offer better than the conventional response to the global Nazi threat to Jewry. Both the Zionists and the laborites were content at first with improvised, sporadic joint action, such as a Madison Square Garden rally with an overflow audience, or a massive parade through the streets of New York to protest Hitler's assumption of power and Nazi atrocities. On the day of the parade many stores, even on Fifth Avenue, shut their doors for an hour in sympathy with its objectives. Flags were flown in Jewish neighborhoods. Christian clergymen and political leaders marched abreast with Stephen S. Wise at the head of the parade. Next day Goebbels fulminated on the German radio, the German ambassador filed a protest with the State Department. The American Jewish Committee alone abstained from these actions. But all the furor brought was headlines, a catharsis for the protestors, and the repetitious pattern of German protests to the State Department.

The labor leaders, in their new roles in the fermentative New Deal atmosphere, were busy around the clock negotiating union contracts, mediating between the CIO and AFL, serving on public bodies appointed by the President, testifying before Congressional committees on economic policy, and responding to summonses to the White House. They thought they helped the anti-Nazi struggle, however, by providing sinecures in America for Aryan Socialist refugees who came out of Germany with reassurances that the German labor movement had gone underground, intact and determined, and with adequate financial help would soon bring the Nazis down. The Jewish labor leaders transmitted generous amounts abroad, which accomplished nothing more than subsidize emigré journals that claimed to have clandestine distribution inside Germany.

The Zionists' leadership of the anti-Nazi struggle was distracted by a variety of tasks related to conditions in Palestine. For example, they protested British restrictions on Jewish immigration and the purchase of land by Jews, and the acquiescence in Arab terrorism which Berlin and Moscow, each separately endorsed. But their primary preoccupations were to raise monies to repair the damage inflicted by Arab attack, to increase the Palestine Jews' capacity to defend themselves, and to override all obstacles to immigration—of Nazi refugees—and to further development of the Jewish National Home.

The Zionists and labor in America began talking of a boycott of Germany almost immediately upon Hitler's assumption of power. But it was first put into effect by none of the established Jewish organizations and leaders, but by three obscure men with a penchant for causes— Ezekiel Rabinowitz, an editor and businessman; Israel Poznansky, a small businessman, and Dr. Benjamin Dubovsky, author of a medical advice column in *The Journal*. All three men had a bent toward militant and unpopular causes. The Yiddish press was still a potent influence, so they enlisted Dr. Abraham Coralnik, *The Day's* feuilletonist who had a universal reputation among Yiddishists, and named him chairman of a new organization, their individual creation, The League to Champion Human Rights. When the three founding fathers scraped together among themselves just enough money to rent an office and print stationery, they published a manifesto, drafted by the grandiloquent Dr. Coralnik, proclaiming a worldwide boycott of German goods and services.

The Yiddish press gave them spacious coverage, and soon pickets appeared outside all German consulates and firms, theaters showing German films, and department stores handling German goods. Men and women of all ages, mostly working class and lower middle-class, shouted in unison "Boycott German goods, boycott German ships," a slogan duplicated on the placards they carried.

But they were aware that the boycott, to gain momentum, required different and more prominent leadership. Like the ancient Hebrews in search of a king, they now went from one national Jewish leader to another offering to surrender their title to those other, hopefully more effective men. None would take up their offer, until they met with Samuel Untermeyer, a notoriously crotchety and arbitrary man, a corporation lawyer of national repute, a voice in the Democratic councils of New York state, who had last been heard of in Jewish affairs in the early nineteen-twenties when, for a brief season, he headed a Zionist fund-raising campaign. He agreed to accept the "crown" that the four Don Quixotes of East Broadway had offered him. Renaming their organization Non-Sectarian Anti-Nazi League to Champion Human Rights, he enlisted a board of prominent Catholic and Protestant laymen, and announced at a press conference that his organization would wage economic war on Germany. He was a Wall Street lawyer. The threat sounded formidable. It made international headlines. The boycott was on its way. Next time pickets appeared en masse before shops handling German merchandise, the cops ordered them away for obstructing access, and when they would not obey carried them off in paddy wagons. The magistrate was about to let them off with a reprimand when, amidst a bevy of reporters and photographers, flash bulbs exploding around him, Samuel Untermeyer entered the cavernous, dimlit, melancholy night court—a small, neat old man, with spats, a brown-dyed moustache, a carnation in his lapel, his voice cracked with age, but his manner firm and autocratic. It was not always that Untermeyer appeared in a magistrate's court. He had come to represent the pickets, and the boycott again hit the headlines.

Jewish leadership, especially the Zionist heads of the American Jewish Congress, became nervous. Untermeyer was a usurper. No longer able to procrastinate, the Congress issued a boycott call and, eventually, with the Jewish Labor Committee, which was supported by the Jewish trade unions, established a Joint Boycott Council.

The boycott created a great deal of newsprint froth. The fact is that the formidable American Jewish community failed to marshal even a fraction of the funds this effort required. It was only in 1939 that B'nai B'rith endorsed and allocated $5,000 for the boycott. The boycott certainly required, but did not obtain, the cooperation of Jewish importers, film distributors, bankers, and department stores. R. H. Macy's struck a patriotic posture, implying that the boycott was un-American. In full-page ads in all the New York City newspapers, Macy's explained that it continued to carry German goods to support Washington's reciprocal trade agreements with Berlin. The Zionists contributed to the disorientation by an agreement their leaders negotiated with Berlin. German Jews, under this plan, were permitted to leave for Palestine with the equivalent of their assets in German consumer goods. The barter of Palestine oranges for German merchandise was a feature of the plan. The value of the Jewish assets was arbitrarily determined by the Nazis. No logical explanation of the distinction between outright trade with Germany and an agreement bartering German products for Jewish lives could alter the fact that the Zionists, while calling for a world-wide anti-Nazi boycott, were trading with Germany themselves.[1]

The American Jewish Committee, under the dispirited leadership of Cyrus Adler, opposed not only the boycott but any hard pressure on Germany. This was not in the Committee's tradition. Under the long rule of Schiff and Marshall, the Committee had been autocratic, disdainful of mass action, but always firm and often audacious. The Czar had offered, through an emissary to relax some of the restrictions on Russian Jewry if Schiff would refuse a loan to Tokyo during the Russo-Japanese war. Schiff replied that nothing less than full rights was acceptable and granted Japan her loan. In 1915 he publicly announced

[1] The dilemma that negotiations for the rescue of Jews might benefit their persecutors had several times divided the Zionist movement. The first time, in 1903, when Theodor Herzl, Zionism's founder, traveled to Russia to persuade Vyascheslav von Plehve, Minister of the Interior, to support the Zionist program as a means of solving the "Jewish problem" in Russia. It was charged that the only result of the Herzl visit would be improvement of Von Plehve's reputation abroad. The Minister was Jewry's arch enemy at the Czarist court and reputedly the architect, which he denied, of the Kishinev pogrom that year. In 1951 David Ben-Gurion overrode fierce parliamentary opposition to a restitution agreement with Germany achieved through direct negotiations. Opponents argued that however financially beneficial to Israel, direct negotiations would help restore Germany's reputation just six years after, under Nazi rule, six million Jews were murdered.

that his firm had not joined in floating an Anglo-French loan because a beneficiary might be "the government of Russia against whose inhumanity the members of our firm have raised their voices." His firm contributed one million rubles towards a loan to Alexander Kerensky's Republican government which came to power after the Czar's overthrow. Anti-Semitic myth has misrepresented this as a loan to Lenin by whom Kerensky was ousted several months later.

The successors of Schiff and Marshall had none of their passion, audacity, and prescience. The National Socialist German Workers Party, until then essentially regional in character, emerged in the September 1930 elections to the Reichstag as a powerful national party. Yet nearly one year later, reviewing the preceding twelve months, *The American Jewish Year Book,* published by the American Jewish Committee, stated: "While several Jewish organizations were deeply stirred by the results of the German elections they took no action, knowing that the sister community in central Europe is well able to deal with the situation, and feeling confident that the sober judgment of the mass of the German people would not permit German honor to be stained by the recrudescence of medieval persecutions."

Cyrus Adler apparently took his cue from Conservative upper middle-class German Jewish leaders who advised caution and disregard of the "prattlings" in *Mein Kampf.* They were of the same social caste as the American Jewish Committee. The JDC (Joint Distribution Committee) of similar social composition, as late as 1934 was confident that with philanthropic assistance a majority of German Jews "could still be accommodated inside Germany."

There was a closeness between the publishers of *The New York Times* and the American Jewish Committee, and Anne O'Hare McCormick, *The New York Times'* perceptive correspondent, interviewed Hitler after he had become Chancellor and came away convinced that he was "indubitably sincere" when he offered to let the Jews go if other countries would receive them and that he was only after the Communists. There were similar assurances from other sophisticated observers. Apparently to help Cyrus Adler placate critics inside the Committee itself, Secretary of State Cordell Hull wrote him in a telegram dated March 26, 1933: "The feeling has been widespread in Germany that following so far-reaching a political adjustment as has recently taken place some time must elapse before a state of equilibrium is re-established . . . such a stabilization appears to have been reached in the field of personal mistreatment and there are indications that in other phases the situation is improving." [2]

The Zionist reaction was different and consistent. Goaded by leaders abroad, who were true statesmen, by a philosophy which maintained that a stateless people can never be secure from persecution, sequestration, and expulsion, and by a constituency of East European immigrants who still carried in their flesh the stigmata of pogroms, the Zionists had a radar sense for Jewish catastrophe. There was disconcerting evidence that Nazism had begun to stir dormant prejudices even in otherwise fair-minded Americans.

Henry Wyman Holmes, Dean of the Harvard Graduate School of Education, stated after a visit to Germany: "I think the reports of Hitler's oppression of the Jews have been exaggerated; some action may have been necessary; [Hitler is] something Germany needed." He later felt impelled to amend his statement by adding that he was "unequivocally on the side of those who oppose the present German policy towards the Jews." [3] The State Department, upset by the accelerated volume and frequency of Zionist and labor protests, apparently began a subtle campaign to silence the protestors. The public prints began carrying ominous hints attributed to "authoritative quarters."

The Literary Digest, then an influential publication widely used in current events classes in American schools, reported: "The impression is growing in some American circles that protests are hurting German Jews and American relations." Schiff and Marshall would have wrathfully responded that American Jewry's protests would not be stifled by such intimidation. Adler, a civil servant trained in obedience, took his cue and behaved accordingly. Yet there was something peculiar about the Zionist militancy. The pedantic Adler and the volatile Stephen S. Wise, who had come to be regarded as the voice of militant anti-Nazi protest, shared a reverence, with a difference: Adler embraced all government, Wise only President Roosevelt. The latter's veneration of F.D.R. was common to nearly all Zionist leaders who with rare exceptions were Democrats and fervent New Dealers. The President's domestic program had strong appeal to the Jews' social passion and demonstrated concern for the working and lower middle-classes to

[2] Cyrus Adler and Aaron M. Margalith, *With Firmness In The Right, American Diplomatic Action Affecting Jews, 1840–1945.* (New York: The American Jewish Committee, 1946), pp. 365–6.
[3] April 8, 1933.

which the majority of American Jewry then belonged. The Zionist leaders attacked both the Nazi government and the State Department's policy of placating Berlin, but for the reasons just mentioned excluded F.D.R. from these strictures, as if Cordell Hull was alone responsible for American foreign policy.

It was in his Quarantine Speech in Chicago in 1937 that Roosevelt first took public notice of the war threat developing in Europe, and it was not until the notorious Crystal Night of November 10, 1938 when the Nazis set fire to all synagogues in Germany that the Roosevelt administration finally spoke up clearly and loudly against the Nazi persecutions of the Jews. The first statement came, as was to have been expected, from Secretary of the Interior, Harold E. Ickes. It was couched in the caustic language that acquired for him the nickname "curmudgeon." The German ambassador promptly delivered a protest note, but this time he received no apologies. Instead, Under-Secretary of State, Sumner Welles, endorsed Ickes' statement.

This was in 1938, by which time Hitler had had four years to accomplish, efficiently, the total social segregation and economic ruination of German Jewry.

Washington's passivity, and the uneven performance of even the most militant Jewish organizations, provided a climate for Communist exploitation. The Communists addressed themselves primarily to the campus and specifically to Jewish students. Communist propaganda cast America alternately as an indifferent bystander and an accomplice and co-plotter of Nazism, and the Kremlin as the guarantor of the rights and safety of Jews, Negroes, and all aggrieved minorities, and as the leader of the forces of light against the forces of darkness in the imminent apocalyptic war against fascism. The glaring international spotlight played on Maxim Litvinov who pounded away at the collective security theme before an immobilized League of Nations, and Georgi Dimitrov, the formidable Bulgarian at the Reichstag Fire trial in Berlin, stepping out of the role of defendant into the role of accuser, causing Hermann Göring, the flatulent, vain, blustering star witness for the prosecution, to perspire, wilt, and finally explode in an outburst of vicious temper.

The Communists were engaged on several fronts. They tried to infiltrate Jewish Establishment organizations and, rebuffed, denounced them as "reactionary" and "collaborators." They also created, especially on the campus, in quick succession, a welter of front organizations which kept the students on a treadmill of constant "anti-fascist" action. They were dispatched to the piers to picket a German liner on one day; on another day, went South to distribute food, clothes, and circulars to Negro sharecroppers, and on a third, to enlist with the Spanish Loyalists. The Communists endowed many and disparate inequities at home and abroad with a nightmarish coherence, like the separate sections of Picasso's "Guernica." Whatever the declared purpose of a Communist-infiltrated demonstration, its placards, carried like icons, always listed a long bill of particulars irrelevant to the immediate issue. The denunciation of F.D.R.'s CCC camps for unemployed youth as concentration camps and/or storm trooper barracks; demands for the removal of the U.S. embargo on arms to Spain, and for a Presidential pardon for Mooney and Billings, two alleged radical terrorists serving life sentences in San Quentin; and protests against Mussolini's assault on Ethiopia, and against the conviction of the Scottsboro Boys, Negro youths found guilty of rape on the testimony of a rail-riding white prostitute; such local issues as rent control, tenant evictions, etcetera—all were a part of the Communist strategy.

The Communists played especially on fear, by no means unjustified, of growing native fascism. *The New Masses* engaged John L. Spivak a former Hearst reporter, to conduct an under-cover investigation of the American fascist groups to reveal their membership strength, the source of their finances, and evidence of their links to Berlin and Rome. He described in dramatic detail how the would-be-führers, confronted with his evidence of their misdeeds, confessed to him like the murderers to the fictional Perry Mason, while their plug-ugly bodyguards stood around ominously polishing their brass knuckles, patting their gun holsters, and watching his every move out of their narrowed eyes.

His articles were issued in a brochure with a lurid cover which screamed "Plotting America's Pogroms" and had a sensational sale. He ruthlessly resorted to guilt by association. His "evidence" consisted mostly of covers, mastheads, and letterheads of anti-Semitic books, periodicals, and organizations. But he did come up with some evidence that irrefutably linked prominent American industrialists, bankers, and politicians to the fascist demi-monde.

Spivak was soon matched by John Roy Carlson, the pseudonym of Arthur Derounian, an Armenian-American reporter. A tense, dark, and bespectacled young man, he had submerged in the fascist lower depths by joining a half dozen of its organizations and corresponding with at least another half dozen, and brought up files of materials which went into two best selling books, *Undercover* and *The Plotters*.

Spivak and Carlson set the pattern. Jewish organizations engaged in combating anti-Semitism developed investigation departments with operatives inside the anti-Semitic network—retired city policemen, pensioned federal agents, "private eyes" whose only previous experience had been collecting evidence in divorce suits, and unemployed reporters who hoped to come up with a series that would restore them to a job on a newspaper and even dreamt of writing a best seller like Carlson. There were volunteers, strictly of amateur standing, Jews who "looked like Christians," and double agents and informers for hire. There was a percentage among them of crackpots, collectors of grievances, pathological liars, and paranoiacs who sometimes would deliberately mutilate themselves and then demand "disability" from the investigative agency employing them and hastily take off for Mexico because "they're after me."

Despite its grotesque elements, this was serious business. A special bureau in Berlin for *Auslandsdeutsche* (Germans abroad) supervised propaganda and organization among German-Americans. Until then, ever since the mid-nineteenth century, Germans and Jews in America had lived harmoniously together. German and Jewish Socialists cooperated in founding trade unions. Jewish immigrants from the German-speaking lands were no less bitterly opposed than other German-Americans to America's entry into World War I. Jews from Germany gravitated to German neighborhoods where they assimilated into the Steuben Society or founded Jewish societies which joined German-speaking verein-federations. They were also among the most zealous sustainers of German *Kultur* in America, helped found literary clubs, choral societies, orchestras, and arrange lecture tours for visiting German dignitaries.

This suddenly changed. From the office of Victor Ridder, one of two brothers who published and edited the daily *Staats-Zeitung*, a Berlin operative, Günther Orgell, directed a campaign to purge the German societies in America of their Jewish members. Discomfited, the Jews resigned, and their resignations were everywhere readily accepted. Acknowledged leaders of the German-American community, professionals and businessmen, founded DAWA (*Deutsch-Amerikanische Wirtschaft-Ausschuss*—German-American Economic Committee) for the professed purpose of defending Germany from the Jewish boycott.

Yet its undeclared purpose seemed to be the expulsion of Jewish stores from German neighborhoods. The DAWA sign in shop windows helped distinguish Aryan-owned stores from others.[4] At German-American rallies the name of German-born United States Senator Robert F. Wagner, one of the few nationally known German-Americans to raise his voice consistently against Nazism, was booed. At nightfall, in the Yorkvilles of the nation, jackbooted, uniformed Storm Troopers with swastika armbands hurried to their weekly drills and nightly meetings, or stood on street corners hawking anti-Semitic publications. Almost every evening German-American lower middle-class families, artisans and shopkeepers, gathered in the beerhalls to "heil Hitler," shout insults at the mention of Roosevelt and Wagner, and applaud inflammatory oratory against the Jews.

Their paramilitary organization, the German-American Bund, solicited allies and found them among the Irish. Yet the behavior of the Irish was not of a piece. Irishmen in high public office unhesitatingly denounced Hitler's persecution of the Jews. A retired American general of Irish extraction, was a marshall of the first anti-Nazi parade in New York City. Michael Williams, then editor of the Catholic liberal weekly *Commonweal*, was among the first who raised their voices against the Nazi outrages, while some leading Protestant periodicals, excoriating the persecutions, coyly suggested that the Jews at times were indeed trying on Christian nerves. Several Catholic bishops of Irish extraction declared themselves unreservedly on behalf of the Jews, but a number of eminent Protestant churchmen, withholding their names from protest petitions, expressed their concern that such intervention might only make it worse for German Jewry.

Yet as many anti-Semitic organizations at that time sprang into being among the Irish as among the German-Americans, and their outdoor rallies drew no smaller crowds than similar meetings in German neighborhoods, the speakers' voices shrill with emotion, the audience seething with passion. Viewed retrospectively, more than three decades later, the phenomenon is still inexplicable. The Jews and the Irish were neither business nor professional rivals, not even in the municipal civil service, and they were generally political allies in Tammany Hall which could count on a heavy turnout for its candidates in Jewish lower middle-class neighborhoods.

[4] Louis Nizer, *My Life in Court* (Doubleday and Company, Inc.: New York, 1961), pp. 287–347.

Possibly, at the root of Irish-Americans' pro-Nazism and anti-Semitism were their hope that Hitler could be the divine instrument to raze the British empire and the deicide-consciousness acquired in their parochial schools which, in the nineteen-thirties, were still strongly under the influence of Ireland's special brand of Catholicism which closely matches the Spanish church in ultra-conservatism.

The role of some Catholic churchmen of Irish extraction was alarming. At least two diocesan newspapers, *The Boston Pilot* and *The Brooklyn Tablet,* were as rabidly anti-Semitic as the worst of the German-American Nazi publications. Father Edward Lodge Curran of Brooklyn, President of the International Catholic Truth Society was a runner-up to Father Charles E. Coughlin of Detroit, without the latter's eloquence, as an advocate of anti-Semitism.

Coughlin was perhaps the most accomplished practitioner of political expediency and demagogy in a decade, the nineteen-thirties, when America was not lacking in masters of the craft. Not long after he launched his national weekly radio broadcasts in 1934, public opinion polls rated him as second to the President in importance in American affairs. A professed admirer of the President, he was, at first, indeed somewhat left of the New Deal, attracting a large liberal audience, of which Jews formed a substantial segment. He edged away slowly, almost imperceptibly, from these early commitments, and suddenly had accomplished a complete aboutface, lashing out at Roosevelt and needling the Jews. Coughlin in 1936 still effectively confused public opinion by protesting American participation in the Olympics in Berlin that year. In 1938, however, he no longer felt it necessary to keep up pretenses. His weekly, *Social Justice,* began serialization of *The Protocols of the Elders of Zion* with commentaries by Coughlin who tried to show that the "Jewish conspiracy" as outlined in that notorious forgery had already, in part, been put into effect. In November 1938, when prescient observers at home and abroad warned that European events were moving towards a fateful climax, Coughlin contributed towards domestic divisiveness in a radio address in which he explained that Nazi anti-Semitism, its dimensions exaggerated by the Jews, was Germany's way of defending herself from Bolshevism; and in July 1939, with Europe hanging over the precipice and Americans plunged in furious debate, he called on his listeners to be prepared to defend America "the Franco way."

The German-American Bund and Coughlin's followers were both

allies and rivals. The Christian Front, also a paramilitary organization, was the Irish-American parallel to the Bund. Photographs, secretly taken at German camps in New Jersey and the midwest and published in American newspapers, showed uniformed Bundists engaged in rifle practice and military drill. Walter Winchell revealed that within the New York State National Guard, a special unit had been formed, called National Guardsmen of German Descent. An official order that it disband followed his exposure. The New York Police Department was reported to have 5,000 enrolled Christian Fronters. Whereas the Germans' DAWA had implicitly asked for a boycott of American Jewish businesses, Coughlin's Christian Front openly urged "Buy Christian Only" and published a *Christian Business Directory* for consumers' guidance.[5]

Jewish storekeepers in Irish and German neighborhoods were then perhaps no less apprehensive than white shopkeepers today in the Negro ghettos. But their psychological condition was far worse. They were not members of the dominant majority whom circumstance had cast among an aggrieved and mutinous minority. They were a minority inside these neighborhoods and everywhere else in the country. The hatred seething about them came not from the underprivileged, uneducated masses, but from otherwise respectable, solid middle-class citizens. Jewish youths clashed with Christian Fronters peddling *Social Justice*. Jewish shops closed early in the hostile neighborhoods, and on evenings when large street corner rallies took place, some owners boarded up their windows and lurked around the corner to call police should their premises be invaded. Although not quite like the Negro and Puerto Rican today, many Jews nonetheless had lost their confidence in New York City's police. There was talk of forming Jewish self-defense units. Some Jewish War Veterans formed The Minute Men to raid Nazi meetings, but were no match for the trained Storm Troopers guarding these meetings.

A reporter [6] for a Yiddish daily became the reluctant carrier one day of a message to Jewish leaders from several men who said they were "from Murder, Incorporated" and wanted a list of "Nazi bastards that should be rubbed out." He brought back a warning that if this plan

---

[5] Promoters of the *Directory* offered, for "a special consideration," to include Jewish firms in their listing. Jews turned down the offer. However, Christian businessmen soon discovered carrying the DAWA insignia, or being listed in the *Christian Business Directory* only lost them customers.

[6] The author of this volume.

were put in motion, the police would be informed promptly. The recipient of the message (this time the contact was by phone) was silent for a moment, then angrily replied, "Tell them to keep their shirts on. OK, we won't ice [murder] the bodies; only marinate them."

"Marination" began within a week. It was a miniature reenactment of the night when God struck all the first-born in Egypt. All Nazi meetings in New York's Yorkville and Ridgewood sections, in Staten Island, in Hoboken and Bergen County, New Jersey were invaded suddenly one evening. Men inside, and strategically deployed outside, glanced at their synchronized watches and went into action everywhere at the same minute. Leaping from their seats, they lunged at the speakers at the precise time that their confederates outside rushed the unsuspecting sentries at the doors and burst inside. A third segment of the invading force had climbed the fire escapes and was entering through the windows. They worked expertly and with dispatch on a ten-minute schedule, causing no fatalities, no permanent injuries, only several dislocated limbs, many bloodied heads and noses, and a great deal of damage requiring dental attention. Like commandos they were gone before the police could arrive. It was sufficient "marination" to have drastically reduced, for a while, attendance at these meetings and to have discouraged Christian Fronters and Bundists from appearing in uniform singly in the streets.

Many Jews felt differently. On behalf of the American Civil Liberties Union, prominent Jewish attorneys appeared in court and at City Hall hearings to defend the Nazis' right to assemble and to parade in uniform in the streets. *The Jewish Morning Journal's* managing editor, Jacob Fishman, could not agree that anyone should be accorded the very rights he would destroy. On the other hand, he angrily rejected evidence offered him, which if submitted to the public prosecutor would have sent the top American Nazi, Dr. Ignatz T. Griebl, to jail as an abortionist. Fishman insisted that the doctor should be sent to jail for inciting racial violence "and not for violating a law that has no business being on the books at all." Shortly thereafter the Yorkville doctor left the country as the FBI closed in to seize him for Nazi espionage. Mayor LaGuardia, whose epithets about the Nazi hierarchy kept the German embassy and the State Department busy alternately protesting and apologizing, supported the civil libertarian view. However, in his whimsical manner, he confined the Bundist parades to Yorkville, the heart of pro-Nazi sentiment, and assigned Jewish and Negro policemen to patrol the route. Thereafter, any Nazi dignitary passing through New York was sure of a mixed Jewish-Negro bodyguard.

One of the most enthusiastic collaborators with the Bund was Abdul Hamid, a forerunner of the Black Muslims of today. A bearded giant of a man, he wore jackboots, a Sam Brown belt and a Turkish fez, which he thought was Muslim headgear, and claimed to be an Ethiopian-born Muslim. He was in fact an American Negro. He had only a dozen followers, but his street-corner rallies in Harlem always attracted a crowd of several hundred to whom he proudly introduced himself as "that man the Jews fear, are scared to death of, and the newspapers call Black Hitler," and explained that Nazi racism was only aimed at "the polluted Jewish race, but not at the princely African blood" which coursed in the veins of every American Negro. He quoted enthusiastically the anti-Jewish statements of Haj Amin el Husseini, the Mufti of Jerusalem,[7] ranted about the "Zionist colonialists" in Palestine and their "stooges, the Jewish storekeepers and landlords of Harlem" and "them Jews in Washington who rules us all, Christian and Muslim, black and white."

Harlem was going through one of its most trying times. None was more furiously hit by the Depression than the American Negro. Unemployment skyrocketed, welfare allotments were small. The Jewish storekeeper, insurance agent, landlord, and pharmacist was the most visible and accessible white presence. When Harlem exploded in summer riots, its fury gutted and pillaged the small Jewish family businesses—the pharmacies, tailor shops, and groceries on Harlem's side streets, and inflicted only minimum damage on the largely Jewish-owned but police-protected large discount houses and other businesses on 125th Street. Harlem's own weekly, *The Amsterdam News,* and the Negro clergy condemned the rioters.

Jewish leaders brought Jewish businessmen and Negro civic leaders to a round-table conference where agreement was reached on a fair distribution of jobs among Harlem's residents. Jewish clerks were replaced in the midst of the Depression by Negroes, and family businesses that had done without any outside help at all now took on Negro clerks. However, some Harlem opportunists tried to make a quick and tidy profit from the situation by demanding more jobs than a store could afford and then, for a fee, calling off the picketline altogether. Expo-

[7] Organizer of the Arab terror in Palestine and wartime Nazi collaborator.

sure stopped the racket which had obviously been learned from Christian Front and German-American Bund "operators."

This obsession with the Jew was not confined to the Yorkvilles and Harlems of the nation. Like the evening in Eliot's poem, the American Jew now lay etherized on the table, subjected everywhere, in the halls of Congress and in respectable journals, to exploratory surgery to see whether or not he was a malignancy in the body of America. Christian opinion ranged from extreme to extreme, and the Jew, were he willing, nonetheless could not possibly meet the contradictory demands upon him: that he assimilate to the point of ethnic extinction, that he cease offending with his excessive efforts at assimilation, that he leave the United States because he was unregenerate and non-assimilative.

The summer of 1941 was a difficult season for the American Jew. He was becoming a pawn in the tense, divisive debate over America's posture toward the European conflict and Lend-Lease aid to Britain. The Jews were accused of interventionism. The world already knew, for Hitler made no effort to conceal it, that in every country she occupied, Germany was segregating the Jews in medieval ghettos. *The Atlantic Monthly* auspiciously and tactfully chose June 1941 to launch a symposium on Jews with the first of two articles by Albert J. Nock and a pontifical editorial note that read: "In this and successive issues, *The Atlantic* will open its columns to the discussion of a problem which is of utmost gravity. We have asked Mr. Nock to begin the inquiry, and we shall invite expressions of opinion from Jew and Gentile alike, in the hope that a free and forthright debate will reduce the pressure, now dangerously high, and leave us with a healthier understanding of the human elements involved."

Nock's articles, in the June and July issues, mixed spurious anthropology, specious history, and mythical statistics to support his thesis that the root of anti-Semitism was neither economic, nor religious, but racial—the Nazi thesis, and also Dreiser's!—because the Jews were "the only Oriental people who ever settled in an Occidental civilization in any large numbers and took any active part in Occidental life." Consequently, the problem is "not essentially Jewish, not essentially Semitic; it is an Oriental problem, Jewish only in so far as the Oriental people concerned in it happen to be Jews rather than Syrians, East Indians, Persians, or some other." He recalled from his boyhood, with some regard several Orthodox Jewish families in a midwestern town who made

". . . no effort or pretense at Occidentalizing themselves; we saw them as first class representatives of an Oriental people with a great history and a great tradition. . . . The mixture was a mechanical one." This *modus vivendi* has since been disturbed, he argued, by Jewish pressure for "chemical mixture, miscegenation." He urged that the Jewish problem be given grave consideration, not by "ex parte pleaders, sentimentalists, propagandisers, disseminators of idle or vicious blackguardism," but by men with "the best professional skill," and warned that if his advice were ignored, "if I keep up my family's record of longevity, I think it is not impossible that I shall live to see the Nuremberg laws reenacted in this country and enforced with vigor."

The Christian Century, then concerned with missionizing the Jews, took a view that was opposite from Nock's, but like him warned that if it were not heeded some horrible fate awaited U.S. Jewry. In issue after issue it excoriated Nazism generally, Nazi anti-Semitism particularly, but schizophrenically reiterated some of the Nazi allegations. On May 3, 1933 its Geneva correspondent, warning that the church must not surrender to the state, and deploring the Nazi persecution of the Jews, added, however, that ". . . the fact that certain types of Jews insist on constituting a nation within a nation creates peculiar difficulties for a country which is threatened with being torn asunder by disunity and internal division." It harshly took to task Dr. Mordecai Kaplan for his monumental two-volume *Judaism as a Civilization* published in 1934 in which, advocating cultural pluralism, he spoke of the Jews' capacity to live in two civilizations, the Jewish and that of the society within which they have become integrated. His theories, if applied—indeed, they had been the condition of Jewish life throughout history—would only make "gentile tolerance more difficult and play into the hands of the non-Christian and non-national forces inherent in every culture."

This preoccupation with the Jew was begun by American journals almost immediately after Hitler assumed power in Germany. It was as if long-inhibited feelings had been given sudden release. Among the first writings that disturbed the American Jewish community deeply were two articles in the December 1933 and the January 1934 issues of *The Christian Century*. Their author was Joseph Ernest McAfee, a lay official of the Community Church of New York City, which had a sizable Jewish membership. Its pastor was the liberal Reverend John Haynes Holmes, friend of Rabbi Stephen S. Wise, and there was an irreverent anecdote in circulation that their two congregations were interchangeable.

Mr. McAfee deplored that among all his Jewish friends over the years he had been unable to find a single one who was "ready to agree that the Jew himself bears a share of the responsibility for the unfortunate social clashes and misunderstandings which have prevailed all down through history. . . ." These were fine euphemisms for the persecution of the helpless by the powerful, for Inquisitions, ghettos, and pogroms. He also lamented "Jewish solidarity," which he left undefined, but clearly it connoted something ominous that evidently was universally acknowledged as such.

Perhaps with the Mormons and/or the Amish in mind, he explained that

> . . . others have either surrendered their overreaching intolerant attitude, and have merged their contribution in the common life of the community, or they have withdrawn to segregated areas where their practice of social and hereditary exclusiveness would not prove a perpetual bane to themselves and to the community by their self-chosen alien status. The Jew stands alone in this particular. The Jew is "different" with a type of difference which is socially baneful, and which cannot ever be aught but that, so long as it is persisted in. No detailed demonstration is required to show that the American Jew is in this socially baneful attitude. He is not, properly speaking, a "menace" to the American community. So impossible an attitude carries with it its own ultimate frustration. The Jew is inviting woes in American society as he has invited through the ages in many lands. The only conditions under which the Jew or anybody else desiring to maintain the group solidarity which even the American Jew continues to insist upon, can do so, is to remove to an area where geographical barriers combine with spiritual aims to preserve the peace.

These views were within a familiar tradition. They were first heard in the French Assembly in its two year debate, 1789–1791, as to whether the Jew should be extended equality. Then, too, conservatives and many liberals alike demanded the Jews' total assimilation as a precondition for civic equality. Yet traditionally his efforts at total assimilation were met with violent rejection.[8] However much Mr. McAfee might have resented the comparison, his proposed alternative was analogous to the Nazis'—the territorial segregation of incorrigibly nonassimilable Jewry—before they launched their genocidal "final solu-

[8] Judd L. Teller, *Scapegoat of Revolution: The Effect of Social Revolutions on Jews Since the Lutheran Reformation.* New York: Scribners, 1954.

tion." Nor was it clear how much more Jews could assimilate than had those who had joined the Community Church. Surely, with Dreiser, Nock, McAfee, *The American Spectator*, *The Christian Century*, and *The Atlantic Monthly* presenting such views, it cannot be argued that anti-Semitism was atypical of a substantial segment of the American liberal community in the nineteen-thirties. This may help explain why America, under a liberal administration, stood passively by when Jews abroad were being purged from the culture, economy, and social life of their countries, compelled to wear the yellow badge and corralled behind ghetto walls. It is this passivity perhaps that emboldened Hitler to conclude that he could, with impunity, ship off six million Jews to the gas chambers.

The German-American Bund had its allies in Congress. Senator Robert R. Reynolds of North Carolina, chairman of the powerful Military Affairs Committee, signed an enthusiastic letter which launched the circulation campaign of the anti-Semitic periodical *The Cross and the Flag*, published by the Reverend Gerald L. K. Smith, a Fundamentalist preacher of racism. Reynolds' own newspaper, *American Vindicator*, was peddled at German-American Bund and Christian Front rallies.

There were other men in Congress, of better repute and dismayingly ambiguous attitudes. Many came from the Midwest with its tradition of isolationism, anti-Semitic tainted Populism, and a Germanic population strongly attached, no matter how many generations removed, to *Das Vaterland*.

The sentiment for U.S. neutrality in the European conflict spread from the Midwest to other sections of the country. It brought together, into a non-interventionist alliance, some odd bedfellows. In 1939, the America First Committee was born out of a welter of isolationist organizations which included Nazi fronts and, after the signing of the Stalin-Hitler pact, Communist fronts, and many of sincere and honest intent. The America First Committee assumed the dimensions of a political force, a formidable movement. Its board was an impressive American coalition. It included interalia Norman Thomas, the revered perpetual Socialist candidate for the Presidency who had been among the first to picket stores selling Nazi merchandise; John T. Flynn, an editor of *The Nation;* Congressman Burton K. Wheeler, an agrarian liberal; the two sons, one a governor, the other a United States Senator, of the late Progressive Senator Bob La Follette, an American legend; H. L. Mencken, Colonel Charles A. Lindbergh, and Lessing Rosenwald, son of the founder of Sears, Roebuck and Company.

Several years later Lessing Rosenwald, whose family is active in the United Jewish Appeal and other pro-Israel causes, helped launch The American Council for Judaism, which defines itself as anti-Zionist but which Israelis and other Jews describe as anti-Israel. His isolationism was anything but typical of American Jewish sentiment.

Of course, a majority of American Jews, with their highly sensitive antennae for the detection of catastrophe, were convinced that intervention was the right course. However, the myth that was being circulated across America was that its Jewish citizens were engaged in a dark conspiracy to compel America into the war. Its authors were Nazi agents and sympathizers, and all manner of anti-Semites who were now able to function under the cover of non-interventionism. Unfortunately even some hitherto untainted isolationists began indulging in anti-Semitic innuendos and outright allegations, their motives often being unclear.

Senator Gerald P. Nye, hero of the liberals and the Left because of his probe of American munitions-makers, alleged in a speech on the floor of the Senate that Hollywood was flooding the country with anti-Nazi films to arouse the nation to war against Germany. Nye and Senator D. Worth Clark asked for a resolution calling for an investigation of the movie industry. Neither senator mentioned the ineffable noun, Jew, yet, all Americans knew that the Jews were being equated with the movie industry, although few knew that the Jewish moviemakers, apprehensive of incurring government displeasure and a falling off at the box office at home and abroad, steered clear of anti-Nazi scripts on the advice of Ambassador Joseph Kennedy.[9]

Congressman Burton K. Wheeler in a startling radio address charged that the campaign for Lend-Lease aid to Britain was financed by "the international bankers with their friends, the royal refugees, and . . . the Sassoons . . . the Rothschilds . . . the Warburgs. . . ." Perhaps this charge should not have startled anyone; Populism had always taken delight in the myth of a conspiracy by international Jewish bankers, and Wheeler was a true Populist.

The severest blow to the Jews was delivered by Charles A. Lind-

[9] Ben Hecht, A Child of the Century. (Simon & Schuster, New York, 1954), p. 520; also Ben Hecht, A Guide for the Bedevilled (Charles Scribner and Sons, New York, 1944), p. 213.

bergh. Addressing an America First Committee rally in Des Moines, Iowa on September 11th, 1941, he warned of attempts to "create a series of incidents which would force America into a central conflict," and charged that "the three most important groups which have been pressing this country towards the war are the British, the Jewish, and the Roosevelt administration," and spelling out the innuendos of Senators Nye and Clark he named the Jews as "the most dangerous" of the three groups because of "their large ownership and influence in our motion pictures, our press, our radio, and our government."

Norman Thomas and John T. Flynn led a roster of liberals who resigned from the America First Committee in protest over Lindbergh's address. But neither Lindbergh, nor the Committee's financial backers, seemed perturbed. The latter were now evidently prepared to match charisma against charisma, the legendary hero-aviator against the thrice-elected President. American Jewry suddenly found itself in the humiliating circumstance of dependence, like the medieval Jewish communities, upon the longevity in office of the reigning prince. F.D.R. became in the Jewish imagination a pillar of fire and a pillar of smoke, a father and a guardian.[10]

Some Jews of high station in American life became so alarmed by this anti-Semitism in high quarters, and its reverberations across the country, that they resorted to a kind of apologia that stripped them of all dignity. Unctuous, specious, it attempted to present the Jew as a man for all seasons, and tailor him to meet criticism from every possible quarter. The prime "defense brief" was published in The Saturday Evening Post. Its author was the late Judge Jerome Frank, a former Harvard Law School Professor of the post-Frankfurter era, a former Chairman of the Securities and Exchange Commission, and, when he wrote his article, a member of the U.S. Circuit Court. He asserted without the slightest reservation that most American Jews "until 1940, were isolationist," citing himself as an example. Admittedly, he was atypical in having "deplored as needlessly provocative the speeches of Secretary Ickes criticizing Hitler." It was only after Hitler's invasion of the European countries that Frank became convinced that Nazism was a menace. He was the original American Firster, the author, in 1938, of

[10] This explains perhaps why American Jews had such total trust in him and dared not protest that he was doing little or nothing to rescue Europe's Jews, or to stop their mass execution.

Save America First from which, he claimed, the America First Committee took its name.

He tried to explain away everything in the Jewish community which, by his lights, might tend to give offense to the general American population, or any segment of it. The Zionists were a small percentage among American Jews and generally sound people, he wrote, and "the intense nationalists among them" are few and, "like the Communist Jews and the American Nazis," mere "sojourners in America." He reassured his readers that Jews ran to both extremes, that there was "a group of wealthy fascist Jews . . . among the leading labor-baiters" (who) "like their gentile friends . . . regard American democracy as sentimental nonsense." Stating that "all true Americans are tolerant of the religious beliefs of others" and that therefore "there need (not) be apologies in America for American-Jewish Orthodoxy," he nonetheless played safe and assured his readers that "the majority of those American Jews who are not immigrants have rejected all or most of the old Jewish customs," that the immigrants were already "in the minority," and that the "relatively recent American restrictions on immigration mean that their number will not be perceptibly increased." He also remembered to comfort *The Saturday Evening Post* audience that the Jews were not "the intellectual superiors of other Americans. The proportion of intellectuals or duds or bores or incompetents or mediocrities among American Jews is just about the same as one would find if he took any group selected at random—say, all red-headed or blue-eyed Americans."

This portrait of the Jew, stripped of all distinctive characteristics, so that he might displease no one, was likely to displease everyone. It certainly displeased large segments of the Jewish community. Protests from Jews were beginning to pour in when an event occurred that united all Americans. The Jerome Frank article was published in the issue of December 6, 1941. The next day, Japanese planes struck at Pearl Harbor.

CHAPTER 6

Struggle for Survival

IN THE SPACE of a single generation, 1921–1941, American Jewry
had become completely transformed. B'nai B'rith provides an excellent example. It was founded in 1843 as a fraternal order of social
peers, middle-class German Jewish businessmen, professionals and
politicians, with a sprinkling of upper-class Yahudim. It also engaged
in philanthropy and interceded, occasionally, for persecuted Jews
abroad.

However, membership applications from East Europeans were
meticulously scrutinized and, generally, unscrupulously blackballed.
Because their revered landsman, Jacob Schiff, the financier, spoke
German-accented English, the German accent was regarded as a crest.
Other accents, particularly with a Yiddish intonation, were treated as
low caste. The East Europeans retaliated. Candidates for public office
in Yiddish-speaking neighborhoods knew better than to list B'nai B'rith
among their affiliations.

Matters were different in the smaller Jewish communities in the
South and Midwest. Marriageable Jewish males were scarce and no
German-Jewish father could afford to reject his daughter's suitor solely
because he was of East European background. These sons-in-law soon
enrolled their friends and relatives, and by 1938 the East Europeans
were able to elect Henry Monsky, one of their own, President of B'nai
B'rith. Monsky, an Omaha-born lawyer and civic leader, was brought
up by Yiddish-speaking parents, and had been a Labor Zionist in his
youth. His charities included a Catholic institution, Boys' Town in Italy.

It was during his incumbency that B'nai B'rith membership leaped
from 60,000 to 150,000, the overwhelming majority being of East Euro-

pean stock, and committed itself to almost the full Zionist program.

Yet, this was not really a revolution. It was accelerated evolution. The old ethnic divisions between Yahudim and Yidn really no longer applied at the time that Henry Monsky stepped into office, although the Yiddish press still hurled the epithet "Yahudim" at the American Jewish Committee. At the end of World War I, the percentage of relatively recent East European immigrants was high in American Jewry. In subsequent years, Jewish immigration was kept down by a restrictionist policy, and not even the Nazi persecutions could persuade the President and Congress to remedy the situation. As a result of this policy, American Jewry had become highly native at the time that World War II broke out. The majority had been here no less than three decades, a high proportion had been brought here as children, and the percentage of native-born was increasing steadily. These circumstances, as well as the prominence of Jews in government, and the rout of the native fascist movements after Pearl Harbor, made the younger Jew more confident and self-assertive than his predecessor had ever dared to be.

His apprenticeship in the radical movements of the nineteen-thirties conditioned him to react spontaneously to issues that aroused his concern and to believe in the capacity of citizens' pressure to alter government policy. When the news of the deportations of European Jews and rumors of their mass asphyxiation began to filter through to America, he began phoning, writing, knocking on the doors of Jewish organizations, inquiring what he could do. He was everywhere greeted with a business-as-usual air, told that the information has yet to be confirmed, assured that the matter was in competent, efficacious hands.

This might have been American Zionism's great moment. For decades the Zionists had prophesied that Jewish statehood was the only solution for moribund European Jewry. Reports in the American press now told of Jews escaping from the very doors of the crematoria and, by the overland route, reaching Palestine, despite a British blockade against Jewish immigration. Yet, while the American Zionist leadership was vigorously protesting against the British, who sealed off Palestine, it was inordinately circumspect in its references to the President of the United States who alone could have pressured Britain to alter her policy.

The British Zionists, even in badly blitzed London, spoke up strongly against their government's policies in Palestine but American Zionists shielded their President. Not that they privately did not demand that America jointly with her allies, and if need be unilaterally, warn the Nazis that there would be immediate and awful retaliation if the crematoria were not shut down; that the President instruct the Treasury to permit the transmission of funds to redeem the Jews, at so much per head, from their Nazi captors.

But these demands, once filed, were permitted to rest with little mobilization of public opinion to support them. Yet, the Zionists had in the past been masters of marshalling public opinion: the Jewish vote had been crucial to Roosevelt in each of his elections, and news of the mass deportation of European Jews to their death had reached the United States in 1942, a Congressional election year, and the penultimate year of Roosevelt's third term. There were rumors, too, that he would be seeking a fourth term.

All this gave the Zionists tremendous bargaining power, but they made no use of it. In fact they prevented the truth about the President's procrastination from reaching the Jewish voter. Perhaps the most important reason for this peculiar policy was the age gap between those who then led American Zionism and the American Jewish constituency. They were at least a generation apart. American Zionism was led by a condominium of old men: Rabbi Stephen S. Wise was sixty-eight and Louis Lipsky was sixty-six in 1942. The average American Jew was then only in his early forties. In Palestine, conversely, David Ben-Gurion, the eldest of the front-line Zionist leaders, a bulldozer of a man, was then only fifty-six, and his second in command, Moshe Shertok (later Sharett) was only forty-eight. Serried behind them were adjutants in their twenties. Another difference was the tasks, the operational methods of the American and Palestinian Zionist leaders between the two world wars. When World War II broke out, the Palestinians had had two decades of experience as professional revolutionaries. They were the leaders, along with Weizmann, Wise, and Lipsky of an internationally recognized legal movement which sent memoranda to the League of Nations and negotiated with the British. But they also presided over an underground movement which consistently sought to supplement that which was denied them in direct negotiations. If the British limited immigration, the underground brought in additional immigrants, if the British denied adequate police protection to Jewish settlements, the underground organized its own clandestine police force.

For nearly two decades American Zionist leadership had been a de-

lightful parochial sinecure. It had only two tasks. One was to raise
funds for the upbuilding of the Jewish National Home. In this, American Zionism was assisted by such visitors from abroad as Einstein and
Weizmann, whose names spelled magic to Jews everywhere. The other
task was to mobilize protests against British policy in Palestine, exer-
cises in public indignation that kept the movement afloat and the
names of its leaders in American headlines. There was nothing daring
about protesting against a foreign government, nor about soliciting
statements denouncing Britain from congressmen and senators who
were delighted to accommodate their Jewish constituents and at the
same time gladden the hearts of Irish voters. The Zionists' only domestic target was the State Department against whose policies they
habitually appealed to the White House, thus conveying the impression that all diplomatic policy that was unsympathetic to their cause
had been formulated without even the President's knowledge, let alone
his consent. This myth made political life easier for them since their
protests involved no risk.

Yet, intramural ferment gave the becalmed Zionist movement an
appearance of being dynamic and provided exciting news for the
Yiddish reader. There were the inner crises within and between the
various ideological groups, and there were, too, the frequent eruptions
of impassioned polemics against the anti- and non-Zionists. American
Zionism was a happy picnic ground for its leaders, their adjutants, and
those who ran before the chariots shouting their praises.

The movement had become so inbred and parochial that there were
mutterings against Wise for his frequent emergence into the main-
stream of American life. Wise, of whom Louis Lipsky had said that "he
reasons with his guts, and prophesies, all too often accurately, like
Jonah from inside the whale," dispersed his passionate concern among
a thousand causes—the Negroes, as a co-founder of the NAACP; labor
(he joined picket lines); civic Reform (he fought Tammany); birth
control, and whatever was the liberal's baker's dozen of causes of the
moment. Yet, his central concern was "Israel." In the rhetoric of the
Reform and Conservative pulpit, before the establishment of the State
of Israel, this meant the Jewish people. He took delight in the intramural Jewish struggles. None could excoriate the American Jewish
Committee or *The New York Times*, sullen in its attitude towards
Zionism, with fiercer eloquence than Rabbi Wise, rocking on his heels,
stretched to his impressive height, his arms spread wide, his voice in
full leonine roar.

However, Wise's primary function was as American Zionism's "Secretary of State." It was his task to "missionize the heathen" to Zionism. Louis Lipsky, his partner in the leadership condominium, was in charge of Zionism's "domestic affairs." A moody man, with a sparse tall frame and elongated skull and features, Lipsky was a rockbound New Englander in appearance. He was a precise English stylist with a great capacity for reasoned argument, draftsman of some of Zionism's major policy statements. Born in Rochester, New York, his enunciation was faultless, yet he felt strangely ill at ease among Gentiles, and he derived his greatest pleasure from devising the tactics for the power struggle within the Zionist movement and the American Jewish community (his talents were fitting for an Italian Renaissance court), and was happiest and most relaxed among his Lower East Side minions.

When not otherwise occupied, he held court every evening, from 8 P.M. until closing time, at the Tip Toe Inn, which until recently was located at Broadway and Eighty-sixth Street. Several tables in the rear were pushed together and reserved as "Mr. Lipsky's corner." Although Zionists were a diversified lot, the waiters recognized his visitors at a glance, even if they saw them for the first time, and directed them promptly to where the master presided, vacillating between loquacity and taciturnity. Around him sat Yiddish editors, big contributors, dignitaries from abroad, spies from the opposition, and the common breed that at public meetings clapped its palms raw in enthusiastic endorsement of Wise's impassioned indignation and Lipsky's reasoned sarcasm. "Mr. Lipsky's corner" became a kind of competitor of the Café Royal for the Zionist trade.

Often seated at Lipsky's side was his court jester, Chone the Famous, a character in Zionist affairs. *The New York Times* reported Chone's death in Israel in 1966 in a long obituary cabled from Jerusalem; Israeli cabinet ministers attended his funeral. A tall sloppy man, with a heavy cane and outsize feet, who lubricated his speech with a generous spray of saliva, he was a bachelor who regarded work as an imposition and lived on handouts which, however, he would not accept "from just any lout." He chose his benefactors well. They were judges, congressmen, rabbis, big businessmen, and he insisted that they each invite him occasionally to dinner (he chewed his food with open mouth, like a cement mixer) to prove that they considered him not a schnorrer, but a mensch (not a beggar, but a dignified human being). To be solicited by Chone was to be admitted into the Brahmin caste of American Zionism.

Chone's great service to Lipsky was as a heckler of the opposition at public assemblies. Federal Justice Julian V. Mack, a close friend of Louis D. Brandeis, was defending the latter's Zionist policies to a convention when Chone waved his cane and shouted, bringing the house down— "*Mack, vos mekest-du?*," a Yiddish play of words which may be translated, "Mack, what are you bleating about?," or "Why are you playing the goat?" Even stalwart persons hesitated to speak up for fear of Chone's abuse.

A Zionist manufacturer of orthopedic shoes used to make Chone's to order because there were none his size. His feet had been stretched to their monstrous proportions on the torture rack in a Czarist jail in a vain effort to solicit from him the names of comrades in the illegal Labor Zionist movement. Chone never mentioned it, he never, in fact, spoke of himself. His favorite subject was other people.

This idyll of American Zionism, with its familial quarrels, was interrupted by events in Nazi Europe. The Zionists had forgotten the distinction between political action, which their founder, Dr. Theodor Herzl, had advocated, and *shtadlanut*, petitioning for grace and favor, which he denounced and which the Zionists ascribed to the American Jewish Committee. Political action, as Herzl understood it, was a combination of petition, negotiation, bluff and mass protest, using the carrot *and* the stick, mating the fact and myth of Jewish influence in finance, journalism, and politics with the pressures of an aroused public opinion. Thus, for example, Herzl offered the Sultan of Turkey a generous loan from the Rothschilds in return for a charter granting the Jews the right of settlement in Palestine; yet, he had earlier broached the idea to the Rothschilds and not been encouraged. He had pointed out to both German and Russian leaders that anti-Semitism blackened their countries' reputations and caused young Jews to join the radical movements, and that Jewish emigration to Palestine would dispose of both problems. He organized world Jewish assemblies to demonstrate the extent of mass support behind him. But American Zionists had unlearned Herzl's lesson. They ceremoniously staged mass meetings and petitioned furiously, but in 1939, Zionist-directed illegal immigration was denounced from the rostrum of a World Zionist Congress as illegal and immoral by an American Zionist, Dr. Abba Hillel Silver, who a few years later was to become a passionate advocate of Zionist uses of political power, even in Presidential elections.

Dr. Stephen S. Wise, American Zionism's primary petitioner, had been a life-long Democrat, and had supported Roosevelt in all his campaigns for the Presidency. Few Jews had better access than Wise to the White House. The President received him each time with the universally familiar Roosevelt charm, and Wise left each time reassured, but nothing ever happened. There was the case of the steamship *St. Louis* tightly packed with German Jewish refugees who held visas for Cuba. Cuba thrice changed its mind about admitting Germany's rejects—it cancelled, re-validated, and again cancelled their visas. Roosevelt's many qualities did not include compassion. He could find no place in the United States for one thousand homeless Jews. France and Britain finally divided the refugees between themselves. Those admitted by France subsequently ended up in Auschwitz.

In July 1938, on the eve of a Congressional election, the President, "deeply concerned," convened an inter-governmental conference in Evian, France, to consider havens for Nazi refugees. To avoid entanglement in "political issues and controversies" he ruled Palestine off the agenda. Unfortunately, no other alternative existed. In 1943, when a second set of British edicts was scheduled to take effect, making further Jewish immigration dependent on Arab consent, the President convened still another conference, exclusively Anglo-American, known as the Bermuda Conference. A court Jew, Sol Bloom of New York, Chairman of the House Foreign Affairs Committee, was assigned the task of announcing that Palestine was off the conference agenda and that "there will be no yielding to pressure groups." Yet the President and all the other conferees were aware since August, 1942, that the only other alternative was the crematorium.

Patently disturbed by the ineffectiveness of the Zionist effort in America, David Ben-Gurion, Zionism's field commander in Palestine and *chef de cabinet* of the world movement, journeyed twice to America during the war, in 1940 and again in 1942, in the hope of stirring up action. In 1942, Weizmann, President of the Zionist movement, was also in America, at the invitation of President Roosevelt to assist in a crucial chemical research project. Aged beyond his years at sixty-eight, his tread heavy, his eyesight failing, Weizmann, in his celebrated role as Zionism's petitioner *par excellence,* also met in America with allied statesmen and with Jewish leaders, Zionist and non-Zionist. From the latter meetings, word quickly spread of disagreement between the two highest ranking leaders of world Zionism. Weizmann maintained his trust in Britain and his confidence that eventually she would keep her frequently breached pledge to the Jews. Ben-Gurion urged accelerated pressure on Britain and a blueprint for Zionist succession to power in Palestine after the war.

Ben-Gurion's mission to U.S. Jewry had failed in 1940; it triumphed in 1942, when an emergency conference attended by 600 American Zionist leaders from across the country, at the conclusion of six days of deliberations, May 6 to 11, at the Hotel Biltmore in New York City unanimously adopted what quickly became known as The Biltmore Program. It included Ben-Gurion's major points—the demand that Britain immediately abrogate the White Paper which restricted Jewish immigration, that she surrender authority over Palestine immigration to The Jewish Agency, that she form a Jewish fighting force of the thousands of Palestine Jewish volunteers already registered with the Jewish Agency, and that a Jewish Commonwealth be established in Palestine at the war's end. Weizmann reluctantly supported the resolution. To him it risked a possible violent showdown with Britain, which he would not support.

It was a great personal victory for Ben-Gurion. Very few American Zionists had up to now thought of him as Weizmann's successor, although he was second in command. Weizmann was a tall man of regal bearing and cosmopolitan manner; Ben-Gurion, as they then saw him, was an aggressive bantam figure, a sort of Jacksonian Zionist, fitting wonderfully into a rustic kibbutz setting or addressing a labor rally in Tel Aviv on a Saturday morning, but not in Zionism's White House and not as its envoy to the chancelleries of the world capitals. His speech was staccato, his voice high pitched, his manner abrupt, and accustomed as he was to khaki shirts and no tie, even an ordinary business suit seemed both awkward and formal on him.[1] Reporters at the Biltmore Conference also had noticed that whenever the leaders lined up to march onto the stage, Ben-Gurion who was always placed with Weizmann and Wise, both towering men, found reason to slip away and enter later with shorter men.

Ben-Gurion's victory resulted from a change, which he no doubt had helped bring about, in American Zionist leadership. It had been forced

[1] Later, as Prime Minister, he rushed one day from a diplomatic reception to a labor rally and apologized to the audience for his formal dress, "These are my working clothes."

primarily by grass roots pressure to end procrastination. The old condominium of Lipsky and Wise was broken up by bringing in Rabbi Abba Hillel Silver of Cleveland. Lipsky had been Weizmann's vicar on American soil. Wise was a man of quick and unpredictable enthusiasms. Now Silver and Wise shared command of Zionist affairs, with Lipsky in a somewhat secondary role.

The Cleveland rabbi, an overbearing man, a powerful but humorless orator, with a reputation for arbitrariness, was about fifteen years younger than Wise and Lipsky. He was already a leader in Zionism in 1921, but resigned all offices when Brandeis' disciples were ousted from leadership. He had never forgiven Wise, who also had resigned, for returning almost immediately. For the next two decades Silver sulked in his sumptuous temple in Cleveland, emerging only rarely to partake of the glories of the Zionist public platform. Distrustful of Wise; as a Republican, immune to Roosevelt's charm, notoriously bull-headed and driven by twenty years of repressed energies, he could be trusted by Ben-Gurion to apply himself relentlessly to the realization of the Biltmore Program, which the Weizmannists would have preferred to treat as a once useful slogan, not as a blueprint.

Strategy called for bringing about the adoption of the Zionist demands by all American Jewry. Henry Monsky of B'nai B'rith, a forceful but infinitely milder man, emerged as the non-Zionists' counterpart to Silver. He was the chief initiator of a call for an American Jewish Conference held in New York at the end of August 1943. In seventy-eight communities across the country, in almost every state, Jews went to the polls to elect delegates to that Conference. All major Jewish organizations were represented. The assembly was estimated to be the authorized spokesman for at least more than half of the total American Jewish population of five million. Delegates from Zionist organizations constituted barely one-fifth of the assembly, yet Silver shared control of the proceedings with Monsky, and Lipsky, determined to demonstrate that the Zionists had anticipated the mood of American Jewry, led those who successfully opposed a modified version of the Biltmore Program.

The dramatic confrontation was between Henry Monsky, President of B'nai B'rith, and Joseph M. Proskauer, leading the American Jewish Committee delegation. Their organizations had always agreed on virtually every issue. Now Monsky argued for endorsement of the full Biltmore Program. Proskauer concurred on all points but one. He requested deletion of the demand for a Jewish Commonwealth. On September 1, Monsky put the full Biltmore Program to a vote. It was carried with only four negative votes and several abstentions. The negative ballots were cast by the American Jewish Committee, which walked out of the Conference soon thereafter.

Evidence that British Intelligence curiously overrated American Zionism is provided by wartime British Foreign Office dispatches to the State Department suggesting that the Zionist effort would work havoc with Anglo-American relations and the progress of the war itself. The truth is that the American Zionist effort, notwithstanding the impression conveyed by the Biltmore Program and the American Jewish Conference, was fitful, irresolute, and that precious energies were wasted on intramural struggles. Wise and Lipsky bristled at Silver's voice. Wise complained of Silver's rudeness. Lipsky muttered that Wise's indecision frustrated and aborted some of the Weizmannist's brightest stratagems against Silver.

Although the plight of Jews was unprecedented in horror and doom, those who handled American Zionist affairs in World War II were no match for the men who had directed American Zionism in World War I. That team had had Louis D. Brandeis as its captain, and included Felix Frankfurter, then only in his thirties; Federal Justice Julian V. Mack, Horace M. Kallen, educator-philosopher, Benjamin V. Cohen, a Frankfurter pupil, who was later to become a member of Roosevelt's "brain trust," and, all of them in full vigor, Wise, Lipsky, and Silver. The non-Zionist supporters of the Zionist program were led by Louis Marshall. The World War II team, led by Silver, Wise, and Lipsky, consisted primarily of mediocre people, common variety businessmen, lawyers, and several highstrung American women catapulted into roles of historic responsibility.

Suddenly a hurricane blew in from Palestine. The eye of the hurricane was a slight, blond young man with a wispy moustache. He was Hillel Kook, nephew of the late Chief Rabbi of Palestine, Abraham Isaac Kook, Orthodox Jewry's foremost philosopher of our time. Not to embarrass his family with his religious and political heterodoxy, Hillel Kook changed his name to Peter H. Bergson. He presided over a small directorate of Palestinians who, like himself, were in their late twenties and early thirties, suave, multilingual, entertaining conversationalists, graceful on the dance floor, and with an aura of international mystery about them. They introduced themselves as emissaries of the Palestinian Jewish underground. Young men of astonishing social mobility, they were soon exhibited at Park Avenue dinner parties, invited for weekends in Connecticut, and enlisted the support of writers, actors, senators, governors, the Hassidic rebbes of Brooklyn, the refugee deans of the European Talmudic seminaries, and to complete the spectrum had even found their way to Las Vegas and Bugsy Siegel and Mickey Cohen, who contributed generously.

Beyond the front line of concerned and informed Jews affiliated with the Jewish organizations and readers of the Jewish press, there was a great hinterland of second- and third-generation American Jews, ranging in age from the twenties to their mid-forties. There were some who had been engaged in liberal and radical causes and previously had been disdainful of any ethnic identification. There were those whose only cause and commitment had been the cultivation of their own careers. They included bestselling authors, screen writers, directors, actors, painters, and scientists. They were now trapped in a nightmare of headlines which told of Jews like themselves in Europe being expelled from society, incarcerated in ghettos and, finally, transformed into ashes. Paranoia was taking its toll. Could they trust their Christian neighbors, their Christian friends on the tennis-courts and at cocktail parties? Would these friends differ from the Germans if Nazism took over America and segregated the Jews from the others?

It is to these that the Peter Bergson group addressed itself; it enlisted the support of a large body of Christian liberal opinion. It spawned a series of front organizations—The Committee for a Jewish Army, The Emergency Committee to Save the Jewish People, The American League for a Free Palestine. All of these were graced by stellar names— Herbert Hoover, Harold E. Ickes, Wendell Willkie, Senator Harry S Truman, Thomas J. Watson, President of IBM; Dr. Samuel Harden Church, President of the Carnegie Institute; Sigrid Undset, the Nobel Prize-winning novelist, a wartime refugee in America; Dorothy Parker, Marianne Moore, Dimitri Mitropoulos, Serge Koussevitzky, Bruno Walter, and a roster of Hollywood and Broadway celebrities.

Bergson and his men represented *Irgun Zvavi Leumi* (National Military Organization), known for short as *Irgun,* one of three Palestine Jewish underground groups. The largest was *Haganah* (Self-Defense), maintained by secret funds from the World Zionist Organization, its members and officers drawn largely from the ranks of Histadrut, the

Israel Federation of Labor and association of cooperatives, and operating from kibbutzim, the collective settlements, the source of Zionist power in Palestine. Its military actions were defensive: protecting the Jewish settlements and cities from Arab attack. It occasionally took the offensive for preventive reasons, to flush out Arab terrorists from the hills or from villages that gave them sanctuary. Haganah also had been engaged, since the nineteen-thirties, in *aliyah bet* (immigration B), the code name, and, when it became too widely known, the nickname for illegal immigration. Its agents were planted in every one of the Palestine Government's departments and bureaus. It possessed fairly complete summaries of every important document in the government files, and myth has it that Ben-Gurion and Shertok, sometimes knew the contents of a confidential communication even before it had reached the addressee.

The ranks of Irgun were comprised of Oriental and East European lower middle-class and *lumpen*-proletariat immigrants, almost exclusively city-based. Its economic philosophy was strictly private enterprise. It was bitterly opposed to Socialist concepts and hostile to Histadrut, the Federation of Labor and association of cooperatives, the bedrock of the Palestine Zionist effort. It was contemptuous of diplomatic jousting with the British, and advocated violent resistance as a means of ousting the mandatory government and achieving Jewish independence. A dissident offshoot of Irgun was the Stern Group, small, tight-knit and sworn to "direct action," to the assassination of all British officialdom in Palestine in any way involved in impeding Jewish effort.

There were occasional clashes between Haganah and Irgun, not over economic issues, but over the strategy and tactics of the struggle for the achievement of Jewish objectives in Palestine. The Zionist majority view held that the campaign of violence conducted by Irgun had disastrous effects—the stiffening of British attitudes, the alienating of non-Jewish supporters from the Zionist cause, the providing of a rationale for harsher policing of the Jews by the Palestine authorities— but the overall and clinching argument against Irgun and the Stern Group was that deliberate violence was "not the Jewish way." Haganah therefore tried to keep Irgun and the Stern Group under surveillance. If it learned in advance of a particularly audacious exploit planned by them, Haganah would try to talk them out of it and sometimes, ironically, used force to prevent it.

When World War II broke out, Irgun suspended its violence (the Stern Group did not) and shifted to propaganda for the formation of a Jewish army, the rescue of European Jewry, and the establishment of Palestine as a sovereign Jewish state. However, even regarding these aims there was an appreciable difference between the Zionists and the Irgun. The former demanded a Jewish fighting force under Zionist colors and British command. Irgun's emissaries proposed a mixed army of Palestinian and stateless Jews under allied command. They declared that the British, in Palestine, were an army of occupation, holding down Palestine with force; they therefore opposed placing Jewish forces under British command. On May 18, 1944 Irgun's emissaries in America founded a Hebrew Committee for National Liberation, a kind of Jewish government-in-exile, which they said spoke for the Jewish population of occupied Palestine, and raising the Zionist flag over their Washington headquarters, they proclaimed its premises the first "Hebrew embassy."

The Irgun's emissaries' establishment of a government-in-exile and opening of an embassy was typical of their boldness and imagination. Even those bitterly opposed to them could not but be deeply stirred by the sudden raising of Hebrew colors on Massachusetts Avenue and the extension of "Hebrew nationality" to the doomed Jews of Europe as a thunderous rebuke to all the countries that had refused them visas.

A distinction was drawn between Hebrew and Jew. The Hebrew might be a Jew, Christian, or Muslim, any resident of Palestine, which was British-occupied Hebrew territory. The Jew was a member of a religious denomination. Some, not all, of the Hebrews have a common religion with the Jews.

On October 13, 1947, announcing Moscow's reversal of previous policy and her readiness to support a Jewish state in a part of Palestine, Andrei Gromyko offered a rationale which corresponded to the definition which Bergson gave in 1944. The Jews outside Palestine have only a religion in common, the Palestinian Jews have all the characteristics of nationhood—a common territory, a common language, a common economy.

In a series of Yiddish radio addresses in September 1944, Isaac Zar, a Yiddish journalist and supporter of the "Hebrew embassy," first proposed a plan for reparations to be collected from Germany and many other European countries after the war. "It would be immoral," he stated, "for any country to claim for itself the damages due its murdered Jews, just as it would be for the small percentage of Jewish survivors to claim all the reparations for the total Jewish property of the respective land. A way must be found which should be just and equitable and the way lies in the recognition of a Hebrew nation, whose nationals the disenfranchised, killed, and robbed Jews had been." His proposals were published in book form in 1945. In 1951, offering almost the same rationale, the Israel government entered into reparations negotiations with Germany, and in 1952 an agreement was concluded granting most of the monies to Israel, and some also to a complex of Jewish organizations outside Israel.

The distinction between Jew and Hebrew, propounded by Irgun's emissaries, comforted the kinds of Jews and Christians who were bothered by the myth of dual Jewish allegiance: to Israel and to the states of which the Jews were citizens. But it alarmed the Zionists because it impugned the basis of their internationally recognized claim to Palestine as Jewry's historic homeland. It alarmed many other kinds of Jews who were not content with a narrow definition that recognized the Jews as exclusively a religious denomination and ignored their long history, which was compounded of both religious and secular components and made them a unique and distinctive people not easily categorized.

The Irgunists followed through with newspaper advertisements and dramatic spectacles that carried the same message, protest, plea, and indictment. They cried out for the rescue of Europe's Jews, struck out at Washington's procrastination, mentioning Roosevelt by name and scoring Britain's callousness. They urged that the Jews be armed to strike back at their Nazi enemies and be restored to political statehood in Palestine. Later, after the war, their advertisements celebrated their resumption of terrorism against the British forces.

The author of these ads and spectacles was Ben Hecht, one of the highest paid writers in Hollywood, who offered his services gratis for this purpose. One of his productions *We Shall Never Die* was directed by Moss Hart, and had a score by Kurt Weill. The cast included Edward G. Robinson, Sylvia Sidney, and Paul Muni. Another spectacle, *A Flag Is Born*, revealed for the first time, perhaps, the talents of an actor named Marlon Brando. Proceeds went to the various Bergson committees. All its advertisements carried coupons requesting contributions. This activity succeeded, temporarily, in eclipsing the Jewish Establishment. Silver urged responsible militancy, unlike that of the

Irgun, but he was pulled back each time by the vacillators. It was probably only the fear of being swept away by the rising popularity of Irgun's American committees that persuaded the Weizmann faction in the Zionist Establishment in America to accede, however reluctantly, to the Silver-Ben-Gurion policies. However, open warfare broke out in the columns of the American press between the Irgun emissaries and the Zionist leadership over the implied claims of the former. They insinuated that they were engaged in a large scale rescue of European Jewry and that they were speaking for multitudes, and not for a small, embattled underground army. In this internecine war, Ben Hecht revealed another side of his nature.

Everyone was impressed, at first, by Hecht's sacrificial service to the Irgun committees. Britain banned his films and, consequently, Hollywood assignments fell off, yet Hecht undeterred continued to produce his inflammatory anti-British ads. Some remembered that in the nineteen-twenties he had published A Jew In Love, probably still the most savage caricature of a Jew in American fiction, an unmatched document of self-hate. He now seemed to be atoning for his past by turning his hate against the British. But when the Irgun and the Zionist Establishment clashed, Ben Hecht rediscovered the Jew as a target. He distinguished between two breeds of Jews. There were the Jews of his romantic imagination—the world of Sholem Aleichem, perishing in the gas chambers; the tough guerrilla fighters of Irgun, the suave Bergson entourage with its mysterious arrivals and departure. To these he sang paeans. But there were also "other Jews," Stephen S. Wise being their prototype, to whom Hecht imputed most of the obnoxious qualities that anti-Semites attribute to the Jew. His diatribes against the Zionist leadership read like a sequel to A Jew In Love. This brought on a crisis in the Bergsonites' ranks. Zionists who had defected to them now turned back. However disappointed in Wise, once the roaring lion of Jewish protest, they still revered him for a lifetime of Jewish service. Ben Hecht was hardly fit to sit in judgment on him, neither was Konrad Bercovici, his associate on the Bergson Committees. Bercovici, a popular fiction writer, by then half-forgotten, had been associated with Yiddish writers on East Broadway. However, when his first English stories on Gypsy life began to sell, this Hungarian Jew evidently decided that sales might be helped if he posed as a born Gypsy, which he did for many years.

Palestine's Zionist leadership, under Ben-Gurion, was distressed as the war ended, over the unpredictability of American Zionist efforts and the progress of Irgun's emissaries to the United States. The latter conveyed the impression that their organization was engaged in a mass effort to bring Jews from Europe illegally into Palestine. Their operation, in fact, was modest, almost negligible. But an enterprise, perhaps without precedent in history, moving thousands of Jews illegally to Palestine from DP (displaced persons) camps in Germany and from East European countries was then, indeed, in high gear, directed by Haganah whose operatives, carrying correspondents' credentials [2] or posing as sales representatives of international concerns, crossed borders with ease, penetrating into war zones and behind that which was soon to be known as the Iron Curtain. At the base of this illegal immigration was The Jewish Brigade, fighting under Zionist colors and British command, the result of years of Zionist pressure that the Jews be granted an opportunity to fight their enemy as Jews.

Through their exaggerated claims, Irgun enlisted generous political and financial support in America and stocked up heavily on arms, which meant accelerated terror. Ben-Gurion and his colleagues were alarmed. Irgun's aim was to raise the price so high in British casualties, military and civilian, that the British would flee Palestine. Zionists feared that this would only turn public opinion against the Zionists and justify British oppression. Haganah's targets were radar and Coast Guard stations, and any installations that interfered with illegal Jewish immigration. British casualties were an inevitable result, as were Jewish casualties, but these were not an objective. It was clear, therefore, that if Irgun accelerated its terror, Haganah would take counter-measures and the result could be civil war in Palestinian Jewry.

Ben-Gurion and his colleagues decided to offset Irgun's young men in Washington with young men from Haganah. The first of Ben-Gurion's team of young Palestinians, drafted from Moshe Shertok's Political Department of the Jewish Agency, arrived in San Francisco in the spring of 1945, when the United Nations was founded. Most of them spoke Arabic and were experts in Arab affairs.

They were a remarkably diverse lot. There was Eliahu Epstein,[3] a tall handsome man graying at the temples. The Soviets had exiled him

---

[2] The author, then editor of an international Jewish news service, accredited a half-dozen such correspondents. To prove that they were indeed correspondents, they sent him cables, from time to time, and these often scooped the large news agencies.
[3] He later Hebraized his name to Elath, was Israel's first ambassador to the United States, and later President of the Hebrew University of Jerusalem.

to Siberia because of his underground Zionist activities. He somehow managed to escape and, by the land route, across Iran, reached Palestine. He at first worked at various proletarian occupations, then enrolled at the American University in Beirut, and subsequently lived for a while among the Arab nomads of the Negev, to study their ways and wrote a book about them. Possessed of dignity, cordiality, warmth and a considerable capacity for making friends, he scored his first great American triumph by winning the confidence of Arthur Hays Sulzberger, publisher of *The New York Times,* The Ochs-Sulzberger families always had been allergic to Zionism. This was reflected in *The New York Times* reports from Palestine for more than two decades, beginning in the nineteen-twenties. Sulzberger was rumored to have been consulted by the founders of the anti-Zionist American Council for Judaism. Now Epstein and Sulzberger were breakfasting together frequently. The effect was evident in the news and editorial columns of *The New York Times.* If not yet friendly, the newspaper had at least become fair to Zionism.

An emissary of another cloth was Tuvya Arazi,[4] slim, slight, with a limp, which he acquired during a wartime intelligence mission in Vichy controlled Damascus. As the police knocked down the door of his hotel room, he jumped out of a window and fractured his leg. He received no medical attention during the many weeks he was in hiding.

Then there was Reuven Zaslani,[5] shortened from Zaslansky, the son of a Jerusalem rabbi. Of average height, squat, flabby, with a scar on his cheek, he was a walking encyclopedia of both essential and trivial information about the devious ways of Arab politics and Arab politicians. He was an excellent, albeit untutored, Arabist, and had served his apprenticeship in intelligence work posing as a Hebrew teacher in Iraq. Most of his assignments were secret, of course. Probably plagued by the silence imposed on him, he communicated his importance in oblique ways. An anecdote had it that he would get into a cab and instruct the driver to hurry, but when asked where to, he would reply that it was classified information, not to be disclosed. He had briefed some of the world's ranking political writers, and confusing his role with authorship he boasted and honestly believed that he was the true author of their pro-Zionist articles and books.

Soon scores of other Zionist emissaries began passing through New

[4] He has since served in diplomatic posts in Turkey and Latin America.
[5] Later Hebraized to Shiloah.

York on all kinds of Haganah missions. Surrounded by mystery, they overshadowed the Irgunists. They were hagglers and traders, scholars and scientists, mechanics, engineers, promoters, and fund-raisers. They included Professor David Bergmann, whose first eminence as a chemist was acquired in pre-Hitler Germany, closely associated with Dr. Weizmann in the latter's wartime research for the allies, and subsequently chief scientific adviser to David Ben-Gurion. Yaacov Dostrovsky-Dori, bespectacled, with a shriveled grandmotherly face, an engineer, later became Commander-in-Chief of the Israel Army in the War of Liberation.

There was also Viennese-born Teddy Kollek, tall, slim, blond, Haganah's champion fund-raiser among American businessmen, member of Kibbutz Ein Gev in Galilee, a fishermen's village which doubles, during the summer, as Israel's Tanglewood, center of international music festivals. Teddy Kollek subsequently served as Director General of the Prime Minister's office throughout Ben-Gurion's tenure, and after that was elected Mayor of Jerusalem. He has acquired weight and a businessmen's taste for cigars and his kibbutz membership for these many years, since Israel's statehood, has been largely nominal.

Irgun's directorate in America presided over the policies and conduct of a series of front organizations, and it could act without the procedural restraints and long-winded debates that hobbled the American Zionist Establishment, because its committees were no more than impressive letterheads, and its public support was not structured, but of the mail-order kind, consisting of contributions sent spontaneously in response to the emotionally charged Ben Hecht ads.

Ben-Gurion's emissaries on the other hand, were under the discipline of a complex democratic organization of global scope. They came, however, to a large receptive American constituency, to Zionist parties and non-Zionist organizations with growing memberships. It seemed as if American Jews, in a kind of delayed reaction to the European catastrophe, were flocking together for solace and comfort, held together by a desperate determination to restore Jewry's dignity from the crematoria ash-hills, and to atone to the survivors for having failed the millions that perished. The war's end weakened the Irgunists and inordinately strengthened the Zionists in American Jewry's favor. American tourists began visiting Palestine, the battlefield of Jewish resistance to the faltering British imperial might. There they could clearly see that it was labor, not Irgun, that was responsible for the

remarkable Zionist achievements, which populated the frontier settlements, maintained the cooperatives, staffed the educational institutions, dominated the Jewish community's governing bodies, and was the
backbone of Haganah which, operating firmly but with restraint, made
its impact felt everywhere.

An excellent team of Zionist professionals, chosen by Wise–Silver
and the Palestinian truth squads, dispatched by Ben-Gurion and Shertok, to travel across the U.S. to deflate Irgun claims cooperated efficiently. Events in 1946 helped their effort to enlist public support for
the Zionist demands that Palestine be opened to the Nazi survivors,
and that it be established as a Jewish Commonwealth. British Foreign
Secretary Ernest Bevin persuaded the United States to agree to a joint
Anglo-American Inquiry Committee to investigate conditions in the
German DP camps, the state of affairs in Palestine, and the attitudes
of the neighboring states. The Committee was accompanied by State
Department and British Foreign Office specialists, briefed and guided
by them, and it seemed a foregone conclusion that its recommendations would be unfavorable to the Zionist cause. Testifying at the Committee's hearings in Washington, Albert Einstein, with the innocent
candor of genius, stated: "I believe that the frame of mind of the
shapers of British colonial policy is so rigid that it cannot be altered.
I think that committees like these are a smokescreen, merely pretending goodwill."

Ben-Gurion's emissaries, however, did not despair entirely. When
the Committee members toured these stockades the multitudes in the
DP camps had been mobilized to demonstrate for "Palestine, no alternative but Palestine." Silver's professionals organized press and radio
coverage of these demonstrations. Moreover, some Committee members began to resent the glib disparaging comment of their Foreign
Office and State Department advisers. The Committee brought in a
series of recommendations. The first of these was that 100,000 DP's be
admitted into Palestine. Unless this was done, the Committee warned,
a revolt would erupt in the DP camps in Germany and, in a parallel
development, the constitutional Zionist bodies in Palestine, would be
superseded by Irgun.

President Truman endorsed the recommendation for the admission
of 100,000 DP's into Palestine but Foreign Secretary Bevin rejected it
out of hand with an angry blast at American Jewry and the snide remark that President Truman's consent was due "to domestic considera-

tions," which was a euphemistic reference to the Jewish vote. Bevin's crude and callous reaction had an explosive effect. It accelerated Irgun terror which, in turn, also forced Haganah to more dramatic resistance. It galvanized American Jewry. It brought about the retirement of Dr. Chaim Weizmann, who had deep trust in Britain, from the Presidency of the World Zionist Organization. This retirement was arranged gracefully at the first post-war World Zionist Congress just several months after Bevin rejected the recommendations of the Anglo-American Inquiry Committee. The post of World Zionist president was left vacant. The movement's essential executive powers were transferred to two co-chairmen, David Ben-Gurion and Dr. Abba Hillel Silver.

In 1949, in his first year as President of Israel whose birth might have been delayed and perhaps forever aborted if his counsel had been followed, Dr. Weizmann published his autobiography, *Trial and Error*. It contains a melancholy postscript to the 1946 World Zionist Congress. "The American group, led by Dr. Abba Hillel Silver, was from the outset the strongest," he writes, and "I became . . . the scapegoat for the sins of the British government." That Congress, he explains, "had a special character, differing in at least one respect from previous Congresses: the absence . . . among very many delegates—of faith, or even hope, in the British government, and a tendency to rely on methods never known or encouraged among Zionists before the war. These methods were referred to by different names: 'resistance,' 'defense,' 'activism.' But whatever shades of meaning may have been expressed by these terms—and the distinctions were by no means clear—one feature was common to all of them: the conviction of the need for fighting against British authority in Palestine—or anywhere else for that matter."

The American Zionists of whom Weizmann complained included many who had hailed him in 1921 in a torchlight parade through Lower East Side streets, as their savior, the exemplar of the Jew's capacity for greatness if granted opportunity. But several additional decades of American experience had altered them. They were now more confident and certain of themselves. Besides, they labored under a burden of guilt for their decimated relatives. There were also their children, who had been conditioned by America's schoolyards not to run away from a fight and who had returned from the wars to discover that their much adulated wartime President had done nothing to halt the Nazi gassing of six million Jews,[6] that Germany was being reconstructed with American monies to which the American Jew contributed his proportionate share as a taxpayer, while frontiers and gates everywhere were still sealed tight against the Jewish survivors of Germany's "final solution."

The Zionist campaign against Britain provided a catharsis for American Jewry's fury, frustration, and humiliation. The truth squads from Palestine, the variegated crew of Haganah emissaries, helped set the dramatic pace for furious fundraising in every Jewish community across the country, at public rallies and in private homes. The United Jewish Appeal raised unprecedented amounts of tax-exempt contributions for relief for the DP camp inmates, the hapless multitudes in the *mellahs* (Jewish ghettos) of North Africa and the remnant Jewish communities in a half-dozen European lands, and for the expansion of Jewish settlement in Palestine in preparation for ultimate Jewish statehood. Audiences from coast to coast turned out night after night to cheer and cry as speakers described the horror of the death camps and the glory of the Palestinian Jewish resistance fighters.

There were also covert contributions, pledged at parlor meetings in elegant Park Avenue and suburban homes. Addressed by Haganah agents, or persons introduced as such, who imparted confidential information, sophisticated men and women gave generous offerings that were not tax exempt and could not even be written off as legitimate business expenditures. Some of the country's best accountants and attorneys offered free advice on how to disguise these outlays of cash, which were transmitted to Swiss accounts or spent right in the United States for the purchase of arms and vessels and for payoffs to hundreds of persons who might otherwise hamper Haganah's illegal traffic in arms and immigrants across the borders of a half-dozen lands on the route to Palestine. Garages of American private estates and resort camps and vacant plants became the storehouses of plane parts and munitions destined for Haganah.

[6] In January, 1944, President Roosevelt issued an executive order establishing a War Refugee Board to speed the rescue of victims from Nazi-occupied Europe. It was established early enough in the year to help his fourth term candidacy, too late in the season to accomplish much for Hitler's victims. It did not single out the Jews, but referred to victims of Nazi persecution generally. It offered to admit one thousand such persons to the United States where they would be kept in a refugee camp in Oswego, New York, and, this being the limit of FDR's compassion and generosity, "upon the termination of the war (would) be returned to their homelands."

In Palestine, debate raged over methods and goals. Haganah was caught in a vise between a moderate wing composed primarily of *bourgeois* German refugees of the nineteen-thirties who urged accommodation to the British at almost any price, and the Irgun whose continuing terror resulted in defections of militants from Haganah's own ranks. The debate revolved around the following: should the aim be removal of immigration curbs, or the immediate establishment of Jewish political sovereignty? Foreign Secretary Bevin early in 1947 took a long gamble, and lost, in announcing that Britain would lay down her mandate and submit the matter to the UN. He probably expected that, faced with the prospect of remaining alone within a hostile sea of Arab multitudes, the Jews would panic and beg London to reconsider. Instead, the Zionist movement proceeded with representations to the UN for an independent Jewish state.

The key role for the enlistment of support at the United Nations fell to American Zionism. The UN headquarters was in America; American Jewry was the most numerous and affluent Jewish community, almost unscathed by the war. Supporters of Zionism were flushed out in the unlikeliest quarters—Jews, half-Jews, and Christian Zionists, men of Irish descent embittered against the British, Latin Americans whose family tradition claimed descent from the *marranos*, Christian sectarians who believed in the imminence of the Jewish Return, industrialists, bankers, labor leaders, professors, diplomats, humanitarians, and adventurers. The result of this remarkable mobilization was that on November 29, 1947 the United Nations General Assembly voted in favor of the establishment of a Jewish state in part of Palestine no later than August 1948. The Soviet Union, to everyone's astonishment, joined with the United States in voting for the resolution.

Immediately thereafter the British and the State Department began a series of evidently complementary maneuvers to frustrate the UN resolution. The British announced that they would withdraw in May, three months ahead of the deadline set in the General Assembly resolution. They permitted the entry into Palestine of armies from the Arab neighboring countries. State Department officials began peddling a proposal to substitute, temporarily, a UN-trusteeship for statehood and thus provide a cooling-off period in which the Jews and Arabs might reconcile their differences and prepare for the responsibilities of self-rule.

The Zionists would not be deterred. For two decades they had developed institutions of self-government in Palestine. They now began to pull the separate fragments together into a unified whole. A Jewish shadow government was in operation even before the British had retired. Jewish volunteers from other countries, not in impressive numbers but with some military specialization, joined Haganah. Volunteers from the United States included the legendary David "Mickey" Marcus. There were also Jewish officers who had defected from the Red Army before the Stalin purge of Jews could strike at them.

London was startled by Dr. Chaim Weizmann, who suddenly emerged from retirement at the request of Ben-Gurion and Silver, his political opponents, and flew to the United States to assist the campaign to prevent the substitution of trusteeship for statehood. In his autobiography, Weizmann writes of this: "The notion of a new trusteeship at this late date was utterly unrealistic. Palestine Jewry had outgrown the state of tutelage. Moreover, everything that had made the mandate unworkable would be present in the trusteeship, but aggravated by the recollection that only a few months before we had been adjudged worthy of statehood. To have accepted this decision would have meant to make ourselves ludicrous in the eyes of history."

His eyes failing, his strength ebbing, he worked doggedly from his hotel suite, cabling, phoning, exerting the magic of his personality on men of his own generation who were still in positions of power and influence—Bernard Baruch, Herbert Bayard Swope, Field Marshal Jan Smuts of South Africa, and "banana king" Samuel Zemurray, President of the United Fruit Company who had tremendous holdings and influence in Central America. No one could be overlooked. Everyone who could enlist even a single vote for the final UN resolution granting Israel statehood had to be approached. Commanding the total American Jewish front was Abba Hillel Silver. American Zionists were working their nerves raw. In Tel Aviv, Ben-Gurion was preparing for that moment in history when he would proclaim the restoration of Jewish statehood after two thousand years.

The State Department was still hoping to persuade the President to approve a draft proposal to delay statehood, without success, however. Within minutes after Ben-Gurion proclaimed statehood in Tel Aviv, President Truman extended recognition to the new state through Eliahu Epstein-Elath, an early member of the truth squads Ben-Gurion had dispatched to America in 1945. He became Israel's first ambassador to the United States or to any country.

American Jewry discharged its functions magnificently. At the UN there was furor. A. M. Rosenthal, now a *New York Times* Assistant Managing Editor, then a member of its UN staff, had been pokerfaced and noncommittal through the many months of the Palestine debate. But when news of Truman's recognition came through, followed by a General Assembly roll call which approved, *post-factum,* Israel's statehood, he flopped into a wheelchair that had been standing nearby and raced down the corridors shouting, "Yippee!" A member of the Jordanian delegation, scion of an aristocratic Arab family, shamefacedly inquired of a Zionist correspondent what an Arab's chances might be for a post with the Israeli diplomatic corps.

At the next session, the American Zionists withdrew and an Israeli appeared before the UN political committee to express his state's appreciation for yesterday's vote. He was young, stoutish, loose-jointed, and spoke in a boyish voice. A correspondent rushed down the corridor, sought out a Zionist press officer and asked: "What is the name of that Johnson's Baby Talcum Powder youth addressing the UN?" Speaking Churchillian rhetoric, Abba Eban, then just turning thirty-three, from that moment captured the affection of American Jews. Immigrants and the sons of immigrants they could envision nothing more appropriate for an Israeli diplomat than a British accent.

In the months ahead the feverish fund-raising went on at an even more accelerated pace. Public collections were paralleled by other, covert requests for money for arms to Israel. Seven Arab states were pouring their armies into Israel. The United States had imposed an embargo on arms to the Middle East. The Czech government offered weapons at usurious rates. Its price was met. Cash was transmitted by circuitous means. The Jews had had many centuries of experience in this kind of effort to redeem their imperiled brethren.

III

THE NATIVE AND HIS ANCESTORS

[1948–1967]

"Such as we were we gave ourselves outright . . .
To the land vaguely realizing westward. . . ."
ROBERT FROST, "The Gift Outright"

"A Jew is somebody who likes living and who puts
up some sort of a fight to stay living."
ALEX COMFORT, On This Side of Nothing

". . . the current trend toward more and more
complete acceptance of the Jew . . . appears unlikely to be reversed by anything short of a catastrophic crisis in American society. . . ."
CHARLES HERBERT STEMBER, in
Jews In The Mind of America

CHAPTER 1

The Hellenists of Suburbia

A T THE END of World War II middle-class America was caught up in two interrelated movements—flight from the central city into new neighborhoods and suburbs, and mass religious denominational affiliation. Cooperative house complexes, split-level and ranch homes, churches, temples, and synagogues rose everywhere in remarkable profusion. The Jews were now more firmly entrenched in the American middle class than ever before. There was no visible Jewish proletariat in the smaller cities, and its rapidly diminishing numbers in the big cities consisted largely of self-employed cab drivers, carpenters, plumbers, glaziers, and similar labor categories.

The Jews' evacuation of the old neighborhoods—in New York, Los Angeles, Chicago, Boston, Cleveland, Detroit—coincided with the influx of Negroes and Puerto Ricans. Yet, its primary impulse was not flight from color. These were second and third generation Jews essentially fleeing their immigrant antecedents and becoming "average Americans." The influx of underprivileged ethnic minorities only cast in sharper focus the conditions they were escaping.

Greater New York City, which contains more than forty percent of the total Jewish population of the United States, provides a grandstand view of the evolution of the Jew from immigrant to native, from tenement to suburbia. Jewish neighborhoods in the central city have been vacated, synagogues sold or boarded up, the bold imprint of the Jewish immigrant culture—newsstands piled with Yiddish newspapers and periodicals; Yiddish posters announcing new plays, lectures, cantorial concerts, liquidation and fire sales, mass meetings and protest marches; store signs in Hebrew lettering; kosher delicatessens, butcher shops, bakeries and the typical two kinds of restaurants, milchigs and fleishigs, shingles with the legend "cantor, marriage performer and circumcizer" —have been replaced by bars and grills, Negro barbecue counters, Spanish grocery stores, fortune tellers and amulet peddlers; storefront churches pouring into the night the liquid sound of cymbals, the rain-spatter of hand-clapping, the shouts, like hot gusts of desert winds, of religious frenzy.

Some of the neighborhoods' old customs have been retained in the new context—matriarchal grandmothers shepherding entire households of children; men and women, after a hard day's labor, hurrying in the twilight to English classes in neighborhood elementary and high schools; newspapers reporting ethnic events; antagonists, transplanting political feuds from their native lands, slugging it out in New York meeting halls; soapbox orators, albeit of more violent disposition than the immigrant Jews, serving up a rich fare of nationalist, racial, and social conceits; fever running through the streets on evenings when one of their own kind is seeking or defending a title in the boxing arena. Unable to afford their own sets, the Jews in the poorer sections used to gather outside radio and TV stores to hear and watch results, while the Irish would gather in the bars. Today's inhabitants of these neighborhoods pour into the streets carrying little transistors which fill the night with simultaneous accounts of the great event.

There have remained behind those with small businesses who are too old to commute, and have acquired enough Spanish words to communicate with their Cuban and Puerto Rican customers; then there are those who know no other America, having lived in these neighborhoods since their arrival in the United States a half-century ago or more; finally, in the once affluent neighborhoods, such as the West Side, for example, there remain the retired well-to-do who are reluctant to surrender their commodious rent-controlled apartments. Some of the old neighborhoods have been repopulated by an influx of post-World War II Jewish immigrants, including many Orthodox and Hassidim, and young couples that neither desire nor can afford the suburbs and East Side apartments.

East Broadway, the Fleet Street of the diminishing Yiddish press, is experiencing a transformation. The construction of cooperative high-rise housing by labor unions has brought new stable elements into a disintegrating neighborhood—Puerto Rican families employed in the garment center, retired Jewish garment workers, and the Orthodox newcomers who represent a high percentage of the remaining active Jewish proletariat. Another reason has been the amended immigration law, which has made possible the reunion of thousands of Chinese families, causing Chinatown to spill over eastward. All this has had a visible effect on the Seward Park Library on East Broadway, one of the Lower East Side's cultural landmarks. Men and women, risen from the Lower East Side to prominence in American life used to do their homework here, a haven from their overcrowded tenement homes. At one time it was celebrated for its Yiddish collection which, however, has declined in recent years. It has been replaced by Chinese and Spanish literature, and expanded its Hebrew collection, which is in demand by the young Orthodox who dip heavily into secular writing as a means of testing both their faith and their Talmudic proficiency at disputation.

The exodus seems to have been arrested also on the West Side, where several new housing developments have risen. One temple has moved to the East Side, but a new one is coming up in the Lincoln Center area. Several colleges, universities, and theological seminaries, Jewish and Christian, on the West Side, have assured a steady level of student and faculty residence. There is an influx too of the Orthodox and Hassidic element, and, concurrently, the Bohemian element. In no other section in New York City, not even Greenwich Village, is there available at newsstands so wide a selection of the little magazines and foreign newspapers and periodicals in many languages including French, Hebrew, Russian, and Spanish.

At first, when the exodus began, it seemed as if the younger generation had jettisoned its entire ethnic heritage. The most striking evidence was its apparent departure from the Jewish cuisine. The Jewish population in the old neighborhoods was no longer sufficiently large to maintain the same number of Jewish restaurants as before, and was afflicted besides with high blood pressure, diabetes and related ailments which come with age and which proscribe indulgence in food. Even the garment center, celebrated for its gourmets, had fewer restaurants now. The older generation of pioneers that always had eaten richly and excessively was under doctors' strictures against misalliances with chopped liver, stuffed miltz and derma, and kreplach, kneidlach, and other gustatory delectations. The younger generation, watching their waistlines, stayed away from these establishments altogether.

From the external evidence in the new neighborhoods and suburbs one might have concluded that the younger people were indifferent to food but were strongly concerned with God and worship. There were few restaurants in these neighborhoods; only supermarkets, which had come into the area with the new residents, featuring frozen TV dinners and bars and seafood restaurants which had preceded the Jews. But arising everywhere, in the confused architectural style of the post-war decades, were churches, temples, and synagogues, some like sprawling one-story industrial plants, others like air-raid shelters, groundhogs, wingspread eagles, birds in a downward swoop.

Probably the true reason for the young Jews' apparent indifference to food and their seeming interest in religion was their determination to fuse into the landscape. The Queens and Long Island neighborhoods and developments where they now settled were either entirely new, or had been almost completely *Judenrein* [1] before the war. The new Jewish residents built temples corresponding to the churches, but apparently deliberately abstained at first from imposing their profusion of restaurants and the Jewish cuisine. However, things gradually changed. The mixed neighborhoods began to acquire a more pronounced ethnic character, becoming either entirely Christian or entirely Jewish by almost unconscious choice. "What happened depended on a multiple of factors," Nathan Glazer writes, "a new synagogue might be built before a church, symbolizing the Jewish character of the development . . . perhaps the proportion of Jews to begin with (by sheer statistical accident) was too high to keep the non-Jews comfortable or too low to keep the Jews comfortable." [2] Fifty percent, he continues, would strike most Jews as "just right," most non-Jews as "too much."

Inhibitions began to drop away. The new Jewish neighborhoods slowly acquired the same rich variety of restaurants, delicatessens, and bakeries as were once found in the parental immigrant ghetto, but with more sumptuous façades and interior décor, and supplemented

---

[1] German expression, literally meaning "clean of Jews." Also the Nazis' slogan in calling for the purge of Jewish influence from German arts, literature, and science.
[2] Nathan Glazer and Daniel Patrick Moynihan, *Beyond The Melting Pot* (Cambridge, The M.I.T. Press, 1963). A classic in its field, it is based largely on surveys of the nineteen-fifties. However, James B. Ringer's *The Edge of Friendliness* (New York: Basic Books, 1967), an American Jewish Committee-sponsored project, indicates, to this reader, little change in suburban Christian-Jewish relations in the past decade, or differences between an East Coast or Midwest, an old or new suburb. The subject of Ringer's study, "Lakeville" (a fictitious name) was a midwest suburb that had been founded in the mid-nineteenth century, had never barred Jews, and is now undergoing new growth and an influx of additional Jewish residents.

with snackbars, called *nosherei* (Yiddish for snack), an institution that originated at Grossinger's [3] and at the Miami Beach hotels. Its purpose is to lift the flagging spirits of guests between meals and to permit the weightwatchers to deceive themselves by skipping meals altogether. The *nosherei* offers a large selection of cheese, knishes, all kinds of Jewish rolls and breads, and the inevitable bagel and lox which is not really an importation from the shtetl, but a purely American creation.

Most of these establishments describe themselves as "kosher-style," which is not synonymous with kosher but is actually a Jewish cuisine which has not been prepared in accordance with the dietary laws. Kosher Jewish foods, frozen and packaged, are now offered in supermarkets across the country, an Orthodox seal of approval guaranteeing that they were prepared under rabbinic supervision. Yet none could care less than the overwhelming majority of suburban Jews whether the food is kosher or not. They buy it because it is Jewish, not because it is kosher.[4]

Curiously, among the elements that have become the ethnic hallmark of the new Jewish neighborhoods and have contributed to the Jews' visibility in the gastronomical culture of America has been Barton's candy shops. The founder, an Orthodox Jewish refugee from Vienna,[5] purportedly brought out his own secret formulas for making chocolates. He introduced sweets for specific Jewish holidays, chocolates for Passover, *hamantaschen* for Purim, and chocolate *dreidlach*

[3] The most famous of New York state's borscht circuit hotels, host to celebrated personages from many lands, Grossinger's has been to weightwatchers what Delilah was to Samson, the sirens to sailors.

[4] The rituals that "have survived do not demand rigorous devotion and daily attention, do not involve an unsupportable isolation from non-Jews, and are acceptable to the larger community as appropriate symbols of the sacred order. Thus, the first to be rejected are the dietary laws," according to Marshall Sklare and Marc Vosk in *The Riverton Study* (New York: The American Jewish Committee, May 1957), which treats an Eastern Jewish community (Riverton is a fictitious name). Sklare and Vosk found that "thirty-one percent [in Riverton] observe some of the dietary laws—they buy kosher meat, but only eight percent have two sets of dishes." Albert J. Gordon's *Jews in Transition* (Minneapolis: University of Minnesota Press, 1949) reveals that out of a sampling of 599 Jewish suburban families in eighty communities across the country, seven percent observed the dietary laws at all times, seventy-six percent did not observe them at home, ninety-three percent did not observe them in public places. Marshall Sklare and Joseph Greenblum, *Jewish Identity on the Suburban Frontier* (New York: Basic Books, 1967), the first of the two volume Lakeville study found that "dietary observance is maintained in but a few of Lakeville homes."

[5] Barton's used to be closed between sundown Friday and sundown Saturday, a policy that changed when the firm surrendered its proprietary rights and began to rent out franchises.

for Hanukkah. Purim, a Jewish children's Halloween, commemorates the death on the gallows of Haman, a Persian royal councillor who had plotted the death of the Jews in his country. Hamantasch, which literally means Haman's purse, is a three-cornered packet of dough filled with poppy seeds, jelly, or cheese. The dreidl is a spinning top whose four sides bear the first letters of the Hebrew phrase "a great miracle happened there," referring to the Maccabean victory over the Graeco-Syrians, and the recapture of the Temple of Jerusalem. The event is marked annually by Hanukkah, the eight-day festival of lights, and the dreidl is used that week as dice in games played by parents and children for small stakes.

The commercialization of the Jewish Holidays gave them an indigenous American character. This occurred at a crucial and auspicious time in the American Jew's history. The Catholic groups—the Irish, the Italians—who had followed or preceded him into contiguous suburban neighborhoods had placed a bold religio-ethnic imprint on their environment. This, in turn, made the Jew feel dislocated, compelling him to surround himself with corresponding external symbols of his own. He retrieved these from the older Jewish neighborhoods. American Christian opinion just then was prepared to defer to Jewish self-assertion. Gnawing guilt over the fate of European Jewry led some contemplative Christians, primarily clergy, to sense an undecipherable apocalyptic-theological meaning in that catastrophe and in the almost concurrent emergence of the state of Israel. This Gentile attitude caused rabbis to accept as unimpeachable the thesis, formulated at approximately that time, by Will Herberg, of a triadic American religion, a coalition of Protestant-Catholic-Jew. The synagogues, bakeries, kosher-style restaurants and Barton's chocolate confections helped the Jew to relax in his new surroundings, and, like the inscription on an amulet at the first sight of hostility, he would recite Will Herberg's theological construction without necessarily knowing its source.

The Jew relates to his environment in two ways, in the secular field he does as his Gentile neighbor although not necessarily together with him, and in the religious field he parallels the Christian's behavior with something similar, although not identical. Christmas and Hanukkah are different in origin; one is rooted in theological myth, the other in national history. Yet, their external symbols are similar. The Hanukkah candles parallel the Christmas tree. "The aspects of Hanukkah observance currently emphasized—the exchange of gifts and the lighting and display of the *menorah* in the windows of homes—offer ready parallels to the general mode of Christmas observance as well as provide a Jewish 'alternative' to the holiday. Instead of alienating the Jew from the general culture, Hanukkah helps to situate him as a participant in that culture. Hanukkah, in short, becomes for some the Jewish Christmas." [6]

The above is an oversimplification. The Jew, in fact, insists on his Jewish alternative. He used to have Christmas trees in his home, but this practice has diminished radically in recent years. He is even seasonally involved in acrimonious debate with some of his neighbors over the introduction of Christmas symbols into the public school. "Sure of themselves as their parents never were," writes a national magazine,[7] "the Jews of the new generation tend to reject Christmas celebrations in Jewish homes as unseemly. 'Twenty years ago, there was hardly a Jewish home that didn't have a tree,' a Beverly Hills, California religious school director remembers. 'Today, there are few that do.'" "Of Jewish students recently polled by the national program director of Hillel Foundation," the magazine reported, seventy-eight percent "disapproved of Christmas trees in their homes." 'After you get somewhere, the trees get smaller,' Rabbi Arnold Wolfe of Highland Park, Ill. explains. 'It's no longer decorous to *goy* it up. Changing names and noses and having trees were inadequate ways of handling the problem. The kids will have nothing to do with it.'"

The suburban Jew's prototype is his remote ancestor, the Hellenistic Jew who in pre-Christian times had unsuccessfully tried to synthesize Judean puritanism and Graeco-Roman paganism and was regarded with suspicion and distaste by Graeco-Roman and Jew alike.

The suburban synagogue, which will be discussed at length in the next chapter, is a striking example of this groping towards synthesis. The difference between the suburban Jew and his parents and grandparents is that they had pronounced attitudes towards religion; many were Orthodox; many were "secularists" who believed that the Jewish people could survive on culture—Yiddish, Hebrew—or ideology—Zionism, Socialism. Reform and Conservative Jews also had strong views and emotions on the differences between themselves and the

[6] Marshall Sklare & Joseph Greenblum, *op. cit.*, p. 58.
[7] *Look*, December 28, 1965.

Orthodox. The suburban Jew is different. God and faith are not part of his basic vocabulary; he gives them fleeting thought at best and may even be said to be unaligned in the eternal debate between believers and agnostics (there are no atheists in suburbia, or so it appears, because that would mean taking sides). Yet, the majority of suburban Jews belong to the synagogue,[8] a high percentage use its facilities, a low percentage attend its services. Its facilities run from hedonist to ritualistic and often include a gym and health club, meeting and game rooms, catering for weddings, confirmations and other familial and public events; a Hebrew school, adult education, and psychiatric pastoral counselling.

One of the features that set the Hellenist apart from other Jews was his preoccupation with athletics, which had affected even segments of the Jerusalem priesthood, and which Jewish tradition regards as narcissistic. Concern with sports similarly sets apart the American, particularly suburban, Jew from his immigrant progenitors and generations of shtetl Jews. The immigrant father's view of life did not provide for sports, and he was distressed by his American son's concentration on sandlot ball in boyhood, tennis in young manhood, golf in his middle and later years. The second and third generation—the grandsons and great grandsons of the immigrant—have adopted their own set of athletic diversions—skiing, boating, surfing, and skin diving, depending on their financial circumstances.

Rites defer to play. Most conservative synagogues, to encourage worship among the young, have adolescent talit and tefillin (prayer shawl and phylacteries) clubs which hold services every Sunday morning. Sometimes the father accompanies his son. About one hour later, at ten in the morning, the fathers have their own event, the Sunday morning brunch which mixes bagels and lox with spiritual sustenance. The rabbi or a visiting lecturer delivers a twenty-minute talk on some Jewish cultural subject or current events, which is followed by ten or fifteen minutes of discussion. Allowing for late-comers, the event starts ten minutes late, and another ten minutes is allowed after the breakfast for lingerers. However, by 11 A.M. the last one has left, the synagogue parking lot is empty, the male congregants are off to the golf course

[8] In Lakeville, more acculturated than the average Jewish suburb, according to Sklare and Greenblum, eighty-seven percent of the parents become synagogue members when their children approach bar mitzvah (confirmation age), and some drop out when the crest period is over.

and other athletic pastimes. This Sunday morning conduct is common to the synagogues of all three denominations—Orthodox, Conservative and Reform.

The Hellenist disposition is evident in rites as well as in play. Some of the former have been altered beyond recognition. The bar mitzvah, the confirmation of the male in his thirteenth year, used to be a solemn but simple ceremony. The confirmant was called to the Torah, generally on the Sabbath nearest his birthday, and was inaugurated as a full-fledged member of the House of Israel, a responsible bearer of God's commandments and henceforth personally answerable for his deeds. The occasion required that he recite a passage from the portion of the Bible read that week in all the congregations. He then delivered a kind of "inaugural address," avowing to be faithful to his mandate as a Jew, after which his relatives showered him with raisins and served refreshments to the congregants.

The well-to-do were not content with such simplicity, however. The bar mitzvah has become a catered affair, a competitive prestigious event, with orchestra and night-club entertainment. It has been carried over, by some, to the Rainbow Room at the Waldorf Astoria, and more recently to the Playboy Club. Some parents have arranged weekend cruises aboard their yachts to celebrate the occasion.

Rabbis inveigh against this to the point of offending powerful congregants, but let the issue rest when members threaten to resign. Others, not too many, have pressed on with occasionally astonishing results. Some congregations will not call a confirmant to the Torah unless his parents pledge beforehand that the event will be celebrated becomingly, as prescribed by a congregational committee headed by the rabbi. Some even insist that a confirmant's parents take a special course on the significance of Jewish confirmation.

The Conservative rabbinate as a body has in recent years initiated a belated effort against the Paganization of the Jewish funeral rite which, as prescribed by tradition and observed today by only the very Orthodox, is sparse, brief, and leaves no margin for caste distinction in death. It provides that the deceased be washed, purged of all impurities, invested in a white linen shroud (males are wrapped also in their prayer shawls), placed in an unpainted, unadorned box and interred before sundown on the day of his demise.

The rite, unaltered through the centuries, has been changed radically in the three generations that accomplished the passage from shtetl to suburbia. Funeral directors, devising extra services and extra charges, have been abetted by the immigrants' eagerness to adopt American ways, the *nouveau riche* passion for ostentation, and the determination of Reform rabbis and principled secularists to "modernize" the ancient customs.

The traveling distance to cemeteries through big city traffic snarls and the inability to inform and assemble kin and friends on short notice has frequently been cited as the reason for suspending the rule on immediate burial. Relatively few Jews today even possess a prayer shawl and only the true traditionalists are interred with it. (The Jewish Socialists in their heyday, afire with anti-religious fervor, replaced the talit with a red flag.) Even the shroud has been largely discarded. Contrary to all Jewish law and custom, but in accordance with American funeral protocol, the deceased is embalmed and laid out, sometimes for several days, in an open casket, surrounded by floral wreaths. Orthodox rabbis have refused to officiate at such funerals. Conservatives have insisted that the casket must be closed during the service. It was not till several years ago, however, that the Conservative movement's United Synagogue and Rabbinical Assembly launched an official campaign to restore some of its tarnished dignity to the Jewish funeral rite.

Traditionally when mourners return from the cemetery, their neighbors offer them hardboiled eggs dipped in ashes. Throughout the mourning period they may be visited briefly, and visitors enter and leave with the Hebrew phrase "May God comfort you with the mourners for Zion and Jerusalem." Someone, probably an enterprising caterer, found this custom inconsistent with the mores of an affluent society. And in recent years a new custom, the catered post-burial wake, made its appearance in communities removed from the large Jewish population areas. Mourners hurried home from the funeral to receive their guests at a formal cocktail party. Even the Orthodox among the young suburbanites were entrapped by advertisements headlined "We cater shivas" (the seven-day mourning period) and offering to deliver and serve sumptuous kosher meals to visitors during the shiva so that they might "long savor this solemn occasion." The pagan and Christological connotations—the Pharaonic funeral feasts, the Last Supper, Easter, and the Eucharist—were inescapable. Rabbis bore down heavily and scored an immediate and easy victory in Springfield, Massachusetts, where, in

1961, all the synagogues denounced the open casket, the flowers (proposing charity instead), the wake and the catered shiva. The March 1962 issue of the funeral industry's peculiarly named organ, *Casket and Sunnyside*, reacted with anything but a sunny disposition. An incredibly illiterate editorial, irrelevantly raised the constitutional issue of separation of church and state, and imputed subversion to the rabbis and the synagogues.[9] It said of the Springfield action:

> It is a direct attempt on human freedom. Contrary to the ways of the American democracy, in which people can decide how they will bury their dead as well as other aspects of their personal life, this is a direct attempt of the church to dictate funerals, stripping away from the bereaved families the right of any free choice. In its way it is as bureaucratic and sinister as anything to be found in the lands where the light of freedom has vanished. . . .

The undertakers evidently had overestimated the peril of subversion. There have been curiously few communiqués from the rabbis in recent years on the progress of their campaign.

This dichotomy between Hellenism and shtetl "Calvinism," evident even in ritual, is related somewhat to the Jew's occupations. The most Hellenized is in an occupation that constitutes his deepest penetration into American culture: advertising, the mass media, and in the universities where only two decades ago he had been unwelcome as a student and is today a vigorous presence on their faculties. The Jew in these occupations adapts to the styles and concepts of the elite that determine the American way of life. The oldtime Jewish "Calvinism," perhaps more typical of the immigrant than of the shtetl, persists in occupations such as housing development, which has replaced the garment industry as a source of American Jewish affluence and which, like the classical Jewish occupations, involves hard labor, risks, and challenge.

The Jews entered the universities, the mass media, and housing development almost simultaneously. In the nineteen-thirties the Jewish middle-class vocations and professions were in a shambles as a result of the Wall Street crash. Lawyers drove cabs; the Jews' relatively small real estate holdings were wiped out; the garment industry was almost bankrupt; the chain stores were forcing out the retail stores. By the end of World War II, the entire American middle class had made an

[9] Samuel H. Dressner, *The Jew in American Life* (New York: Crown, 1963).

astonishing recovery. The lowly Jewish junkdealer began to manufacture auto parts for a giant industry that still bars its executive suite
to Jews. Jewish carpenters, plumbers, and painters scraped together all
the negligible family capital and launched into housing development,
supported by government-guaranteed bank loans. From this they
branched off into two additional fields. Treated disdainfully by the
WASP-controlled commercial banks, they turned to the savings and
loan associations, and soon began founding associations of their own.
As the country's new center of gravity spread to the housing developments and suburbs, the Jews built supermarkets there while the big
chain stores that had forced them out of the retail business were still
anchored in the deteriorating central city.

All this ingenious activity did not require new skills. Sholem
Aleichem's Tevya possessed them, and given the opportunity he would
have done as well. His progeny took these traditional skills as business
brokers and merchandisers, and as engineers and inventors cast them in
larger dimensions. They founded electronics concerns and moved into
advertising, publicity, the mass media, publishing, all of which require
merchandising ability.[10]

A study of a sample community,[11] probably typical, shows that ninety
percent of its Jewish youth attend college, thirty-six percent attend
graduate schools. The percentage in New York City, which contains
nearly half of the entire American Jewish population, is believed to be
only slightly lower. It shows also that as the third generation settles
down into its occupations it has little of the drive that is required of pioneers in private enterprise, and is somewhat embarrasssed by its parents'
and grandparents' compulsive work patterns and obsession with *tachlis*
(goals). It places a lower premium on self-employment and sees no
indignity in salaried security, yet feels no less entitled than its predecessors to the riches of the world. Considering its education and the
advanced technology of our times, it may well be able to tailor its life
according to its own precise specifications.

The study reveals a drop from 72.6 percent to 45.2 percent in self-

---

[10] Nathan Glazer, in the section "The Jews" in *Beyond the Melting Pot;* also
Nathan Glazer, "Social Characteristics of American Jews," *The Jews: Their History, Culture and Religion,* ed. Louis Finkelstein, 2 vols. (New York: Harper and
Row, 1960).
[11] Judith R. Kramer & Seymour Leventman, *Children of the Gilded Ghetto, Conflict Resolutions of Three Generations of American Jews* (New Haven: Yale University Press, 1961).

employment in three generations. An even steeper decline might have been indicated if heirs-apparent working in their fathers' businesses had not been classified as self-employed. There was a pronounced differential between the sons of the country club set and of the fraternal lodge members, the study's terminology distinguishing between the upper-middle and lower-middle class. In the first group, fifty-two percent of the sons chose business, forty-eight percent chose professions; in the second, seventy-eight percent professions, twenty-two percent business. Obviously the first group had the more difficult decision to make, since their fathers were ready to offer them prestigious, high income positions and eventual possession of the family business.

The GI Bill of Rights, Truman's determined effort to put an end to discrimination in higher education,[12] the demands of the Korean and Vietnam wars, and of an expanding automation economy, opened new occupational opportunities for the Jew in professions that once had been only a remote dream. The Jewish physicists, medical researchers, sociologists, and professors of English and American history are obviously drawn from all segments of American society. Yet, since the lower middle-class obviously is more numerous than the upper, and since seventy-eight percent of the sons of lodge members and only forty-eight percent of the sons of country-club fathers chose the professions, it seems apparent which class provides the high proportion of the professional elite. America had overturned the shtetl's social pyramid more than half a century ago. The balebatische, the scholar, the genteel among the immigrants became the "ineffectual man," while an inordinately high percentage of the skilled proletariat became nouveau riche. Now, perhaps, the balance is being restored. Although no survey has been made and no figures are available, even the most casual queries show that a surprisingly large number of men eminent in American academia and letters today had genteel immigrant fathers and rabbinic forebears.[13]

The businessman is losing his social eminence in America to the scientist and professional who combine both the mystique of culture

---

[12] The President's Committee on Higher Education charged in 1947 that "Jewish students do not have equal opportunity with non-Jewish students in the choice of institutions and certain fields of advanced studies. The obstacles created by private institutions of higher education are manifested in tacit and overt quotas."

[13] Saul Bellow, Herzog (New York: The Viking Press, 1961): "Herzog's Yiddish background was genteel. He heard with instinctive snobbery Valentine's butchers', teamsters', commoners' accent, and he put himself down for it. . . ."

and an impressive earning capacity that was not theirs two decades ago. For the Jew this circumstance has resolved a dilemma. He had always been torn between conflicting sybaritic and scholarly inclinations and has had to forfeit one for the other in the many centuries when commerce was the only way of satisfying sybaritic tastes. Another reason why the third-generation Jew generally turns away from business may be its embarrassing association with plebeian antecedents, immigrant beginnings, English spoken with a Yiddish accent that was parodied by vaudeville comedians, sweat and poverty and jugular competition.

Yet, even today, the Jew in America is still barred from some highly esteemed occupations. An American Jewish Committee survey, published in May 1966 revealed that "fewer than one percent of the presidents of America's non-sectarian senior colleges and universities are Jewish, although between 10 and 12 percent of the student bodies and faculties in these institutions are Jewish." [14] Still another AJC study revealed that forty-five of the fifty largest commercial banks in the country have no Jews among their senior officials.[15] There is no report on remedial action regarding the university executive suite, but The American Bankers Association has announced that it has taken steps to correct the banking situation.[16]

The suburban Jew's occupations, although of a different kind, are no more heterogeneous than those of the shtetl Jew, his grandfather. They are all middle class and because of the Jew's ethnic predisposition and because of past and even present discrimination he has gravitated more to some than to others. There is also the element of voluntary social selection. That the concentration of Jews in so-called "Jewish occupations" sustains inbred association and Jewish group consciousness has been brought out in a study that compares the attitude towards affiliations and rituals among Jews who are employed in "Jewish" occupations and those who work among Gentiles. The former had an infinitely higher percentage of synagogue members, observers of rituals, and persons who belonged or thought they should to Jewish organizations.[17]

This raises, of course, the entire painful question of social exclusion, discrimination, and preference. The Jew has grouped many of his secular or hedonist activities inside the synagogue. What motivated him to

[14] *New York Times*, May 15, 1966.
[15] *New York Times*, September 2, 1966.
[16] *New York Times*, May 21, 1967.
[17] Judith R. Kramer and Seymour Leventman, *The Gilded Ghetto* (New Haven and London: Yale University Press, 1961), pp. 200–202

use the synagogue in this way? Perhaps because it is a socially approved cover for secular facilities that are equal but separate. He needs this separation partly because he wishes somehow to sustain a group solidarity (an eminent Jewish historian, Simon Dubnow, called this "the Jewish will to be"), partly because it protects him from the pain of social exclusion which, correctly or not, he expects from his Gentile neighbor. Sociologist Herbert J. Gans observes that "Jews often move into communities where the median income is lower than their own, partly because some prefer to spend a lower share of their income on housing, partly because they fear rejection from their non-Jewish neighbors of similar income and education." [18]

In a town of 50,000, including 1,500 Jews, a poll of Gentiles and Jews belonging to mixed organizations revealed that only nine percent of the Gentiles felt differently towards their Jewish than their Gentile peers, but that 39 percent of the Jews thought the Gentiles felt differently towards them.[19] "The Jew is invited to participate in discussions about spending money, but excluded from inner circles where decisions about making money originate," is the succinct summation of a study which contrasts this with the Jew's welcome participation in civic betterment organizations, in art, opera, symphony societies. The very same people, no doubt, may blackball him for membership, if he is sufficiently audacious to apply, in the private clubs which although essentially of a social character foster relationships that are crucial for business and professional advancement.

Even in the inordinately acculturated Lakeview of the Sklare and Greenblum, and Ringer studies, social intercourse between American Jew and Gentile is still largely confined to professional, business, community and civic organizations and occasions. These kinds of contacts are either an extension of the working day, or like business, focused on specific activities and interests. What inhibits a wider range of involvement, a full social interfamilial relationship—most Jew and Gentile social relationships are between the wives, or the husbands, not between the couples—is not necessarily or only prejudice, but rather an insufficient range of common interests.[20]

---

[18] Herbert J. Gans, *The Levittowners* (New York: Pantheon Books, 1967), p. 82.
[19] John P. Dean in *The Jews, Social Patterns of an American Group*, ed. Marshall Sklare (Glencoe: Free Press), p. 311.
[20] Benjamin B. Ringer, *The Edge of Loneliness* (New York and London: Basic Books, 1967), pp. 263–268. The entire volume deals with these issues.

That the "will to be" in Jews is a strong factor is undeniable. It explains the conflict within the Jewish community whether to extend Jewish center memberships to Gentiles who seek to use its athletic and social facilities. To the Jews the synagogue and Jewish center are an enclave in which they can be themselves. A minority needs such enclaves if it is to survive, especially in a mass media society in which the popular culture equates and levels all valuable differences and distinctions. The suburban Jew subsidizes studies of all kinds to advise him how he can remain a Jew without offending, and whether or not he has reached, through business and professional success, the condition most perilous for a minority—excessive visibility? He does not even know whether it is a qualitative or quantitative condition, whether its cause is numbers or cultural dissimilarity. It is something that worries him nonetheless.

His immigrant grandfather may have worn a caftan and earlocks, spoken nothing but Yiddish. However, tucked away in the Lower East Side he was virtually invisible to other Americans, except to those who went slumming in the tenement neighborhoods or when some ghetto disaster splashed him on the newspapers' front pages. His grandson, the suburban Jew, is infinitely more visible, although in no apparent way different from his neighbors. He commutes by the same train, shops in the same markets, attends PTA meetings, is worried about his golf, assiduously washes and polishes his car on Sundays, consumes no smaller quantities of bacon, ham and shellfish than his Christian neighbors, and his distinctive Jewish foods are stored away in the deep freeze of many suburban homes, Jewish and Gentile alike. He is seen on TV as a panelist and moderator, is celebrated as a playwright, director, and actor, both on and off Broadway, and as an author is featured on the drugstore bookrack. But does this suggest full acceptance by America or excessive visibility? The Jewish community relations agencies, at the cost of several million dollars a year, are seeking the answer which has been eluding the Jewish people for more than two thousand years.

CHAPTER 2

The Rabbi and His Flock

ANY RABBI who regards his office as a career, not a calling, who can navigate the shoals of synagogue politics and is content with creature comforts, job security and increments, and a social life of congregational community, should find fulfillment in an American suburban pulpit.

Some, however, chafe against the sinecure, rear up and try to break the pattern and may indeed succeed some day to alter the American synagogue. Many, even with pensions in sight, resign their pulpits to enter some other occupations, defect to business if their purpose is larger income, or join the faculty of a university if their goal is scholarship and academic status. These defections have a depressing effect on what is today "a seller's market"; the seminaries' supply of rabbis falls short of congregational demands, which is why a congregation of one denomination very often settles for a rabbi of another.

If the American rabbi today is haunted by a variant of Hamlet's "To be or not to be?" it is not because his decision to go into the rabbinate was made hastily, or because he has since lost faith, but because the doubt about the usefulness of his role has been so widespread. The synagogue and the rabbi may have become, as some sociologists contend, part of the American Establishment. In the process, the rabbi has become a more ubiquitous, yet an infinitely less important figure. Two prominent Conservative rabbis, almost a generation apart in age, expressed this separately and well a few years ago. Seated in the study of his recently completed new temple, one of the men confided to visitors: "My Lower East Side father, who was an Orthodox rabbi, as you know, was a more fortunate man than I am. It did not matter to him whether his congregants wanted him. He knew that they needed him. Mine, conversely, want me, but they don't really need me." [1] The other wrote, "A growing neighborhood, with a reasonably affluent Jewish community of child rearing age, produces, as a matter of course, a large busy synagogue. Such synagogues succeed just as well as institutions with rabbis of little personal stature—men of drive and learning are not indispensable to their fortune." [2]

The synagogue in suburban America is a more central institution than it had ever been in the shtetl, or even on the immigrant Lower East Side. It is virtually the only Jewish institution in suburbia, and like the promenades in Italian and Spanish towns, the focus of the Jewish population. The rabbi presides over all that transpires within its walls, dividing his time among administrative functions, fund-raising for a new wing or an entirely new building, and such routine chores as officiating at weddings, circumcisions, bar and bas mitzvahs, funerals, and, of course, extremely poorly attended religious services. If he is at all concerned with the spiritual state of his congregation he may also teach adult classes, generally attended by young mothers and middle-aged "moms"; he may even persuade a dozen or so sophisticated male members to join a study circle. In large temples he is assisted by specialist personnel, an adult education director, a Hebrew school principal and teaching staff, an assistant rabbi who is his detail man for administrative matters and attends those bar mitzvahs, weddings, and funerals that do not merit the senior rabbi's presence.

In addition, the suburban rabbi is involved in civic organizations and interfaith affairs and participates in panel discussions, on and off the air and TV screen. Amidst this whirlwind of activities he has little time for study, yet many rabbis utilize their limited leisure with remarkable economy dividing it between Jewish studies and "must" reading in all the subjects that congregants, sometimes specialists, might broach to them. Besides, reading is the stuff of which sermons are made.

In the shtetl and on the Lower East Side the rabbi was more sovereign. In Europe, he was generally on the payroll of the Jewish community, not of a specific congregation, a civil servant, not the protégé of a powerful patron or group of patrons.

On the Lower East Side he was sometimes attached to a synagogue,

[1] The late Rabbi Morris Adler of Detroit in conversation with this author.
[2] Arthur Hertzberg, "The Changing American Rabbinate," *Midstream* (January 1966). Available in reprint.

sometimes an "independent." To whichever category he belonged, Orthodox Jews in his immediate vicinity regarded him as "our" rabbi; his obligations under either circumstance were few so that from dawn until late in the evening he could study the sacred texts and write his own commentaries which, for lack of funds to subsidize publication, remained in manuscript. However, the door of his apartment was always ajar and not infrequently during the day women would enter carrying blood-soaked paperbags in which were wrapped the innards of a fowl. These women knew enough about the defects, visible only after it had been opened, that made a fowl unkosher, and, suspicion aroused, they rushed to consult the rabbi. His verdict sometimes was dictated less by law than compassion. If the woman seemed poor custom required that the rabbi render these services free. It also required, however, that the women leave some coin with his wife, this being one of the sources of his meager income. A quarter was regarded as fair compensation, a dollar was philanthropy. Synagogues that had no rabbi arranged at their Sabbath services several times a year for all that were called to the Torah to pledge contributions for the neighborhood rabbi. If he had a good voice he would also be engaged on the High Holidays as a *baal tefila,* who performs the cantor's role but in quite another manner. The cantor must be a good vocalist, the baal tefila is judged by his comprehension of the text, revealed by his reading, and by his sincerity and piety. If a baal tefila is also a *baal bekhi,* one who virtually sobs the supplications, he has few peers. Hence synagogues always preferred a rabbi for this.

The Orthodox rabbi's obligations to his congregants and neighborhood were thus very few and imposed no real demand on his time. Yet, he never questioned the importance of his function, although his was largely a passive role. Custom recognized that his function was the study of and communion with the sages of past centuries through the printed text. He was the guardian of the law, protector of ritual, the supreme authority to the pious in his immediate vicinity. His wife, not always impressed with his status, might argue bitterly that were he a wiser man he would seek out a more lucrative and secure vocation, and not be dependent on women with blood-soaked paperbags and on the taxing assignment of leading a congregation through the long, exhausting service of the most solemn day of the year, Yom Kippur.

Today, the Orthodox rabbi in suburbia is as much in quest of a sense of purpose as his Conservative and Reform colleagues. Few congregants consult him on ritualistic matters or draw upon his knowledge of the law. The only difference sometimes between his congregants and the others is that on the Sabbath, deferring to his rabbi, he leaves his car in the parking lot of the Conservative or Reform, not the Orthodox congregation. When a rabbi of any of the three denominations sometimes halts in the midst of his interminable chores to calculate his time, he discovers that most of it is spent on fund-raising, membership drives and executive functions so that a degree in business administration might have been more useful to him than rabbinic ordination.

Israel is represented by its ambassadors who are irritated when American rabbis and Zionist leaders speak publicly as if they were Israel's authorized surrogates; the residual Jewish proletariat is largely concentrated among the Orthodox new immigrants; social legislation (which Jewish labor pressure helped enact) in states with large Jewish populations has reduced the frequency of strikes, making them as unfashionable as the trolley car; the high-powered labor executive cannot stir in the Jewish middle class the same guilt feeling as his wild-mannered predecessor, who was in and out of jail for alleged rowdyism on the picket-line. Although poverty has not been alien to the Jew through the centuries, the Jews never had a poverty culture, cannot comprehend it and therefore respond with less than their traditional spontaneous compassion (although they may feel guilty about it) to Southern "white trash" and the displaced cotton-patch Negro who fit too neatly into the category of the *am haaretz*, the untutored and superstition-ridden with whom Jewish learned tradition had little patience; the urban Negro's plight is of direct concern to the Jew, but it can hardly become the *raison d'être* of the rabbinical function. These circumstances combined have negated two functions—Zionism and the social gospel—to which the Reform and Conservative rabbis, the majority of the American rabbinate today, were conditioned.[3]

On the Lower East Side, when a synagogue's mortgage was paid off, its members celebrated the occasion by marching through the streets with the sacred scrolls and band music; in conclusion, as a symbol of the redemption of their house of worship from the bank, they would set a match to the mortgage document. Those synagogue elders were working men and small shopkeepers who treated all debts as onerous. The

[3] *Ibid.*, Judd L. Teller, *Commentary*, February 1958 and also Judd L. Teller, "Zionism, Israel and American Jewry" in *The American Jew, a Reappraisal* (New York: The Jewish Publication Society, 1954), pp. 301-321.

lay leaders of today's suburban synagogue are substantial businessmen. Applying their worldly experience to its affairs, they never burn its mortgage, they extend and increase it, or take out a new one. They are always involved in planning expansion of its physical plant to accommodate more and more activities unrelated to what had through the generations been the synagogue's major, or perhaps even only function: worship and study. This constant expansion requires raising membership dues and imposing frequent additional levies which makes affiliation to a suburban synagogue fairly expensive. It has been estimated by one officer of a Long Island synagogue that anyone who makes less than twenty thousand dollars a year cannot really afford to belong, which also means, in turn, that his children will not be enrolled in the synagogue's school and will be denied a religious education unless they receive one of the several available scholarships. The officer explained that this was not as harsh as it seemed because "poor people cannot afford homes in our neighborhood."

Many of the suburban synagogues are really upper middle-class preserves, alienating Jewish lower income groups whose number increases as the suburb expands into a township. A study published nearly a decade ago, and there is no reason to suspect that the situation has changed, showed that forty-six percent of the officers of Conservative synagogues were top executives in business, government, and voluntary associations, and thirty percent were eminent in their professions.[4] They have sincere concern for the material welfare, i.e. the budget of the synagogue, but few of them really bother with its religious purpose, since they use the synagogue as a surrogate for their homes and thus, eventually, change its character and function.

It is estimated that some fifty percent of Jewish suburban homes exhibit the mezuzah on the outside doorpost. Besides indicating a Jewish residence, the mezuzah is also ornamental, generally encased in beautiful Yemenite silverwork from Israel. But inside the home there is little to distinguish it from Gentile homes, perhaps only a menorah and several books in English on Jewish subjects, addressed to Jew and Gentile alike. Until several years ago Leon Uris' Exodus was found on shelves in Jewish homes, perhaps more often than the Bible. More recently it has been James Michener's The Source. Candle lighting on

[4] Marshall Sklare, "Aspects of Religious Worship in the Contemporay Conservative Synagogue," in The Jews, Social Patterns of an American Group (Glencoe: The Free Press, 1958).

Friday night and during the eight days of Hanukkah, and matzoh on Passover just about exhaust the range of ritualistic observance, the kind that children might store away in their memories. Many congregants rely even for these on the synagogue. Reform temples and some Conservative congregations have a communal seder. There is also the congregational sukkah on the Feast of Tabernacles. The synagogue's ineffectiveness both in its own domain and as a surrogate for the home must be imputed also to a failure of the contemporary rabbinical imagination. Never have rabbis been so free to experiment, and never have they been so pedestrian and fumbling in their attempts at innovations.

The type of services a synagogue or temple chooses is determined less by its formal denominational affiliation than by its rabbi and/or the consensus of its congregants. The suburban synagogues, especially those with young membership, have no single denominational approach and, like the Roman Empire (to press the Hellenist analogy of the preceding chapter), are tolerant of all forms of worship and are disposed towards an eclecticism. The only difference between Orthodox and Conservative congregations is that the former sometimes seat men and women separately, as prescribed by tradition, behind a curtain or partition. All three kinds of synagogue are reconciled to poor attendance on Saturday morning which for centuries had been the week's primary service, because only Yom Kippur (the Sabbath of Sabbaths) is holier than the Sabbath. The focus now is on an after-dinner Friday night service, a purely American invention, perhaps patterned after *The Reader's Digest,* which crowds hymn-singing, the kaddish (prayer for the dead) and a lecture into a compact ninety minutes, followed by a social get-together in a side room where refreshments are served and the lecturer submits to questions from the audience.

Conservative and Reform services and procedures are improvised from synagogue to synagogue. Although each of the denominations has its own standard prayerbook, there is as yet no mandatory order of prayers, the kind that Orthodoxy had handed down through the generations. The rabbi and cantor consult before each service on the prayers to be chanted, and each prayer is announced by page number from the pulpit. Perhaps devotion requires familiarity and the prayers might be more meaningful if the congregation would chant the same ones week after week.

In recent years there has been evidence of a revolt against the laymen's custom of making the synagogue a home away from home. This has resulted from a trend towards neo-Orthodoxy in the Conservative and Reform rabbinates. In the Reform rabbinate some of the ranking younger men have begun to discuss mitzvot, commandments—meaning by that the observance of rituals, which constitutes a virtual Counter-Reformation considering that the movement's founders had jettisoned almost all rituals as obsolescent superstitions and as tending to segregate Jews from their neighbors.

Eugene Borowitz, Professor of Education and Jewish Religion at the Hebrew Union College, is one of the foremost young thinkers in the Reform rabbinate. He wrote; "The man who seeks the reality of Israel's covenant with God should know that it is far less likely to be found in thinking about it than in trying to live by it. One commandment will do for a beginning, any one which seems to speak to him and which he can undertake in his search to clarify his association with his people and its God. A morning prayer, study of an anthology of rabbinic literature, the blessing over whiskey, the prohibition of gossip—he can begin anywhere. And when the inner embarrassment of doing a *mitzvah* as a *mitzvah* has been overcome, he can then see what the reality of the covenanted existence might mean—and then hopefully go on to another *mitzvah*. Going back will be our best means of going forward." [5]

> Another rabbi, Petuchowski, Professor of Rabbinics and Jewish Theology at the Hebrew Union College, concedes the right of every single Jew to choose his own pattern of religious behavior (a Reform rabbi who would not concede this right, would belong fully in the Orthodox camp) but warns, however, that none ". . . should approach the Torah with a prior notion about the inferiority of 'ritual commandments lacking ethical or doctrinal content.' It is true, the prophets have taught us that ceremonies are blasphemy when those who observe them do not lead a moral and ethical life. But that does not mean yet that religion is exhausted by the ethical (and doctrinal) sphere . . . if religion addresses itself to the entire personality, then it obviously will have to provide something for those levels of our being which lie below the layer of consciousness and that may very well be one of the functions of the so-called 'ritual' commandments. Not every 'ritual' necessarily has to teach an 'ethical' lesson in order to be a valuable component of religion . . . though even such 'rituals,' in their aggregate, could conceivably mould the type of personality that is receptive to moral imperatives. A 'ritual' serving as an expression of the Jew's love for God or as a reminder of a historical encounter, is as much entitled to our consideration as are the more pronounced 'ethical' commandments." [6]

[5] *The Condition of Jewish Belief*, a symposium compiled by the editors of *Commentary* (New York: Macmillan Company, 1966), p. 38.
[6] Jacob J. Petuchowski, *The Condition of Jewish Belief*, p. 160.

242 THE NATIVE AND HIS ANCESTORS [1948-1967]

Rabbis have even reverted, unabashedly, to the term "Chosen people." Rabbi Petuchowski writes: "My possession of the Torah is really all the proof I need for the doctrine of the chosen people—all the proof I need, and also the meaning which 'chosenness' has for me. But there are other indications. There is the miracle of Jewish survival which, but for my belief in the chosen-people doctrine, I would have put down to a freak of history . . . as long as I myself feel the need to make my contribution to the world *as a Jew*, it will be my belief in the chosen people which motivates me to do so." [7]

American Jewish neo-Orthodoxy has drawn from several sources, not always closely aligned, not always even related to Orthodoxy, and whose kinship the neo-Orthodox might wish to deny. It evolved in the nineteen-fifties when Existentialism had become the refuge of the disenchanted supporters of Stalinism, of liberals who became silent to escape the malevolence of McCarthyism, and of executives in high-powered industry unsettled by the ultimate meaninglessness of their lives. There was the strange phenomenon of Will Herberg, a former Marxist, a layman who was actually a sociologist rather than a theologian, better versed in Christian theology than in Jewish sacred works, who frankly admitted in a foreword to *Judaism and Modern Man*, his first book, that "what I owe to Reinhold Niebuhr in the formation of my general theological outlook every page of this book bears witness."

His sociology, outlined in his second book *Protestant-Catholic-Jew* and discussed in the preceding chapter accounts for his popularity then on the synagogue lecture circuit. The Jew, new in the suburbs, needed reassurance that his faith blended with its landscape. Herberg's decline since is traceable to his political conservatism and his theology. After the demise of McCarthyism, the suburban Jew snapped back to his liberal posture in politics. Herberg's dour theology was contrary to Jewish conditioning—his pessimism about the human condition, his obsession with man's sinfulness, his rejection of man's redemptive role in the Messianic process and his unrelenting rejection of secularism were apparently out of joint.

A powerful influence has been Abraham Joshua Heschel, a man of great charisma, who bears the name of one of the leading Hassidic families. Had he tarried in the parochial confines of the Hassidic court,

[7] *Ibid.*, p. 161.

and not gone to Warsaw and then Berlin to further his studies, he might have become a Hassidic dynastic leader. In 1937 Martin Buber named him his successor to the perilous post, under those circumstances, of director of German Jewry's adult education program and of the *Judische Lehrhaus* (Jewish House of Study). The latter institution had been founded by Franz Rosenzweig. Thus, by curious circumstance, three of the foremost Jewish religious thinkers of our time, each distinctive in himself and different from the others, had served with the *Lehrhaus*.

In 1938, the Germans expelled Heschel as a Polish Jew. In 1940 he arrived in the United States at the invitation of Hebrew Union College of Cincinnati, and in 1945 joined the faculty of The Jewish Theological Seminary, the Conservative institution. A slight man, soft-spoken, a scholar's brow erupting from bushy beard and head, he advocates a doctrine of pure Hassidism for modern man. All the more strange then, although perhaps not, that he is cited today along with Niebuhr and Tillich as a proponent of American theology. None of the Reform rabbis ever achieved that status. Those who contend that "theology . . . is alien to Judaism," [8] are guilty of separating law from devotion, the physical from the metaphysical. "In the spiritual crisis of the modern Jew the problem of faith takes precedence over the problem of law." [9] Yet, "to reduce Judaism to inwardness . . . is to dissolve its essence and to destroy its reality." [10] Calling for a symbiosis of law and spontaneous faith he states: "The problem of ethics is, what is the ideal or principle of conduct that is *rationally* justifiable? To religion the problem of living is, what is the ideal or principle of living that is *spiritually* justifiable? The legitimate question concerning the forms of Jewish observance is the question: Are they spiritually meaningful?" [11] "Explanations of the *mitzvot* come and go; theories change with the temper of the age . . . explanations are translations; they are both useful and inadequate." [12]

The difference between Buber and Heschel's thought is impressive. Buber, being German, presented his adaptation of Hassidism as a system. Yet the two most notable attempts in Jewish history, by Saadia and Maimonides, to formulate the Jewish *Weltanschauung* as a systematic

[8] Abraham J. Heschel, *Between God and Man, An Interpretation of Judaism,* ed. Fritz A. Rothschild (New York: Harper & Bros., 1959), p. 169.
[9] *Ibid.*, p. 177.
[10] *Ibid.*
[11] *Ibid.*, p. 182.
[12] *Ibid.*, p. 183.

theology, never achieved universal acceptance. Heschel's thought reflects consistency, but does not pretend to be a formal system: his Hassidism is directly from the source, but it is not his only source; he draws like Hassidism itself upon the vast pluralism of the Jewish heritage, and hence *halakhah*, rabbinic law, is his base. Buber rejected *halakhah* in his accent on spontaneity and failed to comprehend the significance of discipline, rote, the repetitive act, the ritualistic commandment, the mitzvah. Heschel stresses spontaneity and mitzvah, transport and law as polarities: Hassidism reflected this polar condition perfectly; the False Messianism of Sabbatai Zvi resulted from a catastrophic imbalance.

Christianity's conflict has not been with Hebrew prophecy, but with Hebrew law. Buber's rejection of *halakhah* explains his ready acceptance by Christian theologians. Christianity's animus toward the Pharisees has been retained even in the Ecumenical Council's statement on deicide. German-born classical Reform Judaism paralleled Christianity's hostility towards the law, Protestantism's accent on the Prophets. Curiously, the mystic Buber may unconsciously have been influenced by rationalist classical Reform.

In his Foreword to the *Commentary* symposium, and using its contributors as his gauge, Milton Himmelfarb concludes that Buber has had "hardly any" influence on American Jewish theology, despite the publicity attending his name, the popularity of his lectures and books. The reason, he suggests, is that Buber's anti-*halakhah* stand alienated Conservative rabbis and his mysticism estranged Reform rabbis. Another probably valid reason is that Buber's universalism and Israel-centeredness do not correspond with the evident intent of some younger men in the rabbinate to create a distinctive American synagogue. These seem to find affinity with Franz Rosenzweig; in Himmelfarb's opinion, out of the twenty-seven Conservative and Reform (there were also eleven Orthodox) contributors to the symposium, fifteen to seventeen have apparently been influenced by Rosenzweig's thought. Like Arnold Zweig, Rosenzweig had his first encounter with East European Jewry when serving as a German officer on the Galician front in World War I. Like Buber, Brod, Kafka, and Zweig he was deeply affected by its culture; before this he had briefly considered conversion to Protestantism.

The years of his primary influence (he died in 1929, at the age of 43) were spent in the kind of physical agony which, in the church, commends its victim to beatification. Progressive paralysis deprived him of speech and of all movement except in one finger with which he would point to letters on a specially constructed typewriter, and it is from this mute, laborious dictation that his wife transcribed his ordered, concise, and lucid sentences. While receding into this condition, he produced masterful translations from medieval Hebrew literature; a new translation of the Bible, in collaboration with Buber; and correspondence which sets forth ideas, but not a system. His only theological work, *Star of Redemption,* was written before his illness and before he acquired the lucidity of thought and expression that characterizes his letters.

Although in the main so very different, Rosenzweig's "synthetic Judaism" and classical Reform Judaism nonetheless meet at points. Rosenzweig tried to accommodate irrational Jewish theology even as Reform Judaism hoped to accommodate rational Jewish theology into the German cultural environment and make it comprehensible to the German-Jewish intellectual. He celebrated Judaism for having cast off "the curse of historicity," implied that Jewry's true mission had begun with its Dispersion, found Orthodoxy "too narrow," Zionism "too limited," liberalism "too vague." These Rosenzweig dicta apparently have been sufficient to propel some younger men among Reform Judaism's neo-Orthodox to take off on a doctrinal space flight which he might have repudiated, were he living. Striking a posture of non-alignment between liberalism and conservatism, they are engaged in social quietism at a time when the Christian church, conversely, is moving out into the world, they are aggressively anti-secular and disparage Zionism as a secular, hence inferior ideology, and suggest that the State of Israel, the consummation of a merely political purpose, is unrelated to the Messianic design and therefore perhaps wholly irrelevant to Jewry's "mission among the nations." [13]

This deprecation of secularism, this fond hope of the emergence of an American synagogue, distinctive and unique, has not been confined to the neo-Orthodox. There are symptoms of it among very young rabbis, just embarking on their careers, in all three denominations. It is not consciously anti-Israel, or anti-Zionist, and is probably related to Ecumenism and the consequent Christian-Jewish dialogue, and a misreading by the younger men of the terminology used in this connection by their elders, men in their late forties and fifties. "Diaspora," "Covenant" and "Revelation," classical terms in Jewish religious discourse, have been brought into such loose alignment with current Christian

[13] Jacob J. Petuchowski, *Zion Reconsidered* (New York: Twayne Publisher, 1966).

theological discourse that some of the young rabbis walk about in a verbal trance spouting a wild theology to congregations that are secular, liberal, pro-Israel, and without interest in theology.[14]

It is because of this that the synagogue and the rabbi might fail American Jewry. There is ample evidence in the literature produced by American Jewish writers in recent years, in the literature American Jews read, in the few kinds of ritualistic observances most common in Jewish suburbia that there may be an opportunity for a revival of distinctive Jewish rituals if the emphasis were placed on their ancestral, rather than divine character, on their significance as instrumentalities of Jewish survival, symbols of universal Jewish kinship through the ages, rather than on religious fiat. Reconstructionism comprehended this, but instead of acting as a catalyst in Reform and Conservative Judaism, it became a fourth denomination with its own synagogues, its own prayerbook and *Haggadah*.

American Jewish Orthodoxy is more difficult to define. Orthodoxy had been virtually the only denomination in Judaism till the eighteenth century. This longevity suggests at least a great past capacity for adjustment and accommodation to times and fashions. The result has been infinite brands of Orthodoxy and many kinds of Orthodox Jew. In America the gap between profession and performance of faith is so large that there are the nominally Orthodox who are no more observant perhaps than the Reform Jew, flouting the dietary laws and other ritual dogma. What they mean is that they belong to a synagogue whose rabbi conducts Orthodox services. Since very likely they had several synagogues to choose from, their affiliation is probably no accident: a) they had been conditioned in childhood to this kind of service; b) its traditional pattern provides greater uplift; c) they have fallen out with the Reform or Conservative Congregation in their neighborhood, and/or they found that they can be bigger fish in their particular Orthodox pond than in any other.

Apart from these who are casually affiliated, there are many others who indeed take their Orthodoxy seriously. At the extreme end are the Hassidim, clinging to ancient customs that were fading away in the East European shtetl on the eve of World War II. There are many kinds of Hassidim and Hassidic sects. There are floaters in each group,

[14] Judd L. Teller, "Secularists, The Rabbinate and Mitzvot," in *Proceedings of 1967 Rabbinical Assembly Convention.* These attitudes of rabbis have been altered somewhat by the six-day war of 1967.

who are as neglectful of religious practices as the average American Jew, but have a kind of tacit dispensation from their rebbe because they are a source of financial support for the sect. There are, of course, the strict sectarians, sworn to a Fundamentalist code, all wearing approximately the same kind of distinctive garments, but each group clustering around its own wonder rebbe, and often maintaining its own circumscribed economy, members employing members and purchasing from their own kind. Even these are not completely isolated from the times in which they live. The newspapers, radio and TV—some rebbes interdict these as instruments of corruption—account for creeping modernism, especially among the women who cut their dresses shorter, order *sheitlen* (wigs, because the Hassidic women must shave their heads) with teased high pompadours and insist on better housing and neighborhoods.

Within the Hassidic camp itself there are also two extremes. There is the Satmar sect; its leader resides in Williamsburgh and his Jerusalem disciples have never yet voted in an Israeli election because its government, they contend, by assuming power, "has sinfully precipitated the Messiah who will come in his own due time." During a lull in Israel's Independence War in 1948 their leader was halted by Israeli soldiers as he was about to cross into enemy territory carrying a white surrender flag. Israelis have never forgiven the patrol for halting him. In New York, the Satmar, from time to time, picket the Israeli consulate to protest "religious oppression," by which they mean that their members were arrested for stoning traffic moving through Jerusalem on the Sabbath.

At the other end of the Hassidic spectrum is the Lubavicher or Habad sect (see Book II, Chapter IV). Its present head holds a degree in engineering from the Sorbonne. He is consulted personally and by correspondence on issues of faith, and on career, business, and family matters. Mail reaches him daily by the sackful, in French, English, Russian, Spanish, Yiddish, and Hebrew. The volume is so heavy that, although he has four secretaries, it takes two months before a letter is answered, unless it requires an urgent reply. He also presides over a worldwide network of educational institutions and reaches into regions where such activity is frowned upon or even forbidden under the law. Habad engages frankly in "missionizing" efforts among non-religious Jews, addressing itself to the intellectual elite. It hints at large numbers of converts from Jewish secularism. Although it no doubt has had some astonishing successes, these probably are fewer than rumored. Now and then a young man from a third generation suburban home discovers "Habad," drops out of college and eventually marries a Habad girl and they set up a rigidly Orthodox household, which means a large family. Habad womenfolk wear the sheitl; conservative, yet not prim dresses; are permitted mild use of cosmetics and may even smoke; that is the way the rebbe's own family comports itself.

It is said that occasionally a "convert" from Jewish secularism, in a burst of enthusiasm, wants to throw up his profession or academic career and settle down as an anchorite at the sect's Eastern Parkway headquarters in Brooklyn, but the rebbe orders him back into the world to proselytize by example and continually test his faith by encountering temptation.

The European deans who arrived here as wartime refugees (Book II, Chapter IV) are the Roman Curia of global Jewish Orthodoxy. Ruling almost unobtrusively from their sanctuaries, they are virtually unknown to the large number who are casually affiliated. However, the Israeli chief rabbinate consults these deans repeatedly. They are held in reverence by that small segment of affluent Orthodox laity involved in American Jewish community affairs and, as a consequence, cast the fear of their sanction even on Yeshiva University. They are acknowledged to have few peers as interpreters of the law, and none have sufficient courage to dissent publicly from their opinion. Rather than initiate actions the deans, like the United States Supreme Court, hand down opinions on cases presented for their ruling. The Rabbinical Alliance of America, one of several Orthodox rabbinical groups (the Conservative and Reform rabbis each have a single central body), serves as the deans' front, when they choose to intervene anonymously, in non-magisterial fashion. Recently the Synagogue Council of America, which represents all three Jewish religious denominations, gave a dinner and awards to the Presidents of the three denominational schools—Yeshiva University (Orthodox), The Jewish Theological Seminary (Conservative), Hebrew Union College (Reform). Several days later The New York Times carried an advertisement signed by the Rabbinical Alliance. "Hear, O Israel," it stated in bold letters, "An Open Letter to the Jewish Community." The text underneath it charged that Rabbi Dr. Belkin, President of Yeshiva, by attending the dinner and accepting the award with the others, gave his "tacit endorsement" to "movements which are designed to destroy belief in the divine origin of the Torah and which cause our fellow Jews to violate and disregard its laws."

This kind of extremism does not sit well, for example, with many of the several hundred men who are organized in the Association of Orthodox Scientists. Dispersed among science research institutions, including top secret installations and universities across the country, they walk about among their colleagues wearing skullcaps, observe the dietary laws, and attend morning and evening services, impressing or puzzling their subordinates, aides, and students. But they are aware that the technological age poses serious challenges to Jewish law and to Jewish religious philosophy, perhaps greater than the challenges faced in their day by Maimonides and, before him, Saadya Gaon.

The scientists and some of the younger men on the Yeshiva faculty had looked to Dr. Joseph Dov Soloveichik of Boston, a Yeshiva rabbinic dean, to confront these issues which the deans pretend do not even exist. Soloveichik, scion of a dynasty of rabbinic legalists, a Talmudic child prodigy, and trained in philosophy in German universities, could contend with all the deans as their peer. However, he has apparently chosen a course of non-alignment, content with his annual lecture at Yeshiva University, a display of encyclopaedic erudition, insights, and pyrotechnics, that is delivered to a S.R.O. audience drawn virtually from all over the United States and including visitors from abroad.

Yet the Maimonidean quest continues to be engaged in by younger men, although not as an overt challenge to the deans. Notable among the new generation is Rabbi Norman Lamm, Professor of Philosophy at Yeshiva. He writes: "The real challenge to Jewish belief in our day will come, I believe, from the cyberneticians who have been developing a metaphysics of cybernetics in which they attempt to use theories of communication and control to establish criteria for a materialistic conception of meaning and purpose. But challenging though it may well be, I do not fear it." [15]

Wherever this ongoing dialogue within and among the denominations might lead—if it leads anywhere at all—it is evident that the rabbinate is no longer content with being decorative. It wants to become functional. But this depends on whether the rabbis can and really care to de-Hellenize the synagogue and many rabbis indeed are trying.

The Orthodox synagogue is no more immune to Hellenization than

[15] *The Condition of Jewish Belief,* p. 131.

the Reform or Conservative. The rabbis are peripheral members themselves—and indeed are aware of the dilemma—of that affluent section of the Jewish community (Hellenism and wealth are synonymous) that is transforming the synagogue into an institution of the upper-income strata. Its trustees argue, not without justice, that it is the affluent who pay the dues, imposts, and make the contributions that maintain the synagogue. A better alternative might be less concern with physical expansion, and transforming the synagogue from a membership association into a Jewish community agency maintained by the public purse.

The American synagogue is almost the direct successor to the synagogue of the East European Orthodox shtetl. Yet, its conduct and nature place it in the tradition of the Hellenists' temple in ancient Alexandria. In Jerusalem, the populace crowded into the temple's courtyards without any predetermined order, and all, even the king, stood at attention before the Lord of Hosts during the entire service. The Alexandrian Temple seated its congregants, each guild under its distinctive banner, in an order corresponding to the status of its occupation. The shtetl approximated the Jerusalem custom, although not as completely oblivious to class distinctions. The synagogue's elders sat at the East Wall, a high honor because the sun rises in the East and Jerusalem is located there: the order in which men were called to the Torah reflected their social status, which was determined not by their wealth, but their learning. However, the informal Orthodox service scrambled all the social categories as congregants moved freely about the synagogue, the high and the lowly exchanging snuff and greetings, and the untutored consulting the scholar on the meaning of sacred works.

More and more synagogues in America today follow the formal model of the Alexandrian Temple. Yet no guilds were barred. The costs of synagogue maintenance in America are so high, however, that some "guilds," the lower income groups, cannot afford membership at all. Thus the synagogue is among the first to surrender to the "metaphysics of cybernetics" and its "materialistic conception of meaning and purpose."

CHAPTER 3

From Yiddish
to Neo-Brahmin

SECOND AVENUE, heartland of Yiddish culture, was picked by time, bone by bone. First to go were the Yiddish theaters. One year there were seven bright marquees on Second Avenue, then five, then none. The theater season, which would begin on the evening that the Yom Kippur fast ended and last through Passover and even Shevuot, which means sometimes till early June—the holidays follow the Hebrew calendar—withered to sixteen, thirteen, and finally eight weeks. Then one day there was no theater season at all. There have been several attempts in recent years to reclaim Second Avenue for the Yiddish stage, all of them abortive.

The most obvious cause of the demise of the theater has been the passing of the generation who spoke Yiddish as the mother tongue. There was the advent of the Yiddish radio programs, which kept potential theater audiences home. But death came prematurely, and the reasons were not the decline of Yiddish or radio competition. The star system was one cause, theater benefits another. Bidding for stars to attract audiences, the Yiddish producers decided the play did not matter. The stars apparently concurred. The audience evidently did not. But the Yiddish producer was contemptuous of his audience. He did not depend on direct box-office sales, but on tickets sold at a discount *en bloc* to landsmanschaften and charities. True, the profit margin was smaller, but the benefit sales assured his production of a safe run, whatever the critics might say. However, the organizations soon discovered that their members refused to purchase benefit tickets because of the inferiority of the plays.

Producers and actors engaged in recriminations as the theater began to decline, and both blamed the Yiddish critics who had always warned them not to think that *"der oilem is a goilem,"* that the patrons were asses and "can be fed pulp." Everyone agreed that the stagehands and ushers bled the Yiddish theater white. Many had other fulltime occupations, even operated businesses of their own, yet they constantly pressed for salary increases in the theater. The ushers were even more overbearing than the waiters in Jewish restaurants, and with none of the latter's gruff concern for their clientele; patron-usher altercations had become as common in the Yiddish theater as preliminary bouts in the boxing ring.

Second Avenue has been taken over by the off-Broadway theater and the New Bohemia. The former Maurice Schwartz Yiddish Art Theater was dark for many seasons, but in recent years it has alternately housed burlesk shows and productions of Chekhov, Pirandello, and Brecht. Another theater alternates between occasional Yiddish variety and films and LSD revivalist sessions conducted by Dr. Timothy Leary and Allen Ginsberg. Other Yiddish cultural haunts have similarly yielded to new occupants. Labor Temple used to provide capacity audiences not only for Thorstein Veblen, Max Eastman, Harry Waton, and others of that general category, although of lesser caliber, but also for Yiddish intellectuals—political analysts, ideologists, poets, novelists. It now accommodates a Spanish language church and Puerto Rican and Cuban culture societies. Elsewhere on Second Avenue, a ramshackle three story red-brick building that served as headquarters of the Yiddish Culture Society, which befriended younger poets, now bears across its front a sign, in Cyrillic letters, "Ukrainian Culture Center." The whole neighborhood bears the imprint of three distinctive and separate segments—the Puerto Ricans, the Ukrainians who entered the United States from Germany after World War II, and the New Bohemians.

The Café Royal, on Second Avenue and Twelfth Street, was the last to go. At one time it was the Sardi's of the Yiddish actors, the Algonquin of the Yiddish writers. Its occasional clientele included former Premiers (Alexander Kerensky), future Premiers (David Ben-Gurion), and Nobel Prize Winners (Sigrid Undset, Thomas Mann, Sinclair Lewis). It had been wasting away for many years before its demise in the nineteen-fifties. It passed away shortly after the death of Herman, its bus-boy-owner and money-lender. It was like the closing of the lid on a coffin. The corpse was carted away in sections. First removed were the tables and chairs, made of the solid lumber of another era; an antique dealer removed its credenza and chandeliers; an interior decorator, its panels. Outside, the darkened slab, with its name in electric bulbs, hung like a flag over a razed fortress until new occupants reopened the place as a dry cleaning establishment, replaced Royal's fogbound sign with gaudy neon lights, and pasted hand-lettered price lists on colored cardboard on the large windows before which passers-by used to halt to gape at the celebrities who had their meals inside.

Some of the most celebrated Yiddish actors and writers who made the Café Royal's reputation preceded by at least a decade the café's demise. They are interred in Brooklyn and Queens, in the burial grounds of Arbeter Ring and Farband, Yiddish fraternal orders. The growling bravado poet Moshe Leib Halpern predicted in verse many years before that death would beckon him from the waves sweeping in at high tide. He suffered a seizure swimming at twilight off Rockaway Beach. The poet Zisha Landau whose bloated body and fine sensuous features bore a striking resemblance to Oscar Wilde's, was a tender and concerned paterfamilias of steady habit. He had one excess, however—food. An ostentatious gastronome, he collapsed, allegedly after consuming, on a bet, an inordinate quantity of shellfish. Moshe Nadir, poet, political polemicist, lover and poseur, fond of handpainted ties and flowing capes, died an ostracized man after breaking with the Communist Party, which for years had sustained his vanity by scheduling Town Hall celebrations for his every new book. This audience turned away from him abruptly after his break with the Party. His more faithful readers were fewer, less demonstrative, and, being anti-Communists, distrusted his conversion.

Perhaps the greatest of these literary figures was H. Leivick, the mystic playwright-poet who passed away after Royal's closing. A stroke deprived him of his speech and all mobility; death finally redeemed him after several years of a horrible, bed-ridden captivity, which had been metaphorically anticipated in almost all his work whose dominant motif was redemption through immolation.

The Yiddish actors, conversely, would "not go gently into that good night." They have proved amazingly durable. One is startled even today in scanning the obituary columns by the name of a once famous

Yiddish actor or actress whom one believed to have passed away long ago.

There are still in America today some Yiddish writers of extraordinary merit. America is also the home of one of the great Yiddish prose masters of all time, the novelist Isaac Bashevis-Singer whose impact on American Jewish writers has been perhaps as great as Kafka's. The catastrophe of European Jewry, which deprived Yiddish literature of its most dedicated readers, has completely altered Yiddish writing. Almost every new work is an unrelenting reaction to that genocide. Singer presaged the catastrophe in the apocalyptic world of his imagination.

As Yiddish literature began its horrible passion, a new American Jewish literature in English began to emerge, not merely books by Jews about Jews, but something which critics of late have begun to describe uneasily as "a Jewish cult." It was created by the intellectuals' disenchantment with Communism, by the German horrors against Jewry in World War II, and by the emergence of Israel. Its midwife was *Commentary*. Attending its birth was the *Partisan Review* and Schocken Books.

Partisan Review was founded by the "internal expatriates" of the nineteen-thirties. The expatriate of the nineteen-twenties was generally a WASP who boozed and brawled his way across the European continent, absorbing experience and form, but oblivious to the ideological ferment around him, and who having had his share of alien embraces returned home to create striking work. Gertrude Stein was the only eminent Jewish figure among them, and she never returned. Other Jewish writers were not about to become expatriated from an America which had not yet fully become their land.

The expatriate of the nineteen-thirties never left America, except for some who traveled to Spain to fight in the ranks of the Lincoln Brigade. He was twice exiled without having left his soil: first, when he rejected America-as-is with its inequities, debutante balls, and shanty towns, orgies on yachts and street-corner apple vendors, for the America-to-be pledged by Communism; and then when he found out that the Soviet promise of universal redemption was counterfeit. It spoiled him for new enthusiasms. This also infected younger men who arrived on the scene just at the crucial juncture of general disenchantment and had been spared the heartbreak of enlisting and then defecting. The condition of total disengagement from any cause was especially hard on the Jewish intellectual. The Jews had found escape from their millennial exile in a spiritual homeland of mitzvot, commands, commitments; moral purpose ordered their thoughts, emotions, and everyday conduct. It was hard for the Jewish intellectual, disaffected from political Messianism, to be at large.

All these many kinds of internal emigrants assembled around the *Partisan Review*, which retrieved American political writing from the clichés of the Communist *New Masses* and the propriety of the *Atlantic Monthly* and *Harper's*, but except for feints at a purer Marxism had no positive political focus of its own. Similarly, its fiction dissented from the nihilism of Hemingway-Fitzgerald and from pedestrian "socialist realism," but cast around without purpose. Then suddenly some of these writers found direction for their political and fictional work in two Continental Jewish writers—Arthur Koestler and Franz Kafka. Koestler, a political animal, incorrigibly secular, served them well in their early polemical stage with "the gods that failed." Kafka served them at a later stage. He was "religious," talking in parables; dead by the time they discovered him. Koestler and Kafka depict almost identical worlds, but Koestler's *Darkness at Noon* is fictional reportage, Kafka's *The Castle* is parabolic; Rubashov is not *Jedermann* but K. is. It is the difference between dialectics and theology.

The "internal expatriates," especially the Jews, used Kafka in the way Freud used Greek mythology, borrowing his metaphors to depict their own condition. Kierkegaard helped, as did Sartre. Soon fiction, criticism, even sociological literature was flooded with references to the "alienated," to the "marginal man." If Gentile intellectuals with ancestral roots in America could call themselves "marginal," then surely the Jewish writer, whose parents or grandparents had migrated from the shtetl, was fully "marginal." It was a distinctive condition, meriting some kind of celebration. It was celebrated indeed in a symposium on the Jewish writer's relationship to his people conducted by *The Contemporary Jewish Record*, a documentary sociological magazine, published by the American Jewish Committee, whose first editor was Professor Abraham G. Duker, the Jewish historian.[1]

In his contribution to the symposium Isaac Rosenfeld who, like Saul Bellow, had deep roots in Yiddish, stated ". . . generally speaking, the position of Jewish writers illustrated one of the strangest phenomena of modern life. Since modern life is so complex that no man can possess

[1] *Contemporary Jewish Record* (predecessor to *Commentary*), February 1944.

it in its entirety, the outsider often finds himself the perfect insider." [2]
These were not casual opinions. None of the participants in that
symposium was flippant; the year was 1944, the smoke of the crematoria
lingered on the horizon. The Jewish intellectual at any rate could now
no longer pretend total disengagement, nor could he dismiss his Jewishness as extraneous and irrelevant, as he had done before his disillusion-
ment with political Messianism and, above all, before the crematoria.
Lionel Trilling wrote in the same symposium: [3] ". . . it is clear to me
that my existence as a Jew is one of the shaping conditions of my temperament, and therefore I suppose it must have its effects on my intellect. Yet I cannot discover anything in my professional intellectual life which I can specifically trace back to my Jewish birth and
rearing." Although "I would not, even if I could, deny or escape my
being Jewish," he wrote, his perseverance as a Jew is "minimal" and
"graceless" because it "does not want enough and is nothing more than
resistance to an external force." His position was typical, he thought,
of all American Jewry, Establishment or not. "There is, I know, much
show and talk of affirmation," Trilling wrote, "but only to the end that
the negative or neuter elements may be made more acceptable. As I see
it, the great fact for the American Jews is their exclusion from certain
parts of American life and every activity of Jewish life seems to be a
response to this fact." Alfred Kazin [4] rhapsodized the Jews of East
Europe and their Orthodox, Zionist, and Socialist traditions. "I admire
these. I have been influenced as a writer and as a person by the idea
of them—I only wish I knew how much. But I have never seen much of
what I admire in American Jewish culture, or among Jewish writers in
America generally. . . . Who is he (the American Jew)? What is
Jewish in him? What does he believe, especially in these terrible years,
that separates him at all from our national habits of acquisitiveness,
showiness, and ignorant brag? . . . what a pity that he should feel
'different,' when he believes so little. What a stupendous moral pity,
historically, that the fascist cut-throats should have their eye on him,
too, when he asks for so little—only to be safe, in all the Babbitt-
warrens."

Of all the Jewish institutions and agencies in America only two—
Commentary and Schocken Books—were responsive to the Jewish in-

[2] *Ibid.*, p. 35.
[3] *Ibid.*, pp. 15-16.
[4] *Ibid.*, pp. 9-10.

tellectual's aroused self-awareness and undertook to provide for it. Zalman Schocken was a German-Jewish Maecenas. Before Hitler's rise to power he published slim, exquisitely lettered volumes in Hebrew and German. The latter were largely concerned with Jewish mysticism, and included works by Martin Buber, Yitzhak F. Baer, and Franz Rosenzweig. He also published Franz Kafka who, of course, was not concerned with the Hebrew language or Jewish mysticism. Schocken's favorite Hebrew author was S. Y. Agnon, winner of the Nobel Prize in 1967. In the nineteen-thirties he transferred his Hebrew publishing activities to Palestine, and in the nineteen-forties, for the first time, introduced his writers to American audiences in English. The impact of Kafka and Buber requires no elaboration.

Commentary, launched by the American Jewish Committee in 1946, was severely prejudged even before its first issue appeared. It was anticipated that it would be a mere house organ for "Jewish Toryism," because its editor, Elliot Cohen, who conceived the magazine, came to the post from long years of service as the public relations director of the Federation of Jewish Philanthropies of Greater New York. The Federation was regarded as even more of a "Yahudim" institution than the Committee, and its public relations director seemed an odd choice for editor of what was announced as a highbrow magazine. Apparently none of these critics was aware that Southern-born Elliot Cohen had been a child prodigy at Yale, that he had been, when still in his 'teens, managing editor of *The Menorah Journal*, then a Jewish quality periodical, that eminent American literary men were among his close friends, and that he had always maintained a great curiosity about Jewish affairs, and spoke with pride of his Litvak father, an ordained rabbi, Hebrew scholar, and a Mobile, Alabama businessman, at a time when young American Jewish intellectuals generally did not boast of such parochial, genteel origins.

With the notable exception of Ludwig Lewisohn and Maurice Samuel and several other ideologically committed men, Jewish intellectuals were not inclined to contribute to the Jewish periodicals which paid little or no honorarium and whose subject matter was delimited by fixed Jewish ideologies or institutional policies. *Commentary* offered liberal rates and reflected Cohen's wide range of Jewish and general interests. A tallish, heavy-jowled man with a somewhat distracted, but amused and kindly stare, and a habit of hesitant, interrogative speech, he enlisted editorial staff and contributors from the *Partisan Review* and persuaded writers who had never done so before to pronounce themselves on Jewish matters. They did so often and wistfully, sometimes arrogantly and even superciliously. This irritated not only the Jewish Establishment, but also some deeply committed anti-Establishment Jews, who assumed that "alienated intellectuals" should return humbly as penitents, not boldly as social critics. *Commentary's* presentation of obverse sides of the coin—it published Will Herberg's theology, but also carried the first severe critique of him [5]—was beyond the comprehension of a community conditioned to a defensive posture. It sometimes offended the sensibilities of even its publisher, the American Jewish Committee, and although Cohen had been guaranteed editorial freedom and would not compromise it, he did not delight in the post-mortem sessions with his board after the appearance of each issue.[6]

Yet its boldness made *Commentary* stimulating, it accustomed Jewish institutions not to bristle at suggestions that they are not quite infallible and taught "alienated" Jewish writers that Jewish affairs were not to be dismissed as "parochialism." It also cultivated new writers. Among Cohen's early editorial associates were Nathan Glazer, the eminent sociologist, and Irving Kristol, subsequently co-editor of *Encounter* and now editor of Basic Books, both then in their twenties, and Clement Greenberg, the art critic. Cohen's successor, the present editor of *Commentary*, Norman Podhoretz, had also served a brief apprenticeship under him.

Commentary established a frame of reference within which Jewish problems could be discussed intellectually, not institutionally. As a halfway inn for Jewish intellectuals seeking to redefine themselves, *Commentary* was symptomatic of the emergence of a new American Jewish writing. At its best, this prose was in the neo-Brahmin Morningside Heights' style—precise, lean, cerebral, irony-tinged, as was true of a great deal of the new American writing of that day, and mildly flushed from an assignation with Henry James, Paul Valéry and Franz Kafka. It contrasted sharply with most preceding American Jewish writing whose practitioners were determined either to prove their mastery of superlative English, of which Ludwig Lewisohn's magnificent baroque

[5] Judd L. Teller, *Commentary*, February 1958.
[6] Elliot Cohen committed suicide after a long nervous breakdown. Shortly before his breakdown, he told this author that he had just turned down an offer to head the Harvard University Press, that he was not certain he had made the right decision, and added sadly that *Commentary* is a fine magazine, but it had in no way changed American Jewish habit.

is the most striking example, or to conceal their lack of ease with the unpredictable nature of English syntax by interlacing their prose with Yiddish dialect, a tradition which was begun with the *Potash and Perlmutter* comedies and was continued in the proletarian novels of the nineteen-thirties.

There was also, as presaged in the *Contemporary Jewish Record* symposium, evidence of a shifting of posture from Jewish self-consciousness to Jewish self-awareness. However, it was easier to alter writing style than substance. The old apologetics still clung to all categories of American Jewish writing—high, low and middlebrow. Laura Z. Hobson's *Gentlemen's Agreement* and Arthur Miller's *Focus* were novels that dealt with anti-Semitism. In the first, a Gentile writer sets out to investigate anti-Semitism among the country club set which denies its prejudice and nonetheless indulges in it. He deliberately passes for a Jew to experience the disabilities that accrue from this condition. He finds them very real and poignant. In Miller's novel a Christian defends a Jewish shopkeeper from anti-Semitic hooliganism and because he wears glasses, which makes him resemble the stereotype of the anti-Semitic caricatures, he, too, is promptly labeled a Jew and beaten up. Miss Hobson and Miller use the mistaken identity ruse to suggest that anti-Semitism is unreal because the Jew himself is unreal, merely a label that could fit almost any human being of the white race.

Miller's is nonetheless an infinitely superior novel because while he avoids facing anti-Semitism as a serious cultural issue, he does probe the nature of violence. However, this method of evasion in dealing with Jews and Jewish concerns stamps almost all of his work and is its most serious defect. Was there any sound reason for denying Willy Loman's ethnic roots? He is universal of course, but would be more so if placed as a Jewish salesmen, Tevye in his 'nth American metempsychosis. Evasion has become a true obsession with Miller.

In *After the Fall*, the stage is dominated by a concentration camp tower, but there is no hint as to who its major victims had been, although Miller includes even the Spanish Republicans. The overwhelming catastrophe that befell the Jews becomes a mere backdrop for Miller's autobiographical episode with Marilyn Monroe and for the events of the McCarthy era in America. Furthermore, the true rememberer of the atrocities is not a Jew, but Helga, the ostensibly anti-Nazi granddaughter of an anti-Nazi general. And, echoing Hannah Arendt's thesis, which envelops victim and persecutor alike in the banality of evil, Miller states—"Who can be innocent again on this mountain of skulls? The wish to kill is never killed." Perhaps so, in Miller's case—the wish to kill the Jew within himself.

In *Incident At Vichy*, a German major, obviously not in sympathy with the roundup of Jews he had been instructed to supervise, is asked by one of the victims to release him. The major's reply is that this would require risking his own life. However, soon thereafter an Austrian aristocrat, arrested by mistake and certain to be released when the error is discovered, offers his papers to the Jew who makes his escape. Thus we find a perverse reversal of roles, the Gentile risks his life for the Jew, and the Jew lacking the nobility to reject the offer accepts it casually.

This defensive attitude was succeeded by self-assertion in the novels about the Jew as American G.I. and about Israel's struggle for independence. Even on the level of popular fiction, they applied Rosenfeld's rule about the Jew's insider-outsider role. They declared the Jew's likeness to others and simultaneously his right to be different. In Irwin Shaw's *Young Lions*, Noah Ackerman establishes the legitimacy of his intellectual interests by first proving his physical courage; he resorts to Esau's fists to obtain a mandate for Jacob's voice.

This writing slowly conditioned the American reader to think of the Jew not as an esoteric immigrant, but a kindred American. It had an unconscious ideological purpose. Nothing served this purpose better than the novels about Israel's independence struggle, of which two hit the bestseller lists, first Arthur Koestler's sensitive *Thieves in the Night*, which was published before Israel's birth, then Leon Uris' runaway bestseller, *Exodus*, a TV soap opera novel, almost an adaptation of Koestler's, tailored to lowbrows. Both demonstrated that when he seizes upon an opportunity to assert himself, the Jew becomes only more like the others; after all, did he not obtain his independence with "Gentile" means—explosives, ambuscade, guerrilla warfare and battlefield courage?

These novels fixed the image of the fighting Jew in the American imagination, banishing the stereotypes of hunched student, comic opera peddler, garment center wheeler dealer, and verbose, hirsute radical. Herman Wouk's *Marjorie Morningstar* completed the process of persuading America of the Jew's "nativization." There is the perhaps apocryphal story that he was introduced to the audience at a Hadassah convention with a flourish—"Mr. Wouk," the lady presiding at the session reputedly said, "Meet two thousand Marjorie Morningstars."

He could have been introduced the same way to a convention of American women of any faith. Marjorie Morningstar is the perfect stereotype of the American female of her class, irrespective of religious denomination. More recently, the bestselling novel *The Rabbi* is similarly a stereotype of the American clergyman, whatever his faith. The perennial bar mitzvahs, Passover feasts and Yom Kippur fasts which keep the Morningstars delighted, anxious and bustling, and the Rabbi clocking his rounds, are typical of that mixture of commerce, hedonism, and polite faith that constitutes American religion. Both are the fictional enactment of Herberg's Protestant-Catholic-Jew synthesis.

In the nineteen-fifties a new kind of American Jewish fiction began to appear. It was neither apologetic nor accusatory. Yet, unconsciously, or only half-consciously, it was in search of a Jewish myth and Jewish idiom in which it might strike root. Almost all of the best American writing contains the myth and idiom of a definite American caste and region. James, who was an expatriate, and Edith Wharton, who was not, share essentially the same caste and regional culture. Willa Cather belongs to a classless midwestern society of an earlier era. The South's impress has been overwhelming. Surely the Jew would be pretentious and a fool if he attempted to adapt the style of any of these castes or regions. His own American roots were in the immigrant ghetto; drawing upon its myth meant accenting his foreignness, drawing upon its speech meant substituting once again dialect for idiom. The tragedy of European Jewry focused his attention on East Europe and Yiddish. German Jewish writers, including Kafka, Arnold Zweig, and Martin Buber, on a similar quest after World War I, had also turned to East Europe. They communicated with living Jews. The American Jewish writer, one war later, could only commune with their books and their ashes.

Suddenly numerous translations of Sholem Aleichem and anthologies of Yiddish writing began to appear—*A Treasury of Yiddish Short Stories* edited by Irving Howe and Eliezer Greenberg, a Yiddish poet, and Saul Bellow's selection, *Great Jewish Short Stories*, more than one-third of which are from the Yiddish. On the stage, albeit not in correspondingly quick succession, *The World of Sholem Aleichem* was followed by Paddy Chayefsky's *The Tenth Man* (*The Dybbuk* transplanted to suburbia), and, most recently, by *Fiddler on the Roof*. The East European shtetl became the tuning fork for American Jewish novelists and playwrights.

The Jewish intellectual is still irritable and ill at ease with the American Jewish community which reflects him like a mirror, and by surrounding him with a visible, living family with conventional American drives, reduces him among his Christian peers from a metaphysical symbol to human scale. The bearded generations, conversely, decimated by German genocide, are beyond making demands or causing embarrassment. Because they are remote and unreal, like the weightless, levitating figures of Chagall's canvases, one may vaguely relate to them without the risk of being mistaken for them. They are no more strange in appearance, with their caftans, beards, and earlocks, than the signers of the Declaration of Independence with their powdered wigs, laces, and frills. Their legends of saints, fools, and tenaciously persevering commonfolk, contrasts with the American legends of swaggerers, barroom brawlers, hired guns and Indian fighters, self-pitying sodden men and fallen women. Few American Jews are so completely secure or so lacking in ethnic vanity that they do not take pride in these essential differences. Sholem Aleichem celebrates these worldly-otherworldly Jews, while Isaac Bashevis Singer depicts their metaphysical agony, which involves passion and sin and has, therefore, disturbed those Jews who believe that no minority should be presented as other than virginal.

No Yiddish writer has ever achieved the unique prominence in America that has been Singer's for the past decade. He is in great demand as a lecturer both on the campus, by the *avant garde,* and in the gilded ghettos. He has been accepted as a writer's writer, and as fully an American writer as if his language were English. He writes in Yiddish, whose audience is diminishing. *The Jewish Daily Forward* publishes reams of copy by Singer weekly, under his real name and innumerable pseudonyms: social comment, book reviews, popular science articles, and impressions from his lecture tours across the country. His fiction is serialized in the *Forward* in the original Yiddish before it is translated into English. He has aroused in Americans a profound interest in all Yiddish culture, yet he is a controversial figure among Yidn. The *Forward* frequently carries letters from readers accusing him of pornography, and with pointed reference to the newspaper's Socialist tradition, denouncing his "belief in demons and other superstitions" and his "brazen advocacy of black reaction." The frequent and captious attacks on him by fellow Yiddish writers are understandably motivated by jealousy. When he was still unknown outside the realm of Yiddish readers and writers, he was praised by his colleagues as a great master. But when these same works scored successes in English translation, the praise quickly turned to something else. He is now alleged to be a "panderer" to the "self-hating Jews" who "preside" over American letters.

Singer is essentially a writer of parables. This genre seems best suited to our apocalyptic times. America's parabolic tradition, contemporaneously brilliantly represented by John Barth, has its beginnings in Melville. The Jews have contributed to modern letters three distinguished parabolists—Franz Kafka, who wrote in German, Singer who writes in Yiddish, and S. Y. Agnon who writes in Hebrew.

The three belong to a tradition that goes back two millennia. Kafka was only remotely aware of its existence. He learned some Yiddish, which is one of its repositories, by attending performances in Prague of a visiting third-rate theatrical troupe, and began to study Hebrew, the primary source of this tradition, perhaps only months before his death by which time he had become a confirmed Zionist. Agnon and Singer are steeped in the tradition.

Its base is the *Aggadah,* the homiletic portions of the Talmudic canon, which contain Persian-gnostic elements such as the doctrine of transmigration, resurrection, and dualism, the contest between the forces of good and the forces of evil. Some of this ancient literature was so patently gnostic in character that it was kept out of the Talmudic canon altogether. Fragments of the excised literature survived as apocrypha.

This category of Jewish literature grew over the centuries, it includes the *Cabbala* and Hassidic writing, and was always treated warily even when its legitimacy was acknowledged. It was subjected to closest scrutiny during the witch-hunt that followed the apostasy of Sabbatai Zvi, the seventeenth-century pseudo-Messiah. The works of his disciples were interdicted and all mysticism became suspect. Hassidism, at its beginnings in the eighteenth century, met with fierce opposition partly because it was rumored that its ranks harbored clandestine Sabbatai Zvi sectarians.

It is to this combined tradition that Singer and Agnon belong, although to separate subdivisions of it.

Agnon's style leans on two pillars, the Scandinavian Gothic and the simplistic Hassidic folktale. Its meanings are moralistic and plain, and he has a taunting wit characteristic of the Hassidic temperament with its leaning towards levity. Singer's writing is more closely related to the seventeenth-century pseudo-Messianic literature which, like Singer, mixed the sacred and the profane, the sublime and the perverse, and saw the world darkly, inhabited by malevolent forces and erotic fantasies. Pseudo-Messianism lingered on in Hassidism in Poland, where Singer comes from; the Hassidism of the Ukraine and Galicia, Agnon's realm, was less tortured, earthier.

The world of Kafka and the world of Singer are totally different, but they are bound by a pattern of succession. Kafka's is a frighteningly ordered world of irrational law and dispassionate power; Singer's is adrift in apocalyptic chaos, all order eroded. His first novel, *Satan in Goray,* dealt with the chaotic aftermath of the Sabbatai Zvi movement and he has dealt with post-Messianic disenchantment ever since. His novels are not "mysteries," like Kafka's; they are history, past and contemporary, with poignant, albeit unstated, political analogues. Small wonder, therefore, that among his earliest admirers were writers who had reacted to Stalin's apostasy from the Communist Messianism in the way seventeenth-century Jewry had reacted to Sabbatai Zvi's apostasy. He has, furthermore, uncovered for the American Jewish writer treasures of the Jewish myth, and his magnificent Hebraic Yiddish may even have shown them how to obtain from Yiddish a rich and distinctive English idiom all their own.

Singer, whose depiction of "negative" characters and of "eroticism" has perturbed those professionally concerned with the Jewish public image, offers in *Spinoza of Market Street* one of the most sensitive descriptions of a love relationship. A Gentile doctor, returning home after an evening of debauchery, stops at the lighted window of the rabbi and sees the rabbi poring over a Talmudic folio and the rebbetzin entering the room, "rather than walk she scraped along—she crept forward toward the table, silently picked up the chickenfeather fan and fanned the coals under the samovar . . . Strange that the rabbi did not address her and kept his eyes on the book. But his face grew gentle as he half-concentrated on his reading, half-listened to his wife's movements. They lived for no one knows how many centuries in Europe. Their great-great-great-grandfathers were born here, yet they conduct themselves as if only yesterday they had been exiled from Jerusalem."

Thus Singer is both allegorist and realist, and a moralist in disguise. This is true also of some of the best American Jewish writing that draws upon the Yiddish literary tradition, either through direct reading or as handed down by immigrant parents. Saul Bellow and Bernard Malamud are most obviously in this vein.

John O'Hara's characters are not seriously concerned with the possible tragic consequences of extramarital relations, but Bellow's characters, from the narrator in *Dangling Man,* to *Herzog,* are. They are haunted by the guilt of marital infidelity. Yet their's is not Christian fear that sex is sin, but an ethical dilemma, infidelity involves deceit and unfairness in human relations. Another reason may also be their strong Jewish familial tradition.

"I have no appetite for guile,

> The narrator in *Dangling Man* says the strain of living in both camps was too much. And I was unlike myself. I was out of character. It did not take me long to see that at the root of it all was my unwillingness to miss anything. A compact with one woman puts beyond reach what others might give us to enjoy; the soft blondes and the dark, aphrodisiacal women of our imaginations are set aside. Shall we leave life not knowing them? Must we? Avidity again. As soon as I recognized it, I began to bring the affair with Kitty to a close. It died in the course of a long conversation, in which I made it clear that a man must accept limits and cannot give in to the wild desire to be everything and everyone and everything to everyone."

Much of the new American Jewish writing is akin to all previous Jewish literature in its groping for purpose. Norman Mailer, the closest to a pure hedonist among the Jewish writers, is not free of this compulsion. It comes through most boldly in the *American Dream,* a clear piece of parabolic writing. It is never absent from Saul Bellow, haunting all his internal dialogues. Herzog about himself: "Who can make use of him? He craves use. Where is he needed? Show him the way to make his sacrifice to truth, to order, peace." And Bernard Malamud, taking issue with Robbe-Gillet's theory of the new novel, "to present what is there, without interpretation," writes,

> "To say that this is the world and it is present is hardly satisfying or sufficient. What a fool I'd be not to say what I think of the world! . . . That the world is present is only a small portion of the truth available to art. In the novel the world appears in language, itself a form of interpretation. Therefore, why should it not be further valued, explained—experienced? One cannot sit on language; it moves beyond the presence of things into the absence of things, the illusion of things. Art must interpret, or it is mindless. Mindlessness is not mystery. It is the absence of

mystery . . . presentation of the world, or history, or society is not enough when it may be necessary to proscribe them." [7]

Craving to be used, to calibrate, to commend or proscribe has distinguished the Jewish personality since the first confrontation between Judaea and Greece. The Jew has not denied himself experience or abstained from pleasure, but he has looked beyond for some transcendental meaning; to use the vernacular he has looked for "a piece of the action" in a greater universal scheme. This has been the hallmark of Jewish writing—Hebrew, Hellenic, Judaeo-Arabic, Yiddish. Behind and beyond the hedonism of Edward Dahlberg, Paul Goodman, Norman Mailer, and Allen Ginsberg there is an admitted search for ultimate purpose, for order in seeming chaos and for the rule of law. This is not to suggest for a moment that a sense of purpose is the exclusive possession of Jewish writers, or that it is necessarily found in all of them. However, it is of great concern among Jews.

Other characteristics traceable to Yiddish literature (which in turn has been considerably influenced by Russian writing) are the internal dialogue and an obsessive concern with the ineffectual man, the non-achiever in the marketplace. We find this in Bellow, Malamud, and others. It has been carried over from the proletarian literature of the nineteen-thirties but for quite a different purpose: The non-achiever is not lamented as a victim, but almost celebrated.

The internal dialogue which gives *Dangling Man* and *Herzog* much of their strength is an ancient Jewish form. It has been the manner of Talmudic study in East Europe, the scholar reciting aloud to himself, in singsong, the arguments of first one, then another disputant, and alternately performing in each of these roles. In Yiddish it has been used most effectively by David Bergelson,[8] particularly in his ironic novel *Noch Alemen* (*It's All Over*), which depicts the ineffectual provincial Jewish intelligentsia adrift in a disintegrating shtetl with its gossip, hopelessness, and obsolescent customs. *Noch Alemen* followed by little more than three decades the prototype of all Hebrew and Yiddish novels on this theme, Mordecai Ze'ev Feierberg's lugubrious autobiographical Hebrew novel *Le-an?* (*Whither?*).

Herzog, more worldly, more learned, is the direct heir to the Feierberg–Bergelson prototype, but where the American differs is that there is no ambivalence in Herzog's nostalgia. Although obviously he "can't

[7] *The New York Times Book Review,* March 26, 1967.
[8] Liquidated in Stalin's purges of Yiddish writers, 1948–1953.

go home again," he fruitlessly seeks the security of the womb. Ineffective, almost comical, Herzog's father is, by contrast, possessed of a strength, a consistency, and purposefulness of moral quality which is more enduring.

Bergelson's and Bellow's anti-heroes are members of the intelligentsia and also in the tradition of Russian literature which patently influenced both writers. However, even without interaction between the two literatures, it was inevitable that they produce an identical type because the spirit of emancipation found in the shtetlach of Russia was typical of the entire country. Malamud's protagonist is of another kind, the completely naïve common man. This places Malamud in the tradition of the master of the Hassidic folktale, the Yiddish classicist Yehuda Leib Peretz.

Both Malamud and Bellow, celebrating the non-achiever, have thus anticipated the "hippie," although neither they nor the "hippies" are likely to acknowledge the kinship. They have thus rejected a hallowed type of American hero to which most earlier American Jewish writers had subscribed unreservedly—the materially successful man. Even Odets, a champion of the ineffectual man, applied the criterion of success, blaming his failure on the system. But in Bellow's work, and this is true to some extent also in Odets', it is the materially successful men who fail in a deeper sense. Odets saw them as the exploiters and the victims of a system; for Bellow they have created their own trap.

This deliberate downgrading of material achievement as a gauge for success may be motivated by the writers' defense of their "unsuccessful" fathers or grandfathers, their repudiation of the allegation implicit in the American myth that material failure is somehow subversive and is perhaps the result of congenital inferiority, or at any rate a pathological condition of some kind. Above all, Bellow, Malamud, and Isaac Bashevis-Singer take exception to this view. The immediate antecedents of their radically different assessment of man's value are in the shtetl, but predate the shtetl. *Fiddler on the Roof* has projected this attitude into the realm of popular culture. Any middle-class American, harassed by mortgage payments and loan installments, can promptly identify with Sholem Aleichem's Tevya despite his strange garb and the peculiar physical conditions under which he endures. The American might envy the maturity underlying Tevya's genuine innocence. Tevya is worried by his family's obvious and essential needs, and is not engaged in a status race; he preserves his spontaneity and, through wonderfully articulate gestures, expresses his delight in the manifold little miracles of daily living.

There is an element in America's literary culture that condemns innocence as mindlessness, tolerating it only in children (Tom Sawyer), in mythical childlike plantation Negroes, and in the foreign born: Saroyan's Armenian-Americans and Harry Golden's Jews who are really plantation Negroes "in white face." Americans who dissociate themselves—in O'Neill's plays, in Wolfe's novels—from the obsessive quest for power and success, are driven, like Hagar, into the wilderness.

This particular element in American criticism is becoming wary of the Jewish writing. It has begun to mutter darkly about a "Jewish cult," a word with esoteric connotations. His earlocks and caftan thus far have helped the stage Tevya pass as another "Negro in white face," an old country cousin of Golden's immigrants. But beneath his makeup and his clowning Tevya is a messenger to Nineveh, crying from the stage like Jonah inside the whale. He will be thought of some day, even as the characters of Malamud and Bellow have been, as representing the Jewish cultist conspiracy to alter America's mores and literary and stage idiom.

One reviewer thought that Malamud's *The Fixer* was "a matter for some public rejoicing" because "it is not about 'Jewishness'" and he proceeded to explain that "'Jewishness' in a lot of recent American fiction seems to be neither Judaism nor Jewry, neither a definable religion nor a historical people, but a vague quality pretending to mystical virtue but delivering little more than sentimental smugness—tradition deteriorated into props. As presented by many writers, especially by Malamud in his previous books, 'Jewishness' has become what is left when Jews are no longer sure who chose them or for what, but continue, nevertheless, to act as though they had been chosen for a superior destiny." [9] Another review takes, on the very same grounds, an opposite view of *The Fixer*: "It owes a great deal to Kafka, not as much as it should to Arthur Koestler's *Darkness at Noon,* too much to the cult of Jewish sensibility in U.S. fiction, and most significantly, nothing whatever to the current U.S. scene." [10] Both reviewers agree that the new American Jewish writing is "smug," "pretentious," a "cult."

Some have intimated that there is "a conspiracy between 'Jewish'

[9] G. P. Elliott, *The New York Times* Book Review, Sept. 4, 1966. A subsequent issue carried sharp rejoinders.
[10] *Time,* September 9, 1966.

publishers and critics who give undue attention and praise to any writing that bears a Jewish stamp," and "that the Jewish writers—or in the Aesopian language that is used, the 'New York' writers—exert a pernicious influence insensitive to art, so the claim goes, they convert literature to 'ideas' or 'trend' in order to monger them. . . ." [11]

Alfred Kazin has taken a charitable and resigned attitude towards the mutterings against the Jewish writer: "Definitely, it was now the thing to be Jewish. But in Western university and small towns many a traditional novelist and professor of English felt out of it, and asked, with varying degrees of self-control, if there was no longer a good novel to be written about the frontier, about Main Street, about the good that was in marriage? Was it possible, these critics wondered aloud, that . . . Norman Mailer has become the representative American novelist?

"But in the frothy turbulent 'mix' of America in the 60s, with its glut, its power drives, its confusion of values, the Jewish writer found himself so much read, consulted, imitated that he knew it would not be long before the reaction set in—and in fact the decorous plaint of the 'Protestant minority' has been succeeded by crudely suggestive phrases about the 'Jewish Establishment,' the 'O.K. writers and the poor goy,' 'The Jewish American push.' Yet it is mainly a certain success that has been resented, not the Jew. And if the Jew has put his distinct mark on modern American writing, 'tis surely because, in a time when the old bourgeois certainties and humanist illusions have crumbled, the Jew is practiced in what James called 'The imagination of disaster.' " [12]

It fell to Truman Capote to combine the decorous with the vulgar. In an interview he spoke of "the rise of what I call the Jewish Mafia in American letters" which controls "much of the literary scene through the influence of the quarterlies and intellectual magazines. . . . I don't think there is any conscious, sinister conspiracy on their part just a determination to see that members of their particular group rise to the top. . . . It is fine to write about specifically Jewish problems, and it often makes valid and exciting literature—but the people who have other messages to convey should also be given a chance. Today because of the Jewish Mafia, they're not being given that opportunity.

[11] Marshall Sklare and Theodore Solotaroff, introduction to *Jews in the Mind of America* by Charles Herbert Stember et al. (pages 5-6).
[12] Alfred Kazin, introduction to *The Commentary Reader*, ed. Norman Podhoretz (New York: Atheneum, 1966), pp. xxiv–xxv.

This is something everyone in the literary world knows but never writes about." Truman hastened to add that "this Jewish Mafia is based more on a state of mind, than on race; Gentile writers such as Dwight MacDonald who toe the line are made honorary members, while gifted Jewish writers are read out of the club." [13]

Others, conversely, see the Jewish writer as the redeemer of an older American species. A review [14] of Philip Roth's *When She Was Good* suggested that "There has been a notable shrinkage of WASP novels lately. You still get the neutral ones . . . but few soaked to the marrow in White-Protestant culture. When such a novel is written, it may well be written by a Jew, not because Jews are the only people who still believe in the high-strung, socially-impacted novel (it only seems like that) but because it takes someone with a lingering sense of community. . . . The White Protestant, by now has no accent, no specific social forms. . . . It takes an outsider to invest him with characteristics, tribal or geophysical."

Because of his confidence in his own validity as an American and his right to bring "Jewishness" into the mosaic of American literature, the new Jewish writer is less concerned than any of his predecessors with the Christian's opinion of the Jew, and more with the interior world of the Jew. Whereas Lewisohn, Samuel, and Hecht made anti-Semitism the theme of entire books, the new writer gives it specific and trenchant treatment. Bellow does this frequently through Herzog's unmailed letters. To "calm Protestant Nordic Anglo-Saxon Edwig," Herzog writes: "Do you think any Christian in the twentieth century has the right to speak of Jewish Pharisees?" and to his fellow Jew, the encyclopaedic Shapiro, he writes, "It was easy for the Wastelanders to be assimilated to totalitarianism. Here the responsibility of artists remains to be assessed. To have assumed, for instance, that the deterioration of language and its debasement was tantamount to dehumanization led straight to cultural fascism." [15] Earlier Jewish writers, except those leaning on either Marxism or Zionism, would not have presumed to pass value judgment on the nature of Anglo-American culture. The new Jewish writer's free-wheeling way with American myths is additional proof of his nativization. Leslie Fiedler's savage exposé of the most advertised American virtue, male virility, in his critical study, *Love*

[13] Interview with Truman Capote, *Playboy*, March 1968, page 169. Compare Capote's views of Jewish influence on U.S. writing with John Corbin's views on Jews in the American theatre in the 1930s (Book II, Chapter 3).
[14] Wilfred Sheed, *The New York Times Book Review*, June 11, 1967.
[15] Compare to Malamud's, earlier in this chapter.

and Death in the American Novel, is perhaps an unconscious retaliation for the antipathy towards Jews shown by Ernest Hemingway,
celebrant of the male virility myth. Norman Mailer's novel *Why Are
We in Vietnam?* exposes the myth's obscenity and its corrosive effect on
American society.

There is among the Irish Americans a development similar to the
Jewish. Their second and third generation writers show a sudden
heightened ethnic awareness, apparently in reaction to their immigrant
predecessors' ambivalence. This new awareness often expresses itself,
however, in ways that the Irish-American Establishment regards as, to
say the least, indiscreet. Daniel [Patrick] Moynihan writes, "But those
who would most value their Irishness seem least to respond to such
achievements. Irish writers . . . have had few traits that commend
themselves to the Catholic middle class." [16] "In the coming generation,"
he goes on, "it is likely that those persons who have the fewest conventional Irish attachments will become the most conscious of their
Irish heritage. This is already evident in writers such as Mary Mc-
Carthy and John O'Hara; things Irish are to be found throughout their
work. It would seem that any heightened self-consciousness tends to
raise the question of racial origin and to stir some form of racial
pride." [17]

There is evidently a difference between the attitude of the Irish and
the Jews towards their respective writers. It is only the Establishment
that becomes upset when a Jewish author, writing casually, comes up
with some unflattering characters. It cannot understand why Isaac
Bashevis-Singer should feel compelled to reveal that the ghetto had
sex, or Philip Roth, in "Ely the Fanatic," to present a caftaned Orthodox
yeshiva dean as superior to Jewish suburbia's Beautiful People. It
argues that a vulnerable minority merits special dispensation, especially
from its own writers, and that its defects, if presented in languages
other than Yiddish and Hebrew, and for readers other than the "in-
group," should be minimized. However, the younger people of the
Jewish middle class, heavy purchasers of *avant garde* literature and
art, have no such apprehensions. The Establishment is divided against
itself on this issue; while the Jewish community relations agencies may
frown on a writer, the synagogue might pay him whatever fee he commands for a lecture. Jewish audiences are puckish, they delight in

[16] *Beyond the Melting Pot,* p. 253.
[17] *Ibid.,* p. 254.

being outraged, and rabbis like to prove their merit by breaking a lance with a celebrated author. And there is always the Jewish tradition of reverence for the Word. Sacred books, when they have fallen apart, are interred in consecrated ground as if they were human remains. Even a Yiddish newspaper, because it bears Hebrew letters, will not be spread on the floor to be stepped on in ultra-Orthodox homes. The Torah is read in the synagogue not from printed volumes but from parchment scrolls inscribed by a *sofer*, a scribe, which is also the Hebrew word for writer. The sofer made his first appearance in Jewish history in the Fifth Century B.C.E., and was apparently also an interpreter of the law and successor to the prophets. The Jews thus have been conditioned for over two millennia to defer to the writer, and, for longer than that, to the castigator. They have also been handed down the tradition that wisdom is not their monopoly. Their respect for other cultures is expressed in an age-old Hebrew phrase, *"chachmat yavan,"* "the wisdom of Greece." The Jewish writer who remains outside his tradition is still revered as a carrier of *chachmat yavan.*

CHAPTER 4

The Native and His Future

GOVERNMENT service has been a passion with Jews since earliest times. One reason might be that they have been stateless throughout most of their history and had a need to be close to sources of power. Other reasons include their millennia-old tradition commanding that each be his brother's keeper, and a life *anschauung* best defined by two Yiddish terms, that every man must seek a *tachlis*, acquire the capacity to provide for himself and his dependents, and that every life must have a *zin*, a transcendental purpose. Neither of these motivations is confined to Jews, yet both are an ethnic characteristic of the Jew.

Up to World War II, the majority of Jews in high American federal office were Yahudim, of German descent, interspersed with *Sephardim*, of Spanish descent, that vanishing breed, Jewry's equivalent of Mayflower stock, the first of whom arrived in America in 1654, fugitives from the Inquisition in Brazil. Sephardim in high office in our own times included Benjamin N. Cardozo, Associate Justice of the Supreme Court, and Bernard M. Baruch, financier, economic adviser to several presidents, elder statesman, and American myth. Before World War I, Yahudim in high office included Oscar S. Straus, Ambassador to Turkey and the first Jew to hold an American ambassadorial post, and his successor Henry Morgenthau. Since World War I, noted Yahudim in government have been Louis D. Brandeis and Felix Frankfurter, Associate Justices of the Supreme Court; Herbert H. Lehman, who served as both Governor and United States Senator from New York, the first Jew elected to these posts in his state, and Henry Morgenthau Jr., the ambassador's son, who as Secretary of the Treasury through all but the first year, of Franklin Delano Roosevelt's White House tenure, was the first Jew to serve in the Cabinet.

Intermarriage has made the Sephardim very nearly extinct and has taken a heavy toll among the Yahudim, and neither group was ever very large. The overwhelming majority of American Jewry today, estimated at six million, is of East European background, only one or two generations removed from its immigrant origins. It is they who now fill government posts, instead of Yahudim or Sephardim. No previous generation of American Jews, in fact, has held so many high federal offices. They include Jacob S. Javits, the senior United States Senator from New York who, on and off, has been mentioned as Republican Vice-Presidential timber; Abraham Ribicoff, now United States Senator from Connecticut and formerly Governor of that state, who also served as Secretary of Health, Education, and Welfare in the Kennedy administration; Abraham Fortas, Associate Justice of the Supreme Court; Sol Linowitz, Ambassador to the Organization of American States, and Arthur Goldberg who, in the space of a few years, has been Secretary of Labor, Associate Justice of the Supreme Court, and chief of the United States Mission to the United Nations. Few men in American history, and no Jew before him had served in that many high posts in so brief a time span.

Beyond the familial passion for government service, there is little resemblance between these East Europeans and their predecessors in government office, the Yahudim and Sephardim. The latter, with rare exceptions, were of upper-class origin, men of commerce and finance, and heirs to considerable fortunes. This was not so among the East Europeans. The older among them, men in their late fifties and mid-sixties, are of lower-middle class or proletarian origin. They generally have risen from the immigrant ghetto and can still manage a labored conversation in Yiddish. Mostly lawyers, they were often the sole support of their families even while going to college. Almost all of them had begun their public service careers during the New or Fair Deal. Following them is another generation, the sons of middle-class and upper-class professionals and businessmen. These younger men are alumni of Ivy League colleges, they know the immigrant ghetto by reputation only, and if they can unscramble any Yiddish vocabulary at all it is because, when children, they occasionally visited with their grandparents.

The Jews have had an ancient, semi-official institution—the court Jew. It dates back to Joseph, at Pharoah's court, who negotiated the immigration of his father and brothers to Egypt from famine-stricken Canaan, and to Ezra and Nehemiah, at the Persian court, who in the fifth century B.C.E. obtained permission for the Jews to return to Palestine from their Babylonian exile. The court Jew was almost always an interpreter, commercial and financial adviser, or banker at the court. He also intervened for his people in times of peril. Occasionally, to remain in favor at the court, he forced his will upon the Jewish community to abide by the rulers' wishes, however onerous and arbitrary.

America also has had court Jews who interceded not for American Jewry, which could register its protest through the ballot, but for persecuted Jewry abroad. However, the American court Jew was radically different from the classical prototype. He was the product of unique American circumstances. He possessed no official mandate from the community, nor could government confer such mandate upon him; in no way beholden to him, the community could at all times denounce and disavow him. Excepting Associate Justices of the Supreme Court, a sacrosanct lifetime office, the community would not confer even unofficially the intervenor role on a Jew in government office lest he be tempted to use his relationship with the Jewish community for self advancement and come to be regarded in government quarters as the safekeeper of the Jewish vote. American Jewry has always been both proud and wary of Jews in high office, an ambivalence and caution which applied no less to Arthur Goldberg than to his predecessors.

President Truman attempted something new. He appointed his own "court Jew," and cast a Boston Jewish lawyer, one of his White House assistants, in that role. The President was overwhelmed at the time by Jewish problems and pressures. The DP camps in Germany were groaning with Jewish survivors of genocide whom no country would admit. In Palestine, Jews rose in arms against Britain's White Paper restrictions on Jewish immigration and in America they demanded the liberalization of American immigration policy, United States pressure on Britain to abrogate the Palestine White Paper barring Jewish immigration, and the establishment of a Jewish Commonwealth as Britain had pledged to do in assuming the Palestine Mandate in 1922. Truman thought it advisable, therefore, that he have an "expert" on hand to analyze Jewish demands, screen petitions and delegations for him, and to interpret White House policy to the Jewish electorate. This was resented, albeit not publicly, as an attempt to prevent Jews from direct access to the President.

It was under President Eisenhower that American Jews found access to the White House barred almost completely. He followed Truman's example and assigned to a White House aide, also by chance a Boston Jewish lawyer, the responsibility of dealing with Jewish matters. He henceforth referred all Jewish delegations and petitions to his Jewish viceroy and was irritated when Jewish leaders sought audiences with the President directly. Richard Nixon, aware of the situation and nursing his own Presidential ambitions, decided to act as stand-in for the President and began inviting Jewish delegations to dinner when crucial matters arose. Although President Kennedy continued the unofficial post of Jewish adviser, he was readily accessible to his many Jewish supporters, especially from the Boston area. President Johnson abolished the post altogether, which Jews do not regret. He was personally available when conditions warranted it, and otherwise relied on Ambassador Goldberg and Vice-President Humphrey to be his liaison to the Jewish community.

The classical American "court Jew"—Louis Marshall, Jacob Schiff, Stephen S. Wise—was a proud and independent man who dared talk back to Secretaries of State and did not spare Presidents' his candor. However, since 1948 there has been no need for the "court Jews," that group of strikingly individual Jews, colorful figures each of them, who alone among all their brethren had access to high places and could presume to voice matters of Jewish concern. There are two reasons for the obsolescence of this informal office: one relates to the establishment of Israel, the other is indigenous to America.

The obvious and elementary fact that Israel is determined to speak with its own voice in high councils and would not surrender that right to anyone, not even to its staunchest Jewish supporters in America, was not readily comprehended by some American Jews, and particularly by the Zionists. It was not easy for Zionist leaders, in America or elsewhere, to step out of their accustomed roles as spokesmen on Palestinian affairs and they continued to declare themselves on matters of vital concern to Israel, before Tel Aviv had even formulated its policy. Abba Eban, recalling his years as ambassador to Washington and to the United Nations, once confided that his most trying day of the week was Monday when he read newspaper accounts of what

Zionist leaders had declared to be Israel policy at meetings in New York City the day before. These newspaper accounts kept him busy all day explaining to the State Department and his peers on Ambassadors' Row that utterances by American rabbis and Presidents of Zionist organizations must not be taken as either Israel's policy or Israeli trial balloons.

Another reason for the extinction of the American "court Jew" is that access to the White House is no longer the privilege of a small, select number. A large segment of American Jewry today is upper middle-class—attorneys, industrialists, merchants, inventors, urbane and well-traveled men, passionately involved in politics, mostly liberal, on all levels—municipal, state and federal. They are among the movers of the President's Club of contributors to the National Democratic Committee. They have entertained Democratic Presidential candidates at their homes where record sums were raised for campaign purposes. They have helped in local elections that so often have national repercussions. Like most Americans of their class who have chosen politics as an avocation, they are delighted to serve as dollar-a-year men in Washington or as members of United States delegations to international conferences which endows them with pseudo-diplomatic status. In times of crises, such as that which afflicted Israel in 1967, preceding the Six-Day War, Jewish leaders assemble and dredge their memories for men across the country who might be called upon to persuade recalcitrant senators and accelerate pressure on the White House itself.

Most of these politically influential men have no role at all in Jewish affairs, except as leaders, upon occasion, in philanthropic enterprises such as the United Jewish Appeal and the Israel Bonds Organization. Very few are involved in that organizational welter which formulates American Jewish policy. Most of these agencies have moved, by stages in the past five decades, from dingy flats on the Lower East Side to midtown skyscraper offices and, finally, into vacated rich men's mansions on the Upper East Side, between Fifth and Park Avenues, known as "diplomats' row" because of the many foreign consulates and United Nations' missions located there. Except for a few "old timers" of the immigrant generation who still linger on, the framers of so-called American Jewish policy are men of the same socio-economic strata as their Jewish peers engaged in general politics. Somehow they have chosen, or have drifted into that aspect of Jewish affairs loosely classified as "community relations," although not so very long ago it was known as "Jewish defense" activity. The new term corresponds better with their view of themselves as no longer an imperiled minority but as integral members of the American Establishment.[1]

Although two decades are, at most, only one generation, American Jewish leadership since 1948 has passed from a first to a second to a third generation. Each assayed itself and its relations with the larger community differently than the other two. It was as if American Jewry viewed itself in a three-way mirror, each revealing or accentuating another aspect of its personality.

The first, the immigrants, had been an embattled generation. Theirs had been a life of hand-to-hand combat against the shtetl's endless poverty and religious strictures and, in America, against the degradation of life in urban slums, labor exploitation, economic setbacks, and all kinds of New World diseases. Above all, however, they experienced anti-Semitism, in all its rich variety, both abroad and here, and this left an indelible mark upon them. The goy was the eternal persecutor. Their one sure weapon against him was protest, and they had persuaded themselves that overflow rallies at Madison Square Garden and the Hippodrome, and parades thru the streets of New York, could affect government policy. Yet, it was through the labors and persistent pressures of that generation that the Zionist effort in Palestine was brought to a stage where, after World War II, it could challenge the British and, when they evacuated, establish orderly Jewish government there.

A younger generation, seemingly more militant than its predecessors, began to claim its place in American Jewish leadership in the final stage of the Palestine struggle and took over almost completely after 1948.

These were men in their early forties, American-born, the first suburban generation, with a vivid memory of the immigrant ghetto and still picking its lint off their garments. Theirs had been a lifelong struggle to persuade the Gentile not to confuse them with the stereotype of the Jew as alien-mannered, displaced, and universally rejected. In the early nineteen-forties, still on the campus or just departed from it,

---

[1] The first to present the thesis that the Jew has been integrated into the Establishment was Will Herberg in his book, *Protestant-Catholic-Jew*. For dissenting opinions see Ben Halpern's book, *The American Jew*, and Judd L. Teller's essay, "The Changing Status of the American Jew," in *Midstream Reader* (New York: Thomas Yoseloff, 1960), pp. 13–26.

they enthusiastically acclaimed the new fighting Jew in Palestine, the antithesis of the stereotype and easily the match of the bravest goy in courage. In suburbia, they pursued the same aim by adopting all the mores and fashions in apparel, furnishings, and hobbies recommended by quality magazines as being sophisticated American. The stereotype Jew was transformed, by this alchemy, into the stereotype American.

Israel, the boldest projection of the new image of the Jew, continued to be at the center of their concerns. They raised enormous amounts annually through the United Jewish Appeal, Israel Bonds and a score of auxiliary pro-Israel funds, and responded with "extra giving" whenever emergencies arose. They dutifully drafted memorandums and adopted resolutions calling on the United States government to support Israel whenever the new state seemed militarily or politically threatened. Yet, there was a cleavage between the older generation, still clinging to its offices, and the younger men, which was almost as serious as that which divided the Yahudim and East Europeans a generation ago, and it was essentially of the same nature as then, a difference over tactics. The older men, when Israel was threatened, urged public demonstrations and that *"die Yiddishe gass"* [2] be summoned "to pour out its righteous wrath." The younger men rejected these proposals as wasteful and unavailing, and as needlessly recalling the earlier image of the universally unwanted and rejected Jew. These younger men struck diplomatic postures, unconsciously mimicking the Israeli diplomats who visited suburbia regularly on fund-raising missions. They had come a long way, although still in their middle-age, from the immigrant ghettos and were overwhelmed by an invitation to dinner with the Vice-President of the United States and an hour-long "candid talk" with the Secretary of State. Poised, but not self-possessed, they often fumbled these occasions; eager to appear objective and cool, they failed in their role as advocates. Two events will illustrate this point.

David Ben-Gurion's fateful decision to withdraw Israeli forces from the Sinai Peninsula in 1956 was in response to two pressures, from President Eisenhower who threatened punitive action, and from American Jewish leadership, who panicked and urged Israel to bend to the President's will. Faced with possible desertion by his most loyal ally,

[2] Yiddish expression: literally "the Jewish street," its real meaning—the Jewish masses.

American Jewry, Ben-Gurion's courage failed him. There was a similar reaction among some American Jewish leaders to Israel's seizure of Adolf Eichmann. Warning of worldwide violent anti-Semitism, frightened by the swastikas daubed on some suburban synagogues, distressed by the charge against Israel, of international lawlessness, they urged that Eichmann be released to (non-existent) international custody or to the German authorities. This time Ben-Gurion stood his ground, Israel behaved as befits a sovereign state, but the first generation of American suburban Jewry proved in both instances that it felt less secure and less accepted than it professed to be.

The generation that had been engaged in the campus rebellion of the nineteen-thirties and in supporting the Palestine Jewish underground of the nineteen-forties was perhaps never truly rebellious. Its major goal, even in the nineteen-thirties, was accommodation to what it assumed to be the prevailing American mood and fashion at the time. In the nineteen-fifties, it pressed the cause of accommodation through its community relations agencies. Investigators and private detectives gave way to lawyers and sociologists; probes of anti-Semitic conspiracies were second only to studies of Gentile attitudes, and there was general optimism that legislation and education would succeed where protest had failed.

Discrimination against Jews in education, employment, and housing was already rapidly diminishing at the time the Jewish community relations agencies launched their campaign to outlaw religious and racial discrimination in these fields. The Jewish agencies also joined as *amicus curiae* in NAACP suits against violators of the newly passed laws. The Negro stood to benefit most from these efforts.

The Jews struck out with vigor in still another direction, interfaith relations. Almost immediately after the war, liberal rabbis and Protestant clergy plunged into interfaith dialogues which accented the common roots of Christianity and Judaism. A new phrase, or concept was introduced—"Judeo-Christian civilization." The rabbis' involvement had the enthusiastic approval of their congregants. It corresponded with suburban Jewry's passion for accommodation.

The Jewish community spent lavishly on this combined effort of anti-discrimination legislation and interfaith relations. The first generation of suburban Jewry had moved far from historical Jewish positions in a brief span of time. In 1927 there were few defenders, even in the Reform rabbinate, for the statement imputed to Stephen S. Wise that Jesus was in the direct line of Hebrew prophets.[3] Threatened with an ouster from Jewish leadership, Wise denied having made the statement. The Yiddish novelist, Sholem Asch, was ostracized, one decade later, for a series of novels on New Testament themes which anticipated the Christian-Jewish dialogues that became the vogue in the nineteen-fifties. Translated into English, his novels were American best sellers in the nineteen-thirties, but Abraham Cahan, editor of the Socialist *Jewish Daily Forward* which had first publication rights, rejected them out of hand as "missionary tracts." [4]

There evolved a new relationship between Catholic and Jew. It began almost imperceptibly in the nineteen-thirties. Roosevelt had been its godfather. Only four years after religious bigotry brought about the execrable defeat of Al Smith in the race for the Presidency, Roosevelt brought Catholics and Jews to Washington to serve as his braintrusters, staff his alphabet bureaus and join his Cabinet. Since then the Catholics generally have been with the Jews in the liberal camp on economic issues.

Catholic and Jew moved, almost simultaneously, into the suburbs and into The New Class which has been defined [5] as composed of "technologists and administrative intellectuals," "non-property-holding individuals" who "with some exceptions . . . arrive at their positions— or at least are permitted to enter the race—mostly by virtue of academic qualifications." Not content that their odds are slightly better than the Jews' for advancement in the giant industrial corporations, Catholics have turned, like the Jews, to that other sector of the American corporate order—governmental and non-governmental social welfare agencies, and educational and scientific institutions.

But the suburban New Class Catholic found some of the doctrine

[3] Rabbi Samuel Schulman, a leader of the anti-Zionist forces in the Reform rabbinate, declared: "I know that I am a Reform rabbi, and in the eyes of my Orthodox brethren, am considered no rabbi at all. Nevertheless, on this question, I stand with them."
[4] Internal evidence supporting Cahan's judgment may be found in Asch's ambiguous statement of faith, *One Destiny*—An Epistle to the Christians (New York: G. P. Putnam's Sons, 1966), pp. 51-52, in which he suggests that "Jesus divided his mission into two 'advents,'" "the first coming of the Messiah was not for us but for the Gentiles"; "only in the second advent, when he would appear in the clouds, would the kingdom of heaven begin, the rule of the Messiah" and "for the second coming, that is today, for the coming of the Messiah, we wait together with the rest of the tormented world."
[5] David T. Bazelon, *Power in America, The Politics of the New Class* (New York: New American Library, 1967) p. 308.

governing relations with Jews and other Christian denominations highly embarrassing. It prevented him, for example, from joining his Protestant and Jewish neighbors' interfaith dialogues. Pope John XXIII's call for a revision of attitudes and a spirit of ecumenism was, therefore, ecstatically greeted by the new breed of American Catholic for it could no longer be said, after Pope John and the Ecumenical Council, that "the true church need never stir to gather its dividends." Realizing that stir it must, even arch-Conservative American prelates deferred to the laity and assumed a liberal position in some of the Ecumenical Council deliberations.

The Ecumenical Council's declaration on deicide dampened some of the Jewish enthusiasm for interfaith dialogues, although these increased in number because of Catholic initiative. The Jewish defense agencies, to justify the effort invested in obtaining the declaration, celebrated it as a triumph. Jewish scholars generally labeled it disappointing. To be sure, it admonished that the Crucifixion "cannot be charged against all Jews without distinction, then alive, or even against the Jews of today," but it also stated that "the Jewish authorities and those who followed their lead pressed for the death of Christ," which only reaffirms that which the Council was expected to excise, and in the words of an eminent Jewish authority "shows a singular disregard for the historical realities of life in Palestine under Roman occupations." [6]

The meager results of the laborious Jewish lobbying effort in Rome was one of the reasons for the strengthening of the trend, evident before this, among Jewish organizations toward greater concern with the Jewish community's inner direction, its self-image rather than its public image. Statements of policy, or those expressions of Jewish opinion most frequently quoted in *The New York Times,* accented "Jewish identity," "Jewish living," and "Jewish survival."

The leadership and staff of the Jewish Establishment had evidently realized that they had moved in an orbit different from that of the average American Jew, that the issues on which they had focused their attention were often of only peripheral interest to their constituencies. Those that had been preoccupied with the Ecumenical Council had suddenly become aware that most others had only a vague interest in its deliberations, that suburban young parents were concerned with how to bring up their children as Jews; and those with sons and daughters on out of town campuses, were worried about intermarriage. The

[6] Ben Zion Bokser, *Rabbinical Assembly's Convention Proceedings,* 1967.

younger generation generally differed from its immediate predecessors in two respects: it neither sought to escape its Jewish identity, nor was it content with the definition that being a Jew meant being a liberal and contributing generously to philanthropies; the latter may, in fact, become obsolescent in America's affluent society, according to some indices.[7]

Younger men, reflecting these new concerns, have in fact begun to take their place in the ranks of Jewish leadership. Still in the minority, they seem to have already influenced the attitudes of some of the older men. They are a mixture of the grandsons of immigrants, and first generation Americans, the sons of the better educated immigrants who entered this country after World War I. In their forties, they are today the same age as their immediate predecessors had been on assuming leadership in 1948. Their attitude is neither defensively bellicose, like the immigrant's, nor excessively accommodating like that of the first suburban generation.

Their attitude is one of calm self-confidence. How infectious this can be was demonstrated in the summer of 1966. *The New York Times* reported from Washington that President Johnson had intimated his displeasure with the views on Vietnam of some prominent Jewish individuals and had suggested that they might find themselves in the awkward position someday of petitioning the United States to defend Israel under similar circumstances.

The Jewish organizations responded promptly and unhesitatingly that the Jewish community was as divided as was America generally on the Vietnam issue, and that the Jews, like all other American citizens, might be expected to take individually or collectively any position they wished without being censured by the President. The episode hit *The New York Times'* front page several times that week. The President and the Executive Vice-President of B'nai B'rith emerged from a meeting with President Johnson stating that the offensive re-

[7] As government assumes more responsibilities in the social welfare field, the area of operations of private philanthropy is narrowed down. In the words of a leader of the National Conference of Jewish Communal Service, President Johnson's Great Society programs are on "a collision course" with private agencies (Jewish Telegraphic Agency Bulletin, May 16, 1967). One study found, and any observer can confirm this, that "philanthropy emerges as the most common expression of Jewish identification. . . . Even the Jew with no synagogue affiliation, no Jewish organizational membership, no degree of cultural distinctiveness, still walks in step with the Jewish community in this one respect—he gives." (Marshall Sklare and Mark Vosk, *Riverton Study*, American Jewish Committee, 1957.)

marks had been falsely imputed to him. Ambassador Goldberg offered similar assurances to representatives of more than twenty major Jewish organizations at a conference at his Waldorf Astoria suite. It was a sharp departure from the wary attitude of some of the very same people during the Sinai crisis of 1956 and when the news first broke that Israel had seized Eichmann. The American Jewish Establishment evidently had come of age.

The fact that the Jewish Establishment of the nineteen-sixties possessed so high a degree of self-confidence and was prepared to speak and act with a boldness inconceivable in the nineteen-fifties was further confirmed during the Israel crisis in May–June 1967.

During the Sinai campaign, apprehensive about being charged with dual allegiance, forewarned by Israel's own envoys that President Eisenhower was hypersensitive, arbitrary, and vindictive, the leaders of the American Jewish organizations labored for days on each statement they issued, excising any intimation of rebuke to the White House.

Not so in May–June, 1967. The American Jewish organizations promptly declared themselves and demanded that the Administration declare itself. Had not America induced Ben-Gurion to withdraw his forces from Sinai in 1956 by pledging to guarantee the territorial integrity of Israel and free passage for Israel's ships through the Tiran Straits? They demanded that the pledge be kept. They were aware of what the involvement might be, of what the public repercussions might be, and that President Johnson, albeit accessible to Jews and with a record of friendship for Israel, was also short-tempered, explosive, and desperately entangled in Vietnam.

The 1967 Israel crisis proved also that the sociological studies and polls commissioned over the years by the various Jewish organizations on the attitudes of American Jewry towards Israel had been absurdly off base. Most of these studies and polls were agreed that interest in Israel was declining among American Jews, and was almost completely fading away among the younger generation to whom it was a remote territory not sufficiently radical to be exciting, too developed to be challenging. The sociologists predicted also that the mystique of Jewish brotherhood had lost all meaning for the younger American and Israeli Jew.

Thus the Jewish Establishment, both the community relations agencies and the fund-raising bodies, were overwhelmed by the response of American Jewry when the alarm for Israel was sounded. This was early summer when fund-raisers take off on vacation, yet within hours monies were streaming in incessantly. Synagogues froze their building and expansion funds; contributors sent in twice and triple the amounts they had pledged earlier in the year; businessmen applied for loans to tide them through, and transmitted their bank accounts to UJA; word spread that "even the doctors are giving like mad," and physicians generally are known in "the trade," to professional fund-raisers, as reluctant contributors.

Men and women of the lower-middle and working class, whom UJA hardly bothers to solicit, queued up at its offices with "the poor man's bread," in some cases their life's savings, and when their small contributions were added up, the silver coin and the crumpled bills and the twenty-five dollar United States government bonds represented a substantial sum.

American Jewry's philanthropies have long astonished their Gentile neighbors. [8,9] *Fortune* (June 1966) called it "the miracle of Jewish giving." But never before had there been anything like it, not even in 1946 when Nazi genocide was revealed in all its horror to the world and American Jews contributed to sustain the lives of the survivors; not even in 1948 when the State of Israel came into being. There was biblical grandeur about this as there was about the six-day war. The UJA published daily bulletins, like baseball scores, listing the amounts raised the day before. At other times cautionary voices would have advised, and prevailed, that publication of these figures might convey an exaggerated estimate of Jewish wealth and lend support to allegations of dual allegiance.

Not the least surprising to Jewish organizations was the response from the campus. A call went out for volunteers for non-military duties

[8] The authors of the Riverton Study (1957) found that "Jewish giving is not limited to Jewish causes . . . we talked with a number of non-Jewish community leaders; almost all remarked that Jews are generous givers and that they tend to be more generous than non-Jews, especially considering that they support both Jewish and community-wide philanthropies." The primary impulse behind Jewish philanthropy is the Jews' ethos; biblical law had already instructed them to be equally charitable to their own poor and to the stranger at their gate. When Amsterdam (Dutch) Jewry, in 1654, gave its pledge that none of the Jewish refugees from Brazil whom Governor Stuyvesant was reluctant to admit to New York would become wards of that city, it acted in accordance with a tradition that makes every Jew responsible for his fellow Jews.
[9] Sociologist George A. Lundberg, in an address to the anti-Zionist American Council for Judaism, caused considerable agitation among Jewish agencies in the nineteen-fifties with his admonition that Jewish philanthropy was one of the boldest assertions of "ethnocentricity."

in Israel, and soon thousands phoned, wrote, telegraphed, and personally appeared at Israeli consulates and Jewish organizations offering to leave immediately for Israel to assist in combatant and any other duties. There was also a small percentage of non-Jewish youth among the volunteers. A call went out to Jewish faculty members to sign a petition, published in the leading American newspapers, demanding that America keep her pledge to Israel, and within several days—although this was a time of the year when it is difficult to reach teachers at their customary addresses—more than three thousand, or ten percent of the estimated thirty thousand Jewish faculty members, responded, among them men and women of great eminence in their fields. Experts in Russian and Arab affairs, economics and manpower, formed teams to study Israel's problems and to blueprint recommendations for her in these fields. Yet the Jewish Establishment had been moaning for years that Jewish academia while spontaneously responding to all liberal and radical causes, was chronically indifferent to Jewish affairs.

All this shows that there has long been a failure of communication between the Jewish Establishment and the majority of American Jewry. The professionals and laymen involved in the Jewish Establishment have never been eager to share policymaking with its members, although determined to increase their number, and the membership, in turn, indicated no special desire for participation. The large fund drives functioned on the premise that it was more expeditious and economical to raise large sums from relatively few people than small funds from the multitudes. The upper middle-class policymakers, had persuaded themselves that they knew what was best for the Jews here and everywhere. The rest of American Jewry, if it stopped occasionally to read and contemplate the published policy pronouncements, assumed that there was nothing terribly wrong with the Jewish situation and that at any rate it was being handled by experts. The late spring of 1967 was a watershed in the history of American Jews.

With liberals divided on the Vietnam issue, with Black Power advocates ejecting the white man from their ranks and seething with judiciously restrained anti-Semitism (SNCC's newsletter in August removed all bars), the Jewish liberal, hitherto unconcerned with Jewish affairs, suddenly finding himself without shelter, his righteous passion unspent and unsatisfied, discovered Israel in a crisis that seemed custom-tailored to his emotional needs. The interfaith movement, put to the test, produced melancholy results. Several million Jews, the

Israeli Jewish population, were threatened with genocide for the second time within a quarter of a century and for the second time the Church was neutral. With a few exceptions, none of the high Catholic and Protestant prelates could be persuaded to issue an appeal for Israel. Genocide was prevented by the audacity of Israel's military command which, leaving the country's cities unprotected, risked its entire air force on a single concentrated attack on the enemies' airfields. Many rabbis have, as a result, lost their enthusiasm for ecumenical dialogues.

In 1948, Israel also fought alone, but at least there was the illusion of Big Powers' and United Nations' concern for her fate; in 1956 it had France and Britain, traditionally a most slippery ally, with her although America was against her; in 1967 Israel was terribly alone. But at this juncture a book published several years before and widely denounced by the American Jewish community, Hannah Arendt's *Eichmann in Jerusalem*, had a belated catalytic effect. She had imputed co-responsibility for the genocide of the six million Jews to the East European Jewish culture which allegedly had conditioned them to self-degradation and self-immolation. Her hasty and selective research, confirmed the prejudicial basis of Miss Arendt's thesis. With the average reader unaware of the voluminous evidence to the contrary, her indictment became the subject of discussion among Jews and between Jews and Christians. This was perhaps the first generation in all Jewish history placed in an ambiguous relationship with its martyrs because of the indictment that they had been accomplices in the evil that had destroyed them and that the evil was so universal, or banal, that it was rooted in their own as well as in the Nazi culture.

This charge haunted the consciousness of numerous Jews. The events of May–June 1967, therefore, seemed to present to every Jew another fateful test, which he must not fail for it might confirm the charge in the eyes of all.

The 1967 Israel crisis forced to the consciousness of American Jews an issue that had long been shunted aside, although it had been the subject of impassioned debate among the cognoscenti of the American Jewish Establishment and between Americans and Israelis in the years immediately after 1948. Israelis based their appeal for Jewish immigration from America on the premise that catastrophe stalks the Jews wherever they are, that America was no "exception," that it could happen here. This was angrily rejected by American supporters of Israel, including Zionists, who claimed that America was in all respects an exception in all Jewish history. The Israelis soon realized that to press the issue was impolitic, would offend some of their best supporters, adversely affect fund-raising, and perhaps appear to corroborate, as some American Jews contended, the anti-Semitic allegation of dual allegiance leveled against Jews engaged in assisting Israel.

American Jewry produced a voluminous literature, largely socio-logical, to prove that America *was* different. The first of these reassur-ing works was Will Herberg's *Protestant-Catholic-Jew*. The latest, pub-lished shortly before the 1967 Israel crisis, is *Jews in the Mind of America* by Charles Herbert Stember and others, a study sponsored by the American Jewish Committee. These books set out to prove that the American Jew was today a full-fledged member of the American Estab-lishment. The Stember volume even suggested that a new trend was becoming manifest in America, anti-Semitism was being replaced by asemitism, complete unawareness on the part of the Gentile of any difference between Christian and Jew.

The interfaith dialogues and the Jewish organizational lobbying at the Ecumenical Council apparently conveyed to Christian clergy, both Protestant and Catholic, an erroneous impression of a Christian-Jewish consensus. This was illustrated by the statement of Cardinal Bea, the chief proponent of the deicide declaration, to an American Jewish Committee delegation, in the words of a *New York Times* dispatch from Rome, that "the two faiths can profitably work together on such prob-lems as Church aid to education, textbook support for religious-run schools and other common interests." [10] In other words, he expects the Jews, because of the Declaration, to abandon some of their most deep-seated principles.

Sharing the platform with Rabbi Marc H. Tenenbaum, of The American Jewish Committee, a young scholar deeply engaged in the dialogues, was Bishop Fulton J. Sheen who predicted the growth of Christian-Jewish amity in their "common struggle against contemporary secularism." [11] There is an apparent effort under way by segments of the Christian clergy of all denominations to desecularize America and to persuade the Jews, especially the rabbis, to become its accom-plices.[12] Yet, modern Jewry owes its emancipation to the eighteenth- and nineteenth-century secular revolutions, the revival of Hebrew, the

[10] *The New York Times*, February 24, 1967.
[11] *The New York Times*, March 17, 1967.
[12] Judd L. Teller, *Proceedings of the Rabbinical Assembly Convention*, 1967.

emergence of Yiddish literature, and Israel's sovereignty—all secular achievements. An eminent American Jewish historian-sociologist, Professor Ben Halpern, who challenges the Stember thesis (in his contribution to the Stember volume and elsewhere) underscores the vast difference between Christian and Jewish views of, and experiences with secularism, and hence the impossibility of cooperation in a sphere which Cardinal Bea, Bishop Sheen and others regard as the foundation of evolving Christian-Jewish amity. Protestant and Catholic have been brought together by Ecumenism "in common defensiveness" because "among Christians it is considered practically a truism that secularism reduces the scope of the religious community," Halpern writes, whereas its effect on Jews has been "to widen rather than reduce the scope of the community"; it "may have weakened the hold of the Christian church and caused it to lose many of its faithful . . . but it bolstered the hold of the community, if not the synagogues, on many Jews." [13]

"In cold fact," he says elsewhere,[14] "the acceptance of Judaism as an American faith, when voiced by Christians, frequently implies a degree of confidence that Judaism is progressing towards submergence," while "in Jewish mouths, talk of a Judeo-Christian civilization or of a peer relationship among Catholics, Protestants, and Jews often tacitly anticipates an eventual merger in a joint American religion." There is a concealment of substantive differences under the umbrella of semantics which suggest consensus but really represent disagreement. The seasonal fracas over Christmas in the public schools never outlasts the month. But it proves something that is keenly felt in normal times, too, even by Jewish intellectuals who have no formal affiliation whatsoever with the Jewish community: "No Jew living in a society as saturated with the forms and language of Christianity as America is can fail from time to time to be reminded of the fact that he is a Jew. One doesn't fear anti-Semitism, one doesn't fear in fact anything at all—but one is reminded: when political conventions are opened with a prayer, when one meets the expression 'Christian' country or 'Jewish vote,' when hymns are sung at the opening or closing of meetings whose purpose is totally non-religious. In fact anything that smacks of religion at all will do the trick. The curious thing is that these things should remind you of being Jewish." [15]

Notwithstanding these various symbols, America is essentially a

---

[13] *The Jewish Frontier*, February 1967.
[14] *The Jews in the Mind of America* by Stember et al.
[15] Judith Jarvis, in symposium on Jewish identity, *Commentary*, April 1961.

secular society and tensions on purely religious grounds have none of the Old World potency here. They are like damp gunpowder. However, the dissolution of the line of demarcation between church and state involved in the Blaine Amendment fight in New York State, will lead to litigation in which the majority of Jews will be aligned with the liberals against church forces that seek to support the parochial school system with public funds. This may create some discomfort for suburban Jewry but need have no lasting effect, although it might ignite a conflagration prepared for by other circumstances. Many American Jews probably wondered, after Israel's six-day war, what American public reaction might have been if American forces had come to Israel's defense and had become involved in a shooting war with Russian volunteers? The polls showed that almost all Americans had become Israel's rooters after the six-day war, but that, a majority, before that, had supported Johnson's policy of non-intervention.

The Jewish involvement in the Ecumenical Council coincided with the high season of the Civil Liberties struggle. Yet events in the American South were of far more fateful significance for this country, hence for American Jewry, than anything emanating from Rome. This was not evident, however, from the Jewish Establishment's preoccupation with the Ecumenical Council. It issued pronouncements, to be sure, aligning itself with the Negroes' struggle. Rabbis and Jewish college students represented better than a fair percentage of the Freedom Riders. The American Jewish community even offered up two victims to the white citizens' councils' lynch mob. But as Leslie Fiedler summarized it so well, "No Jew can selflessly dedicate himself to fight for the equality of the Negro; when he pretends that he is not also fighting for himself, he is pretending to be indistinguishable from a goy." [16] Ben Halpern [17] emphasized that the most effective help to the Negro would come not from the "benefactor who engages in social action primarily in order to express his own values," but from "activists who have an interest of their own in social justice."

However, it is psychologically most difficult for the American Jew to admit that besides being idealistically motivated he has a legitimate, poignant self-interest in the triumph of the Negro struggle. To admit this, even to himself, is to concede that which he has so passionately denied in discussions with Israelis: that America is not all *that* different,

[16] *The Midstream Reader* (New York: Thomas Yoseloff, 1960), p. 44.
[17] *The Jewish Frontier*, February 1967.

that the race struggle has invested his situation here with the classical ingredients of Jewish catastrophe, that in the violent struggle between a Christian ruling majority and a Christian oppressed minority (in the Old World, Christian divisions were ethnic; in America they are racial) he may once again be cast as a scapegoat because of a situation not of his creation and beyond his control.

The Jewish Establishment has produced another one of those sociological studies on Negro anti-Semitism, based on polls, that seek to persuade the American Jew that history has invested him with total immunity from the fate that befell other Jewish communities. Subsidized by the B'nai B'rith Anti-Defamation League and conducted at the University of California Study Research Center, it has come up with findings that most Negroes' attitude towards Jews are comparable to the attitudes towards whites generally, that those who detect a difference tend to favor the Jew, and that Negroes are more opposed than non-white Christians to anti-Jewish discrimination.[18]

Sociologists have been proven, by the events of May–June 1967, to have been ridiculously wide of the mark in their conclusions that the younger American Jew is becoming increasingly alienated from his origins and has lost all kinship for Israel. There is no reason why sociologists should be more correct in their evaluation of Negro attitudes towards Jews. The study is based on polls, and America has transformed the Negro into an ingenious dissimulator before the white man and his black agents. But even assuming the absolute reliability of the study, its findings offer less comfort than its sponsors seem to think. Negroes generally *are* bitter towards whites, the ghettos *are* in a state of unpredictable and desperate ferment. If twenty-four percent of those queried found Jewish landlords better than other white landlords, and seven percent said they were worse, it leaves sixty-nine percent who see no difference, and the Jew, unfortunately, happens to be the Negroes' closest white target. Eighty percent of those queried said they had never been treated unfairly by Jewish merchants, yet the study also found that Negroes are more likely than other Americans to accept the economic stereotype of the Jew, an ironic paradox which only proves that experience yields to myth.

---

[18] Gary T. Marx, *Protest and Prejudice: A Study of Belief in the Black Community* (New York: Harper and Row). Martin Duberman, Princeton historian and author of the play *In White America*, expressed strong skepticism of Marx's findings in *The New York Times* Book Review, Jan. 21, 1968.

The facts are that the American Negro and Jew have been brought into a fateful confrontation. As of 1960, one-third of the American Negro population was centered in thirteen metropolitan areas, almost all of them in the north.[19] The high ghetto birthrate and the continual Negro exodus from the rural South to these particular northern areas have no doubt increased their Negro population considerably beyond the 1960 figure. The cities with the greatest magnetic pull—New York, Detroit, Chicago, Los Angeles—also contain the bulk of America's Jews. This brings the Jew and Negro into daily encounter, and in these tinderbox times, into conflict. The Jew is, first and above all, the most visible white man. He is also the most visible and ubiquitous white liberal in the interracial civil rights organizations. Liberalism and the interracial civil rights movement are condemned by the Negro militant, even as Socialism is condemned by the Communist, as diverters of valuable energy and as subverters of the true revolution. According to Negro extremists, liberalism is the Jews' conspiracy to thwart the struggle for Black Power. Central in these tensions is that which unites the Negro *with,* and separates the Jew *from,* the American majority. The Negro is Christian. The Jew is the classical scapegoat in Christian iconology. He becomes, additionally, the voodoo pin cushion in the extremist black Christian's iconology.

The ghetto riots have conveyed the erroneous impression that the source of Negro-Jewish tensions is the slum dweller. However, his energies are sparse and quickly spent in several riotous nights a year and, like the white Appalachian, and for similar reasons, he is devoid of all hope and ambition and therefore less subject to the frustrations that generate hate than is the emergent Negro middle class. It is this latter group that has produced most of the young Negro militant leaders. It is this class that, reaching out for economic and political power, especially in the northern areas, finds, as the emergent white Christian middle class has found in other times, and other lands, that the Jew has preceded it. It encounters him everywhere—as landlord, shopkeeper, social worker, school teacher, in the courts, on the campus, at City Hall, and in the mass media. Like the Christian middle class elsewhere, on previous occasions, some might try to make up for lost time and find a shortcut to success by dislodging the Jew. The Jewish landlord is yielding to the white university and the Negro bank. The

[19] Charles Silberman, *Crisis in Black and White* (New York: Random House, 1964).

Jewish merchant has similarly been abandoning the ghetto. With the exception of a discount house here or there, the majority of Jewish merchants in the ghetto are holding on simply because their businesses are so small, that liquidation would bring them little equity. They make just about enough to keep their families off the relief rolls. But Jewish teachers constitute some fifty percent of all teachers in the New York school system, for example (and nearly half of American Jewry lives in Greater New York). The percentage of Jews among the social workers is also disproportionately high. Many of these persons have accepted Negro ghetto assignments, rather than less turbulent neighborhoods, because of a feeling of profound commitment, a passionate idealism. The teachers now find themselves accused of deliberately under-educating the Negro child,[20] the social workers of discriminating against Negro peers in their profession and of contempt for their clients. Suddenly two new organizations have been formed, the African-American Teachers Association and the Association of Black Social Workers, to defend themselves from alleged discrimination, but in reality to seek preferential treatment. The division is ostensibly along color lines, but the Jew is too obvious a target in Christian and black nationalist iconology for anti-Semitism not to assert itself in these two organizations, as it has already in SNCC.

A key impediment to Negro-Jewish understanding is that half of the Negro population in America has been born since World War II. Some of the young Negro militants were, at best, only starting school when the American Jewish Congress and the American Jewish Committee very nearly crippled their specific Jewish programs by focusing their concern on the Negro and sending their legal and social science research staffs into battle for his rights. Philip Randolph, Bayard Rustin, Roy Wilkins, and Whitney Young remember this, but it is beyond the memory range of the young Negro nationalists, and even when this early Jewish participation in the Negro struggle is recalled to them, they reply that it is only additional evidence that the Jew has been "using" the Negro movement and that the Establishment leaders listed above were his pliant tools.

[20] Nathan Glazer, in Beyond The Melting Pot, perceptively observed: "The very large number of Jewish teachers affects the character of New York schools. It is not easy to figure out what the impact of a largely Jewish teaching staff is on students. . . . Whether, in their expectation of intellectual competence, the Jewish teachers overwhelm and discourage Negro and Puerto Rican migrant children, or encourage them to greater efforts, would be hard to say."

There is a peculiar, ironic contemporaneity between the progress of the Jew and the regression of the Negro. But these two processes are in no way related, and the former did not result from the latter. Jewish mass immigration to America began in 1881, just four years after the Reconstruction period had ended and the South had begun to coerce the Negro back to his former, pre-Emancipation status. Yet, even as the Negro was being stripped of his rights and ghettoized in medieval fashion, the Jew was rising from steerage and sweatshop to higher middle-class status, not without setbacks but with inordinate application and relentless sacrifice. The Negro was centered in the South, the Jew in the North, and a large scale confrontation between them started only in the nineteen-twenties when the first exodus from the South took place. At no time, neither then nor today, has Jewish commerce with the Negro been anything but an infinitesimal part of the gross income of American Jewry. But because he has been a latecomer to America, and is not of the same religion as the majority, black and white, the Jews' achievement has been used by the Negro militant as a measure of Negro under-achievement and he has been blaming the Jew for the disparity.

It has been forgotten that the Jew, traditionally color-blind, traded and served the Negro inside his ghetto when the white Christian would not, that the Jewish landlord and shopkeeper were not carpetbaggers who invaded the Negro ghetto. These had been their neighborhoods long before the Negro arrived. They dealt with their own landsmen, the Jewish immigrants, and with other ethnic immigrants, no differently than with the Negro newcomer. They enabled the poor to furnish their homes and clothe their families by substituting credit for outright cash. However, all installment buying involves an overcharge, which may occasionally be excessive and abusive, of course. The overcharge makes up for loss through consumers' defaults on payments and disappearance with the merchandise, and also for the higher interest rates this type of merchandiser pays because he requires credit over a longer period than does the seller who is in a cash across the counter business. Nor is it true that the Jew has from the outset (although it may be more true now) fled his old neighborhoods because of the Negro influx. His evacuation began long before the Negroes' arrival. It was a consequence of his socio-economic advancement, which enabled him to afford better housing. There is no doubt also that this evacuation was accelerated when the Negro mores began to replace his own. The evidence is irrefutable that even in lily-white suburbs the Jew shows a preference for neighborhoods in which his customs, habits, patterns, in other words his identity, are not completely eclipsed. The Jew is still today the predominant white element in the interracial apartment house neighborhoods.

However, the irrational does not yield to reason and myths are more potent than reality.

Harold Cruse has produced a kind of *Mein Kampf* for the black race. His *The Crisis of the Negro Intellectual* is a volume of 594 pages. He sees Israel as a world conspiracy against the black race. "For the emergence of Israel as world-power-in-miniscule meant that the Jewish question in America was no longer purely a domestic minority problem growing out of the old immigrant status tradition. A great proportion of American Jews began to function in America as an organic part of a distant nation-state." Cruse sees that in America "a fateful triangular tension among national groups is coming to the fore. . . . This triangle consists of Anglo-Saxon nationalism, Black nationalism and Jewish nationalism." The Jews are nationalists yet they advocate integration of the Negro as a means of stripping him of his nationality, only because they fear that Black nationalism will drive "Anglo-Saxon nationalists into the radical rightist political camp" and thus jeopardize the Jews alliance with the white Establishment.[21]

The extreme Negro nationalist, having lost all hope in America and advocating the territorial separation of the races, could never have conceived of driving a wedge between the Jew and other white Americans. This has been attempted, however, by an integrationist and moderate, Louis Lomax, author, and TV personality who draws generous lecture fees from Jewish temples and centers. He has suddenly injected into the Negro-Jewish dilemma the thesis that the Jew is alien to America. This has always been the thesis of anti-Semitism everywhere, in America and in East Europe, and was the foundation of Hitler's racism. After alleging that the Negro writer is denied his proper recognition by Jews (although the new Negro writing was discovered largely by Jewish editors, publishers, critics and *Commentary*, a Jewish magazine) he argues, with a pretense at authority, that the Jewish tradition "as both a theoretical and practical matter, offends Negroes," "contradicts everything (the Negro) understands

[21] Harold Cruse, *The Crisis of the Negro Intellectual* (New York: William Morrow, 1967), pp. 480–481.

democracy to be for . . . (Jewish) groupness, particularly when augmented by power, is the mortal enemy of democracy" and "we find ourselves discriminated against in employment not because we are Negroes, but because we are Gentiles." [22]

This kind of theorizing is akin to the grumblings of some white critics and reviewers about a "Jewish cult" in American writing and the supposed power of the Jewish critic on the fate of American books and authors. It has all the ingredients of potential danger. An attempt has already been made, at the New Politics convention in Chicago in September, 1967, to unite Negro and white in a revival of Populism, which has a long anti-Semitic tradition. That attempt has floundered because of the ineptness of its architects. More seasoned designers will attempt it next, perhaps with greater success. The Populist myth was compounded of aversion for the city, isolationism, and a belief in Jewish power, whose purpose was to foment world conflicts in which Jews might benefit. American Jewry's involvement with Israel evidently serves the same purpose in the New Politics and SNCC isolationism as American Jewry's opposition to Nazi Germany served in the isolationism of the nineteen-thirties. Their position on the Israel-Arab conflict, although they set out from different premises, is similar to that of the John Birch Society, as was the position of the American Communists and the right-wing American isolationists after the Stalin-Hitler pact.

The present circumstances, although in an incipient stage, are more dangerous for American Jewry than any previous Populism. In the past, Populism was regionalized. It was largely midwestern, Southern and rural, areas of sparse Jewish population. The isolationism of midwestern Populism was a projection into foreign policy of grievances and attitudes whose source was domestic. The Jews were wholly irrelevant to those domestic crises. Today, however, matters are different. The mass media quickly transforms regional issues into national dilemmas. The heart of the domestic crisis is the conditions in our great metropolitan centers: the Negro revolt, the breakdown of law, the ineptness of government in dealing with Negro despair. For the first time in American history the Jew is relevant to the domestic crisis and is located in the areas of most intense ferment. Even so optimistic an appraiser of the future of the Jew in America as Charles Herbert Stember, who sees

[22] Louis Lomax, *The Negro Revolt* (New York: Harper and Brothers, 1962), pp. 185–186.

asemitism replacing anti-Semitism, nonetheless has his reservations. "Plans and hopes like these hinge, of course, on the assumption that the tendencies we have observed will continue in years to come," he writes, "To take this for granted would be reckless as well as presumptuous, for throughout the long history of the Jews, periods of acceptance and security have alternated with periods of rejection and oppression. But we may confidently state that the current trend toward more and more acceptance of the Jew—both individually and in the abstract—appears unlikely to be reversed by anything short of a catastrophic crisis in American society." [23]

Who can say with confidence that the eruption of our cities and the Negro revolt are not shaping up into such "a catastrophic crisis"? The Jew has been the traditional scapegoat in the struggle between an oppressed Christian minority and an oppressor Christian majority. In the past the differences between Christians were ethnic or denominational, in America today they are racial.

In many ways the Jew must take an existentialist view of the situation. Forces other than the Jewish minority will determine the course of events, which threaten American society and government. However, within the existential situation and before history hands down its final verdict, the Jew must use all his resourcefulness to improvise accommodations with the Negro. He must seek to extend the principle of the balanced ticket to all other areas of urban life in which Jew and Negro confront one another. This requires, among other things, the evacuation of Jewish business from the Negro ghettos where it serves as a living symbol of Jewish exploitation. It requires the redistribution of roles in politics, business, economics, and the professions between Negro and Jew on the basis not of merit, or economic realities, but political expediency. It does not propose the exclusion of other ethnic groups from such arrangements if they are willing and sincere. It requires wisdom and there is regrettably little evidence of this in the Negro and Jewish Establishments alike, which find comfort in the deception that the crisis is not as severe as it seems. Another serious handicap is the absence of a universally recognized Negro negotiating authority. The Negro community is too polarized. However, these steps must be taken before political carpetbaggars descend on Jew and Negro alike

[23] *The Jews in the Mind of America*, p. 217.

and utilize the tensions between them to divide them, politically at any rate, into warring camps.

American politics has traditionally been determined (and the arrangement has worked fairly well) by ethnic, religious, and economic pressure groups. Jewish political influence has derived from the concentration of the Jewish electorate in several key states. The high Negro and the declining Jewish birthrate, together with the diminution of the Jewish voter's ethnic consciousness now that he thinks of himself as part of the Establishment, can lead to a complete dissipation of American Jewry's political power should the politician be compelled to choose between the Jewish and the Negro vote. Indeed this would be a consummation *not* to be wished for as its effects would transcend America's frontiers, and be felt in Israel and in other communities that have relied on American Jewry for support. While what is possible is not necessarily probable, too often in his history the Jew discovered that the very people who would tolerate him as a stranger refused to suffer him as a native. To ignore the lessons of Jewish history would be to run the risk of repeating its most tragic episodes.

Index

Abramovich, Binna, 54–55
Acceptance of Jews, future, 296
Accidents, lawyers and, 81
Actors and actresses; at Café Royal, 54–55; See also specific actors and actresses
Adler, Cyrus, 172, 175, 176
Adler, Jacob P., 23
Adler, Luther, 143
Adler, Rabbi Morris, 236n
Adler, Sarah, 54
Adler, Stella, 143
Advokats, see Lawyers
AFL (American Federation of Labor), anti-Nazi struggle and, 173
African-American Teachers Association, 293
After the Fall (Miller), 259
Aggadah, 263
Agnon, S. Y., 257, 263
Albert Einstein Medical Center, 74, 126n
Aleichem, Sholem, 32, 207; appearance of translations of, 261; as master of Yiddish fiction, 10
Alexandrian Temple, 250
Alreitniks, 38
Alte moid, 88
Am haaretz, 238
Amalgamated Clothing Workers, 129
America First Committee, 189, 190–92
American Bankers Association, 232
American Civil Liberties Union, 184
American Council for Judaism, 190
American Dream (Miller), 265
American Federation of Labor (AFL), anti-Nazi struggle and, 173
American Hebrew, 46
American Israelite, 46
American Jewish Committee, viii, 45, 126, 258; anti-Nazi stance of, 171, 173, 176; B'nai B'rith and, 201; economic boycott of Germany and, 175; employment survey of, 232; fight against anti-Semitism by, 94, 96; fight against racist ideology by, 100; focus of concern on Negro struggle by, 293; paradox in actions of, 96; publications of, 255, 257, 288; similarity of, to Negro organizations, 97; Wise and, 196; Yidn and, 96; Zionists and, 96
American Jewish Congress, 13; economic boycott of Germany and, 174; focus of concern on Negro struggle by, 293; Zionists' call for an, 12
American Jewish Joint Distribution Committee (JDC), 11, 17; anti-Nazi stance of, 176; Depression and, 122; representative in U.S.S.R. of, 106; Stalin and, 107
American Jewish Year Book, The, 121, 176
American League for a Free Palestine, 203
American Palestine Campaign, 122
American Spectator, 189
American Vindicator, 189
Amsterdam News, 185
Anarchists, as hostile to Orthodox, 62
Andreyev, Leonid Nikolayevich, 21
Ansonia Hotel, 154
Anti-Defamation League, 102
Antin, Mary, 148
Anti-Semitism, 94–100, 288; AJC's fight against, 94, 96; diminishment of, 280; of Dreiser, 188–89; effect upon immigrants of, 278; Eichmann and, 280; in Harlem, 185; of Henry Ford, 59, 95, 102, 103; Hobson and, 259; of isolationists, 189–90; of McAfee, 187–89; Marshall's fight against, 94, 96, 176, 177; Miller and, 259; Negro struggle's similarities with, 97; Taft on, 102; as theme, 270; in U.S.S.R., see U.S.S.R.; before World War II, 170–92; Yidn and, 96; Zionists and, 96
Apatoshu (writer), 46
Appel, Benjamin, 147

Arazi, Tuvya, 209
Arbeter Ring, 253
Arbeter Theater Farband (Artef), 55, 144–45; Communist Party and, 144n
Arendt, Hannah, 259, 287
Arent, Arthur, 143
Arlosoroff, Chaim, 131
Aronson, Boris, 141
Arsonists, lawyers' defense of, 81–82
Artef (Arbeter Theater Farband), 55, 144–45; Communist Party and, 144n
Asch, Nathan, 147
Asch, Sholem, 32, 46; Cahan and, 35–36; as master of Yiddish fiction, 10; ostracizing of, 281; unionization of garment industry and, 149
Association of Black Social Workers, 293
Association of Orthodox Scientists, 249
Atheism, 40
Athletics, 89–91, 226
Atlantic Monthly, 186, 189, 255
Attorneys, see Lawyers
Aufbau, 157, 160

Baal bekhi, 237
Baal tefila, 237
Babbitt (Lewis), 134
Babylonian exile, 275
Bader, Gershom, 53
Baer, Max, 90
Baer, Yitzhak F., 257
Baerwald family, 106
Baiting of Jews, 148
Balebatischer, 19, 88
Balfour Declaration, 12, 13; Weizmann and, 14
Bands, Boiberiker, 86
Bank of the United States, 113–17; failure of, 117; founding of, 115–16; run on, 114
Bar Kokhba, 90
Bar mitzvah, 63, 227
Baratov, Ben Zion, 55
Baratz, Joseph, 131
Barbusse, Henri, 133
Barth, John, 263
Barton's candy shops, 223
Baruch, Bernard M., 215, 273
Bea, Augustine Cardinal, 288, 289

Beards, Orthodox and, 75
Behrman, S. N., 140, 146
Bein, Albert, 146
Belkin, Rabbi, 248–49
Bellow, Saul, 255, 264–67;
anticipation of "hippie" by,
267; description of West
Side by, 154; specific
treatment of anti-Semitism
by, 270
Ben-Ami, Jacob, 21, 23
Ben-Gurion, David, 12, 17,
162, 252; description of,
200; Israel's labor move-
ment and, 131; Palestinian
truth squads and, 211;
trade with Germany and,
175n; trips to U.S. by,
199–200; Weizmann and,
207, 210, 215; withdrawal
of Israeli troops from Sinai
Peninsula by, 279–80;
Zionist leadership and, 195,
200–1, 207–8, 212
Ben-Zvi, Itzhak, 11, 17
Bercovici, Konrad, 207
Bergelson, David, 266
Bergmann, David, 210
Bergson, Peter H. (Hillel
Kook), 202–7
Berkeley, Calif., Jewish in-
tellectuals in, 127
Berlin, Irving, 140
Berlin, Isaiah, 169
Bermuda Conference (1943),
199
Bernstein, Henri, 161
Bernstein, Herman, 31
Bevin, Ernest, 211, 214
Bialik, Chaim Nachman, 56,
58
Bialystoker Congregation,
72–73
Bible, Yiddish version of, 32
Bierstube, 151
Biltmore Program, 200, 202
Biro Bidjan (U.S.S.R.), 106
Birth control, 40
Blaine Amendment, repeal of,
290
Blitzstein, Marc, 143
Bloom, Sol, 199
B'nai B'rith, 283; American
Jewish Committee and,
201; economic boycott of
Germany and, 175; trans-
formation of, 193
Boiberiker Kapelie (band),
86
Booksellers, 56–57
Borden's (milk company), 82
Borowitz, Eugene, 241
Borscht circuits, 141, 223
Boston Pilot, 182
Bowery Theater, 20
Boycott of German goods,
174–75
"Brain drain," 160
"Brain trust," FDR's, 202
Brandeis, Louis D., 3; at-
traction of non-Establish-
ment Yahudim to, 13; in
government, 273; reputation
in garment industry, 12;
Zionism and, 34, 202
Brandeis University, 126n
Brando, Marlon, 206
Brecht, Bert, 252
Breitbart, Zisha, 90
Brice, Fanny, 140
Brisbane, Arthur, 102
British Intelligence, 202
Broadway, Jewish restaurants
on, 38

Brod, Max, 244
Bronx, the; East, 37; Jewish
population of, 125
Bronx Park, 138
Brooklyn; cemeteries in, 4;
Jewish population of, 125
Brooklyn Tablet, 182
Buber, Martin, 243, 257, 261;
in Commentary, 256–57; as
Galician, 8; on Hassidism,
243–45
Buchalter, Lepke, 89
Buloff, Joseph, 25n, 144
Bund, German-American,
181, 183, 185, 186
allies in Congress of, 189
Buttons, Red, 142

Cabarets on Upper West
Side, 156
Cabbala, 263
Café de la Paix, 156
Café Royal, 50–55; actors'
section of, 54–55; clientele
at, 252; competitor to, 197;
disappearance of, 252–53;
German refugees at, 161;
Herman the busboy at, 52–
53, 253; sections of, 51
Cafés, 156
Cahan, Abraham, 30, 34–36;
as editor of Jewish Daily
Forward, 281; Palestine
issue and, 108
Caldwell, Erskine, 133, 147
Camps, summer, 141–42, 144
Canal Street, 55
Cantor (chazan), 70; record
cutting by, 71; shames
and, 120
Cantor, Eddie, 140
Cardozo, Benjamin, 273
Carlson, John Roy (Arthur
Derounian), 179–80
Carnegie Hall, 39
Carnovsky, Morris, 144
Catastrophe, Jews' disposi-
tion to, 287
Castle Garden, 37
Cather, Willa, 261
Catholics: Jews' relationship
with, 281–82, 288–90; new
jobs of, 281; political
power of Irish, 46
CCNY (City College of New
York), 127, 171
Cemeteries, 4
Centralverein, 152
Chachmat yavan, 272
Chagall, Bella, 162
Chagall, Marc, 161, 162, 262
Chalah, 64
Chalef, 166–67
Chaliapin, Feodor, 51
Chanukov, L., 46
Charities: during Depression,
121–22; overseas, 101, 121–
22
Chayefsky, Paddy, 261
Chazan (cantor), 70; record
cutting by, 71; shames and,
120
Chekhov, Anton Pavlovich,
21, 133, 252
Cherem, 165
Chess champion, 85
Chevra ein yaacov, 68
Chevra kadisha, 93
Chevra mishnayot, 68
Chevra shas, 68–69
Chevra tehilim, 68, 69
Chicago, University of, 170
Child prodigies, 85
Children, naming of, 87

Chinese, renewed immigra-
tion of, 221
"Chone the Famous," 197,
198
Chossen, 63
Christian Business Directory,
183
Christian Century, 187, 188,
189
Christian Front, 186, 189;
members of, in N.Y.C.
Police Department, 183
Christmas, Hanukkah's
similarity to, 224–25
Christmas trees in Jewish
homes, 225
Church, Samuel Harden, 203
Churchill, Winston, 169
Churgin, Pinchas, 76
CIO (Congress of Industrial
Organizations), 170; anti-
Nazi struggle and, 173
Circumciser (mohel), rever-
end as, 92
City College of New York
(CCNY), 127, 171
Civic Repertory Theater, 21
Claessens, August, 41
Clark, D. Worth, 190
Cloakmakers, 125
Clurman, Harold, 143, 145,
147
Coffee houses, Romanian, on
Lower East Side, 9
Cohen, Benjamin V., 13, 202
Cohen, Elliot, 257-58
Cohen, Mickey, 203
College degrees, percentage
of Jews obtaining, 230
Colleges and universities:
clashes between Commu-
nists, Socialists, and
Zionists at, 131; Jews'
entry into, 229, 230
Comfort, Alex, 218
Commentary, 254, 257, 295
Committee for a Jewish
Army, 203
Commonweal, 181
Communism: expatriate dis-
enchantment with, 254;
Jewish Daily Forward's at-
tacks on, 28; universal
simplistic faith in, 26
Communist Messianism, 264
Communist Party: Artef and,
144n; Moshe Nadir's break
with, 253
Communists: anti-Nazi cam-
paign of, 178–79; attempt
to seize control of garment
center unions by, 108; dual
unions of, 108; Jewish,
107; soliciting funds by, 43;
Zionist clashes with, 131
Congress, Bund allies in, 189
Congress of Industrial Organizations (CIO), 170;
anti-Nazi struggle and, 173
Congress of Racial Equality
(CORE), 97
Conservative Judaism, 60, 61;
changes in, 163–64; major
theologians of, 62; suburban services of, 240
Conservatories of music, 87
Contemporary Jewish Rec-
ord, 255, 259
Cooper Union, 39
Cops: Catholic, 85; occupation as, 84–85
Coralnik, Abraham, 32; in
League to Champion Hu-
man Rights, 173; on Wise,
77

Corbin, John, 24, 140
CORE (Congress of Racial Equality), 97
Coughlin, Father Charles E., 182
Court Jew, 275–76
Crane, Stephen, 147
Cronkite, Maj. Alexander P., 94
Cross and the Flag (Smith), 189
Cruse, Harold, 295
Culture explosion, 19
Culture invasion, 139–52
Cummings, E. E., 51
Curran, Father Edward Lodge, 182
Cushings's Manual of Parliamentary Rules, 15

Dahlberg, Edward, 147, 266
Daily News, 136n
Dangling Man (Bellow), 265, 266
Darkness at Noon (Koestler), 268
Darrow, Clarence, 103
Dassin, Jules, 142
Dating, 63
DAWA (Deutsch-Amerikanische Wirtschaft-Ausschuss), 180, 183
Day, 28, 31–33
   on Wise, 77
Dearborn Independent: anti-Semitism of, 95, 102–3; libel suit against, 103
Debating and discourse, 20, 40–41
Deicide issue, 282
Delancey Street, 6
Dentist, occupation as, 80–81
Depression, 111–27; back-to-the soil movement in, 125; Bank of the United States and, 114; effect on Yeshiva of, 118; Hoover and, 114; landsmanschaft in, 122–23; overseas charities in, 122; refugee influx to Palestine in, 122; shifts in population caused by, 125–26; synagogues during, 119–21; unemployment in, 122; use of welfare agencies in, 121–22; Yiddish newspapers on, 13
Der Kundes (*The Wild One*), 27
Der Meitcheler Eeloui, 74
"Der oilem is a goilem," 252
Derounian, Arthur (John Roy Carlson), 179–80
Deutsch-Amerikanische Wirtschaft-Ausschuss (DAWA), 180–81, 183
Dewey, John, 132
Dickson, Thomas, 24
Die Schnorrers, 47, 48
"Die Yiddishe gass," 279
Die Yunge poets, 32, 47–49
Die Zukunft, 44
Dietary laws, observance of, 85
Dillon, A. M., 49
Dimitrov, Georgi, 178
Depilatory powder, 75
Discourse and debating, 20, 40–41
Discrimination in housing, 38
Displaced persons (DP), 208; camps of, 275
Division Street, 55
Doctors: occupation as, 79–

80; in the shtetl, 79
Dos Passos, John, 133, 134, 140, 147
Dostoevski, Feodor Mikhailovich, 133
Dostrovsky-Dori, Yaacov, 210
Dowries, 88
Dreidlach, chocolate, 223
Dreiser, Theodore, 133, 134, 147, 151; anti-Semitism of, 189
Druggist, occupation as, 80
Dual (parallel) unions as organized by Communists, 108
Dubinsky, David, 129, 171
Dubnow, Simon, 233
Dubovsky, Benjamin, 173
Duker, Abraham G., 255
Dybbuk, The (Ansky), 261

East Broadway, 20; as newspaper center, 28
East Bronx, 37
East European Jews: American Jewry and, 273–74; from Austro-Hungarian empire, 5; from Czarist territories, 5; division between Yahudim and, 279; ethnicism among, 9–10; in government office, 274; history of, 5; trade unionism and, 10; war for hegemony between Yahudim and, 11–12; Yahudim and, 4–5, 47; Zionism and, 10; *See also* Yidn; *specific ethnic groups*
East Wall, 250
Eastman, Max, 252
Eban, Abba, 216, 276–77
Eclair (restaurant), 156
Ecumenical Council, 282, 288, 290
Edgar Allan Poe House, 138
Education, *see* Colleges and universities; Schools
Eeloui, 74
Eichmann, Adolf, 104, 280, 284
Eichmann in Jerusalem (Arendt), 287
Ein Harod, 131
Einstein, Albert, 18, 161, 196, 211
Eisenberg, Emanuel, 143
Eisenhower, Dwight D., 276, 279, 284
Eisenstein, Rabbi Ira, 163
Eisler, Kurt, 158
"Eli, Eli," 72
Eliot, T. S., 135
Ellis Island, 37, 98
Elman, Mischa, 87
Ely the Fanatic (Roth), 272
Emergency Committee to Save the Jewish People, 203
Employment, *see* Occupations
Encounter, 258
Encyclopaedia Britannica, 96
Engels, Friedrich, 87
Enoch Arden Law, 92
Epstein, Eliahu, 208, 209, 215
Eron Prep School, 41
Establishment, Jewish: coming of age of, 284; failure of communication between constituencies and, 286; *See also* Leadership
Establishment, Jews in the, 287
Eternal Road, The (Reinhardt), 158

Ethical Culture Society, 128
Ethnic characteristics, 273
Ethnicism among East European Jews, 10
European Jews, *see* East European Jews
Evian, France, 199
Excommunication of Kaplan, 165
Existentialism, 242, 297
Exodus (Uris), 239, 260
Expatriates, Jews as internal, 255
Ezra, 275

Fabian Socialism, 35
Fair Deal, 274
Farband, 253
Farm conditions, 143
Farrell, James T., 133, 147
Feast of Tabernacles, 163, 240
Feder, Abe, 141
Federal Theater, 139, 143
Federation of Jewish Philanthropies, 118; of Greater New York, 257
Feierberg, Mordecai Ze'ev, 266
Feldshers, 79, 80
Fermi, Enrico, 161
Feuchtwanger, Lion, 21, 158
Fiction: American Jewish, 260–69; contemporary English, about immigrant Jew, 58; Yiddish, 46
Fiddler on the Roof, 147, 261, 267
Fidele, 86
Fiedler, Leslie, 148, 149, 270, 290
Films, anti-Nazi, 190
Finishers, women employed as, 87
Fish, sugared, 8
Fishman, Jacob, 18, 29, 30; American Nazi rights and, 184; Weizmann and, 30
Fitzgerald, F. Scott, 255
Fixer, The (Malamud), 268
Fleischigs, 66
Flexner, Bernard, 13
Fluden, 63
Flynn, John T., 189, 191
Focus (Miller), 259
Fokine, Michel, 51
Food: American recognition of ethnic, 155; chalah, 64; fluden, 63; holobtzies, 66; Hungarian goulash, 8; karnetzlach, 8; knishes, 39; kosher style, 223; kreplach, 66; mameliga, 8; pletzlach, 63; sugared fish, 8
Ford, Henry: anti-Semitism of, 59, 95, 102; apology to Jews by, 104; libel suit against, 103; Marshall's fight against, 103
Fortas, Abraham, 274
Fortune, 285
Forward, see Jewish Daily Forward
"Fourth Reich," 155–58
Francis Joseph, Emperor, 5, 53
Frank, Jerome, 191, 192
Frank, Waldo, 152
Frankfurter, Felix, 13, 202, 273
Free love, 40
Freiheit, see Morning Freiheit
Freud, Sigmund, 8, 255
Freudianism, 135

Frost, Robert, 218
Funeral director, 228; marrying a, 93; as occupation, 91
Funeral industry, exposé of, 93
Funeral practices, 92, 227–28

Gabel, Max, 20
Galician Jews, 6, 7; manners of, 8; Yiddish spoken by, 8
Gaon, 74n
Gaon, Saadya, 249
Garfield, John, 142
Garment industry, 87–89; unions in, 3, 10, 43, 87, 108–10
Gellis, Isaac, 91
Gentiles (Goys): feelings toward Jews of, 233; recent similarities of Jews to, 260; use of protest against, 279
Gentleman's Agreement (Hobson), 259
Georg, Manfred, 157
German-American Bund, 181, 183, 185, 186; allies in Congress of, 189
German Jews: assimilation of, 160; contributions of, 160; "Fourth Reich," 155–58; Yidn and refugee, 159
Germany: refugees from, 153–61; See also Yahudim
Gershwins, the, 140
GI Bill, 231
Ginsberg, Allen, 252, 266
Girls as pianists, 86
Gitlow, Ben, 132
Glass, Montague, 58
Glatshtein, Yaacov, 49
Glazer, Nathan, 222, 232n, 258
Glazman, Baruch, 46
Goals of Jews, 266
Goebbels, Joseph, 172
Gogol, Nikolai Vasilyevich, 21
Gold, Herman, 50–51
Gold, Michael, 147, 148, 150
Goldberg, Abe, 136–37
Goldberg, Arthur, 274, 276, 284
Golden, Harry, 58, 268
Goldstein, Jennie, 20–21
Goodman, Paul, 266
Gordon, A. D., 131
Gordon, Julie, 146
Gorelik, Mordecai, 141
Göring, Hermann, 178
Gorki, Maxim, 21, 211
Goulash, Hungarian, 8
Government service, 273–77; Sephardim in, 273; Yahudim in, 273–74
Goys (Gentiles): feelings toward Jews of,, 233; recent similarities of Jews to, 260; use of protest against, 279
Grand Concourse, buildings on, 39
Grand Street Neighborhood Playhouse, 32
Great Jewish Short Stories (Bellow), 261
Greenberg, Clement, 258
Greenberg, Eliezer, 261
Greenberg, Hayim, 43
Greenblum, Joseph, 223n, 233
Greenwich Village, 221
Griebl, Ignatz, T., 184
Gromyko, Andrei, 205

Grossinger's Hotel, 223
Group Theater, 139, 140, 143, 145
Guide to the Perplexed (Maimonides), 76

Habad (Lubavicher) sect, 249
Habimah, 25–26, 144
Haganah, 105; accomplishments in Israel of, 211, 212; Histadrut and, 203; Irgun and, 204, 208; smuggling immigrants into Israel by, 207, 208; U.S. missions of, 210, 213; World Zionist Organization support of, 203–4
Haggadah, new, 163, 246
Hakoah, 91
Halakhah, 244
Halper, Albert, 147, 150
Halpern, Ben, 289, 290
Halpern, Moshe Leib, 48–49, 108, 253
Haman, 163
Hamantaschen, 224
Hamid, Abdul, 185
Hamsun, Knut, 133
Hanukkah, 163, 224, 240; Christmas' similarity to, 224–25
Harlem, anti-Semitism in, 185
Harper's, 255
Harrison, William Henry, 172
Hart, Lorenz, 142
Hart, Moss, 142, 146, 206
Hassidism: Agnon's relationship to, 263–64; birthplace of, 5; Buber on, 243; fanaticism of, 7; Heschel on, 243; opposition to, 263; parabolism and, 263; Pseudo-Messianism in, 263; Scandinavian Gothic and, 263; sects of, 247–48; wonder-rebbes of, 72
Havdalah, 64
Hebraists, 55–58; as booksellers, 56–57; location of, 55; ranking figure of, 56
Hebrew, U.S.S.R.'s suppression of, 45, 105
Hebrew Committee for National Liberation, 205
Hebrew Free Loan Society, 87
Hebrew Immigrant Aid Society (HIAS), 99
Hebrew literature, satire in, 150
Hebrew National, 91
Hebrew Teachers Institute, 118
Hebrew Union College, 243, 248
Hecht, Ben, 150, 210; anti-Semitism and, 270; Irgun and, 206–7, 210; Wise and, 207
Heifetz, Jascha, 87
Heimischer Yid, 115
Heine, Heinrich, 112
Hellenist disposition of suburban Jews, 219–34
Heller, Dr., 54
Hellman, Lillian, 146
Hemingway, Ernest, 255, 271
Herberg, Will, 258; Niebuhr and, 242; Protestant-Catholic-Jew thesis of, 224, 261, 288
Herman the busboy (Café Royal), 52, 253
Herzl, Theodor, 33, 175n, 198

Herzog (Bellow), 265, 266, 267, 270
Heschel, Abraham Joshua, 242, 243–44
HIAS (Hebrew Immigrant Aid Society), 99
High holidays: Rosh Hashanah, 64, 70, 95; Yom Kippur, 64, 65, 70, 240, 251
High schools, girls in, 88
Hillman, Sidney, 17, 129, 171
Himmelfarb, Milton, 244
"Hippies," 267
Hirschbein, Peretz, 22, 32
Histadrut: founding of, 17–18; Haganah and, 203
Hitler, Adolf, 191; Ickes' criticism of, 191; New York Times interview of, 176
Hobson, Laura Z., 17, 259
Hoffman, B. (Zivyon), 73
Hoffman, Richard Beer, 158
Holidays: Christmas, 225; commercialization of, 224–25; Feast of Tabernacles, 163, 240; Hanukkah, 163, 224, 240; Passover, 163, 223, 251; Purim, 163, 224; Rosh Hashanah, 64, 70, 95; Shevuoth, 65, 240, 251; suburbia's observance of, 239, 240; Sukkoth, 65, 66; Yom Kippur, 64, 65, 70, 240, 251
Hollywood, anti-Nazi films and, 190
Holmes, Henry Wyman, 177
Holmes, Rev. John Haynes, 187
Holobtzies, 66
Hook, Sidney, 132
Hoover, Herbert, 113–14, 203
Hospitals: Spivak Sanitarium, 126; Yidn's fear of, 80
Hotels: Ansonia, 154; bar mitzvahs in, 227; Grossinger's, 223
Houseman, John, 143
Housing: Amalgamated project, 129; discrimination in, 37; exposé of conditions in, 143; Lincoln Center, 156
Housing developments, Jews' entry into, 229
Howe, Irving, 261
Huett, Richard, vii
Hull, Cordell, 176, 178
Hull, Helen, 171
Humphrey, Hubert, 276
Hungarian goulash, 8
Hungarian Jews, 7
Hurok, Sol, 87
Husseini, Haj Amin el, 185
Hutchins, Robert C., 171

I Can Get It for You Wholesale (Weidman), 150
Ibsen, Henrik, 21
Ickes, Harold E., 178, 203; criticism of Hitler by, 191
I'd Rather Be Right (Kaufman and Hart), 142
Ideologists, 42; generation of, 128
Ignatov (writer), 46
ILGWU (International Ladies' Garment Workers' Union): increasing influence of, 129; Labor Stage, 139; 1921 court ruling in favor of, 3; Unity House, 142
Immigrants, political use of, 99
Immigration of Jews to U.S.,

19; contemporary English fiction on, 58; difficulties of, 98; "experts" for, 99; restrictions on, 3, 98, 153, 275; separation caused by, 98

Immigration law, amendment of, 220

Immigration to Palestine: by smuggling, 207, 208; White Paper on, 275

Incident at Vichy (Miller), 260

Intellectuals: California's population of Jewish, 127; Stalin's death drive against Jewish, 107

Interfaith relations, 280, 282

Intermarriage, 274

International (Hearst's magazine), 95

International Catholic Truth Society, 182

International events, Jews' sensitivity to, 101–3

International Ladies' Garment Workers' Union, *see* ILGWU

Inzich poets, 32, 47, 49, 50

Irgun Zvai Leumi (National Military Organization), 105, 203–10; American support of, 208; distinction between Hebrew and Jew by, 205; Haganah and, 204, 208; Hecht's newspaper ads for, 206–7; threat to Palestinean Zionist bodies by, 210; U.S. embassy of, 205; Weizmann and, 207

Irish: American literature of, 271; belligerency of, 6; move to Upper West Side by, 37; political power of, 46; pro-Nazi position of, 181

Irving Place Theater, 21

Isolationist policies of U.S., 101

Isolationists, anti-Semitism of, 189

Israel, 42; American Zionists, and, 276; attitude of American Jews toward, 284; as center of Jewish concern, 278; contributions to, during 1967 crisis, 285; fight for statehood by, 202–15; Haganah's accomplishments in, 211, 215; immigrants smuggled into, 208; 1967 crisis in, 277, 284; wars in, 284; *See also* Palestine

Israel Histadrut Campaign, 130

Israeli Bonds Organization, 277

It Can't Happen Here (Lewis), 143

Italians, relations between Jews and, 6

It's All Over (*Noch Alemen*; Bergelson), 266

Jager's (restaurant), 40

James, Henry, 261

Javits, Jacob S., 274

JDC (American Jewish Joint Distribution Committee), 11, 17; anti-Nazi stance of, 176; Depression and, 122; representative in U.S.S.R. of, 106; Stalin and, 107

Jerusalem, Mufti of, 108

Jessel, George, 140

Jew in Love, A (Hecht), 150

Jewish Agency for Palestine, 200; formation of, 18

Jewish Agricultural Society, 125

Jewish Brigade, 208

Jewish Commonwealth, 275

Jewish Daily Forward, 28, 34–36; attacks on Communists by, 28; labor leader support by, 42–43; Palestine issue and, 108; rejection of Asch by, 280; remuneration by, 44; Saphire in, 137; on Wise, 77

Jewish House of Study (Judische Lehrhaus), 243

Jewish Labor Committee, 175

Jewish Morning Journal, 18, 28–30, 38; classified ads in, 117; medical advice column in, 173; Saphire in, 138; on Wise, 77

Jewish National Home, 43, 196

Jewish Reconstructionist Foundation, Inc., 163, 165

Jewish Theological Seminary, 128, 163–65, 172, 243, 248

Jews in America, The, 95

Jews in the Mind of America (Stember), 288

Jews Without Money (Gold), 148, 150

John XXIII, Pope, 282

John Birch Society, 296

Johnson, Lyndon Baines, 279, 283, 284

Joint Boycott Council, 174

Jolson, Al, 140

Joseph, 275

Journal, see *Jewish Morning Journal*

Journals and Newspapers: *Day*, 28, 31–33, 77; *Der Kundes*, 27; *Freiheit*, 43, 45, 108, 144; *Jewish Daily Forward*, 28, 34–35, 43, 44, 47, 108, 138, 262, 280; *Jewish Morning Journal*, 18, 28–30, 36, 77, 117, 138, 173; *Tageblat*, 28, 77; Weltschmerz in, 33

Judaism: Conservative, *see* Conservative Judaism; origin of, 60; Orthodox, *see* Orthodox fundamentalism; Reform, *see* Reform Judaism; Yahudim and, 60

Judaism as a Civilization (Kaplan), 187

Judaism and Modern Man (Herberg), 242

Judenrein, 222

Judeo-Christian civilization, 280, 289

Judge, occupation as, 84

Judische Lehrhaus (Jewish House of Study), 243

Kafka, Franz, 254, 255, 257, 258, 261, 263, 264, 268

Kallen, Horace M., 202

Kanin, Garson, 142

Kapelie, 86

Kaplan, Mordecai M., 62, 163–65, 187

Karnetzlach, 8

Kashrut Association, 167–68

Katz, Manne, 161

Katzenelson, Berl, 131

Kaufman, George S., 140, 142, 146

Kaye, Danny, 142

Kazan, Elia, 139, 144

Kazin, Alfred, 256

Kennedy, John F., 274, 276

Kennedy, Robert, 38

Kerensky, Alexander, 105, 252

Kerensky government: Russia's Jews and, 45; Schiff's loan to, 176

Kerstein, Lincoln M., 13

Kibbutzim, 42

Kiddush, 63

Kierkegaard, Søren, 255

Kingsley, Sidney, 146

Kishinev pogrom, 175n

KKK (Ku Klux Klan), 114; exposé of, 95

Klezmer, 86

Knishes, 39

Kober, Arthur, 142

Kobrin, Leon, 22

Koestler, Arthur, 255, 260, 268

Kohn, Rabbi Eugene, 163

Kollek, Teddy, 210

Kook, Rabbi Abraham Isaac, 202

Kook, Hillel (Peter H. Bergson), 202–7

Kopilevich, Dr., 54

Kosher poultry, 166–68

Kotler, Yosel, 26–27

Koussevitzky, Serge, 203

Kreplach, 66

Kristol, Irving, 258

Kunitz, Joshua, 76

Labor movement, 34; Yiddish and, 137; *See also* Trade Unionism

Labor riots, police and, 109

Labor Stage, 139, 142

Labor Temple, 132–33, 252; ideological orthodoxies on display at, 133

Labor Zionism: chief theoretical spokesman of, 43; founder of, 42

Labor (Socialist) Zionists, 11; Ben-Gurion, *see* Ben-Gurion, David; Ben-Zvi, 11, 17

LaGuardia, Fiorello, 166, 184

Lamm, Rabbi Norman, 249

Land, movement to, 125

Landau, Zisha, 253

Landsman, 115

Landsmanschaft, 15, 17, 39; in Depression, 122; "interventionists" in, 123; "isolationists" in, 123

Languages, *see* Hebrew; Yiddish

Lassalle, Ferdinand, 87

Lawson, John Howard, 146

Lawyers (advokats), 8; accidents and, 81; as immigration experts, 99; occupation as, 81–83; as students, 82; unions and, 83

Leadership, 276–90; attack on discrimination by, 280; changing of, 277–80; in interfaith relations, 280–82; and Johnson's criticism of Jews on Vietnam, 283; loss of contact with constituencies by, 282–86; politically influential Jews' role in, 277; preoccupation with Ecumenical Council by, 290; self-confidence of, during 1967 crisis, 284; as spokesmen on Israel, 276; *See also* Court Jew; Es-

tablishment, Jewish; Zionist leadership
League of Nations, 101, 195; Nazism and, 178
League to Champion Human Rights, 173
Le-an? (Whither? Feierberg), 266
Leary, Timothy, 252
Lecture circuit, 159
Le Gallienne, Eva, 21
Lehman, Herbert H., 273
Lehman family, 106
Leib, Mani, 52
Leivick, H., 47, 49, 108, 253
Lend-Lease financing of, 190
Lenin, Vladimir Ilyich, 105, 106
Leonard, Benny, 90
Leve, Sam, 141
Levin, Meyer, 147, 150
Lewis, Sinclair, 133, 143, 147, 150, 252
Lewisohn, Ludwig, 148, 152, 259; anti-Semitism and, 270; as contributor to Jewish periodicals, 257; in polemic against Gentiles, 58–59; as ranking American Jewish writer, 135; reaction to danger of Nazism by, 151
Liebknecht, Karl, 162n
Liessin, Abraham, 44
Lincoln, Abraham, 39
Lincoln Brigade, 254
Lincoln Center housing, 156
Lindbergh, Charles A., 190, 191
Linowitz, Sol, 274
Lipchitz, Jacques, 161, 162
Lipsky, Louis, 195–97, 201, 202
Literary Digest, 140, 177
Literature, American Jewish: Commentary and, 254, 256–57; conspiracy in, 268–69; creation of, 254; criticism of, 268; emergence of, 254; fiction and, 260–61; groping for purpose in, 265; Irish Americans and, 271; Partisan Review and, 254; satire in, 150; Schocken Books and, 254
Litvaks (Lithuanian Jews), 6; description of, 9
Litvinov, Maxim, 178
Living Newspaper, 143
Lodge, John Cabot, 100
Lomax, Louis, 295
London, Jack, 46, 126
Lope de Vega, Felix, 21
Los Angeles, Calif., Jewish population in, 127
Love and Death in the American Novel (Fiedler), 270–71
Lovestone, Jay, 132
Lowell, Amy, 170
Löwenstein, Prince Hubertus von, 159
Lower East Side: Rabbis on, 236; Romanian businesses on, 8; Sabbath services on, 70; waiters of, 40; See also specific streets and theaters
Lozovsky, Solomon A., 107
Lubavicher (Habad) sect, 247
Lubavitcher Rebbe, 168–69
Luchow's, 40
Ludwig, Emil, 158
Lumet, Baruch, 142
Lumet, Sidney, 142

Lutsky, Aaron, 49
Lynchings, Negro, Yiddish poetry on, 47

Macbeth, 139
Mack, Julian V., 198, 202
Macy's, R. H., 175
Maecenas, 257
Magid, 73
Magidoff, Jacob, 30
Mailer, Norman, 265–66, 271
Maimonides, 243, 249; legal commentaries of, 76
Malachi, A. R., 57
Malamud, Bernard, 264–66, 267
Maltz, Albert, 146
Mameliga, 8
Manhattan, Jewish population in, 125–26
Mann, Paul, 144
Mann, Thomas, 252
Marcus, Bernard, 116–17
Marcus, David "Mickey," 215
Marcus, Joseph S., 115–16
Marinoff, Jacob, 27
Maritain, Jacques, 162
Marital infidelity, 265
Marjorie Morningstar (Wouk), 260
Marranos, 214; definition of, 10
Marriage brokers (shadchanim), reverends as, 92
Marriages, quick and quiet, 92
Marshall, Louis, 12, 13, 172; as Court Jew, 276; death of, 128; fight against anti-Semitism by, 94, 96, 175, 177; in fight against Ford, 103; Lower East Side and, 13; Yidn and, 96; Zionists and, 96
Marx, Karl, 87, 152, 169
Marx Brothers, 140
Mass media, Jews entry into, 229
Massena, N.Y., Rosh Hashanah incident in, 95
Maud, Zuni, 26, 27
Maupassant, Guy de, 21
Maurois, André, 161
Mayakovsky, Vladimir, 45
McAfee, Joseph Ernest, 187–88, 189
McCarthy, Mary, 271
McCarthyism, 242
McCormick, Anne O'Hare, 176
Medical School, Albert Einstein, 126n
Medicine as a profession, 79–80
"Mein Greene Kuzine," 71
Melamadim, 75
Mellahs, 213
Melville, Herman, 263
Mencken, H. L., 133, 189
Menorah, 225
Menorah Journal, 257
Mensheviks (Social Democrats), 105
Menuhin, Yehudi, 85
Mercury Theater, 143
Merezhkovski, Dmitri Sergeyevich, 21
Meshumad, 52
Mestel, Jacob, 55
Metaphysical agony of Jews, 262
Metropolitan Opera, 49
Meyer, Eugene, Jr., 13
Meyer (painter), 47

Mezuzah, 85
Michener, James, 239
Midwives, 80
Mikva, 17
Milchigs, 66
Miller, Arthur, 259–60
Mitropoulos, Dimitri, 203
Mitzvot (mitzvah), 87, 241
Mohel, reverend as, 92
Moishe Kapoyer, 71
Molière, Jean Baptiste Poquelin, 21
Molnar, Ferenc, 161
Moneylending: by Hebrew Free Loan Society, 87; by Herman at Café Royal, 52
Monsky, Henry, 193, 201
Mooney and Billings, 179
Moore, Marianne, 203
Morgenthau, Henry, 273
Morgenthau, Henry, Jr., 273
Morning Freiheit: labor leader support by, 43; literary policies of, 44–45; Mufti incident and, 108; Nitgedaiget and, 144; remuneration by, 44
Moscow Art Theater, 25
Moshavim, 42
Mosholu Park, 128
Moynihan, Daniel, 271
Mufti of Jerusalem, 108
Muni, Paul (Muni Weisenfreund), 23–24, 206
Murder, Inc., 89, 183
Murray, Philip, 170
Musclemen (shtarke) in garment industry, 89
Music, conservatories of, 87
Musician, occupation as, 86–87
Mussolini, Benito, assault on Ethiopia by, 179
Muste, A. J., 132
Mutual aid, 15

NAACP (National Association for the Advancement of Colored People), 97, 196, 280
Nadir, Moishe (Isaac Reiss), 44, 115, 253
Names given children, 87
Nation, 152
National Democratic Committee, 277
National Guard, N.Y.S., 183
National Military Organization, see Irgun Zvai Leumi
"Nativization," 260–61
Nazi refugees, 153; FDR and, 199
Nazism, 122, 176; Communist campaign against, 178–79; films on anti-, 190; Irish position on, 181, 182; trade union response to, 173; Zionism and, 171, 173, 177, 178
Nearing, Scott, 132
Negroes, 290–97; anti-Semitism of, 185; anti-Semitism's similarities to struggle of, 97, 291; impediment to understanding between Jews and, 293; Jews' achievements as used by militant, 294, 295; Jews and, at New Politics convention, 295; Jews' self-interest in struggle of, 290; opinion of Jew by, 291; Yiddish writings' concern for, 46
Negro organizations: AJC's similarity to, 97; CORE,

97; NAACP, 97, 196, 280; SCLC, 97; SNCC, 97, 286, 293, 295; Urban League, 97
Nehemiah, 275
Neo-Orthodoxy, 240–42
Neumann, Dr., 53
New Class, 281
New Deal, 143, 274; participation of Jews in, 171
New Masses, 179, 255
New Politics convention (1967), 295
New School for Social Research, 158
New York City: Jewish population in, 4, 125–26; See also specific areas and boroughs
New York City Board of Orthodox Rabbis, 167
New York Public Library, Jewish Room in, vii
New York Telephone Company, 97
New York Times, 136; advertisement by Rabbinical Alliance in, 248; Chone's obituary in, 197; Christian-Jewish relations in, 288; expressions of Jewish opinion in, 282; interview with Hitler by, 176; Jews and Vietnam in, 283; reports from Palestine by, 209; Wise and, 196
Newspapermen, 51
Newspapers and journals: Day, 28, 31–33, 77; Der Kundes, 27; Freiheit, 43, 45, 108, 144; Jewish Daily Forward, 28, 34–35, 43, 44, 47, 108, 138, 262, 280; Jewish Morning Journal, 18, 28–30, 36, 77, 117, 138, 173; Tageblat, 28, 77; Weltschmerz in, 33
Niebuhr, Reinhold, 242, 243
Nigun, 169
1921, events of, 3
Ninety-niners (Orthodox congregation), 75
Nitgedaiget, 144
Nixon, Richard, 276
Noch Alemen (It's All Over; Bergelson), 266
Nock, Albert J., 186, 189
Non-Sectarian Anti-Nazi League to Champion Human Rights, 174
Norris, Frank, 147
Nosherei, 223
Nye, Gerald P., 190

Occupations, 79–93; athlete, 89–91; cloakmaker, 125; cop, 84; denied to Jews, 232; dentist, 80; doctor, 79–80; druggist, 80; feldsher, 79, 80; funeral director, 91; in garment industry, 87; judge, 84; lawyer, 81; midwife, 80; musician, 86–87; politician, 83–84; reverend, 91–92; shames, 119–20; tailor, 88
Odets, Clifford, 144, 145, 146, 267
Of Thee I Sing (Kaufman), 142
O'Hara, John, 265, 271
Old Bunch, The (Levin), 150
One Third of a Nation, 143
O'Neill, Eugene, 268
Orators, 40–42; Socialist, 40–41

Ornitz, Samuel, 147, 148
Orthodox fundamentalism, 60, 246; beards and, 75; chevra ein yaacov in, 68; chevra mishnayot in, 68; chevra shas in, 68–69; chevra tehilim in, 68; deans of, 248–49; developments in, 162; domination of physical environment by, 62; Hellenization and, 249–50; hostility of anarchists to, 62; hostility between Yiddishkeit and, 62; Kashrut Association and, 167–68; modern challenge to, 249; Ninety-niners congregation, 75; pledges in synagogues of, 61; Reconstructionists and, 165; suburban services of, 240
Orthodox Jews, opinion of Schwartzbard case of, 104
Orthodox rabbinate: creation of an elite by, 168; test of, 165

Palestine: American settlers in, 130; Arab terror in, 110; Britian's White Paper on, 275; creation of a shadow state in, 17; first Zionist commune in, 131; Haganah in, see Haganah; Histadrut and, 17, 203; Irgun in, see Irgun Zvai Leumi; Jewish Daily Forward and, 108; Jewish refugees from Germany in, 122; New York Times reports on, 209; Stern group in, 105, 204; truth squads in, 211; U.S.S.R.'s UN vote on, 214; Weizmann and, 130; See also Israel
Palestine Mandate, 275
Palo Alto, Calif., Jewish intellectuals in, 127
Pankin, Jacob, 41
Paradise Lost (Odets), 146
Parallel (dual) unions, 108
Paris Peace Conference, 12
Parker, Dorothy, 203
Parks, 138
Parliamentary Rules, Cushing's Manual of, 15
Partisan Review, 257; birth of American Jewish Literature and, 254; internal emigrants and, 255
Passover: good on, 223, 240; preparations for, 66–67; Reform Judaism and, 163; theater season and, 251
Pelley, William Dudley, 151
Peretz, Yehuda Leib, 32, 267
Permissiveness, shtetl's increasing, 31
Persky, Daniel, 57
Petliura, Semyon, 103
Petuchowski, Rabbi Jacob J., 241, 245n
Pgam, 166
Pharmacists, see Druggists
Philanthropists, U.S.S.R. and American Jewish, 106
Philanthropy, 34
Philosophy, Jewish: on Americanization of Jew, 260–61; on concern with ineffectual man, 266; on extramarital relationships, 265; in Hassidic works, 263–64; on Jew in agony, 262; on "Jewishness,"

269; on love, 264; on materialism, 267; on necessity of existentialist view, 297; return to East Europe, 262; on search for purpose, 265; on unreal Jew, 259
Phylacteries, 169
Pianists, girls as, 86
Picon, Molly, 21
Pins and Needles, 143
Pinski, David, 22, 32
Pirandello, Luigi, 252
Piscator, Erwin, 158
Playboy Club, 227
Plehve, Vyascheslav von, 175n
Pleiner Yiddish, 35
Pletzlach, 63
Plotters, The (Carlson), 180
Podhoretz, Norman, 258
Podlie, 19
Poe, Edgar Allan, house of, 138
Poetry: on Negro lynchings, 47; revolutions in, 32
Poets, 47–52; Die Yunge, 32, 47–49; Inzich, 32, 47, 49, 50; youths' difficulty in relating to, 135
Pogroms: Kishinev, 175n; Russian, 105; Ukrainian, 104
Poland, unemployment of Jews in, 122
Poles, 6
Police Department, New York City: Christian Fronters in, 183; Jews' loss of faith in, 183; labor riots, and 109
Policemen, see Cops
Policy framing, 277
Polish Jews, 6, 9
Political power: Irish Catholic, 46; Jews' loss of, 297
Politicians: role in Jewish affairs of Jewish, 277; use of immigrants by, 99
Politics, 297; Jews in, 83–84, 276–77
Polo Grounds, 91
Population, Jewish: in America, 4; in New York City, 4, 126; in Russia, 105
Populism, 275
Potash and Perlmutter, 259
Pound, Ezra, 135, 151
Poznansky, Israel, 173
Pragmatists: generation of, 128; leadership of Zionism by, 130
Press, see Newspapers and journals
Presser, occupation as, 88
Prodigies, 85
Professions: Jews in, 231–32; See also specific professions
Proskauer, Joseph M., 201
Protestant-Catholic-Jew (Herberg), 288
Protocols of the Elders of Zion, 102, 151, 182
Puppet theater, Yiddish, 27
Purim, 163, 225
Purim shpiel, 22

Queens: cemeteries in, 4; Jewish population of, 125
Quota law, immigrant, 3, 100

Rabbi Jacob Joseph school, 85

Rabbinical Alliance of America, 248
Rabbis: diminishing need for, 235; diminishing sovereignty of, 237; great, 74n; on Lower East Side, 237; shames and, 120
Rabinowitz, Ezekiel, 173
Raboi, Isaac, 46
Racist ideology, AJC's fight against, 100
Radical ideologies, debating of, 40
Randolph, Philip, 293
Raphaelson, Samson, 146
Ratner's, 39
Reader's Digest, 240
Real estate, Yidn in, 38–39
Rebbetzin, 55
Reconstructionism, 163–65, 246
Record hits, 71
Reflex, 93
Reform Judaism, 60–61, 162; changes in, 162; citadel of, 65; services in suburbia of, 240
Refugees: categories of, 153; German, 154–61; in Palestine from Germany, 122; restriction of immigration of, 153
Reik, Theodor, 158
Reiner Yiddish, 35
Reinhardt, Max, 158
Reisen, Abraham, 35, 36
Reiss, Isaac (Moishe Nadir), 44, 115, 253
Religion, 60–78; See also Conservative Judaism; Orthodox fundamentalism; Reform Judaism
Remarque, Erich Maria, 133
Reshevsky, Sammy, 85
Restaurants: on Broadway, 38; disappearance of, 221; Jager's, 40; Luchow's, 40; in new Jewish neighborhoods, 222–23; Ratner's, 39; Romanian, on Lower East Side, 8; Tip Toe Inn, 197; unlicensed, 157; waiters in, on Lower East Side, 40; See also Café de la Paix; Café Royal
Reuther, Walter, 170
Revel, Bernard, 76
Reverends, 91–92
Reynolds, Robert R., 189
Ribicoff, Abraham, 274
Rice, Elmer, 140, 146, 152
Richmond (Staten Island): cemeteries on, 4; Jewish population of, 125
Ridder, Victor, 180
Ringer, James B., 222n, 233
Riots, labor, 109
Ritt, Martin, 142
Ritual murder, Massena incident as, 95
Rituals, 241n
Robbe-Grillet, Alain, 265
Robbins, Jerome, 142
Robinson, Edward G., 206
Rockefeller, John D., 106
Role of Jews: insider-outsider, 260; reevaluation of, 257
Rolland, Romain, 21, 133
Rome, Harold, 143
Roosevelt, Franklin Delano, 129, 139; Adler and, 172; "brain trust" of, 202; Jewish advisers of, 171;

Morgenthau, Jr. and, 273; Nazi refugees and, 199; Quarantine Speech of, 178; Silver and, 201; special position in Jews' eyes of, 177–78; War Refugee Board established by, 213n; Weizmann and, 199; Zionists and, 194–95
Roosevelt, N. J., 125
Roosevelt, Theodore, 171, 172, 281
Rosenblatt, Cantor Yossele, 70, 126
Rosenbluth, Capt. Robert, 94
Rosenfeld, Isaac, 255, 260
Rosenfeld, Yona, 35, 36
Rosenman, Samuel, 171
Rosenthal, A. M., 216
Rosenwald, Lessing, 190
Rosenzweig, Franz, 243, 244–45, 257
Rosh Hashanah, 64, 70; Massena incident, 95
Roth, Henry, 147
Roth, Philip, 270, 272
Rothschilds, 198
Rothstein, Arnold, 109
Rubashkas, 26
Rumanian Jews, 6, 8; businesses of, 9
Rumpelmeyer's, 156
Russell, Bertrand, 35
Russia: effect on Jews of Communist seizure of power in, 105–8; Jewish population of, 105; Kerensky's government in, 46; See also U.S.S.R.
Russo-American Treaty of 1832, 16
Rustin, Bayard, 293
Ryskind, Morris, 146

Saadia, 243
Sabbath, dating on, 63
Sabbath services in Lower East Side synagogues, 70
Sacco-Vanzetti execution, 133
Samuel, Maurice, 58, 148, 257, 270
Sandburg, Carl, 47, 135
Sanger, Margaret, 40
Santa Barbara, Calif., Jewish intellectuals in, 127
Saphire, Saul, 137–38
Saroyan, William, 139, 268
Sartre, Jean Paul, 255
Satan in Goray (Singer), 264
Satire in Yiddish and Hebrew literature, 150
Satmar sect, 247
Saturday Evening Post, 191–92
Satz, Ludwig, 22, 23
Sausage, fried, 8
Scandinavian Gothic, 263
Schachtman, Max, 132
Schary, Dore, 142
Schiff, Jacob, 11, 16, 17, 34, 102; American Jewish Committee and, 175, 177; as Court Jew, 276; death of, 128
Schildkraut, Rudolf, 23
Schiller, Friedrich von, 21
Schlager, 115
Schlagsahne, 155
Schmalhausen, Daniel, 132
Schneider, Benno, 145
Schneider, Isidor, 147, 148
Schnitzler, Arthur, 21
Schocken, Zalman, 257
Schocken Books, 254; re-

sponsiveness to Jewish intellectuals of, 256
Schools: Albert Einstein, 74, 126n; Eron Prep, 41; girls in, 87–88; Rabbi Jacob Joseph, 85; Yeshiva, 74, 75, 118, 249, 250
Schrank, Joseph, 143
Schulberg, Budd, 150, 151
Schulman, Rabbi Samuel, 77
Schundroman, 134
Schwartz, J. J., 46
Schwartz, Maurice, 21; as actor, 22; Art Theater of, 252; as director, 22, 23, 24
Schwartzbard, Sholem, 103–4
Schweid, Mark, 55
SCLC (Southern Christian Leadership Conference), 97
Scottsboro Boys, 179
Second Avenue: decline of Yiddish culture on, 251; numbers of theaters on, 251; theater headquarters at, 20–21
Secularism, deprecation of, 245
Secularists, domination of public platform by, 62
Sefarim, Mendele Mocher, 32
Self-employment, 230
Sephardim: in government office, 273; intermarriage and, 274
Sereni, Enzio, 131
Seward Park Library, 221
Shabes, 115
Shadchanim, reverend as, 92
Shakespeare, William, 21
Shames, 119–21
Shapiro, Gurrah, 89, 270
Sharett, Moshe (Moshe Shertok), 195, 208, 211
Shaw, George Bernard, 21, 35
Shaw, Irwin, 146, 260
Shecter, Solomon, 62
Sheen, Bishop Fulton J., 288
Sheffield's (milk company), 82
Sheitelen (sheitel), 138, 247
Shertok, Moshe (Moshe Sharett), 195, 208, 211
Shevuoth, 65, 251
Shipley, Joseph T., 76
Shishi, 120
Shiva, 15, 120; catering for, 228
Shma, 85n
Shochtim (shochet), 166
Sho'er, Abraham, 57
Shofar, 163
Shpiel, 21–22
Shtadlanut, 198
Shtarke, 89
Shtetl, relations between Jew and Christian in, 124
Shtreimlach, 86
Siddur, 165
Sidney, Sylvia, 206
Siegel, Bugsy, 203
Silver, Rabbi Abba Hillel, 198; as American Zionist leader, 201, 211, 212, 215; FDR and, 201
Silvers, Phil, 142
Sinai Peninsula, 279
Sinclair, Upton, 133
Singer, I. J., 35
Singer, Isaac Bashevis, 262–64; on agony of Jews, 264; impact on American Jewish writers, 254; prominence

of, 264; reaction to view on material failure by, 267; revelation that ghetto had sex by, 272

Singer, Saul, 115

Six-Day War, 277, 284–88; contributions to Israel during, 285; reaction by American campus youth during, 285–86

Sklare, Marshall, 223n, 233

Skulnik, Menashe, 22

Slonim, Yoel, 33

Smith, Al, 114, 119, 281

Smith, Gerald L. K., 189

Smithsonian Institution, 172

Smuts, Field Marshal Jan, 215

SNCC (Student Non-violent Coordinating Committee), 97, 286, 293, 296

Soccer, 91

Social Democrats (Mensheviks), 105

Social Justice, 182

Socialism, Fabian, 35

Socialist Party's Camp Tamiment, 142

Socialist (Labor) Zionists, 11

Socialists: campaign debating by, 40; funeral practices of, 93; Old Guard, 17; oratory of, 40–41; Zionist clashes with, 131

Sofer, 272

Soloveichik, Joseph Dov, 249

Southern Christian Leadership Conference (SCLC), 97

Soviet Union, see U.S.S.R.

Speakers, 40–42

Spewack, Bella, 146

Spewack, Sam, 146

Spier, André, 161

Spinoza, Baruch, 152, 165

Spinoza of Market Street (Singer), 264

Spivak, John L., 179, 180

Spivak Sanitarium (Denver), 126

Sports, 89–91, 226

Springfield, Mass., 228

Spritz, 157

Staats-Zeitung, 180

Stalin, Joseph: Communist Messianism and, 264; death drive against Jewish intellectuals by, 107

Stamgast, 52

Stanislavski, Konstantin, 25, 144

State Department, U.S., 178

Staten Island (Richmond): cemeteries on, 4; Jewish population of, 125

Stein, Gertrude, 254

Steinbeck, John, 147

Steinberg, Rabbi Milton, 164

Steinhardt, Laurence, 13

Stember, Charles Herbert, 218, 296

Stern Group, 105, 204, 205

Stereotypes, 279

Steuben Society, 180

Straus, Nathan, 13, 45

Straus, Oscar S., 273

Streicher, Julius, 148

Strindberg, August, 21

Student Non-violent Co-ordinating Committee (SNCC), 97, 286, 293, 296

Students, law, 82

Suburbia, 219–34; Americanization of Jew in, 279; Jewish leaders from, 279;

movement to, 219–22; observance of holidays in, 240; Orthodox rabbi in, 238; synagogue membership in, 225–26; synagogues in, 238–39

Sukkoth, 65, 66

Sulzberger, Arthur Hays, 209

Summer camps, 141–42, 144

Suspicion of Jews, 102

Swan, Oliver, vii

Swope, Herbert Bayard, 215

Synagogue Council of America, 248

Synagogues and temples, see Temples and synagogues

Syrkin, Nachman, 42

Szilard, Leo, 161

Tachlis, 230, 273

Taft, William Howard, 16, 102, 172

Tageblat, 28; on Wise, 77

Tailor, occupation as, 88

Talmud, study of, 69

Talmudical (Rabbinical) Academy, 118

Talmudists: arrival of outstanding, 74; at theater, 25

Talner, David—Reb Dovidl, 86

Tamiment, Camp, 142

Telephone Company, New York, 97

Teller, Benjamin, viii

Teller, Judd L., 238n, 258n

Temple Emanu-El, 65

Temples and synagogues: Alexandrian Temple, 250; barring of guilds from 250; Depression's effect on, 119–21; Emanu-El, 65; Hellenization of, 249; postwar building of, 222; services in Lower East Side, 65; suburban, 238, 239; suburban membership in, 226

Tendler, Lew, 90

Tenenbaum, Rabbi Marc H., 288

Tenth Man, The (Chayefsky), 261

Terrorists, Irgun and Stern, 105

Theater, American: during Depression, 139; Jews in, 140, 141, 143

Theater, Yiddish, 20–27; American drama critics' opinions of, 24; borscht circuits, 141; branch lines of, 20; culture explosion and, 19; decline of, 251–53; during Depression, 139; long life of actors in, 253; origin of, 21; producers in, 251; Second Avenue headquarters of, 20; See also Yiddish Art Theater

Theater groups: Artef, 55, 144; Group Theater, 139, 140; Habimah, 25–26, 144; Labor Stage, 139, 143; Mercury Theater, 143; Theater Union, 139; Theatre Guild, 21, 139

Theater Union, 139

Theaters, Yiddish: Artef, 55; Bowery, 20; Irving Place, 21; Labor Temple, 252; recent use of, 252

Theatre Guild, 21, 139

Theologians of Conservative Judaism, 62

Thieves in the Night (Koestler), 260

Thomas, Norman, 41, 189, 191

Tichel, 138

Tillich, Paul, 243

Time, 140

Tip Toe Inn, 197

Toller, Ernst, 21, 158

Tolstoi, Leo, 21, 133

Town Hall, 39

Trade unionism: role in bringing Yahudim and East Europeans together, 10–11; See also Garment industry; Labor movement

Trade unions: dual (parallel), 108; lawyers and, 83; response to Nazism of, 173; See also specific unions

Treasury of Yiddish Short Stories, A (Howe and Greenberg), 261

Trilling, Lionel, 256

Triple A Plowed Under, 143

Trotsky, Leon, 126

Truman, Harry S, 203, 211, 216, 231, 276

Tully, Jim, 46, 126

Tuvim, Julian, 161

Twain, Mark, 147

Tworkow, Jack, 27

Tzadik, 148

Ukrainian Culture Center, 252

Ukrainian Jews, 5

Ukrainian pogroms, Petliura and, 103–4

Ukrainians, 6

Uncle Moses (Asch), 149

Undercover (Carlson), 180

Underground, Zionist, 105

Underworld in garment industry, 89

Undset, Sigrid, 203, 252

Unemployment in Depression, 122

Union of Orthodox Rabbis, 164, 167

Union of Soviet Socialist Republics, see U.S.S.R.

Unionism, see Garment industry; Labor movement; Trade unionism

Unions, see Trade unions; specific unions

United Jewish Appeal, 279, 285; establishment of, 122; funds for Palestine and refugees raised by, 213; politically influential Jews and, 277; Rosenwald in, 190

United Palestine Appeal, Wise and, 77, 78

United Synagogue and Rabbinical Assembly, 228

Unity House, 142

Universities and colleges: clashes between Communists, Socialists, and Zionists at, 131; Jews' entry into, 229

Untermeyer, Louis, 135

Untermeyer, Samuel, 18, 45; economic boycott of Germany and, 174

Upper West Side: cabarets on, 156; cafés on, 155–56; changing of, 38; German refugees on, 154–58; Jewish realtors in, 38–39; lower-class invasion of, 37

Urban League, 97
Uris, Leon, 239, 260
U.S.S.R. (Union of Soviet Socialist Republics), 45; American Jewish philanthropists and, 106–7; Biro Bidjan, 106; economic problems of Jews in, 106; JDC's representative in, 106; Lenin's attitude toward Jews in, 105, 106; persecution of rabbis in, 105; persecution of Zionism in, 46, 105, 106; Stalin's drive against Jewish intellectuals in, 107; suppression of Hebrew in, 46, 105; UN vote on Palestine of, 214; U.S.'s refusal to recognize, 101; See also Russia

Vakhtangov, Yevgeni, 144
Valéry, Paul, 258
Varenikes, 66
Veblen, Thorstein, 132, 252
Vilna Troupe, 25
Violence in garment industry, 89
Violinists, 86
Vitlin, Josef, 161

Wagner, Robert F., 181
Waiters on Lower East Side, 40
Waldorf Astoria, 227
Walker, James J., 109, 119
Wall Street crash, 113
Walter, Bruno, 203
War Refugee Board, 213n
Warburg, Felix, 11
Warburg family, 106
Washington Heights, 155
WASPS (White Anglo-Saxon Protestants), 37, 230, 254, 270
Waton, Harry, 132, 252
Watson, Thomas J., 203
We Shall Never Die (Hart), 206
Webb, Mary, 35
Webb, Sidney, 35
Weidman, Jerome, 150, 151
Weill, Kurt, 158, 206
Weisenfreund, Muni (Paul Muni), 23–24, 206
Weizmann, Chaim, 14, 18, 162, 169, 200; Ben-Gurion and, 207, 210, 215; Bergmann and, 210; FDR's invitation to, 199; Fishman and, 30; handpicking of American leadership by, 130, 207, 210; Irgun and, 207; retirement from World Zionist Organization of, 212; Silver and, 202; Zionist leadership of, 195
Welfare agencies, use of, in Depression, 121
Welles, Orson, 139, 143
Welles, Sumner, 178
Weltanschauung, 243
Weltschmerz in newspapers, 33
Werfel, Franz, 158
West, Nathanael, 147
West Side, see Upper West Side
Western Union, 97
Wexley, John, 146
Wharton, Edith, 261
What Makes Sammy Run? (Schulberg), 150

Wheeler, Burton K., 189, 190
When She Was Good (Roth), 270
White House, 275–77, 284
Whither? (Le-an?; Feierberg), 266
Whitman, Walt, 135
Why Are We in Vietnam? (Mailer), 271
Wiernik, Peter, 29–30
Wilde, Oscar, 21, 253
Wilkins, Roy, 293
Williams, Michael, 181
Williamsburgh, 7
Willkie, Wendell, 203
Wilson, Edmund, 57
Wilson, Woodrow, 50, 172
Winchell, Walter, 183
Wine-cellars, Romanian, on Lower East Side, 9
Wise, Rabbi Stephen S., 13, 77–78, 202, 280; American Jewish Committee and, 196; as American Zionism's "Secretary of State," 195–97; in anti-Nazi parade, 172; anti-Nazi protest of, 77; as Court Jew, 276; Hecht and, 207; Holmes and, 187; Palestinian truth squads and, 211; support of FDR by, 199
Wolfe, Rabbi Arnold, 225
Wolfe, Thomas, 134, 148, 268
Women, employment of, 87
Wonder-rebbes, 72
as violinists, 86
Work, see Occupations
Workmen's Circle, funeral practices of, 93
World of Sholem Aleichem, The, 261
World Zionist Congress, 198
World Zionist Organization, 212; Haganah's support by, 203
World's Work, 95
Wouk, Herman, 260
Writers, 43–47, 49–50, 58–59, 253–68; Yiddish, 253–56

Yahrzeit, 63
Yahudim: concern for Yidn by, 45; decline in power of, 128; definition of, 3; East European Jews and, 4–5, 47; funeral practices of, 93; in high federal office, 273–74; history of, 4–5; intermarriage and, 274; Judaism of, 60
Yarid, 117
Yehoash (poet), 32
Yehuda (Levin), 150
Yeshiva, 74; effect of Depression on, 118; Ninety-niners' children in, 75; teachers at, 76
Yeshiva University, 74, 248
Yeshivot (yeshiva), 164
Yesenin, Sergei Aleksandrovich, 52
Yezierska, Anzia, 58
Yichus, 19
Yiddish: decline of, 136; decline of Yiddish theater and, 251; fiction in, 46–47; high, 8; labor movement and, 137; pleiner, 35; Polish, 9; as verbal instrument of culture exploision, 19; version of Bible in, 32; Zionists and, 136–37
Yiddish Art Theater, 20–24;

birth of, 21; paternity of, 21; premieres at, 21; recent use of, 252
Yiddish Culture Society, 252
Yiddishism, Zhitlovsky as high priest of, 42
Yiddishists, 55
Yiddishkeit, 60; hostility between Orthodox and, 62
Yidn (East European immigrants), 37, 46; anti-Semitism and, 96; awareness of American continent by, 124; fear of hospitals by, 80; Marshall and, 98; in power, 128; as realtors, 38–39; refugee Germans and, 159; Yahudim's concern for, 45; See also East European Jews
Yivo, viii
Yom Kippur, 64, 65, 70, 240, 251
Yona Shimmel's, 39, 91
Young, Whitney, 293
Young Lions (Shaw), 260
Young people, 131–35; favorite authors of, 133–35

Zametkin, Mikhail, 17
Zar, Isaac, 205
Zaslani, Reuven, 209
Zemach, Nahum, 25
Zemurray, Samuel, 215
Zhitlovsky, Chaim, 42
Zin, 273
Zionism: American Jewish affairs and leaders of, 162; American leadership of, 196; attacks on U.S. State Department by, 178, 196; Brandeis and, 34; ideological discussions in, 130–31; Irgun threat to, 211; Nazism and, 171, 173, 177; parochial attitude of, 196; persecution of, in U.S.S.R., 45, 105; pragmatists' leadership of, 130; reaction to Nazi threat by American, 194–201; role in bringing together of Yahudim and East Europeans, 10, 11; See also Labor Zionism
Zionist Archives, viii
Zionist leadership: Ben-Gurion and, 195, 200, 208; Lipsky in, 195–98, 201; Shertok in, 195, 208, 211; Silver in, 201–2, 211, 212, 215; Weizmann in, 195
Zionists: anti-Semitism and, 96; call for American Jewish Congress by, 12; challenge to AJC by, 96; Communist clashes with, 131; debating by, 40; in dilemma over U.S.S.R., 106; end of World War II and, 210; FDR and, 194–95; first commune in Palestine of, 131; Israel and American, 276; Marshall and, 96; Socialist clashes with, 131; Socialist (Labor), see Labor (Socialist) Zionists; soliciting funds by, 43; underground of, 105; Yiddish and, 136–37
Zivyon (B. Hoffman), 73
Zvi, Sabbatai, 244, 263
Zweig, Arnold, 244, 261
Zweig, Stefan, 158